THE CAMPER CONVERSION MAI

How to convert **Volkswagen**

T5 VAN to CAMPER

Lindsay Porter

Speedpro Series
4-Cylinder Engine Short Block High-Performance Manual – New Updated & Revised Edition (Hammill)
Alfa Romeo DOHC High-performance Manual (Kartalamakis)
Alfa Romeo V6 Engine High-performance Manual (Kartalamakis)
BMC 998cc A-series Engine, How to Power Tune (Hammill)
1275cc A-series High-performance Manual (Hammill)
Camshafts – How to Choose & Time Them For Maximum Power (Hammill)
Competition Car Datalogging Manual, The (Templeman)
Cylinder Heads, How to Build, Modify & Power Tune – Updated & Revised Edition (Burgess & Gollan)
Distributor-type Ignition Systems, How to Build & Power Tune – New 3rd Edition (Hammill)
Fast Road Car, How to Plan and Build – Revised & Updated Colour New Edition (Stapleton)
Ford SOHC 'Pinto' & Sierra Cosworth DOHC Engines, How to Power Tune – Updated & Enlarged Edition (Hammill)
Ford V8, How to Power Tune Small Block Engines (Hammill)
Harley-Davidson Evolution Engines, How to Build & Power Tune (Hammill)
Holley Carburetors, How to Build & Power Tune – Revised & Updated Edition (Hammill)
Honda Civic Type R High-Performance Manual, The (Cowland & Clifford)
Jaguar XK Engines, How to Power Tune – Revised & Updated Colour Edition (Hammill)
Land Rover Discovery, Defender & Range Rover – How to Modify Coil Sprung Models for High Performance & Off-Road Action (Hosier)
MG Midget & Austin-Healey Sprite, How to Power Tune – New 3rd Edition (Stapleton)
MGB 4-cylinder Engine, How to Power Tune (Burgess)
MGB V8 Power, How to Give Your – Third Colour Edition (Williams)
MGB, MGC & MGB V8, How to Improve – New 2nd Edition (Williams)
Mini Engines, How to Power Tune On a Small Budget – Colour Edition (Hammill)
Motorcycle-engined Racing Car, How to Build (Pashley)
Motorsport, Getting Started in (Collins)
Nissan GT-R High-performance Manual, The (Gorodji)
Nitrous Oxide High-performance Manual, The (Langfield)
Race & Trackday Driving Techniques (Hornsey)
Retro or classic car for high performance, How to modify your (Stapleton)
Rover V8 Engines, How to Power Tune (Hammill)
Secrets of Speed – Today's techniques for 4-stroke engine blueprinting & tuning (Swager)
Sportscar & Kitcar Suspension & Brakes, How to Build & Modify – Revised 3rd Edition (Hammill)
SU Carburettor High-performance Manual (Hammill)
Successful Low-Cost Rally Car, How to Build a (Young)
Suzuki 4x4, How to Modify For Serious Off-road Action (Richardson)
Tiger Avon Sportscar, How to Build Your Own – Updated & Revised 2nd Edition (Dudley)
TR2, 3 & TR4, How to Improve (Williams)
TR5, 250 & TR6, How to Improve (Williams)
TR7 & TR8, How to Improve (Williams)
V8 Engine, How to Build a Short Block For High Performance (Hammill)
Volkswagen Beetle Suspension, Brakes & Chassis, How to Modify For High Performance (Hale)
Volkswagen Bus Suspension, Brakes & Chassis for High Performance, How to Modify – Updated & Enlarged New Edition (Hale)
Weber DCOE, & Dellorto DHLA Carburetors, How to Build & Power Tune – 3rd Edition (Hammill)

RAC handbooks
Caring for your car – How to maintain & service your car (Fry)
Caring for your car's bodywork and interior (Nixon)
Caring for your bicycle – How to maintain & repair your bicycle (Henshaw)
How your motorcycle works – Your guide to the components & systems of modern motorcycles (Henshaw)
Caring for your scooter – How to maintain & service your 49cc to 125cc twist & go scooter (Fry)
Efficient Driver's Handbook, The (Moss)
Electric Cars – The Future is Now! (Linde)
First aid for your car – Your expert guide to common problems & how to fix them (Collins)
How your car works (Linde)
Motorcycles – A first-time-buyer's guide (Henshaw)
Motorhomes – A first-time-buyer's guide (Fry)
Pass the MoT test! – How to check & prepare your car for the annual MoT test (Paxton)
Selling your car – How to make your car look great and how to sell it fast (Knight)
Simple fixes for your car – How to do small jobs for yourself and save money (Collins)

Enthusiast's Restoration Manual Series
Beginner's Guide to Classic Motorcycle Restoration YOUR step-by-step guide to setting up a workshop, choosing a project, dismantling, sourcing parts, renovating & rebuilding classic motorcyles from the 1970s & 1980s, The (Burns)
Citroën 2CV, How to Restore (Porter)
Classic Large Frame Vespa Scooters, How to Restore (Paxton)
Classic Car Bodywork, How to Restore (Thaddeus)
Classic British Car Electrical Systems (Astley)
Classic Car Electrics (Thaddeus)
Classic Cars, How to Paint (Thaddeus)
Ducati Bevel Twins 1971 to 1986 (Falloon)
How to restore Honda CX500 & CX650 – YOUR step-by-step colour illustrated guide to complete restoration (Burns)
How to restore Honda Fours – YOUR step-by-step colour illustrated guide to complete restoration (Burns)
Jaguar E-type (Crespin)
Reliant Regal, How to Restore (Payne)
Triumph TR2, 3, 3A, 4 & 4A, How to Restore (Williams)
Triumph TR5/250 & 6, How to Restore (Williams)
Triumph TR7/8, How to Restore (Williams)
Ultimate Mini Restoration Manual, The (Ayre & Webber)
Volkswagen Beetle, How to Restore (Tyler)
VW Bay Window Bus (Paxton)
Yamaha FS1-E, How to Restore (Watts)

Expert Guides
Land Rover Series I-III – Your expert guide to common problems & how to fix them (Thurman)
MG Midget & A-H Sprite – Your expert guide to common problems & how to fix them (Horler)

Essential Buyer's Guide Series
Alfa Romeo Giulia GT Coupé (Booker)
Alfa Romeo Giulia Spider (Booker)
Audi TT (Davies)
Austin Seven (Barker)
Big Healeys (Trummel)
BMW E21 3 Series (1975-1983) (Reverente)
BMW E30 3 Series 1981 to 1994 (Hosier)
BMW GS (Henshaw)
BMW X5 (Saunders)
BSA 350 & 500 Unit Construction Singles (Henshaw)
BSA 500 & 650 Twins (Henshaw)
BSA Bantam (Henshaw)
Citroën 2CV (Paxton)
Citroën ID & DS (Heilig)
Cobra Replicas (Ayre)
Corvette C2 Sting Ray 1963-1967 (Falconer)
Ducati Bevel Twins (Falloon)
Ducati Desmodue Twins (Falloon)
Ducati Desmoquattro Twins – 851, 888, 916, 996, 998, ST4 1988 to 2004 (Falloon)
Ducati Overhead Camshaft Singles, "The Book of the (Falloon)
Fiat 500 & 600 (Bobbitt)
Ford Capri (Paxton)
Ford Escort Mk1 & Mk2 (Williamson)
Ford Mustang – First Generation 1964 to 1973 (Cook)
Ford Mustang – Fifth generation/S197 (Cook)
Ford RS Cosworth Sierra & Escort (Williamson)
Harley-Davidson Big Twins (Henshaw)
Hinckley Triumph triples & fours 750, 900, 955, 1000, 1050, 1200 – 1991-2009 (Henshaw)
Honda CBR FireBlade (Henshaw)
Honda CBR600 Hurricane (Henshaw)
Honda SOHC Fours 1969-1984 (Henshaw)
Jaguar E-Type 3.8 & 4.2-litre (Crespin)
Jaguar E-type V12 5.3-litre (Crespin)
Jaguar Mark 1 & 2 (All models including Daimler 2.5-litre V8) 1955 to 1969 (Thorley)
Jaguar S-Type – 1999 to 2007 (Thorley)
Jaguar X-Type – 2001 to 2009 (Thorley)
Jaguar XJ-S (Crespin)
Jaguar XJ6, XJ8 & XJR (Thorley)
Jaguar XK 120, 140 & 150 (Thorley)
Jaguar XK8 & XKR (1996-2005) (Thorley)
Jaguar/Daimler XJ 1994-2003 (Crespin)
Jaguar/Daimler XJ40 (Crespin)
Jaguar/Daimler XJ6, XJ12 & Sovereign (Crespin)
Kawasaki Z1 & Z900 (Orritt)
Land Rover Series I, II & IIA (Thurman)
Land Rover Series III (Thurman)
Lotus Seven replicas & Caterham 7: 1973-2013 (Hawkins)
Mazda MX-5 Miata (Mk1 1989-97 & Mk2 98-2001) (Crook)
Mercedes Benz Pagoda 230SL, 250SL & 280SL roadsters & coupés (Bass)
Mercedes-Benz 280-560SL & SLC (Bass)
MG Midget & A-H Sprite (Horler)
MG TD, TF & TF1500 (Jones)
MGA 1955-1962 (Crosier)
MGB & MGB GT (Williams)
MGF & MG TF (Hawkins)
Mini (Paxton)
Morris Minor & 1000 (Newell)
Moto Guzzi 2-valve big twins (Falloon)
New Mini (Collins)
Norton Commando (Henshaw)
Peugeot 205 GTI (Blackburn)
Porsche 911 (964) (Streather)
Porsche 911 (993) (Streather)
Porsche 911 (996) (Streather)
Porsche 911 Carrera 3.2 (Streather)
Porsche 911SC (Streather)
Porsche 924 – All models 1976 to 1988 (Hodgkins)
Porsche 928 (Hemmings)
Porsche 930 Turbo & 911 (930) Turbo (Streather)
Porsche 944 (Higgins)
Porsche 986 Boxster (Streather)
Porsche 987 Boxster & Cayman (Streather)
Rolls-Royce Silver Shadow & Bentley T-Series (Bobbitt)
Subaru Impreza (Hobbs)
Triumph 350 & 500 Twins (Henshaw)
Triumph Bonneville (Henshaw)
Triumph Herald & Vitesse (Davies)
Triumph Spitfire & GT6 (Baugues)
Triumph Stag (Mort)
Triumph Thunderbird, Trophy & Tiger (Henshaw)
Triumph TR6 (Williams)
Triumph TR7 & TR8 (Williams)
Vespa Scooters – Classic 2-stroke models 1960-2008 (Paxton)
Volvo 700/900 Series (Beavis)
VW Beetle (Cservenka & Copping)
VW Bus (Cservenka & Copping)
VW Golf GTI (Cservenka & Copping)

Those Were The Days ... Series
Alpine Trials & Rallies 1910-1973 (Pfundner)
American 'Independent' Automakers – AMC to Willys 1945 to 1960 (Mort)
American Station Wagons – The Golden Era 1950-1975 (Mort)
American Trucks of the 1950s (Mort)
American Trucks of the 1960s (Mort)
American Woodies 1928-1953 (Mort)
Anglo-American Cars from the 1930s to the 1970s (Mort)
Austerity Motoring (Bobbitt)
Austins, The last real (Peck)
Brighton National Speed Trials (Gardiner)
British and European Trucks of the 1970s (Peck)
British Drag Racing – The early years (Pettitt)
British Lorries of the 1950s (Bobbitt)
British Lorries of the 1960s (Bobbitt)
British Touring Car Racing (Collins)
British Police Cars (Walker)
British Woodies (Peck)
Café Racer Phenomenon, The (Walker)
Don Hayter's MGB Story – The birth of the MGB in MG's Abingdon Design & Development Office (Hayter)
Drag Bike Racing in Britain – From the mid '60s to the mid '80s (Lee)
Dune Buggy Phenomenon, The (Hale)
Dune Buggy Phenomenon Volume 2, The (Hale)
Endurance Racing at Silverstone in the 1970s & 1980s (Parker)
Hot Rod & Stock Car Racing in Britain in the 1980s (Neil)
Last Real Austins 1946-1959, The (Peck)
Mercedes-Benz Trucks (Peck)
MG's Abingdon Factory (Moylan)
Motor Racing at Brands Hatch in the Seventies (Parker)
Motor Racing at Brands Hatch in the Eighties (Parker)
Motor Racing at Crystal Palace (Collins)
Motor Racing at Goodwood in the Sixties (Gardiner)
Motor Racing at Nassau in the 1950s & 1960s (O'Neil)
Motor Racing at Oulton Park in the 1960s (McFadyen)
Motor Racing at Oulton Park in the 1970s (McFadyen)
Motor Racing at Thruxton in the 1970s (Grant-Braham)
Motor Racing at Thruxton in the 1980s (Grant-Braham)
Superprix – The Story of Birmingham Motor Race (Page & Collins)
Three Wheelers (Bobbitt)

Truckmakers
DAF Trucks since 1949 (Peck)
Mercedes-Benz Trucks (Peck)

Auto-Graphics Series
Fiat-based Abarths (Sparrow)
Jaguar MKI & II Saloons (Sparrow)
Lambretta Li Series Scooters (Sparrow)

Rally Giants Series
Audi Quattro (Robson)
Austin Healey 100-6 & 3000 (Robson)
Fiat 131 Abarth (Robson)
Ford Escort MkI (Robson)
Ford Escort RS Cosworth & World Rally Car (Robson)
Ford Escort RS1800 (Robson)
Lancia Delta 4WD/Integrale (Robson)
Lancia Stratos (Robson)
Mini Cooper/Mini Cooper S (Robson)
Peugeot 205 T16 (Robson)
Saab 96 & V4 (Robson)
Subaru Impreza (Robson)
Toyota Celica GT4 (Robson)

WSC Giants
Audi R8 (Wagstaff)
Ferrari 312P & 312PB (Collins & McDonough)
Gulf-Mirage 1967 to 1982 (McDonough)
Matra Sports Cars – MS620, 630, 650, 660 & 670 – 1966 to 1974 (McDonough)

Biographies
A Chequered Life – Graham Warner and the Chequered Flag (Hesletine)
Amédée Gordini ... a true racing legend (Smith)
André Lefebvre, and the cars he created at Voisin and Citroën (Beck)
Chris Carter at Large – Stories from a lifetime in motorcycle racing (Carter & Skelton)
Cliff Allison, The Official Biography of – From the Fells to Ferrari (Gauld)
Edward Turner – The Man Behind the Motorcycles (Clew)
Driven by Desire – The Desiré Wilson Story
First Principles – The Official Biography of Keith Duckworth (Burr)
Inspired to Design – F1 cars, Indycars & racing tyres: the autobiography of Nigel Bennett (Bennett)
Jack Sears, The Official Biography of – Gentleman Jack (Gauld)
Jim Redman – 6 Times World Motorcycle Champion: The Autobiography (Redman)
John Chatham – 'Mr Big Healey' – The Official Biography (Burr)
The Lee Noble Story (Wilkins)
Mason's Motoring Mayhem – Tony Mason's hectic life in motorsport and television (Mason)
Raymond Mays' Magnificent Obsession (Apps)
Pat Moss Carlsson Story, The – Harnessing Horsepower (Turner)
Tony Robinson – The biography of a race mechanic (Wagstaff)
Virgil Exner – Visioneer: The Official Biography of Virgil M Exner Designer Extraordinaire (Grist)

Toys & models
Britains Farm Model Balers & Combines 1967-2007, Pocket Guide to (Pullen)
Britains Farm Model & Toy Tractors 1998-2008, Pocket Guide to (Pullen)
Britains Toy Models Catalogues 1970-1979 (Pullen)
British Toy Boats 1920 onwards – A pictorial tribute (Gillham)
Diecast Toy Cars of the 1950s & 1960s (Ralston)
Ford In Miniature (Olson)
GM In Miniature (Olson)
Plastic Toy Cars of the 1950s & 1960s (Ralston)
Tinplate Toy Cars of the 1950s & 1960s (Ralston)

General
Caravan, Improve & Modify Your (Porter)
Caravans, The Illustrated History 1919-1959 (Jenkinson)
Caravans, The Illustrated History From 1960 (Jenkinson)
Drive on the Wild Side, A – 20 Extreme Driving Adventures From Around the World (Weaver)
Dune Buggy, Building A – The Essential Manual (Shakespeare)
Dune Buggy Files (Hale)
Dune Buggy Handbook (Hale)
Volkswagen Bus Book, The (Bobbitt)
Volkswagen Bus or Van to Camper, How to Convert (Porter)
Volkswagens of the World (Glen)
VW Beetle Cabriolet – The full story of the convertible Beetle (Bobbitt)
VW Beetle – The Car of the 20th Century (Copping)
VW Bus – 40 Years of Splitties, Bays & Wedges (Copping)
VW Bus Book, The (Bobbitt)
VW Golf: Five Generations of Fun (Copping & Cservenka)
VW – The Air-cooled Era (Copping)
VW T5 Camper Conversion Manual (Porter)
VW Campers (Copping)
You & Your Jaguar XK8/XKR – Buying, Enjoying, Maintaining, Modifying – New Edition (Thorley)
Which Oil? – Choosing the right oils & greases for your antique, vintage, veteran, classic or collector car (Michell)
Works Minis, The Last (Purves & Brenchley)
Works Rally Mechanic (Moylan)

From Veloce Publishing's other imprints:

Battle Cry!
Soviet General & field rank officer uniforms: 1955 to 1991 (Streather)
Red & Soviet military & paramilitary services: female uniforms 1941-1991 (Streather)

Hubble & Hattie
A dog's dinner – Practical, healthy and nutritious recipes for REAL dog food (Paton-Ayre)
A tale of two horses – A passion for free-will teaching (Gregory)
Among the wolves – Memoirs of a wolf handler (Shelbourne)
Animal Grief – How animals mourn (Alderton)
Camper vans, ex-pats and Spanish hounds – The strays of Spain: from road trip to rescue (Coates)
Cat Speak – recognising and understanding behaviour (Rauth-Widmann)
Charlie – The dog who came in from the wild (Tenzin-Dolma & Bekoff)
Clever Dog! – life lessons from the world's most successful animal (O'Meara)
Dieting with my dog – One busy life, two full figures ... and unconditional love (Frezon)
Dinner with Rover – Delicious, nutritious meals for you and your dog to share (Paton-Ayre)
Dog Cookies – Healthy allergen-free treat recipes for your dog (Schops, Pick)
Dog Games – Stimulating play to entertain your dog and you (Blenski)
Dog Relax – Relaxed dogs, relaxed owners (Pilguj)
Dog Speak – recognising and understanding behaviour (Blenski)
Dog-friendly Gardening – Creating a safe haven for you and your dog (Bush)
Dogs on wheels – Travelling with your canine companion (Mort)
Emergency first aid for dogs – at home and away (Bucksch)

For post publication news, updates and amendments relating to this book please visit: www.veloce.co.uk/books/V367

www.veloce.co.uk

First published in 2007 by Veloce Publishing Limited, Veloce House, Parkway Farm Business Park, Middle Farm Way, Poundbury, Dorchester DT1 3AR, England. Fax 01305 268864 / e-mail info@veloce.co.uk / web www.veloce.co.uk or www.velocebooks.com. Reprinted May 2015. ISBN: 978-1-904788-67-6 UPC: 6-36847-00367-8 Readers with ideas for automotive books, or books on other transport or related hobby subjects, are invited to write to the editorial director of Veloce Publishing at the above address. British Library Cataloguing in Publication Data – A catalogue record for this book is available from the British Library. Typesetting, design and page make-up all by Veloce Publishing Ltd on Apple Mac. Printed in India by Nova Publications & Printers Pvt. Ltd.

THE CAMPER CONVERSION MANUAL

How to convert **Volkswagen**

T5 VAN to CAMPER

Lindsay Porter

VELOCE PUBLISHING
THE PUBLISHER OF FINE AUTOMOTIVE BOOKS

Contents

Introduction & acknowledgements

Every Volkswagen Camper ever made is a real enthusiasts' vehicle. Right from the first 'Split-Screen' Campers from the Fifties, right up to the T5 of the 'Noughties', Volkswagen Transporters have a quality that has never been equalled by commercial vehicles from any other manufacturer.

The special appeal of these vehicles isn't a fluke. It's because of the fact that Volkswagen Transporters have always been innovative, well designed and well built. The rear-engined versions built for the first 40 years of the Transporter's life were a revelation in terms of both carrying capacity and build quality while the 4WD Syncro, based on the T3, remains a sensational vehicle though a rare one these days. The T4, as the first of the front-engined Transporters was a touch conservative though even more tough and reliable than its predecessors. But the T5, the subject of this book, is another Transporter trailblazer. Even in short-wheelbase form, it has a greater load capacity than the T4, it has a genuinely car-like – or, more-accurately, MPV-like – driving feel to it. The build quality is better than ever. And the performance is amazing! The higher powered 2.5 litre TDI engine has the exact same 0-60 acceleration figures as the Mk 1 Golf GTI but is capable of up to 40mpg in general driving, even with the full Camper conversion inside.

As I've said elsewhere in this book, we bought our T5 after attending a press launch event and being so impressed, I bought one, as soon as the waiting list would then allow. You'll see in this book all the work we've since had carried out on it as well as work that's been carried out on a number of other vehicles, so that you can see the full range of conversion options and techniques available to T5 owners. We both love our T5 Camper so much that we fully intend keeping it 'for ever'...

Most books are a bigger slog than you ever think they're going to be (though why that should be after all these years beats me!) and this one was no exception. First, I'd like to thank Shan, my long-suffering wife, for putting up with all the weekdays, weekends and evenings that have been taken up in my working on it. She also took quite a few of the pictures that were taken at our home; she had her hands in quite a few of the shots that I took and she also contributed to some of the work we carried out ourselves. She's not only steeped in patience, she's uniquely versatile with it!

Zoë Palmer has worked for us for 16 years at the time of writing though, as our publishing activities have reduced, works for us now for fewer hours than ever before. She worked really hard on this book and is responsible for the excellent way in which the material was organised, set out and presented to Veloce Publishing.

At Veloce, my good friends Rod and Judith have displayed the patience of saints as I have kept their company waiting time and again as the material for this book has accumulated. Editor and layout artist Tim Barden has worked stoically and with enormous skill at producing a fine-looking book and I'm very pleased with what he's done.

The great majority of the conversion work described in these pages was carried out by my friends at Leisuredrive. This is the second vehicle they've done for us which, I think, speaks for itself. I'll finish off this section with a bit more information about them. First, though, a word about some of the dozens of suppliers we have been fortunate in dealing with in connection with this book, looking at them in alphabetical order. Other specialists featured here all come highly recommended by me. (Any specialists that failed to impress were simple left out!) I've just picked out here the ones I've had most to do with.

The unforgettably named CAK, (Caravan Accessories, Kenilworth and manufacturers of the well-known CAK Tanks) have always come up trumps (so to speak). Owner Jonathan Frost is a thoroughly nice bloke and, since he and his wife are keen motorhome users, he's an extremely knowledgeable bloke and has been a great source of recommendations of what to use and what not to use. Dometic Ltd continues to manufacture what I consider to be the best fridges and other electrical equipment on the market, as it has done for decades past. It's really smashing to deal with, too. (It's funny how top quality products and nice people usually go together.) Hodgson & Hodgson is a company I have never seen featured in a motor caravan publication before. It manufactures top class vehicle insulation and I 'found' it after an extensive internet search.

JP Exhausts is a company I've used several times over the years and I'm impressed not only by the quality of its stainless steel exhausts but by the friendly, top quality service it provides. Maxview is another great company to deal with and makes TV viewing possible in just about any location by use of its affordable, portable satellite TV systems. Michelin Tyres hardly need any introduction. It's just that it manufactures one of the T5's original equipment tyres and, in my view, makes the best tyres in the world. Morris Lubricants is small in global terms but big on quality. I've visited its factory and use only its products in my T5. Pentagon Glasstech fits the class-leading window tinting and protection systems. I've seen cars from the stars and the 'special services' having their windows made secure there; they really are that good! Towcraft Ltd, suppliers and fitters of tow brackets and trailers, is another bunch of people I've come to know and like enormously over the years. The company is top quality and totally honest. So is Vehvac Ltd, who fits air conditioning and many other electronic accessories. Kent is quite a long way from where I live but I am one of those prepared to travel in order to benefit from its quality service. ViaMichelin are Michelin men (and women) but also produce the very best sat. nav. software I have used. Unlike some sat. nav. software, it really works! As, I suppose, you would expect from the people behind the Michelin Guides. Würth UK Ltd is the British arm of a company which produces German quality consumables. Like the T5, it is the best there is and I use the company in preference to any others.

Finally, though, I come back to Leisuredrive who converted our T5, having converted our T3 Transporter a good few years earlier. Although Leisuredrive's designs have evolved and improved over the years, a consistent thread is found in its no-nonsense designs. Leisuredrive's designs really work because the owners/managers Derek Andrews and Jennifer Seddon, as well as many of the staff who work there, actually use the products they build and have done so for years. As a result, they know what works and what doesn't work and have refined their designs to be practical and useable. And I know from personal experience, having used their conversions for a number of years myself, that they are based on exceptionally well-built furniture which lasts extremely well. But then, you can see for yourself just what Leisuredrive can offer, since they've opened themselves up to inspection through the pages of this book.

Photographing and writing this book has been demanding but enjoyable. However, the greatest enjoyment has come from the pleasure gained from working with the super people who have helped and contributed throughout. My grateful thanks are due to them all, including those I haven't had space to mention here by name.

Lindsay Porter
Herefordshire, England

DEDICATION

It's a real pleasure to dedicate this book to our very good friend, highly efficient co-worker and one of the very nicest people you could ever wish to meet, Zoë Palmer.

Safety first!

You must always ensure that safety is the first consideration in any job you carry out. A slight lack of concentration, or a rush to finish the job quickly can easily result in an accident, as can failure to follow the precautions outlined in this Chapter. Whereas skilled motor mechanics are trained in safe working practices, you, the home mechanic, must find them out for yourself and act upon them.

Remember, accidents don't just happen, they are caused, and some of those causes are contained in the following list. Above all, ensure that whenever you work on your vehicle you adopt a safety-minded approach at all times, and remain aware of the dangers that might be encountered.

Be sure to consult the suppliers of any materials and equipment you may use, and to obtain and read carefully any operating and health and safety instructions that may be available on packaging or from manufacturers and suppliers.

PART I. IMPORTANT POINTS

Vehicle off ground

• **Always** ensure that the vehicle is properly supported when raised off the ground. Don't work on, around, or underneath a raised vehicle unless the axle stands are positioned underneath secure, load bearing underbody areas.

• **Never** work on a vehicle supported only by a jack.

• **Never** attempt to loosen or tighten nuts that require a lot of force to turn (e.g. a tight oil drain plug), with the vehicle raised, unless it is safely supported. Take care not to pull the vehicle off its supports when applying force to a spanner. Wherever possible, initially slacken tight fastenings before raising the vehicle off the ground.

Safety 1. ALWAYS ensure that the safe working load rating of any jacks, hoists or lifting gear used is sufficient for the job, and that lifting gear is used only as recommended by the manufacturer.

• **Always** wear eye protection when working under the vehicle and when using power tools.

Using trolley jack and axle stands

If someone pops out at regular intervals to see how you are getting on, it could be enough to save your life!

Safety 2. Whenever you're working beneath a vehicle, have someone primed to keep an eye on you!

Working on the vehicle

• **Always** seek specialist advice unless you are justifiably confident about carrying out each job. The safety of your vehicle affects you, your passengers and other road users.

Safety 3. DON'T lean over, or work on, a running engine unless it is strictly necessary, and keep long hair and loose clothing well out of the way of moving mechanical parts. Note that it is theoretically possible for fluorescent striplighting to make an engine fan appear stationary – double check whether it is spinning or not! This is the sort of error that happens when you're really tired and not thinking straight.

• **Don't** work on your vehicle when you're overtired.
• **Always** work in a well ventilated area and don't inhale dust – it may contain asbestos or other harmful substances.
Remove your wrist watch, rings and all other jewellery before doing any work on the vehicle – and especially when working on the electrical system.
• **Don't** remove the radiator or expansion tank filler cap when the cooling system is hot, or you may get scalded by escaping coolant or steam. Let the system cool down first, and even then, if the engine is not completely cold, cover the cap with a cloth and gradually release the pressure.
• **Never** drain oil, coolant or automatic transmission fluid when the engine is hot. Allow time for it to cool sufficiently to avoid scalding you.
• **Always** keep antifreeze, brake and clutch fluid away from vehicle paintwork. Wash off any spills immediately.
• Take care to avoid touching any engine or exhaust system component unless it is cool enough not to burn you.

Running the vehicle

• **Never** start the engine unless the gearbox is in neutral (or 'Park' in the case of automatic transmission) and the handbrake is fully applied.
• **Never** run catalytic converter equipped vehicles without the exhaust system heat shields in place.
• Take care when parking vehicles fitted with catalytic converters. The 'cat' reaches extremely high temperatures and any combustible materials under the vehicle, such as long dry grass, could be ignited.

Personal safety

• **Never** siphon fuel, antifreeze, brake fluid or other such toxic liquids by mouth, or allow contact with your skin. There is an increasing awareness that they can damage your health. Best of all, use a suitable hand pump and wear gloves.
• Before undertaking dirty jobs, use a barrier cream on your hands as a protection against infection. Preferably, wear thin gloves, available from DIY outlets.
• Wear impervious gloves – disposable types are ideal – where there is a risk of used engine oil or any other harmful substance coming into contact with your skin.
• Wipe up any spilt oil, grease or water off the floor immediately, before there is an accident.
• Make sure that spanners and all other tools are the right size for the job and are not likely to slip. Never try to 'double-up' spanners to gain more leverage.
• Seek help if you need to lift something heavy which may be beyond your capability. Don't forget that when lifting a heavy weight, you should keep your back straight and bend your knees to avoid injuring your back.
• **Never** take risky short-cuts or rush to finish a job. Plan ahead and allow plenty of time.
• Be meticulous and keep the work area tidy – you'll avoid frustration, work better and lose less.
• Keep children and animals well away from the work area and unattended vehicles.
• **Always** tell someone what you're doing and have them regularly check that all is well, especially when working alone on, or under, the vehicle.

PART II. HAZARDS

Fire!

Petrol (gasoline) is a dangerous and highly flammable liquid requiring special precautions. When working on the fuel system, disconnect the vehicle battery earth (ground) terminal whenever possible

Safety 5. There are several types of fire extinguisher. Take advice from your accredited supplier to make sure that you have the right type for workshop use. Note that water fire extinguishers are not suitable for workshop or automotive use.

Safety 4. Würth produces a huge range of workshop products, including the safety-related items shown here.

and always work outside, or in a very well ventilated area. Any form of spark, such as that caused by an electrical fault, two metal surfaces striking against each other, a central heating boiler in the garage 'firing up', or even static electricity built up in your clothing can, in a confined space, can ignite petrol vapour causing an explosion. Take great care not to spill petrol onto the engine or exhaust system and never allow any naked flame anywhere near the work area. Above all, don't smoke!

Pressure

• **Don't** disconnect any fuel pipes on a fuel injected engine while the ignition is switched on. The fuel in the line is under very high pressure – sufficient to cause serious injury. Remember that many injection systems have residual pressure in the pipes for days after switching off. Consult the workshop manual or seek specialist advice before carrying out any work.

Fumes

• In addition to the fire dangers described previously, petrol (gasoline) vapour and the types of vapour given off by many solvents, thinners and adhesives, are highly toxic and under certain conditions can lead to unconsciousness or even death, if inhaled. The risks are increased if such fluids are used in a confined space so always ensure adequate ventilation when handling materials of this nature. Treat all such substances with care – always read the instructions and follow them scrupulously.

• **Always** ensure that the vehicle is out of doors and not in an enclosed space when the engine is running. Exhaust fumes contain poisonous carbon monoxide, even when the vehicle is fitted with a catalytic converter, since 'cats' sometimes fail and don't function when the engine is cold.

• **Never** drain petrol (gasoline) or use solvents, thinners, adhesives or other toxic substances in an inspection pit, as the extremely confined space allows the highly toxic fumes to concentrate. Running the engine with the vehicle over the pit can have the same results. It is also dangerous to park a vehicle for any length of time over an inspection pit. The fumes from even a slight fuel leak can cause an explosion when the engine is started. Petrol fumes are heavier than air and will accumulate in the pit.

Mains electricity

Before using any mains-powered electrical equipment, take one more simple precaution – use an RCD (Residual Current Device) circuit, breaker. Then, if there is a short, the RCD circuit breaker minimises the risk of electrocution by instantly cutting the power supply. Buy one from any electrical store or DIY centre. RCDs fit simply into your electrical socket before plugging in your electrical equipment.

Safety 7. Never work on the ignition system with the ignition switched on, or with the engine being turned over on the starter, or running.

The ignition system

• Touching certain parts of the ignition system, such as the HT leads, distributor cap, ignition coil, etc., can result in a severe electric shock. This is especially likely where the insulation on any of these components is weak, or if the components are dirty or damp. Note also that voltages produced by electronic ignition systems are much higher than those produced by conventional

Safety 6. Avoid the use of mains electricity whenever possible when working on the vehicle. For instance, you could use rechargeable tools and a DC inspection lamp, powered from a remote 12V battery – both are much safer. However, if you do use mains-powered equipment, ensure that the appliance is wired correctly to its plug, that where necessary it is properly earthed (grounded), and that the fuse of the correct rating for the appliance is fitted. For instance, a 13 amp fuse in a lead lamp plug will not provide adequate protection. Do not use any mains-powered equipment in damp conditions or in the vicinity of fuel, fuel vapour or the vehicle battery.

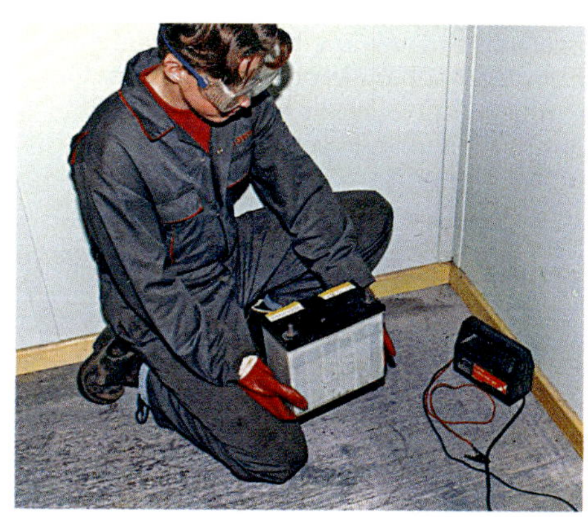

Safety 8. Never cause a spark, smoke, or allow a naked light near the vehicle's battery, even in a well ventilated area. A certain amount of highly explosive hydrogen gas will be given off as part of the normal charging process.

systems and could prove fatal, particularly to people with cardiac pacemaker implants. Consult your handbook or main dealer if in any doubt.

• An additional risk of injury can arise while working on running engines, if the operator touches a high voltage lead and pulls his or her hand away on to a sharp, conductive or revolving part.

The battery

• Battery terminals on the vehicle should be shielded, since a battery contains energy and a spark can be caused by any metal object which touches the battery's terminals or exposed connecting straps.

• Before working on the fuel or electrical systems, always disconnect the battery earth (ground) terminal.

• When using a battery charger, care should be taken to avoid causing a spark by switching off the power supply before the battery charger leads are connected or disconnected. A spark can enter on of the vent holes causing the battery to explode and throw acid a surprising distance. Keep a stored battery well away from work areas.

• Before charging the battery from an external source, disconnect both battery leads before connecting the charger. If the battery is not of the 'sealed-for-life' type, loosen the filler plugs or remove the cover before charging. For best results, the battery should be given a low rate trickle charge overnight. Do not charge at an excessive rate or the battery may burst.

• **Always** wear gloves and goggles when carrying or when topping up the battery. Even in diluted form (as it is in the battery) the acid electrolyte is extremely corrosive and must not be allowed to contact the eyes, skin or clothes.

Brakes and asbestos

• Obviously, a vehicle's brakes are among its most important safety-related items. **Only** work on your vehicle's braking system if you are trained and competent to do so, **unless** you have someone who is a trained mechanic thoroughly check and approve your work and your vehicle's braking system as a whole, before the vehicle is used on the road.

• Whenever you work on the braking system's mechanical components, or remove front or rear brake pads or shoes: i) wear an efficient particle mask; ii) wipe off all brake dust from the work area after spraying on a proprietary brand of brake cleaner (never blow dust off with compressed air); iii) dispose of brake dust and discarded shoes or pads in a sealed plastic bag; iv) wash your hands thoroughly after you have finished working on the brakes and certainly before you eat or smoke; v) replace shoes and pads only with asbestos-free shoes or pads. Note that asbestos brake dust can cause cancer if inhaled.

Brake fluid

Brake fluid absorbs moisture rapidly from the air and can become dangerous, resulting in brake failure. Castrol (UK) Ltd. recommend that you should have your brake fluid tested at least once a year by a properly equipped garage with test equipment and you should change the fluid in accordance with your vehicle manufacturer's recommendations. You should buy no more brake fluid than you need, in smaller rather than larger containers. Never store an opened container of brake fluid. Dispose of the remainder at your Local Authority Waste Disposal Site, in the designated disposal unit, not with general waste or with waste oil.

Engine oils

• Take care to observe the following precautions when working with used engine oil. Apart from the obvious risk of scalding when draining the oil from a hot engine, there is the danger from contaminates that are contained in all used oil.

• **Always** wear disposable plastic or rubber gloves when draining the oil from your engine. Note that the drain plug and the oil are often hotter than you expect. Wear gloves if the plug is too hot to touch and keep your hand to one side so that you are not scalded by the spurt of oil as the plug comes away; ii) There are very real health hazards associated with used engine oil. In the words of one manufacturer's handbook "Prolonged and repeated contact may cause serious skin disorders, including dermatitis and cancer". Use a barrier cream on your hands and try not to get oil on them. Always wear gloves and wash your hands with hand cleaner soon after carrying out the work. Keep oil out of the reach of children.

Plastic materials

• Work with plastic materials brings additional hazards into workshops. Many of the materials used (polymers, resins, adhesives and materials acting as catalysts and accelerators), contain dangers in the form of poisonous fumes, skin irritants, and the risk of fire and explosions. Do not allow resin or 2-pack adhesive hardener, or that supplied with filler or 2-pack stopper, to come into contact with skin or eyes. Read carefully the safety notes supplied on the can, tube or packaging and always wear impervious gloves and goggles when working with them.

MOST IMPORTANT! PLEASE READ THIS SECTION!

Fluoroelastomers

• If you service your vehicle in the normal way, none of the following may be relevant to you. Unless, for example, you encounter a vehicle which has been on fire (even in a localised area), subject to heat in, say, a crash-damage repairer's workshop or a vehicle breaker's yard, or if any second-hand parts have been heated in any way.

• Many synthetic, rubber-like materials

Safety 9. Keep your inspection lamp well away from any source of petrol (gasoline) such as when disconnecting a carburettor float bowl or fuel line.

used in motor cars contain a substance called fluorine. These materials are known as fluoroelastomers and are commonly used for oil seals, wiring and cabling, bearing surfaces, gaskets, diaphragms, hoses and 'O' rings. If they are subjected to temperatures greater than 315°C, they will decompose and can be potentially hazardous. Fluoroelastomer materials will show physical signs of decomposition under such conditions in the form of charring of black sticky masses. Some decomposition may occur at temperatures above 200°C, and it is obvious that when a vehicle has been in a fire or has been dismantled with the assistance of a cutting torch or blow torch, the fluoroelastomers can decompose in the manner indicated above.

• In the presence of any water or humidity, including atmospheric moisture, the by-products caused by the fluoroelastomers being heated can be extremely dangerous. According to the Health and Safety Executive, "Skin contact with this liquid or decomposition residues can cause painful and penetrating burns. Permanent irreversible skin and tissue damage can occur". Damage can also be caused to eyes or by the inhalation of fumes that may be created as fluoroelastomers are burned or heated.

After a vehicle has been exposed to fire or high temperatures, you must observe the following precautions:

• **Do not** touch blackened or charred seals or equipment.

• Allow all burnt or decomposed fluoroelastomer materials to cool down before inspection, investigations, tear-down or removal.

Safety 10. When you drain your engine oil – don't oil the drain! Pouring oil down the drain will cause pollution. It is also an offence.

• Preferably, don't handle parts containing decomposed fluoroelastomers, but if you must, wear goggles and PVC (polyvinyl chloride) or neoprene protective gloves whilst doing so. Never handle such parts unless they are completely cool.

• Contaminated parts, residues, materials and clothing, including protective clothing and gloves, should be disposed of by an approved contractor to landfill or by incineration according to national or local regulations. Oil seals, gaskets and 'O' rings, along with contaminated material, must not be burned.

PART III. GENERAL WORKSHOP SAFETY

• **Always** have a fire extinguisher of the correct type at arm's length when working on the fuel system – under the vehicle, or under the bonnet. If you do have a fire, **don't panic**. Use the extinguisher effectively by directing it at the base of the fire.

• **Never** use a naked flame near petrol or anywhere in the workplace.

• **Never** use petrol (gasoline) to clean parts. Use paraffin (kerosene), white spirits, or best of all, a proprietary brand of degreaser.

• **No smoking**. There's a risk of fire or of transferring dangerous substances to your mouth and, in any case, ash falling into mechanical components is to be avoided.

• Be methodical in everything you do, use common sense, and think Safety First! at all times.

PART IV. ENVIRONMENT FIRST

• The used oil from the sump of just one car can cover an area of water the size of two football pitches, cutting off the oxygen supply and harming swans, ducks, fish and other river life.

• **Don't** mix used oil with other materials, such as paint and solvents, because this makes recycling difficult.

• Take used oil to an oil recycling bank. Telephone **free** in the UK on 0800 663366 to find the location of your nearest oil bank, or contact your local authority recycling officer.

Chapter 1

Choosing, buying & engine servicing

1-1-1. This is our Leisuredrive Volkswagen T5 late one sunny winter's day. Most of the embellishments have been fitted and finished by now and, at first glance, our vehicle looks more like a Caravelle than a Camper, which is what we were aiming for. The T5 is just like Volkswagens from time immemorial; the options are available from Volkswagen and from independent suppliers to customise them any way you want.

My wife, Shan, and I are long-standing VW fans and I've written quite a lot about VW vehicles over the years. In 2003, we owned a venerable but superb Volkswagen T3 Camper of 1985 vintage – not old by VW Camper Van standards I know, but at 18 years old it was way past the sell-by date of most ordinary vehicles though still going strong.

Then in August of 2003, I was honoured to be invited to a Volkswagen UK launch of the T5 Transporter (the van had already been around in LHD form for some months).I can honestly say that, at the launch, I was so smitten that on my return home, Shan and I decided we'd sell the T3, mortgage the cat and buy ourselves a brand new T5. It turned out that this was easier said than done, the waiting list being so long that it wasn't until October of 2004 that we received the specification we wanted. And boy, was it worth the wait!

We then arranged with Derek Andrews, the man behind Leisuredrive, to

1-1-2. Our van had originally looked much like this, although without the internal bulkhead or snazzy wheel trims. It's worth bearing in mind when buying a used van that if a bulkhead is in place, extra work will be involved in removing it. Moreover, many commercial vans have no glass in their rear door for security reasons, so you may be better off looking out for a van with a fully glazed rear door.

1-1-3. A van with high mileage but lots of regular maintenance and a full service history will generally be more desirable than one that shows a lower mileage but which has been knocked about and not properly maintained.

carry out the conversion to a camper for us. After all, Leisuredrive had converted our previous VW Camper and six years of use had seen nothing break, come loose or fall off! And that's where this book began.

There was once an advert for razors where some smug-looking feller held up a razor to the camera and said something like, "I tried this razor and liked it so much, I bought the company." Well, I'm fortunate enough to test drive quite a few vehicles in the course of my work as a motoring writer and I can honestly say, "I test drove the van and liked it so much, I bought one!" Not as spectacular a claim, perhaps – but at least it's true ...

1-1-4. The window van which has windows behind the cab but not at the very rear could be a good basis for a conversion, but this is the Shuttle which has a sliding door on each side that makes it unsuitable.

1-1-5. This cutaway of the Caravelle's internal components gives a good idea of the vehicle's structure.

SECTION 1. MODEL TYPES

Ninety-six models – which is right for you?

A VW press release of 2006 posed the above question of the T5 Transporter – and it wasn't even including the Caravelle MPV range! However, it's not as daunting a choice as you might think and, buying second-hand, you won't have the detailed choice that the new vehicle buyer enjoys. However, there are several major categories of Transporter available at the time of writing and you'll need to know which version you want before you start looking because their detail characteristics are quite different.

All the engines are powerful and economical TDI engines and feature Volkswagen's 'Pumpe Duese' (PD) unit-injector technology. Other main features include: long service and maintenance intervals; independent suspension on all four wheels and agile handling; superb, slick gear change; ergonomic cab design with car-like qualities and comfort levels.

Gross vehicle weights, at time of launch, ranged from the T26 (2.6 tonne); T28 (2.8 tonne); T30 (3.0 tonne) to T32 (3.2 tonne). The vehicle we chose is a T28, to provide 200kg more carrying capacity than the base vehicle, plus, we assumed, more resilient suspension for a vehicle carrying the kitchen sink around with it the whole time but at very little extra cost.

All have:
- two wheelbases: 3m or 3.4m.
- three roof heights (only one for the Shuttle).

VW's designated model types are currently:
- The Transporter Panel Van.
- four gross vehicle weights.
- load compartment volumes of 5.8m^3 to 9.3m^3
- seating for 3

The Transporter Kombi

- designed to carry up to 6 people in comfort, and a sizeable load at the same time.
- two gross vehicle weights.
- payloads of 1200kg or 1400kg.
- a range of door and window options.
- rubber flooring in load compartment.

The Transporter Window Van

- Volkswagen's heavy duty answer to passenger-carrying for up to nine people.
- range of seating up to nine, arranged in up to three rows.
- a range of door and window options.
- tough rubber flooring.
- suitable base for conversions.

1-1-6. Less common but more likely to be well looked after, especially if you're buying from the original owner, is the Sportline, which comes with all sorts of accessories ready fitted and shows just how much pride many Transporter owners take in their vehicles. This would make an excellent basis for conversion to motor caravan.

The Transporter Shuttle

- designed to transport occupants in style.
- spacious interior with comprehensive choice of optional extras and versatile seat configuration.
- space for 8 to 9 people plus luggage
- easy access, with two sliding doors
- two trim levels, S or SE
- 'car-like' equipment – passenger airbag, electric front windows, electric heated/ adjustable mirrors, comfort seats
- fully trimmed side and head linings
- air conditioning on the SE

Then there are the Transporter Chassis and Double Van options. Neither of these are covered in this manual since it is intended for those converting versions with a conventional rear body.

Of these model types, the Shuttle effectively rules itself out because of the fact that it has two sliding doors and you need an uninterrupted 'wall' against which to fit Camper furniture. The other three versions are all equally worthy of consideration with the following provisos:

- You will usually pay more for a van with factory-fitted side windows than you would for a panel van. The presence of windows means that you will save having to carry out some of the conversion work yourself, however, or you will save the cost of having someone else do it for you. However, early Transporter sliding windows were prone to leaking, whereas, oddly enough, the aftermarket ones fitted by Leisuredrive certainly don't. They look almost identical, though the latter have visible, exterior drain holes in the glass – presumably a price worth paying.

You need to go for a van with an adequate payload. You will be permanently carrying around the entire weight of your chosen furniture, plus accessories, and you will want to have some in hand for load and passenger carrying.

In my view, the engine you choose will make a greater difference to the character of the vehicle, from the driver's perspective, than any other single aspect of the vehicle. Look at the following list of options and choose accordingly.

Engine options

At the heart of every Transporter sits one of Volkswagen's impressive TDI 'Pumpe Duese' (PD) diesel engines. Each of the TDI PD units features unit injector technology, that was new to the T5, with greatly improved fuel consumption **and** increased power and torque

- 85PS 1.9 TDI PD: 4-cylinder producing 200 Nm maximum torque with a 5-speed manual gearbox.
- 104PS 1.9 TDI PD: 4-cylinder producing 250 Nm maximum torque with a 5-speed manual gearbox.
- 130PS 2.5 TDI PD: 5-cylinder producing 340 Nm maximum torque with a 6-speed manual, 6-speed Tiptronic or 6-speed manual gearbox with 4MOTION®.
- 174PS 2.5 TDI PD: 5-cylinder producing 400 Nm maximum torque with a 6-speed manual gearbox. At the time of writing, and odd though it seems, Tiptronic and 4MOTION 4WD versions are not available with this more powerful engine in the UK.
- PETROL/GASOLINE ENGINES: No petrol engine versions are available in Europe, only in the Caravelle MPV version.

1-1-7. The Caravelle is the MPV version of the Transporter.

Differences between these engines are more notable on the road than they are on paper. The gearchange on all T5s is one of the very best you will encounter (and that includes cars) because of its location on the dash. Incidentally, this is a wonderful feature for Campers because it improves walk-through access to the rear of the vehicle no end. But the 6th gear on the more powerful engines is a great aid to economy and relaxed long-distance cruising. You don't

1-1-8. Volkswagen clearly had a leisure connection in mind right from the start, as this press picture indicates. Note the painted bumpers and mirrors, along with the slightly different lower grille shape and touches of chrome work, all of which are additional features when compared with the van.

MODEL IDENTIFICATION

Transporter models are named according to engine and gross vehicle weight, so it's easy to understand what's on offer. For example, the T28 130 TDI PD van is a 2,800kg panel van with the 130PS 2.5-litre engine. (The German term 'PS' is approximate – in fact very close indeed – to the 'bhp' used in the UK and USA.)

1-1-9. The T5 short wheelbase is the most popular for conversions because it is so much easier to use as an everyday vehicle. It can be parked in most car-based parking spaces.

1-1-10. The long wheelbase (LWB) version has an extra 15% or so of interior load space, and this can make a noticeable difference when you're on holiday – provided you don't mind the extra difficulties in driving and parking the longer vehicle, as well as the higher ferry costs if you regularly cross the Channel.

1-1-11. In spite of what the sign behind it might seem to be telling you, this is not a VW Golf but a VW California. It's Volkswagen's factory-built camper and is, of course, fabulous!

have to be at high speed to use it either. On our 174PS engined version, you can pootle along at 40mph in 6th quite happily.

The four-cylinder engines are perfectly okay. They are developments of the T4 engine and thus go back a generation, though in terms of longevity, there's nothing wrong with that. In fact, I'd have been perfectly happy with a 4-pot engine until I drove the others. The 5-cylinder engines are jewels of engines. They are classics that set completely new standards for van engines which is unsurprising when you note that they were shared with the highly sophisticated Audi A6. They are smooth, quiet, have loads of torque (low-down pulling or towing power) and are so economical!

Two points worthy of note here:

- The 174PS engine is actually slightly more economical than the 130PS 5-cylinder engine.
- At launch, VW's witty and enthusiastic Press Officer Paul Bucket started by comparing the VW's performance figures with that of the Golf Mk1 GTI, the original hot-hatch. Top speed of the 174PS van was a little lower (caused almost entirely by greater wind resistance). The 0-60mph acceleration times were, astonishingly, almost identical. But fuel consumption of the van was far better than that of the hot hatch! Could this be two vehicles in one? Well yes, because the T5 van is a real 'driver's' vehicle, with handling and brakes to match the power. Mind you, I haven't seen a convertible version yet ...

More features

With an Anti-lock Braking System (ABS), Electronic Differential Lock (EDL) and Traction Control System (TCS) (not 4MOTION®), all T5s come with a comprehensive safety package. This is complimented by Engine Braking Control (EBC) which prevents the driving wheels breaking away on slippery surfaces when taking your foot off the accelerator, or re-engaging the clutch – handy on a campsite. As standard, the 130PS 4MOTION® window van model is equipped with Electronic Stabilisation Programme (ESP) with a brake assist system for added safety. This is also available as an option on some other van models of 130PS upwards. Other options in the cab include front passenger airbag plus two side and two curtain airbags. A driver's airbag is of course standard, as are 3-point belts on all seats.

4MOTION

This is VW's name for its 4x4 version of the Transporter, the Syncro name used on earlier versions falling oddly out of favour. Shan says it would be a good brand name for a laxative! But that aside ...

The 4MOTION® all-wheel drive system is designed to react to even the slightest wheel slip at which it distributes power and drive to the wheels with the most grip. All this happens in milliseconds, through control units that are linked to the vehicle's dynamic sensors, engine management system and gearbox. For the more extreme circumstances, there's also a locking rear differential fitted as standard.

1-1-12. The California's interior boasts swivelling front seats and the fold-away table you can see here. When not needed, it fits into a space in the sliding door – a neat touch!

This is a real benefit giving greatly increased traction, though it can only be used on loose, slippery surfaces. On a hard, gripping surface, the vehicle would be difficult to control because of the lack of a differential. It is easily controlled via a switch on the dash. For safety, 4MOTION® comes complete with the standard ABS (Anti-locking Braking System) and EDL (Electronic Differential Lock) systems. In addition, some 130PS 4MOTION® models are equipped with ESP (Electronic Stabilisation Programme) as standard.

Converters often dislike converting the 4MOTION because of the lack of room beneath the vehicle for possible access and for the location of water tanks. You also have to bear in mind the extra weight and the loss of fuel economy, plus the fact the system has not been available with all engines fitted to the panel van in the UK. It's a very nice thing to have for all-year-round campers, though!

1-1-13. As with all T5s, the driving position and equipment are of a superbly high quality and make for a thoroughly enjoyable driving experience.

1-1-14. The California's cooking facilities are very stylish, though limited to two rings and no grill, as with most continental campers. The fridge works from electricity only.

1-1-15. The wardrobe and rear storage areas are of a supremely high quality in the California, but not everyone will appreciate such a thin mattress.

Buying right

When buying a second-hand van, you will be constrained to some extent by what is available, so it might help to make yourself a list of features in descending order of importance. Draw yourself a line where the 'must haves' turn into the 'would like to haves' and restrict your search to those you can find from above the line.

At the time of writing, there are no obvious weaknesses in the construction of the vehicle of which you need to be aware; the 12-year body warranty is ample evidence of Volkswagen's confidence in the longevity of the bodywork. The steering is known to give the odd 'clunk,' but there may by now be a factory fix for this slight and cosmetic problem. You will need to check all the usual wear points, for example wheel bearings. Check for engine wear (which can be caused by running it without coolant or running it too low on lubricant), and for transmission problems. Worn, 'crunching' synchromesh is not unknown on 6-speed gearboxes.

The main problems you may encounter could be from damage. Has a 4MOTION been abused off-road? Has the load area, the sliding door, door gear or rear door(s) been damaged by rough handling? Is the rear suspension sagged or suffering from broken springs because of repeated over-loading? These are the most likely problems you may encounter on a former work-horse and it is definitely an advantage to know who the previous owners have been and what sort of use they gave the vehicle. In general, large companies and utilities look after its vehicles best, with maintenance schedules being adhered to, while one-man builders' vans (for instance) may not always receive the most careful use!

Two more points worth bearing in mind:

- If the rear of the van has been fitted out with plywood liners or shelving, the side-walls are less likely to be damaged, but do bear in mind that some or all of the window panels will be removed in any case, though not the box-sectional structures between them. (If these are bent, you would be well advised to look elsewhere!)
- You will also need to decide whether you want a van equipped with double rear doors or a single, lift-up door. Either type can be converted using the Leisuredrive units shown in this manual. The single-door model makes the vehicle look neater and

1-1-16. Another delightful touch is the way that the rear door stores a couple of lightweight folding chairs.

1-1-17. With a power-operated roof and an optional awning specially developed by Omnistore for the T5, the high cost of this vehicle is justified by the high quality of its fittings. Note that the sliding door is on the right-hand side, even on UK versions.

more MPV-like and provides shelter from the rain when the door is open. On the other hand, it requires more clear space behind the vehicle, when parked, in order to gain access to the rear. The great majority go for a single-door and it could be that this style will hold its value best, but in the end (or at the back!) the choice is yours.

SECTION 2. CONVERSION CHOICES

Before starting work, you'll need to decide what type of roof you want to have. All have 'pros'; all have 'cons,' So it's a matter of seeing which one is likely to suit you best.

Important notes:
The roof on the T5 has to be strengthened with VW-approved strengthening sections. Unless you are qualified in such work, the job must be carried out by a qualified technician.
The work shown, being carried out by Leisuredrive, is for information purposes only – fitting the roof-strengthening sections is **not** a DIY job!

HIGH-TOP OR RAISING ROOF?

High-top

- You've always got lots of headroom, making moving around easier.
- You won't be able to get into any car parks with height barriers.
- You won't have to go outside to raise the roof when it's raining.
- The wind will blow you around more, and your top speed will be lower and fuel economy worse.
- Bear in mind that some high-tops are higher than others. Some have room for (cramped) kids' beds 'upstairs,' while others are just high enough to stand up in.

Raising roof

- You'll park more easily and speed, stability and economy will hardly be affected.
- It gets colder inside at night with the top up, because you have, in effect, a tent over you. (It's better if you close the top at night, if there are two of you.)
- You can park in some car parks with height restrictions, although by no means all.
- There may be a little more maintenance needed, long-term, as struts wear or if the fabric becomes damaged.

The beauty of building your own T5 motor home is that you can put in it exactly what you want. This manual concentrates on units that are available from Leisuredrive and here you can see the various options available. This may give you ideas for how to build your own from scratch, or you may want to modify some of the kits supplied by Leisuredrive. You could do as we have done and go along with a complete Leisuredrive 'build' as it stands. After all, it has been building motor caravans for several decades and have ironed out most of the problems. So, here's a selection of the major options.

Self-build or not self-build?

You are recommended to have a high- or lifting-top fitted for you (see above), although some owners also like to have the work of fitting the side windows carried out for them, leaving the rest to do themselves. Companies such as Leisuredrive cater for all requirements, giving you the choice between having:

- All the work carried out for you. You deliver the bare van then later, you collect the finished motor caravan.

Time: Two-to-three weeks.

- The hardtop or raising roof and windows fitted for you. You buy the internal furniture and kitchen equipment in kit form and fit them yourself.

Time: A week for fitting; several weeks of solid work to fit out the interior, the details such as trimming taking longest.

- You buy all of the parts: windows, trim and interior, and fit the lot yourself.

Time: Several months of part-time work, if you've never done it before, though Leisuredrive won't supply you with the major body-related parts.

Leisuredrive Vivante – Plan A

1-2-1. The Vivante is the high-top version of Leisuredrive's Volkswagen T5 motor home. There are many variations and many options available but here are some of the basic features.

1-2-2. If you removed the right-hand side of the vehicle and looked through to the left, this is what you would see. The kitchen area at the rear with seating and table arrangement in front.

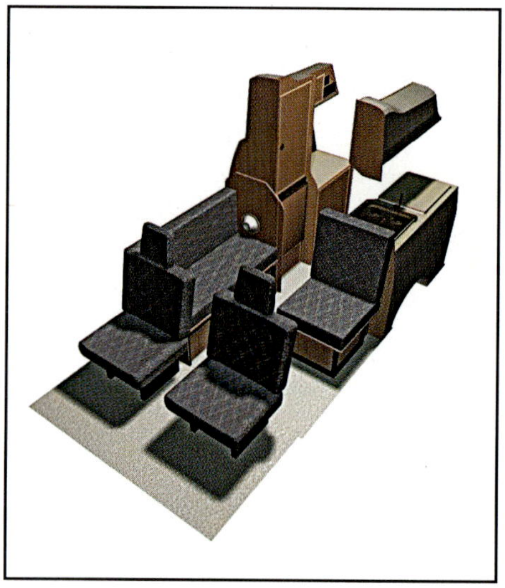

1-2-3. The front two seats here are for driver and passenger. There is just one extra forward-facing passenger seat with seatbelt, but there is more rear seating for use when the vehicle is stationary.

1-2-4. If you select the option of swivelling seats, the front seats can be turned as shown and a dining table erected.

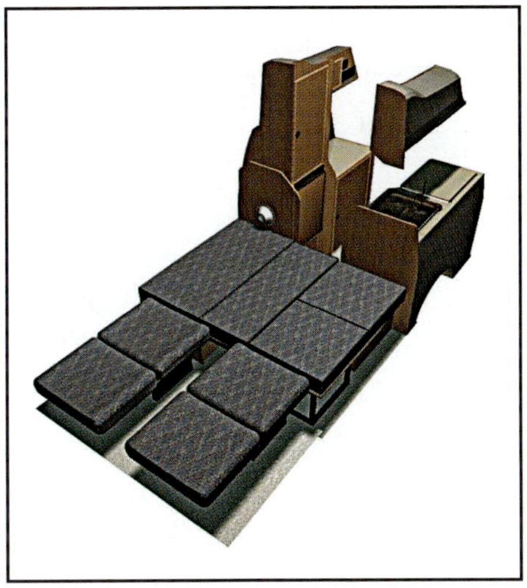

1-2-5. At night, the front seats – though not as flat as shown in this schematic plan – fold down and make part of the linked-twin beds.

1-2-6. This is another overall view with the front of the vehicle to the left of this illustration.

1-2-7. The kitchen area is opposed by the wardrobe and WC with a low door leading out through the tailgate.

1-2-8. This is a 'real world' view of the Vivante with the optional swivelling passenger seat facing to the rear.

1-2-9. The tailgate up and the rear door open allows you to see into the rear of the vehicle. Note the extra storage space on the left and the access to the WC holding tank on the right.

1-2-10. The seating arrangements are not exactly as those shown in picture 1-2-5, as you can see. The backrest for the front seats remains upright.

1-2-11. This is the galley and WC area at the rear with the fridge situated beneath the wardrobe.

1-2-12. For a vehicle of its size, the kitchen area is of excellent proportions.

Leisuredrive Crusader – Plan B

1-2-13. This is the Reimo elevating roof fitted to our vehicle ...

1-2-14. ... and this is the alternative elevating roof offered by Leisuredrive.

1-2-15. This is the driving or daytime arrangement of the Plan B layout. The rear seats have two seat belts; one a lap-diagonal and the other a lap-only.

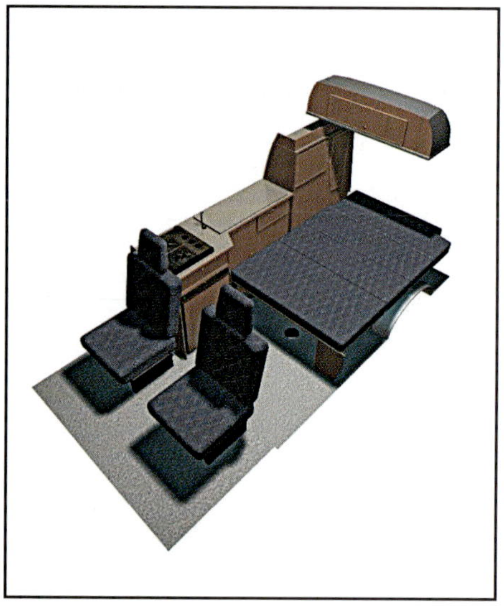

1-2-16. At night, the rear seats fold flat to make one excellent bed.

1-2-17. In the real world again, this is the view of the Plan B interior as you might use it on-site, although without the optional table.

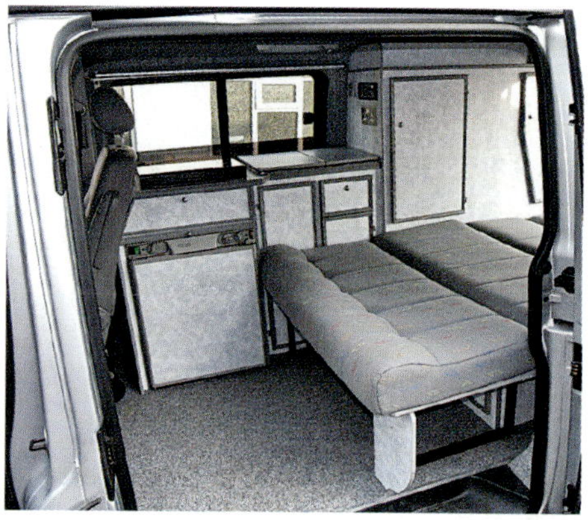

1-2-18. With the rear seats folded flat to make the bed, there is good access to the fridge, although two of the cupboards become obscured. In practice, you get used to it!

1-2-19. When the rear seats are up, the backs of the seats make luggage space, while there is more storage space beneath.

1-2-20. The cooking area is similar to that of Plan A and is fine for short trips.

1-2-21. The main differences between Plan A and Plan B are that Plan A is designed to take advantage of the fixed high-top and includes an integral WC area, while Plan B is more spacious and is perhaps more practicable for everyday use.

SECTION 3. OIL CHANGE

When you've purchased your van for conversion, the first thing you'll want to do is to change the engine oil. But before you do, stop right there! If there is a service history, check it out. You might just find that the correct grade of long-life oil has been used and the oil change only needs to take place every 20,000 miles. (There is a sensor which is intended to detect the type of oil and the service interval and inform you, via the dashboard, when the oil needs changing. But I would be reluctant to rely on that on a vehicle I didn't know.)

However, let's assume the worst and that the oil needs changing. Swapping the oil is not a problem but I've known strong men driven to drink after spending hours searching hopelessly for the oil filter on the 5-cylinder engine. Here's how to locate it and how to change the oil once you've found it:

SAFETY FIRST!

Diesel engine oil is known to be potentially carcinogenic and you must always wear suitable protective gloves while carrying out this work.

1-3-1. Unscrew the fixings – there appear to be six on some; eleven on others – holding the undertray in place and remove it.

1-3-2. The drain plug is clearly seen on the front of the sump.

1-3-3. Note that the five-cylinder engine has seven litres of oil in it (plus the oil filter's 0.4 litres), so you will need more than one five litre container to drain the oil into.

1-3-4. While you get on with the rest of the work, leave the sump to drip as much oil out as possible. Note that if you have raised the front of the vehicle, you won't be able to drain all of the oil until the vehicle is level.

1-3-5. *Now you've got the job of removing the oil filter. You will need a box spanner or socket of 35mm.*

1-3-6. *Here's how to find the position of the oil filter. In this picture, the front of the vehicle is to the right. Try placing your forehead on the top of the air filter (position A) and look underneath the fluid reservoir in the direction of the arrow.*

1-3-7. *This is the socket spanner shown in picture 1-3-5, with a ratchet drive attached to it, placed on the hexagonal head of the oil filter.*

1-3-8. *In effect, this is what you are doing in the engine bay. The socket is placed on the hexagonal head at the top of the oil filter and the oil filter housing is unscrewed. When it comes free, you can completely unscrew and remove it by hand.*

1-3-9. Back with the protective gloves because of the oil on the oil filter, this shows the filter and housing being removed from the engine bay.

1-3-10. On the bench, pull the oil filter out of the housing and change the rubber seal, supplied with the new filter, in the top of the housing.

1-3-11. Push the new filter into the housing and make sure that the oil seal (arrowed) on the end of the stem, on what will be the bottom of the oil filter, is in place.

1-3-12. The cap of the housing tells you to refit it to 24Nm. It's made of plastic so don't over-tighten!

1-3-13. It doesn't come with the new oil filter but you should always buy a new drain plug, fitted with its integral sealing washer, every time you change the oil to ensure there are no leaks.

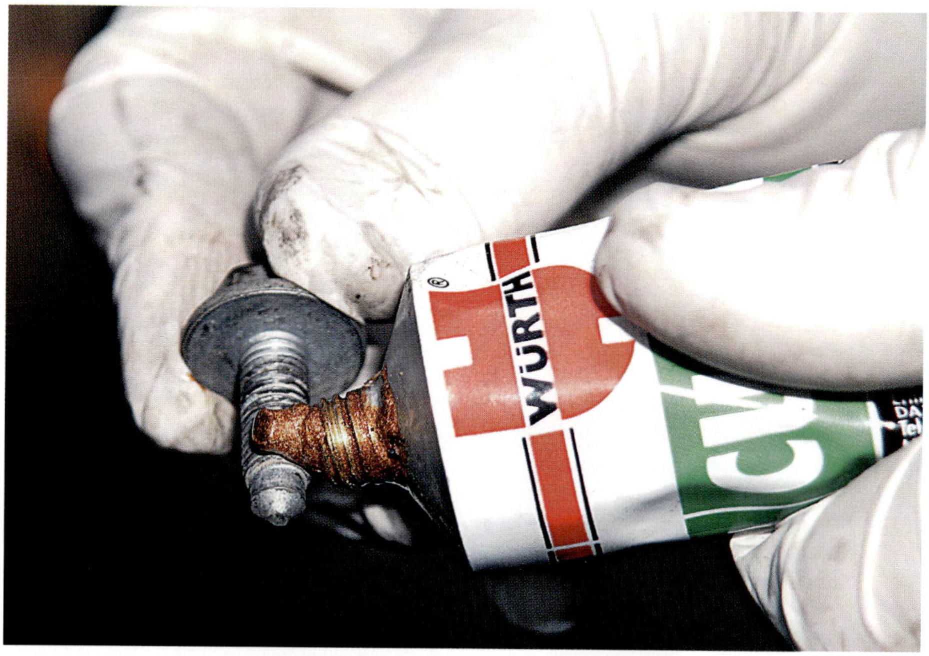

1-3-14. Just to make sure that the thread doesn't seize at its outer end where the oil from the engine might not penetrate, you could use Würth copper grease to lubricate the thread.

1-3-15. Use a torque wrench and tighten the drain bolt to the figure shown in your handbook.

1-3-16. Before tipping in the fresh oil, wipe out the oil filler neck because road and engine dirt does tend to gather in there.

1-3-17. We used the British-made Morris' Multilife Fully-Synthetic 0W/30 'Fuel Efficient' motor oil. It is produced to the correct specification for this engine, it gives the full 20,000 miles service life and, in theory at least, provides greater fuel economy because of its lower viscosity.

Chapter 2
Exterior structural work

Intro 1. Derek Andrews, Leisuredrive's proprietor, gives the go-ahead to adding our T5 to the vehicles in the Leisuredrive workshop at Bolton.

Intro 2. This is the last time we will see a basic T5 van in its current form.

Intro 3. Leisuredrive's huge workshop tends to be awash with T5 Volkswagens alongside the other vehicles it converts.

INTRODUCTION

There are several stages to converting the bodywork of a VW Transporter into a suitable shell for a motor caravan.
If you're converting a van that's had a hard life, there may be bodywork repairs to carry out first. There's an argument for respraying the vehicle after the conversion has been carried out because of the risk of paintwork damage during the conversion process. On the other hand, there will be less preparation, less to mask off and less risk of getting overspray onto your new interior if the respray is carried out first.

First: You always start by stripping the interior out. On a van with a bulkhead, there is more to do than on those without. Window vans tend to have more interior trim, though you'll obviously save the time taken to fit some or all of the windows, depending on the model.

Second: Any internal structural work – and indeed, any bodywork repairs that may be needed – can best be carried out now. Welding is most safely carried out without flammable trim in the area, but do remember to cover up any exposed glass, including dashboard and mirrors, before using an angle grinder. The sparks etch themselves immovably into any nearby glass or paintwork.

Third: Now it's on to some of the most dramatic parts of the conversion job. This stage involves making fundamental changes to the vehicle's bodywork so that it can fulfil its new purpose.

Important notes:
In all cases (except the most Spartan of conversions – not the sort covered here) the van will be fitted with windows. You really do need experience before carrying out this work yourself.

Don't carry out the work shown in this chapter or in any individual section without reading the rest of this manual. There are many jobs that are associated with other work. This manual has been divided up into logical sections of the vehicle but these are not necessarily the order in which you will carry out the work. Please study the whole of the manual before commencing work.

Intro 4. Most working vans have accumulated lots of 'muck' inside them and so, once all the seats and trim are out of the way, you can pressure wash or steam clean the interior so that you're starting off with something that's completely clean.

SECTION 1. STRIP AND PREPARE VAN

Remove interior trim

The plastic studs holding the trim panels in place can theoretically be screwed out but in practice, you will be better off removing them, as shown here.

Sun visor and roof console (Multivan) removing

See Chapter 3, Section 1.

2-1-1. Leisuredrive's foreman, Barry Roberts, uses a home-made trim-removing tool to lever free each trim clip. Purpose-made tools can be purchased but it's easy to make such a tool from a very cheap wood chisel using a bench grinder.

2-1-2. In many cases, trim panels are simply lifted free.

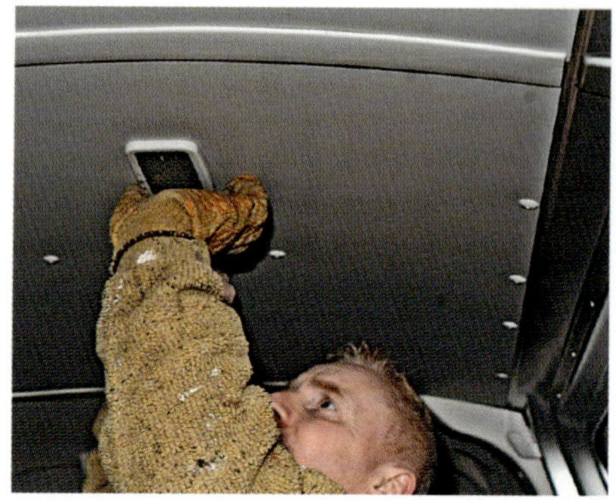

2-1-3. In others, there are obstructions in the way. The interior lights are carefully levered out of their recesses ...

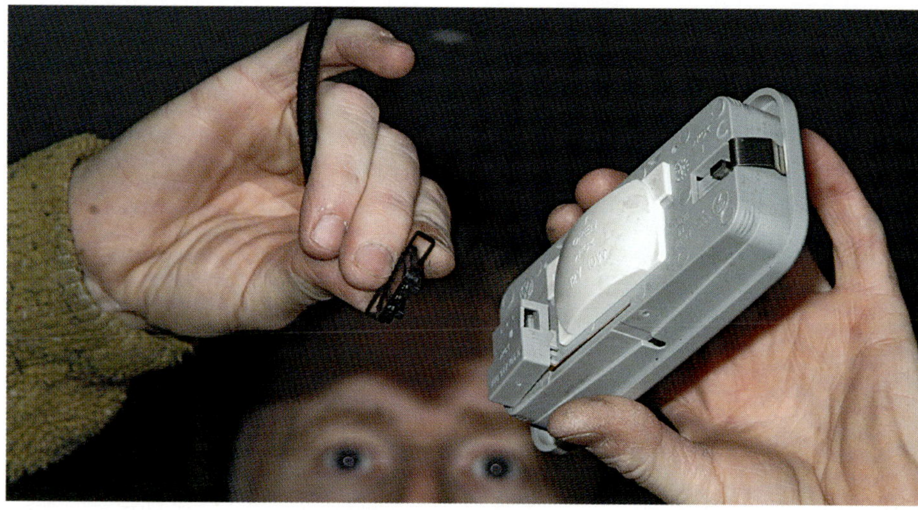

2-1-4. ... and then the wiring connectors unplugged from behind them.

2-1-5. The edges of the roof trim are removed in a similar fashion to that shown in picture 2-1-1 except that the lever goes behind the trim panel ...

2-1-6. ... this is because the clips on the trim strips are pushed into slots on the inside of the trim, as shown here.

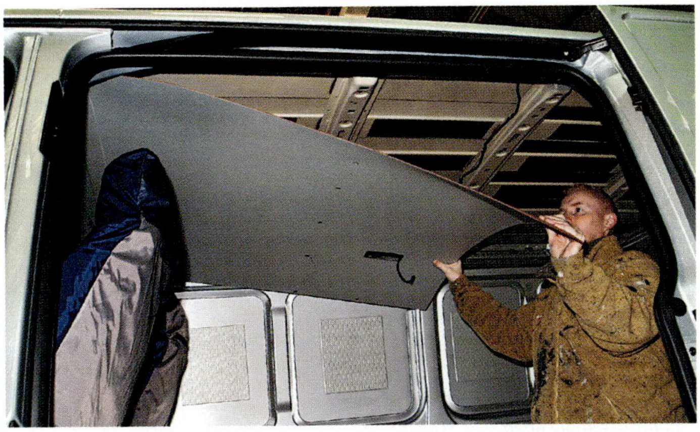

2-1-7. Barry releases one of the roof trim panels before removing it from the vehicle.

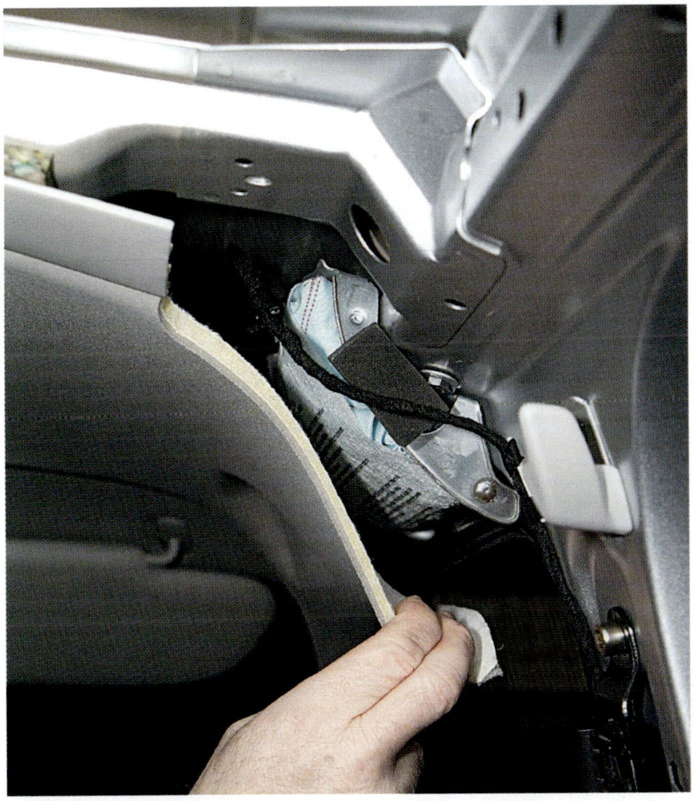

2-1-8. Vans fitted with side air bags have the airbags located behind the front cab trim.

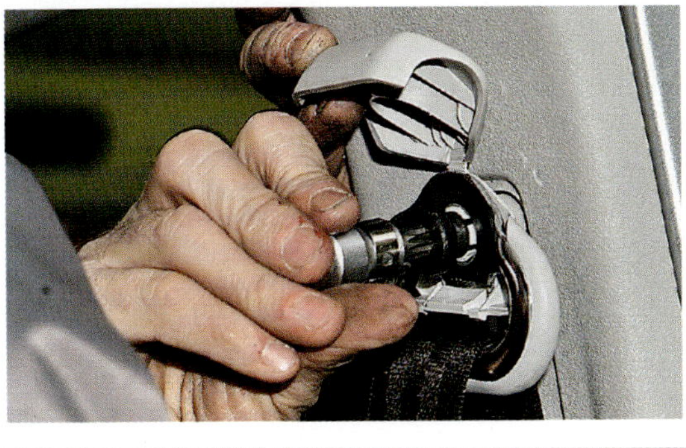

2-1-9. Before removing the B-post trims, the seat belt upper mountings need to be undone.

2-1-10. The B-post trims are unclipped …

2-1-11. … and removed.

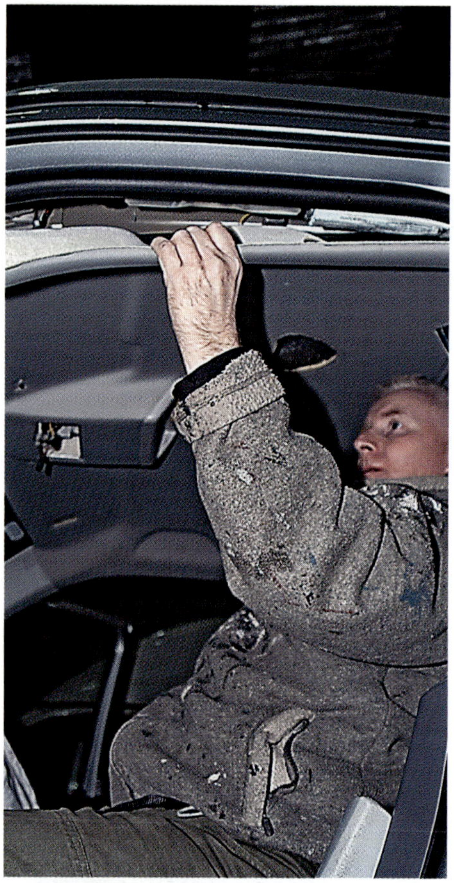

2-1-12. Once the sun visors and centre section have been removed (see Chapter 3, Section 1) the headlining can be sprung ...

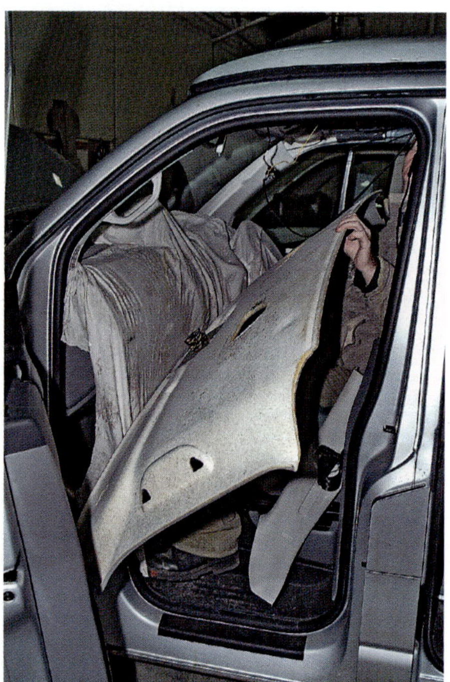

2-1-13. ... and carefully eased from the cab.

Airbag removal

AIRBAG WARNINGS

There are certain specific precautions that must be taken before removing an airbag. Electrostatic discharges may result in unintentional triggering of an airbag. Therefore, the mechanic must electrostatically discharge him/herself before disconnecting the igniter and earth wires. This can be done by briefly touching the body or striker plate of the door.

If the vehicle needs to be driven with an airbag removed, a VW dealer plug needs to be fitted in its place. This is not available to non-VW staff so please follow the following procedure.

- Before starting to detach the airbag, disconnect the battery.
- Refer to your handbook and make sure that you have radio codes, that any auxiliary alarm can be disconnected in this way and that any other proceedings that are required before disconnecting the battery have been carried out.
- The airbag can now be removed, as required.

Do not under any circumstances reconnect the battery with the air bag removed or the vehicle's ECU will register a fault and you will need to have a VW main dealer reset it.

Airbags contain explosive devices and must be stored extremely carefully, preferably in a locked steel cupboard. Only leave them off the vehicle for the shortest amount of time practicable.

When refitting, reconnect the airbag to the vehicle, refitting the electrical plug and socket together.

Only reconnect the battery after all airbags have been reconnected.

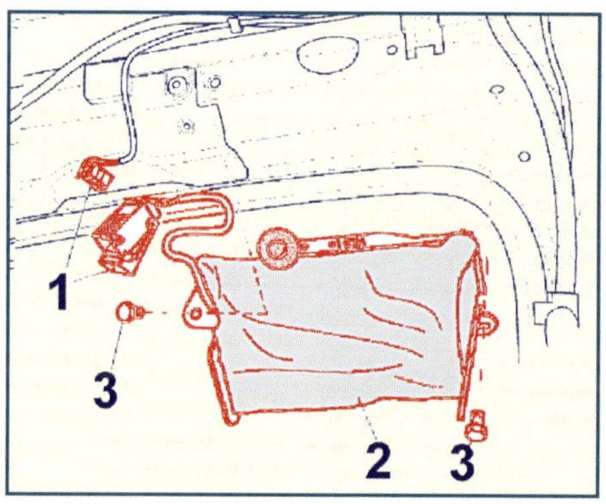

2-1-14. These are the airbag connections, mechanical and electrical. Refer to this diagram in the next four steps.

Important notes:

- When refitting, tighten to 8Nm.
- The bolts are microencapsulated and must be renewed each time they have been loosened.
- Before new bolts are installed, the threads of the corresponding nuts must be cleaned.

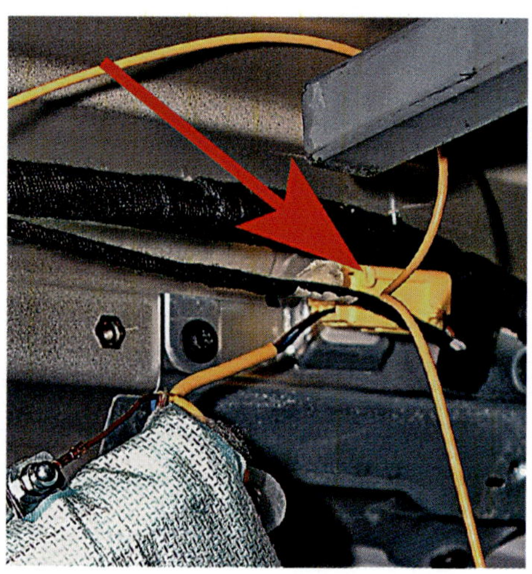

2-1-15. If the electrical connector (1) can be accessed, follow the Volkswagen recommendation and release this first.

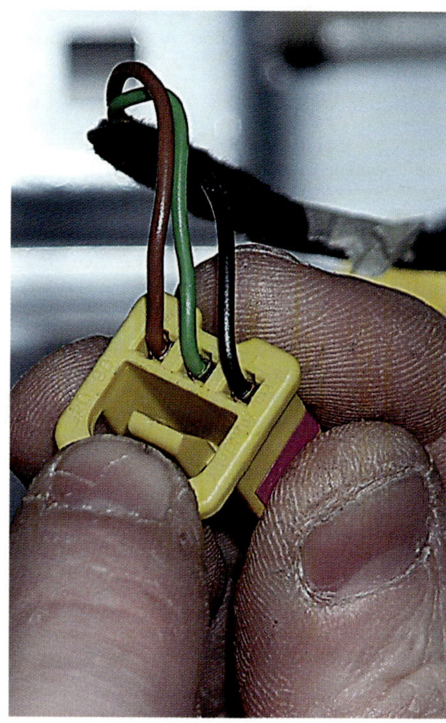

2-1-16. The connector (1) can be released after lifting the latch on the larger part of the clip, then pressing in the catch shown here on the smaller part.

2-1-17. Remove the two bolts (3).

2-1-18. Carefully remove the airbag unit (2) from the vehicle.

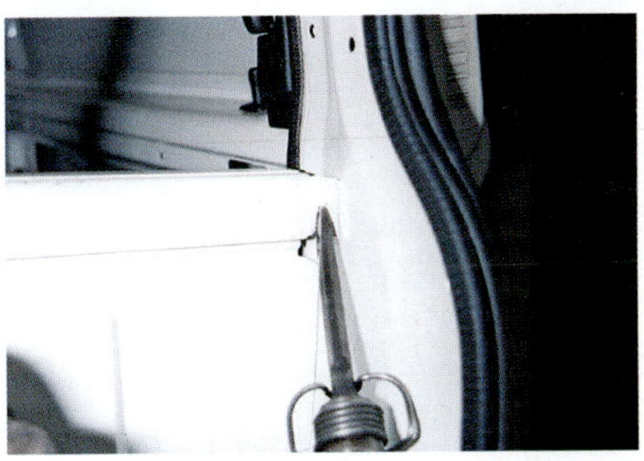

2-1-19. Barry starts by cutting away the top of the panel from its mountings on the door pillar. The welded-on tabs of metal are left attached to the door pillar for now.

2-1-20. He now cuts down the length of the bulkhead panel from top to bottom.

SAFETY FIRST!

- **Always** wear industrial-type protective gloves when cutting sheet metal.
- **Always** wear eye protection whenever using power tools for cutting metal.

Note: If you're not using an air chisel, don't fold the panel down: instead, use the saw to cut right across the panel from side to side.

2-1-21. The panel can now be folded down into the back of the van.

Remove bulkhead panel

On many vans, there is a bulkhead panel fitted behind the front seats and running right across the van. This must, of course, be removed before the conversion can be commenced.

In this section we will show Barry using an air chisel to cut away a typical bulkhead. If you are not experienced in carrying out this work, there may be some risk of damaging the van's outer panels and a better alternative would be a Clarke compressed air-powered panel saw. There will be a little bit more cleaning up to do with the angle grinder but a much reduced risk of causing damage. It will cut much closer to the edge of a panel than an electric jigsaw.

2-1-22. Barry cuts the joint between the bulkhead panel and the floor.

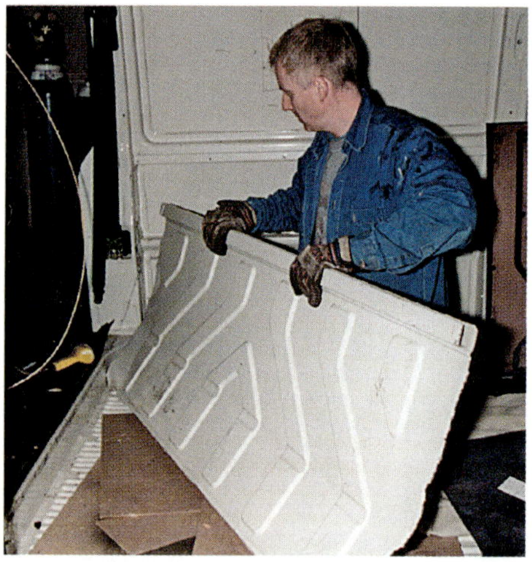

2-1-23. The redundant bulkhead panel can now be lifted out of the vehicle.

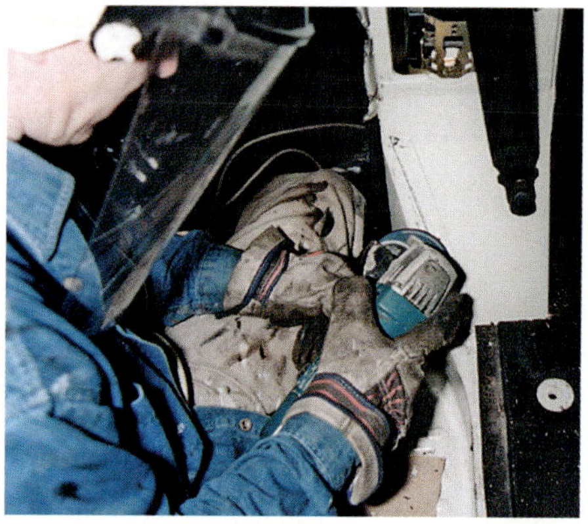

2-1-24. In some cases, there will be seams remaining on the vehicle, held in place with spot welds. Use the angle grinder to grind carefully through each spot weld but take great care not to cut into the panel beneath.

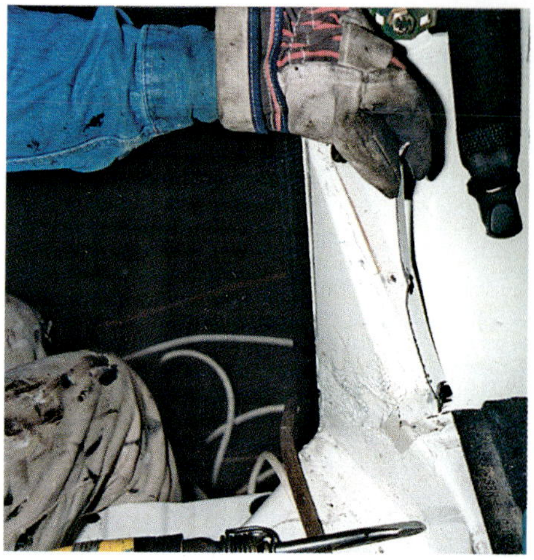

2-1-25. Use a screwdriver to lever the seam off the remnants of its spot welds and lift it away.

SECTION 2. FITTING STANDARD SIDE WINDOWS

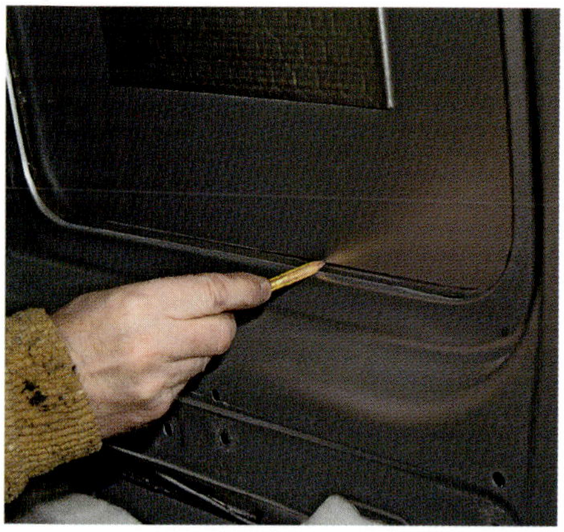

2-2-1. Barry Roberts pointed out that the window glass needed to be cut just inboard of the strengthening ribs.

2-2-2. Wearing an appropriate face mask, Barry drilled a series of small holes of about 3mm diameter (though the size is not crucial) …

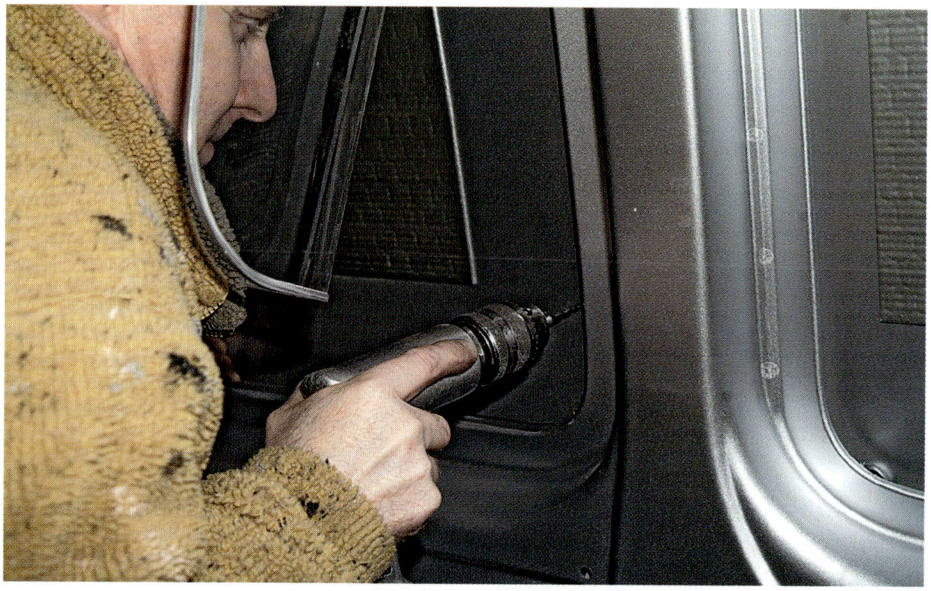

2-2-3. … to mark the edges of the reinforcing panels …

2-2-4. … all the way around.

2-2-5. He then transferred his attention to the outside of the vehicle and using a straight edge …

2-2-6. … transferred the positions indicated by the drilled holes to the outside of the van.

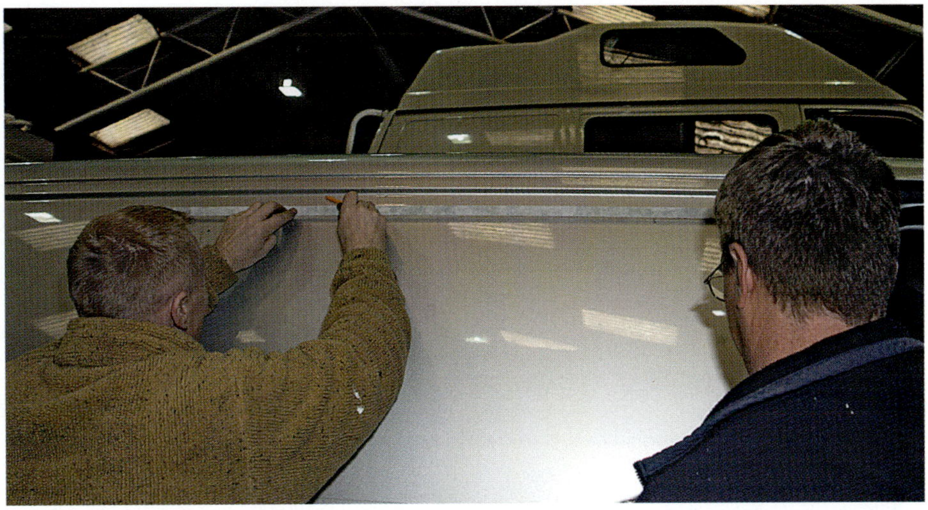

2-2-7. Because the paintwork is slippery, it's best if you have someone else to lend a hand in order to prevent the straight edge from slipping while you mark your cut lines.

2-2-8. Before starting work, Barry placed thick tape all the way around the outside of the cut lines so that the jigsaw can't cause any damage to the bodywork that will remain in place.

2-2-9. Barry drilled a series of holes adjacent to each other …

2-2-10. … so that he could make a start with the full width of the jigsaw blade.

2-2-11. Note how he started inboard of the cut line and then curved out to meet the cut line.

2-2-12. From inside the vehicle, you can see how the jigsaw blade was just skimming the reinforcing panel. It's a good idea to have someone on the inside watching to make sure that you don't stray from your cut line.

2-2-13. Barry cut the top, bottom and one end …

2-2-14. … leaving the other end until last …

2-2-15. … so that the person lending a hand was able to hold on to the panel being removed. It's important that the person who is removing the panel also wears heavy duty industrial gloves because the edges of the steel are very sharp indeed!

2-2-16. Even Barry, with all of his experience, deliberately cuts fractionally inboard of the line that he finally wants to make sure there is no risk of cutting into the reinforcing panel. Here he has gone all the way back around the aperture checking the position of the line and he has used the jigsaw to remove any surplus material.

2-2-17. Finally, he filed all the edges to get rid of burrs and roughness.

2-2-18. Before leaving the job, Barry used VW brand metal primer to prime all the bare edges of the steel that he had just cut. This, on the driver's-side of the vehicle, is the only window that needs to be fitted.

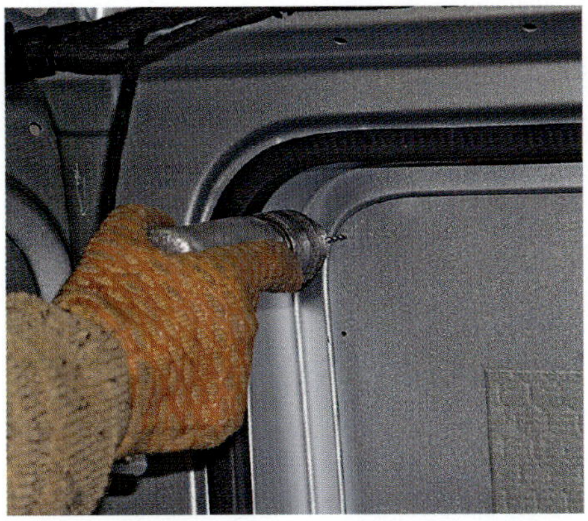

2-2-19. On the other side of the vehicle, Barry used exactly the same approach …

2-2-20. … to mark up and prepare for cutting out the two windows to be fitted. One goes in the sliding door and one in the rear section.

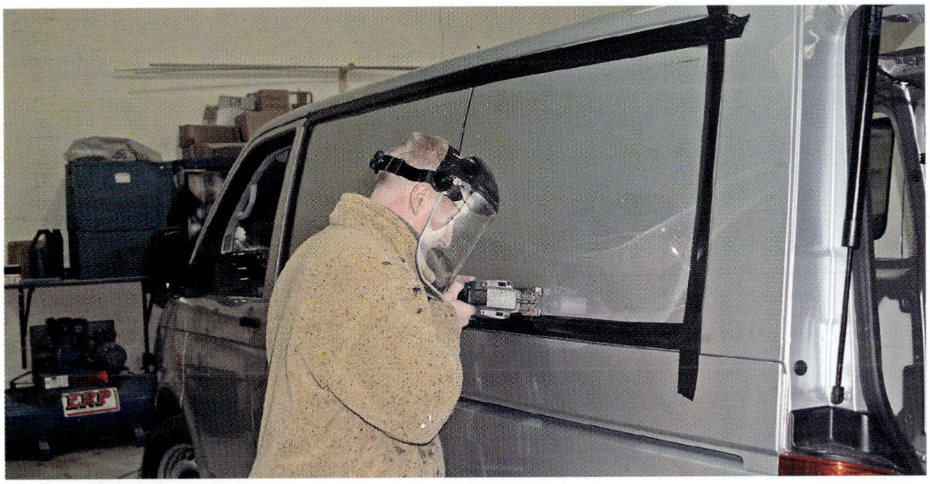

2-2-21. Barry followed exactly the same approach as for the other side of the vehicle but note that it isn't necessary to mask off between the sliding door and the rear panel because the whole area will be covered with glass.

2-2-22. The two panels were cut free and removed from the vehicle as before.

2-2-23. At this point, company owner Derek Andrews turned up and pretended that he was furious at Barry for having removed the 'wrong' piece of steel! Barry offered to weld it back in again for him!

2-2-24. Already, the erstwhile delivery van is looking less commercial because of the cutouts for the rear windows.

2-2-25. This is the rubber trim that needs to be fitted to the cut edges on the insides of the window apertures.

2-2-26. Barry pushed it on ...

2-2-27. ... then tapped it fully home, working along the strip as he went.

2-2-28. Next, he prepared to fit the glass. The glass was simply bonded to the vehicle's bodywork and Barry used masking tape to define the edges of the areas to be bonded.

2-2-29. The bonding material is extremely strong and tenacious and if you haven't used it before, you may want to apply even more masking tape than this, covering a greater width.

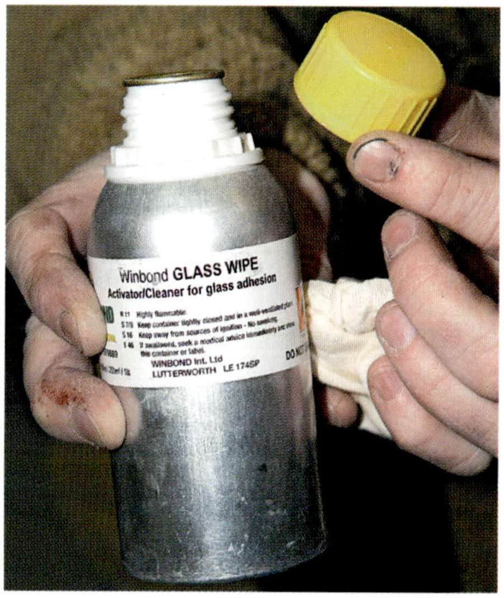

2-2-30. This was the special activator/cleaner that Barry used ...

2-2-31. … all the way around the edge of the glass sliding window that he will be fitting to the vehicle.

2-2-32. The special primer for painted metal …

2-2-33. … was applied to the whole of the area inboard of the masking tape.

2-2-34. Note that the primer 'sticks' extremely well, so you have to beware of spots that get on the paintwork.

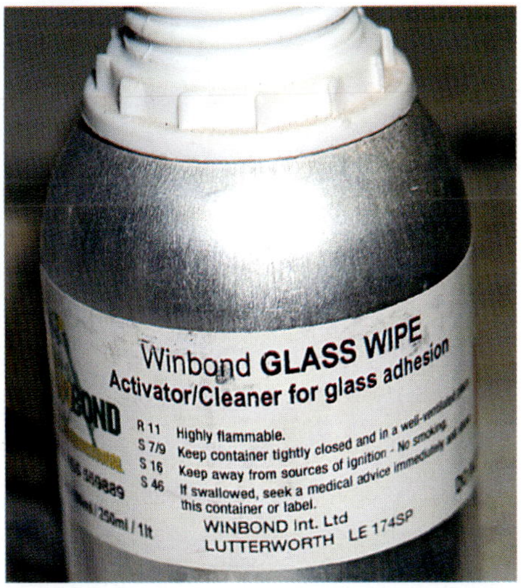

2-2-35. Barry goes back to the activator/cleaner …

2-2-36. … and used some of it to wipe the primer from the bodywork before it hardened. This is most important!

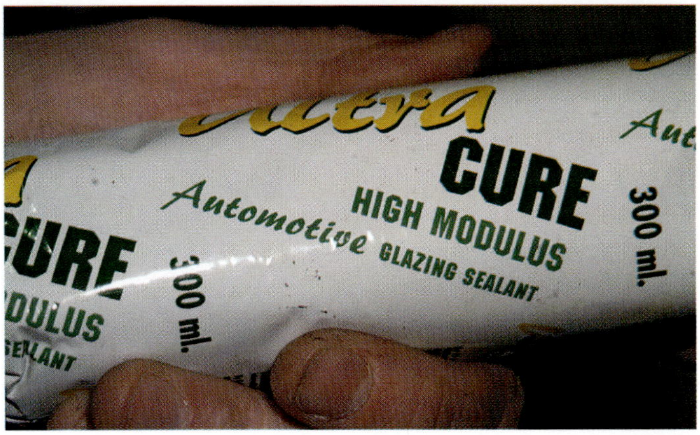

2-2-37. The next product to be used was the special adhesive for bonding the glass in place.

2-2-38. When this work was carried out, it was in the middle of February and before using it, Barry placed the adhesive in a bucket of hot water to soften it.

2-2-39. The nozzle on Barry's applicator gun had a special cutout in the end so that the adhesive formed an inverted 'V'-shape.

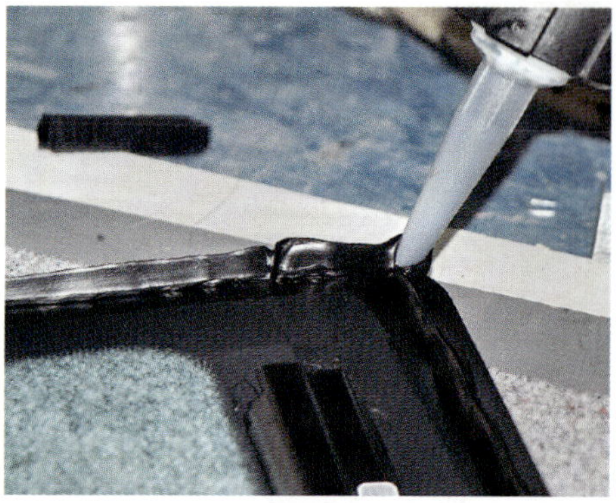

2-2-40. Barry took special care that there were no gaps anywhere around the line of the adhesive.

2-2-41. It is in the corners where you have to take special care that there are no gaps.

2-2-42. Barry and Roy working together lifted the sliding door glass into position …

2-2-43. … before pushing it home.

2-2-44. The glass tends to slide so Roy held onto it for a while …

2-2-45. … while Barry got hold of a clamp and lightly clamped it into place. After fitting the clamps, Barry recommends that there is an even gap filled with adhesive between the glass and the door panel of about 1.5 to 2mm all the way around.

2-2-46. Barry evenly clamped the glass in each of the four corners but note that the clamps each had a plastic pad on its head so that it didn't risk cracking the glass.

2-2-47. You also have to watch that the clamp is clear of the fixed bodywork when the sliding door is open.

2-2-48. This is the sliding glass on the opposite side of the vehicle which was fitted in the same way …

2-2-49. … except that this time it was held with tape.

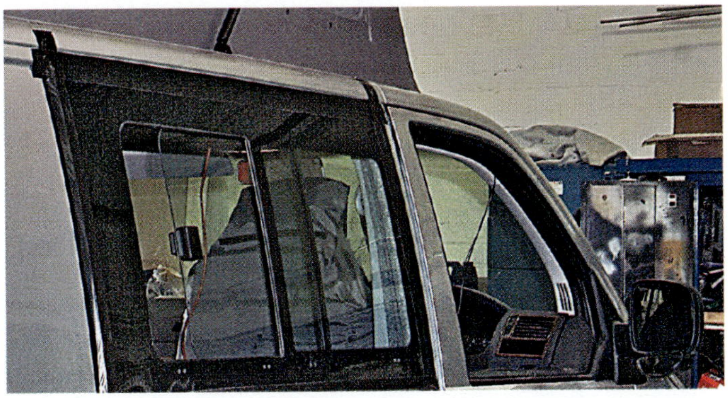

2-2-50. The glass was left overnight (at this cold time of the year) for the bonding agent to set before removing the tape. Theoretically, you don't need to leave it as long as this as you can see from the time taken on roadside windscreen repairs, when bonded windscreens are replaced in a similar fashion. However, there is no urgency and it's best to allow plenty of time.

SECTION 3. FITTING A DUMMY WINDOW

The rear-right panel is covered by the wardrobe and, if you are converting a window van, you'll have to make a trim panel to cover the inside of the window so that the raw back of the wardrobe doesn't show. However, in our case a van was being converted and I didn't like the appearance of the plain panel in the side of the vehicle. The general approach has been to make our vehicle look as much like a Caravelle as possible and to this end, Autoglass came out and showed how it fits a glass panel. Prior to that, I had some preparation to carry out.

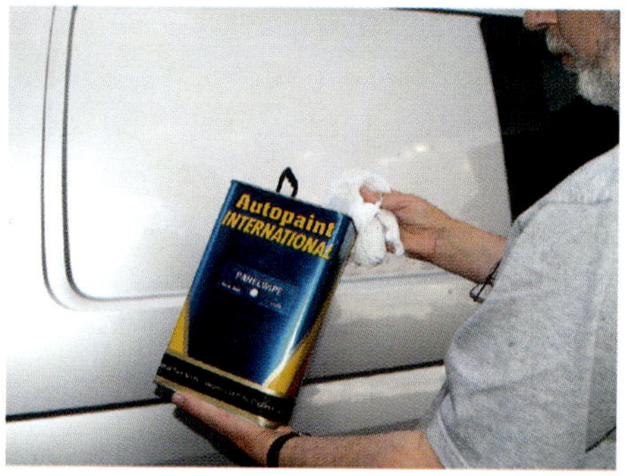

2-3-1. The first job was to degrease the whole area of the panel using Autopaint International's Panel Wipe.

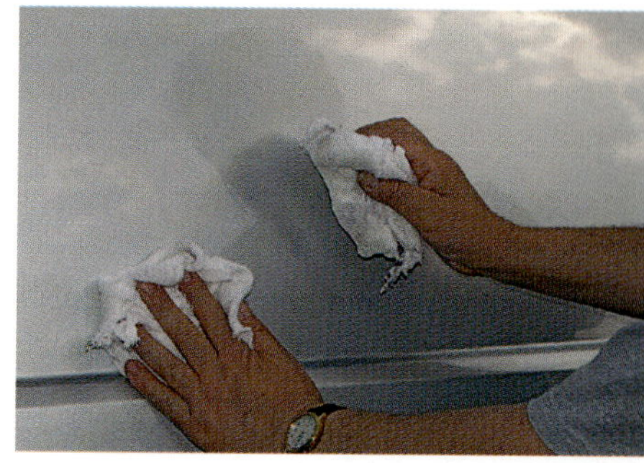

2-3-2. The correct way is to use two cloths: one to apply the wipe and one to rub the surface clean. This is the most effective way of removing silicones and other contamination.

2-3-3. I then held up the glass to see where the edges would come to …

2-3-4. … and masked all the way around …

2-3-5. … including the edge of the sliding glass panel fitted by Leisuredrive.

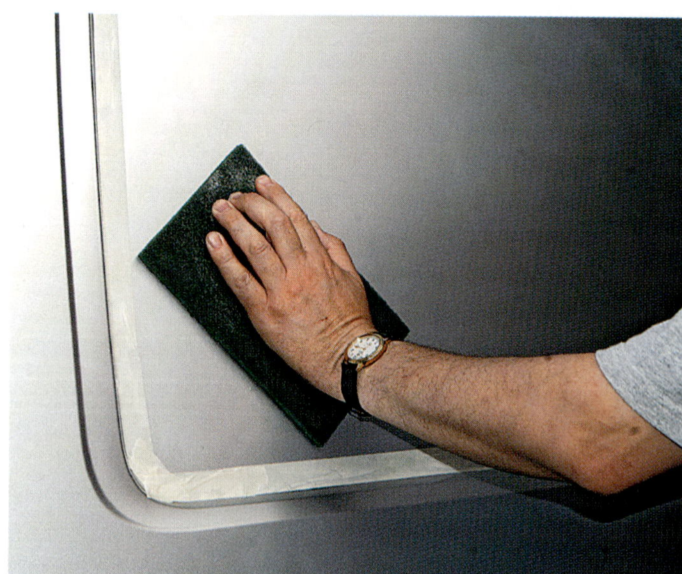

2-3-6. Also from Autopaint came one of these abrasive pads, rather like a kitchen cleaner and I used this to lightly abrade the entire surface of the panel that would be behind the glass.

2-3-7. Next I went to town on masking off the rear of the vehicle. Overspray can carry quite a long way, especially when you are working outdoors even when there is no wind obviously blowing. You certainly don't want the type of paint that I was going to be using blowing over the rest of the bodywork.

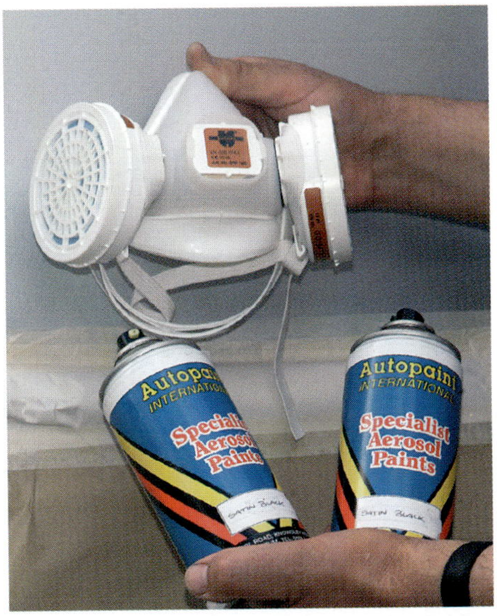

2-3-8. From Autopaint International, I obtained cans of satin black aerosol.

2-3-9. Wearing the appropriate Würth face mask, I applied thin coats of satin black paint in horizontal strips …

2-3-10. … followed by vertical ones.

2-3-11. When my old mate Mel from Autoglass arrived, the masking tape had been removed and Mel admired the several coats of satin black paint that I had applied to the vehicle.

2-3-12. Mel sprayed glass cleaner onto the inner surface of the window …

2-3-13. … wiped it off carefully …

2-3-14. … and spent some time making sure that there was no speck of dust on the inner surface of the glass. There won't be any access to this part of the glass and so any dirt you leave on there will be on there for keeps.

2-3-15. He used an air line to make doubly sure that no dust remained on the surface.

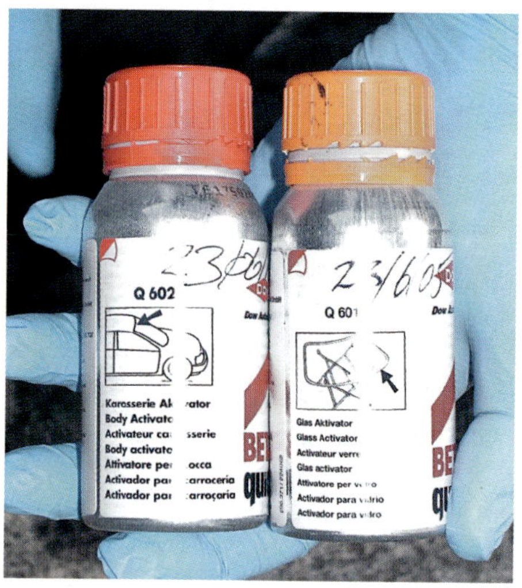

2-3-16. These are the two activator products used by Autoglass. On the left is the activator for the bodywork and on the right that for the glass.

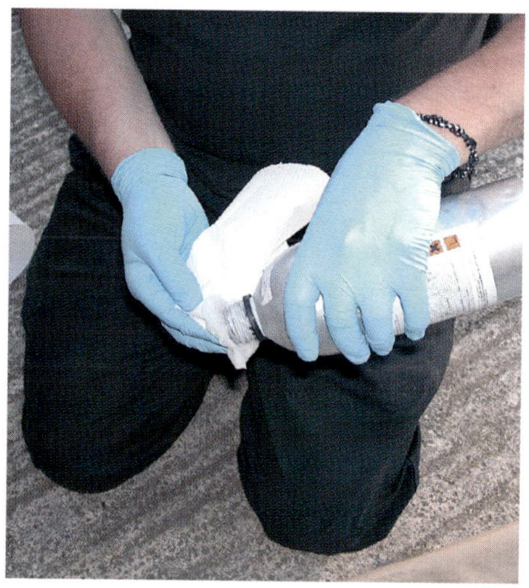

2-3-17. Using a slightly different product to that used by Leisuredrive, Mel poured some special cleaner onto a rag …

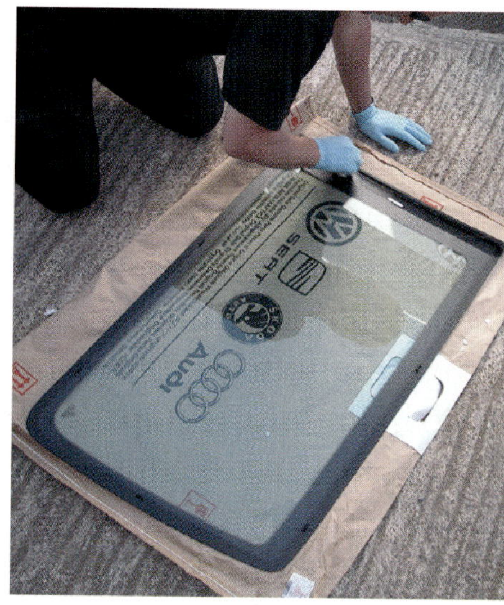

2-3-18. … and wiped the edge of the glass to make sure that it was chemically clean.

2-3-19. Mel used the applicator in the can to apply activator to the edge of the glass.

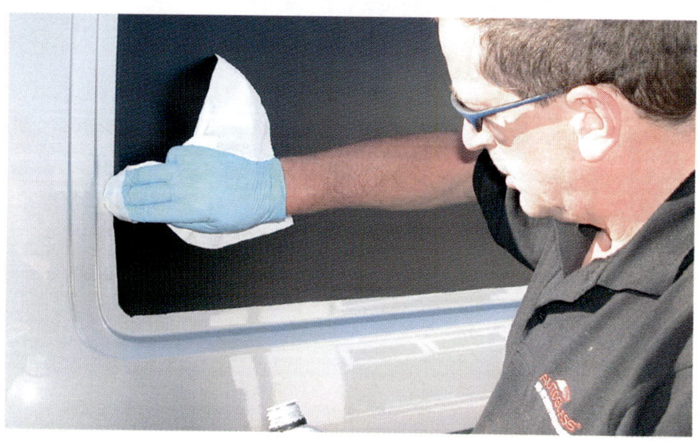

2-3-20. He then cleaned the edge of the bodywork just as he had done the glass.

2-3-21. Activator was then applied to the bodywork also.

2-3-22. Mel used his rechargeable power applicator to put a bead of bonding material all the way around the panel on the vehicle.

2-3-23. Mel used these two sucker handles on the glass …

2-3-24. …turned the glass over and blew off the surface to remove any dust that might have landed on there in the last few minutes…

2-3-25. …and lifted the glass into position on the side of the vehicle.

2-3-26. He aligned it correctly …

2-3-27. …then held it in place with masking tape.

2-3-28. After a few minutes in the warm sunshine, the glass adhesive had gone off sufficiently for the tape to be removed.

2-3-29. I now had my wish and the right side of the vehicle had the look of a Caravelle about it. The satin black paint behind the glass fools the eye into thinking that you are looking into a darkened interior. When combined with the tinted glass that we show being fitted later, this becomes indistinguishable from a normal window.

SECTION 4. MAKING AND FITTING A HIGH-TOP

2-4-1. Leisuredrive makes all of its own fibreglass panels. This is a new high-top roof being laid-up (as the fibreglassing term is), in the appropriate mould.

2-4- 2. After rolling on the gel coat and letting it go off, another layer of resin is rolled inside the mould and fibreglass added.

2-4-3. More resin is placed on top …

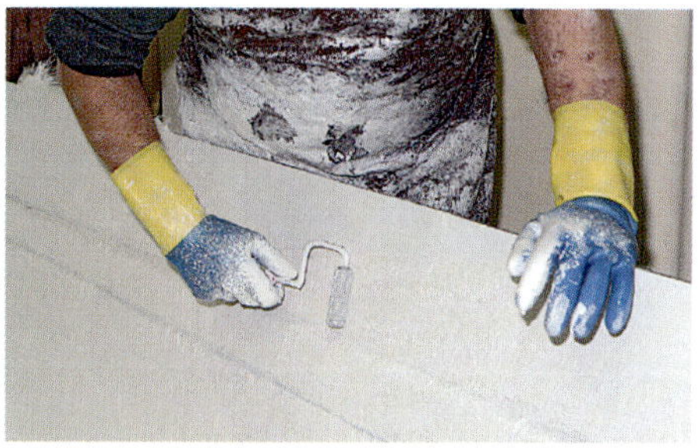

2-4-4. … and rolled out with a metal roller so that the fibreglass is fully saturated by the resin.

2-4-5. For this top, wooden reinforcements are stapled in place …

2-4-6. … then more wooden reinforcements added where a skylight will be fitted.

2-4-9. More fibreglass is laid up over all of these reinforcing sections.

SAFETY FIRST!

It is essential to always wear an efficient particle mask or air-fed breathing mask when machining fibreglass because the particles are potentially extremely injurious to health.

2-4-10. This is a different top but the principle remains the same. The position of the side window is being marked with a template …

2-4-7. This wooden section with a metal plate bonded onto it is added …

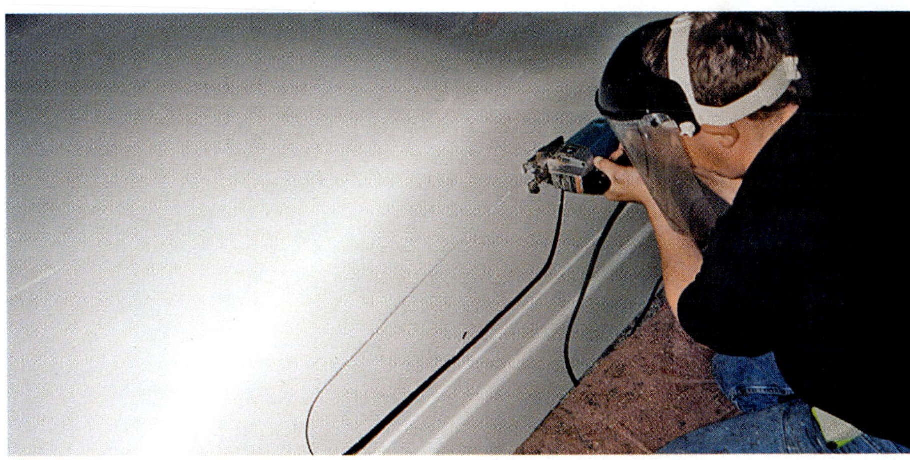

2-4-11. … before being cut out with a jigsaw.

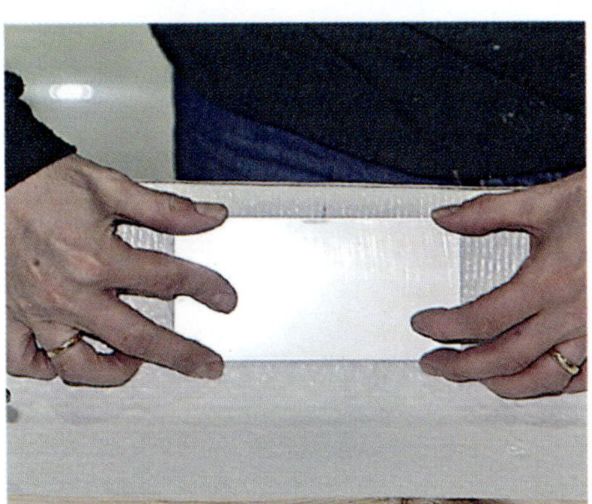

2-4-8. … to provide extra reinforcement where needed.

2-4-12. The inside of this top is now prepared for fitting the interior trim by coating it with adhesive.

2-4-13. The new trim material is lowered into place …

2-4-14. … and carefully rolled flat to promote good adhesion and provide a smooth finish.

2-4-15. Now it's time to fit the side trim boards.

2-4-16. All hands to the high-top as another one is lifted out of its mould at Leisuredrive.

2-4-17. Window apertures are cut through the side trim boards and then the insides of the hard top can be finished off with trim material.

2-4-18. The rubber is cut to length so that the ends provide a tight fit. The ends are then glued together with Superglue.

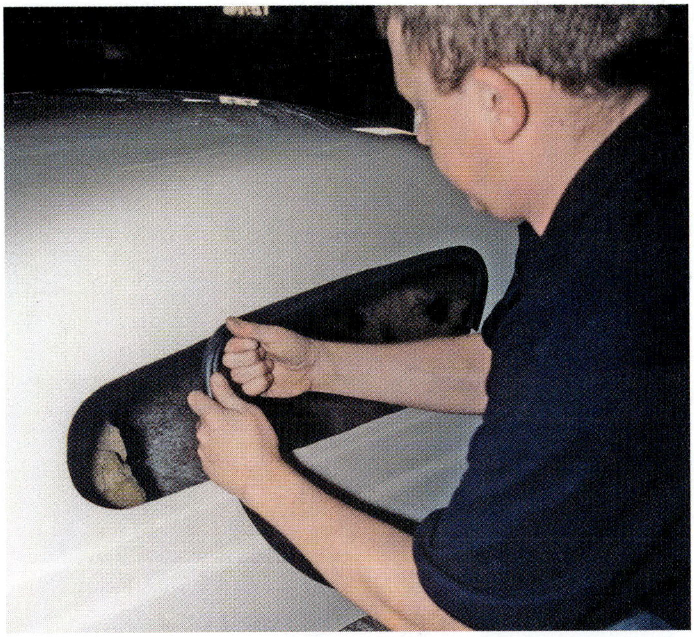

2-4-19. Glazing rubber is added to the edge of the window aperture.

2-4-20. With the aid of silicone lubricant, the glass is inserted into the base of the rubber …

2-4-21. … and eased into the slot in the rubber all the way round.

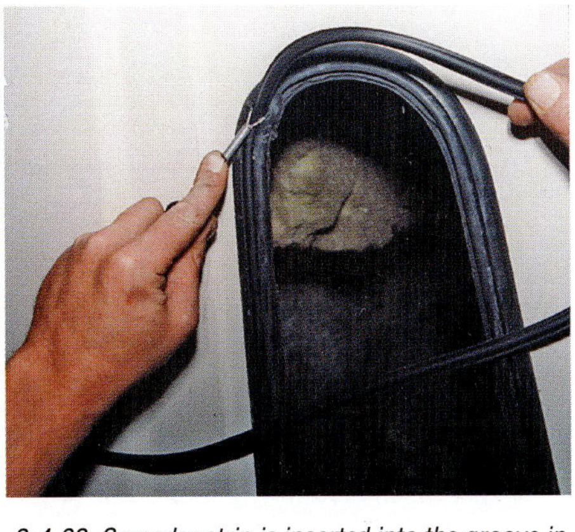

2-4-22. Spreader strip is inserted into the groove in the outer edge of the rubber to spread it and hold the glass tightly in place. It's almost impossible to do this without the correct insertion tool, shown here.

2-4-23. The spreader strip is cut to length and the ends butted carefully together. The high-top is now ready for fitting to the vehicle.

2-4-24. The high-top is lifted into place and it is essential to make sure that the top is seated precisely in the correct position before moving on.

Fitting the high-top

The vehicle shown here is not a T5 but an earlier Volkswagen. The principles employed by Leisuredrive are similar, however.

2-4-25. This is another larger van with a Hi-Top roof being fitted but the principle is exactly the same. The fitter starts by applying masking tape all the way around the lower edge of the roof so that excess sealer is easier to get off. Once again, you should check with your roof supplier on the type of sealer that is recommended for this particular work. My own preference would be to use a Würth sealer and you can ask your Würth supplier for data sheets which will advise on the correct sealer to use with GRP and steel, and also on the correct way of using it. In general, it's essential that all the surfaces to be bonded are thoroughly cleaned with panel wipe so that no trace of dirt of grease – even invisible grease from your fingers – can remain on either of the surfaces to be bonded together.

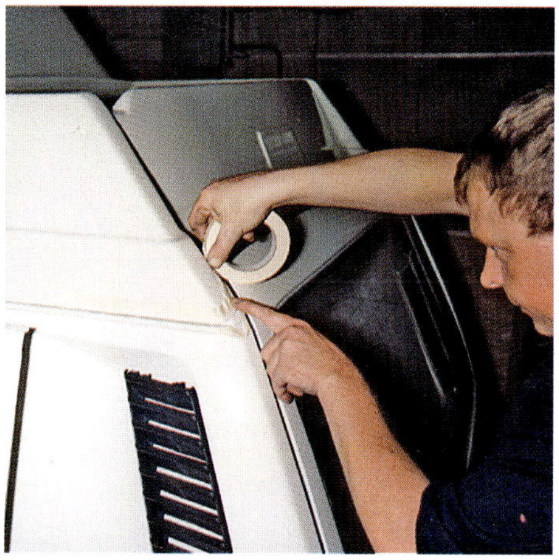

2-4-26. The fitter takes his time with the masking tape, especially around the tricky shapes where the doors are fitted.

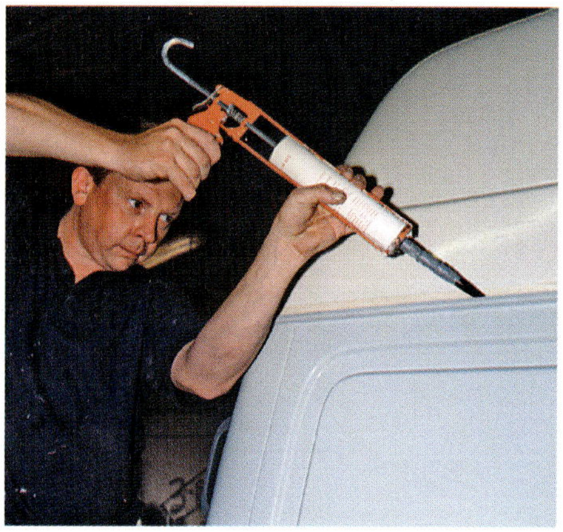

2-4-27. If you are retaining the colour of the vehicle's bodywork and also that of the high-top, it's a good idea to try to use a sealer which is the same colour as the bodywork.

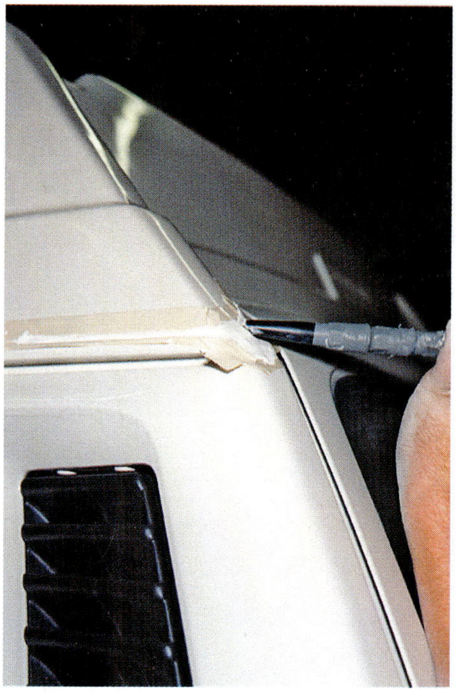

2-4-28. In this case, the whole of the van will be resprayed, so it's possible to use regular black sealer. It's most important to achieve a consistent run of sealer with no gaps and with lots of sealer in place to not only prevent the ingress of water, but also to add the strength of the two panels being bonded together.

2-4-29. From the point of view of strength, sealer applied to the inside, where it can be injected between the van's bodywork and the high-top, is even more important. Once again, make absolutely certain the there are no gaps and that there is sufficient sealer to bond the top in place.

Top tip!
- *Just in case you won't be able to get sealer down between the two panels once the top is in place, be sure to apply a large quantity of bonding sealer to the roof of the van at the point where the high-top will sit.*

2-4-30. The outside is finished off by peeling off the masking tape and then wiping down the bodywork where excess sealer may have oozed out.

2-4-31. The interior trim is fitted in place so that the high-top matches the rest of the van.

2-5-A1. There had been a delay while the Reimo roof was delivered and this had led to some of the jobs being carried out on our T5 being done in an unusual order. However, all of the work remains the same, whichever order you choose to do it in.

SECTION 5. ELEVATING ROOF

Part A. Fitting roof reinforcing frame

Derek Andrews, the man behind Leisuredrive has made the important point that the work shown on the vehicle's bodywork – and in particular in this chapter – is not to be undertaken by amateurs.
If you are not accomplished and trained in this type of work, don't be tempted to just 'have a go'! This part of the manual in particular deals with the structural rigidity of the vehicle. Cutting away the roof removes some of that structural rigidity and it can only be replaced if the strengthening panels shown here are fitted in a skilled and appropriate manner.

2-5-A2. Inside the box, now at the top of the picture, is the well made Reimo elevating roof panel. In front of it, you can see the strengthening section, the hydraulic struts and, on the left, some of the sealing strip and sealant used when fitting the assembly.

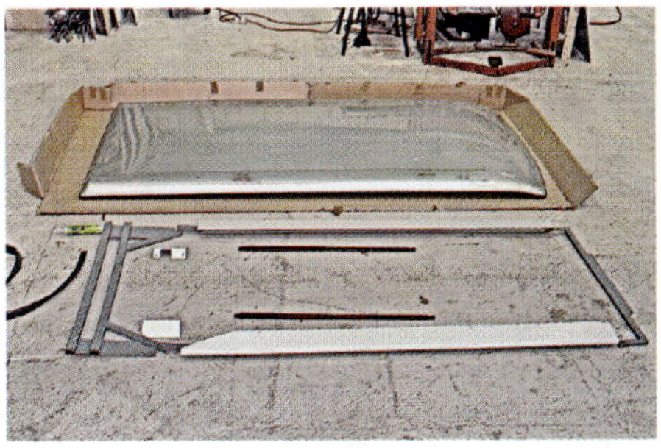

2-5-A3. It is important to remember that, as the roof is cut away, filings will drop inside the vehicle and so the seats, if not removed, must be carefully covered.

2-5-A4. Leisuredrive's foreman, Barry, recommends that for the same reason, the windows are closed, preventing any filings from dropping down into the door cavities.

2-5-A5. This is the rear section of the reinforcing framework with the four captive threads arrowed.

2-5-A6. Barry offered up the frame into the roof space on our van and showed how the captive threads line up with four pre-existing holes in the van body.

2-5-A7. With the frame in its correct location, Barry marked out, with a pencil, where the edges will be.

2-5-A8. He used a small diameter drill to mark the corner of where the cut will have to be made, using the same technique that he followed when fitting the windows. These holes, when viewed from above, will tell him where the extremities of each cut need to be made.

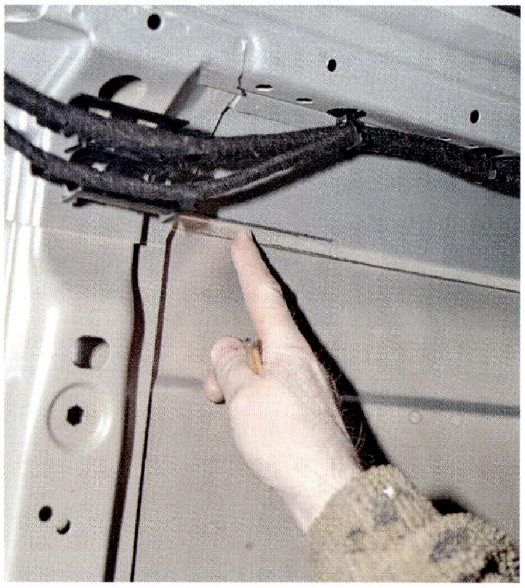

2-5-A9. Before going any further, Barry reminded us that there are cables clipped to the roof space and these must be avoided at all costs!

2-5-A10. Barry knows that this particular roof frame needs a cutout 25mm inboard from the roof box section and he makes a mark accordingly.

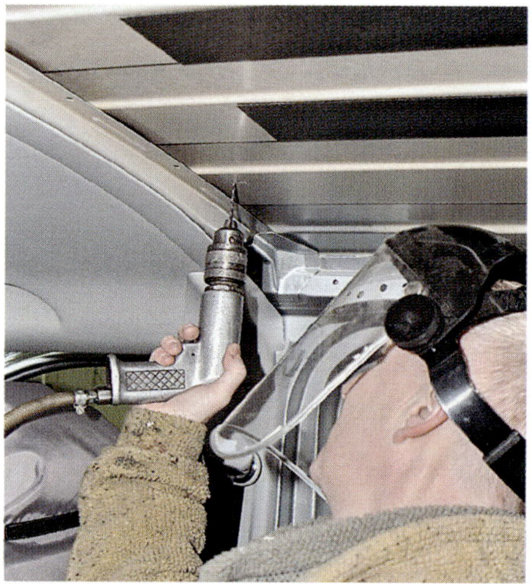

2-5-A11. Once again, a hole is drilled from beneath so that, when on top of the roof, he can see where the cut lines will be.

2-5-A12. Those cut lines are now connected up, across the back of the roof …

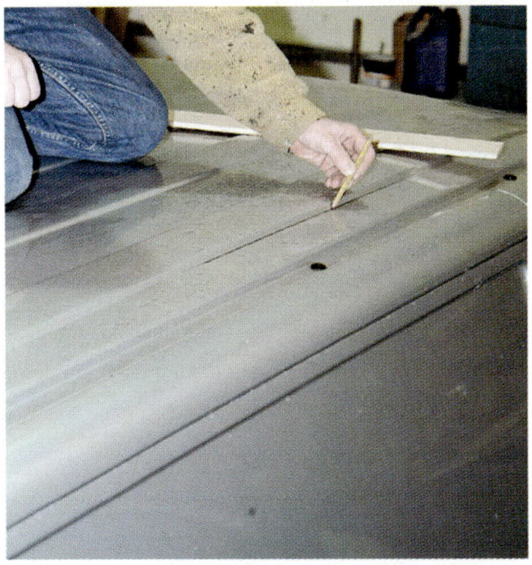

2-5-A13. … following this rib down the length of the roof …

2-5-A14. … and across the front, just behind the front door. Anyone carrying out this work for the first time will need to refer to the Reimo fitting instructions and the dimensions of the reinforcing sections supplied, as well as noting the variations that Barry built into this particular job as shown later in this chapter.

2-5-A15. Barry used his drill to make a series of holes which he then linked together by pushing sideways carefully on the drill (if you're not careful the drill will break!). Note that in this instance, where he needed to begin cutting through a double-sided panel, a slot needed to be made in both sections.

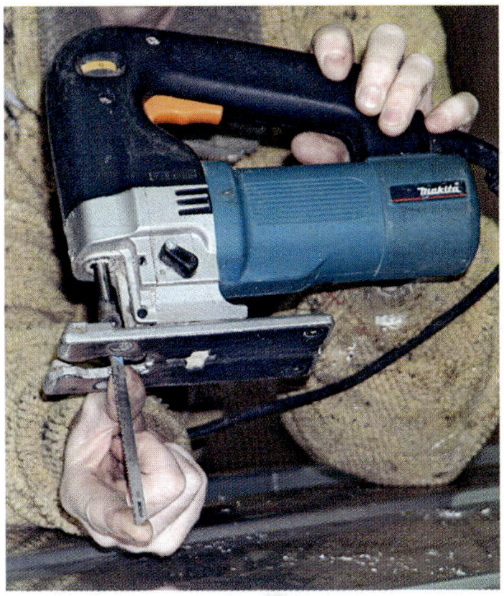

2-5-A16. Barry pointed out that the jigsaw blade he used had to be long enough to cut through the widest box section.

2-5-A17. Barry started at the front …

2-5-A18. … and cut straight across to the other side.

2-5-A19. He cut down the length towards the back …

2-5-A20. … and then continued the cut round the corner …

2-5-A21. … and across the back of the van.

2-5-A22. Before going any further, he supported the redundant roof panel with strips of suitable plywood across each cut corner.

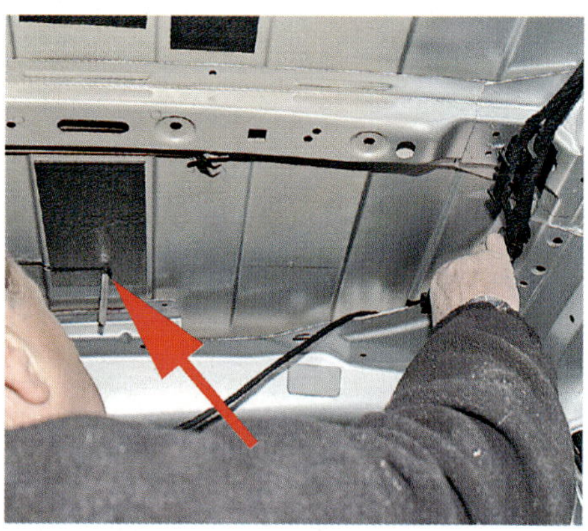

2-5-A23. Also, you can see that the blade (arrowed) was heading for the other side of the van where the wiring loom was situated.

Important note:
• The work carried out on our vehicle was slightly different to that carried out on most and for that reason, this sequence switches to another van, as shown here.

2-5-A24. Derek lent a hand by staying inside the van while Barry cut through the remainder of the roof and used a length of timber to make sure that the wiring loom was held well out of the way of the blade.

2-5-A25. By now, the entire roof section had been cut out all the way round.

2-5-A26. With gloved hands inside the roof and standing to one side, he carefully removed the redundant panel over the top …

2-5-A27. … and over the side, obviously taking great care not to damage the side of the vehicle.

2-5-A28. You can see that the front-most cut was carried out just behind the roof crossmember which is positioned approximately above the seat headrest.

2-5-A29 This is how the cutout area will look AFTER it's done, so you can see where the cut goes and – most important! – the wires to be avoided.

2-5-A30. If the area above the seats is going to be cut out, this is how Leisuredrive proceed: wearing suitable face mask and gloves, Barry cut through the cross-section with an angle grinder.

2-5-A31. Because of the position of the sliding door gear and the wiring loom, Barry had to use an air chisel on this side of the vehicle.

2-5-A32. He then took the crossmember away from the roof.

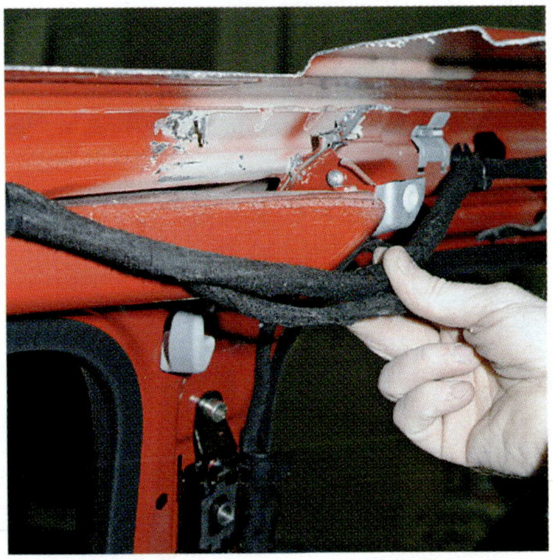

2-5-A33. The area around the sliding door had to be cleaned up, untidy sections of steel having to be made smooth with the angle grinder.

Starting to fit the frame

Whether or not the front part of the roof is going to be cut away, the next stage is to fit the rear and sides of the reinforcing frame.

2-5-A34. The first part of the reinforcing frame to be fitted is the rear section that we saw earlier. However, before going any further, Barry filed all of the cut edges smooth, blew all swarf away using an air line and then painted all the edges of bare metal.

2-5-A35. Barry inserted the rear section into the roof space. You can see that he had already primed the ends of this section where they fit inside the sidemembers.

2-5-A36. Barry screwed the crossmember in place through the four holes in the roof shown earlier.

2-5-A37. In this (untypical) case, the side reinforcing section was going to have to be cut short because the roof was not extended over the front seats. Barry started by measuring up …

2-5-A38. … then transferring the measurements to the side panel …

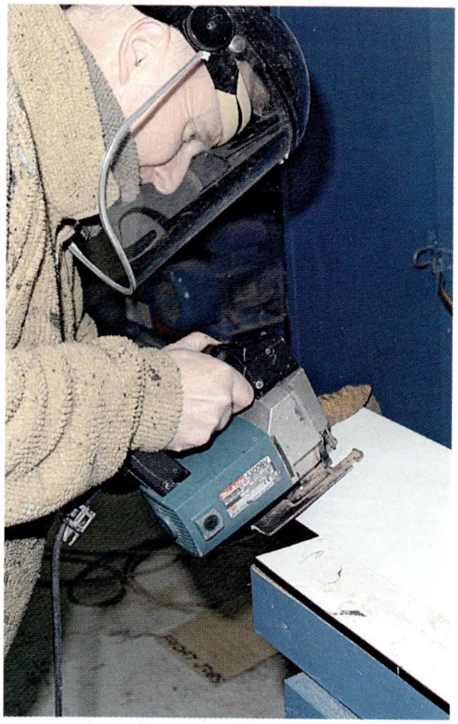

2-5-A39. … before cutting off to length.

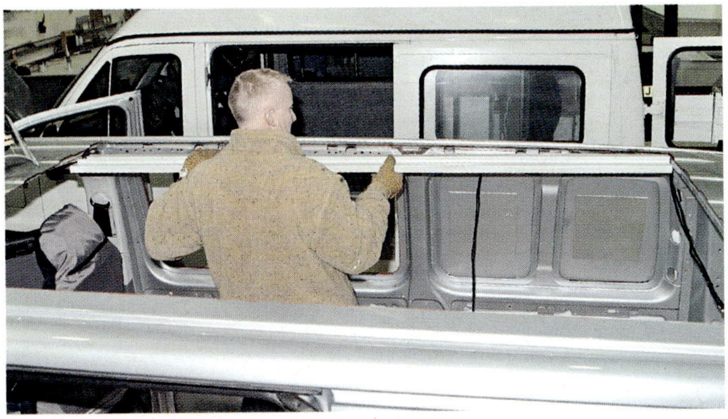

2-5-A40. Barry offered up the side panel into position, slotting it over the leg on the end of the rear crossmember.

2-5-A41. This is a length of cable that Barry already fitted so that it would be in position for the strip light in the cooking area. He measures its location …

2-5-A42. … transferred the position to the side reinforcing member …

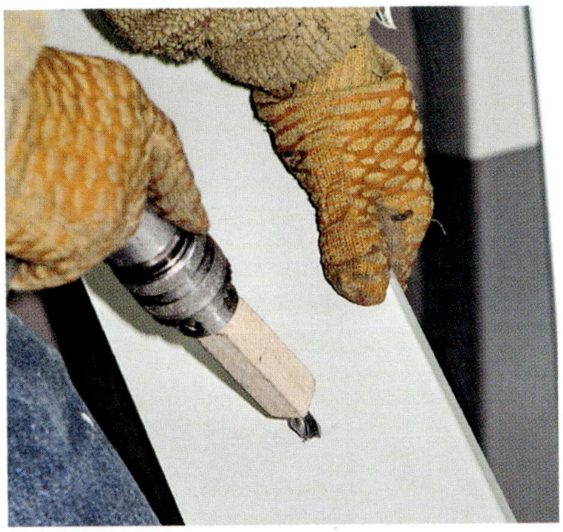

2-5-A43. … and drilled a suitable hole. Note Barry's use of a piece of wood with a hole drilled right through it to act as a depth stop.

2-5-A44. Barry made some final adjustments to the shape of the end of the panel …

2-5-A45. … and then primed all cut edges in the usual way.

2-5-A46. Before locating the side member on the van roof, Barry applied sealant liberally along the edges to be joined.

Top tip!
- Würth's Bond & Seal fulfils the dual purpose of both sealing the gap and bonding the panels together, imparting extra strength.

2-5-A47. Barry slotted the side reinforcing section in position.

2-5-A48. At the rear, Barry drilled and pop riveted the panel in place.

2-5-A49. Then, with the first pop rivet fixed, he drilled the rest of the holes required ...

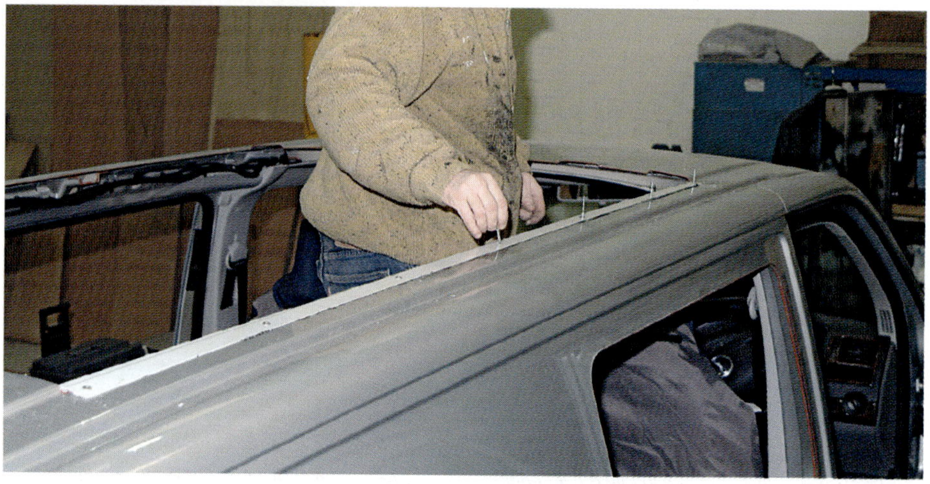

2-5-A50. ... inserted the line of pop rivets ...

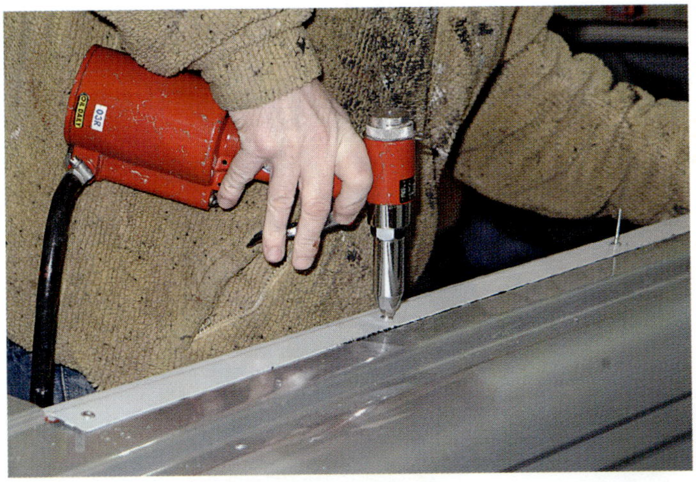

2-5-A51. … and riveted them all in place using his power rivet gun.

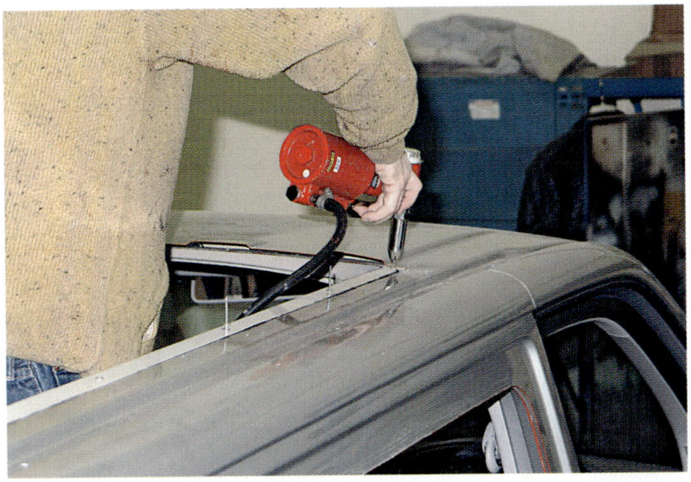

2-5-A52. The last rivet was applied at the front of the side reinforcing section.

2-5-A53. Excess sealant could then be cleaned off.

2-5-A54. The next step was to rivet the reinforcing section to the underside of the van roof. Again, it is best to apply Würth Bond & Seal to double-up on the strength.

2-5-A55. Note that the cable for the light has been pushed through the panel ready for a grommet to be slid over the bare edges of the metal on the reinforcing section.

2-5-A56. Now, Barry has gone back to the rear end of the panel and drilled into the reinforcing section which sticks out from the strengthening rear crossmember. These sections are also bonded and riveted together.

2-5-A57. More drilling, bonding and riveting is carried out between the lower ribs on the roof just ahead of the tailgate and the reinforcing rear crossmember.

2-5-A58. Barry gets some help with offering up the front reinforcing section to the front of the cab.

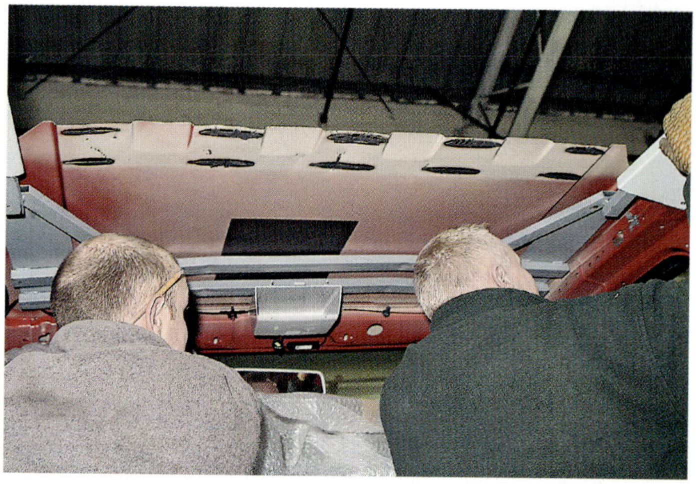

2-5-A59. The reinforcing section was carefully pushed above the housing in the top of the roof …

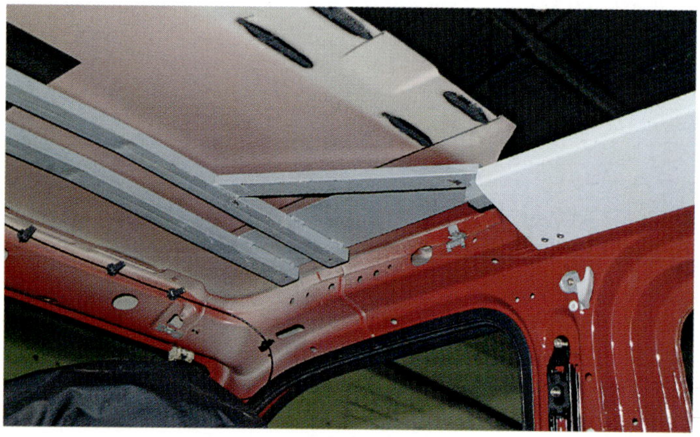

2-5-A60. … and then fed back into the side reinforcing sections.

2-5-A61. Barry drilled just two holes, one on each side to enable him to pop rivet the front reinforcing section in place for now holding it in position.

2-5-A62. He measured the distance to be cut from the earlier cut line. He could just as easily have drilled from beneath as he did previously to indicate the cutting positions.

2-5-A63. Barry transferred those positions to the top of the roof …

2-5-A64. … and then drew his cut lines on the top of the roof.

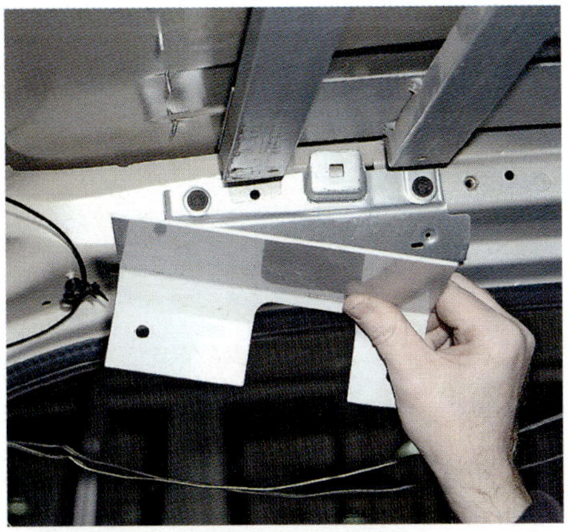

2-5-A65. Next, these separate strengthening plates were to be fitted between the van roof and the reinforcing box sections.

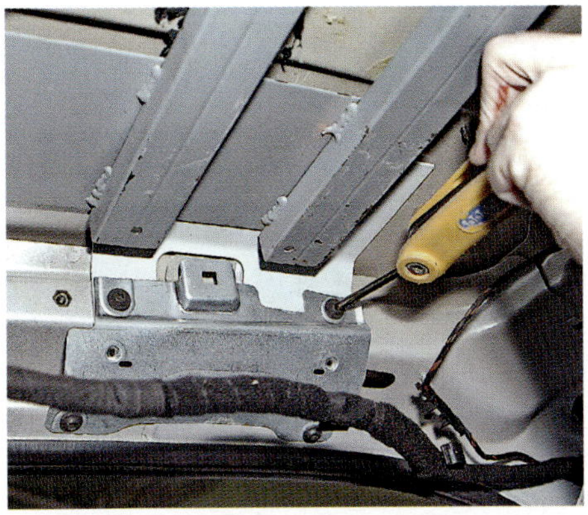

2-5-A66. On some vehicles, this reinforcing plate is found only on the grab-handle side; on others, there's one on each side. When fitted, it has to be unscrewed ...

2-5-A67. ... and the bottom screws loosened so that the top can be eased away ...

2-5-A68. ... and the strengthening plate inserted.

2-5-A69. Where no reinforcing plate was fitted, and making sure that the reinforcing plates were snug against everything to which they would be fitted, Barry drilled ...

2-5-A70. ... then pop riveted each plate to the sides of the van ...

2-5-A71. ... and then right through the reinforcing sections and into the original van roof above.

2-5-A72. All of the remaining drilling and pop riveting then took place between the reinforcing sections and the roof that remains in place.

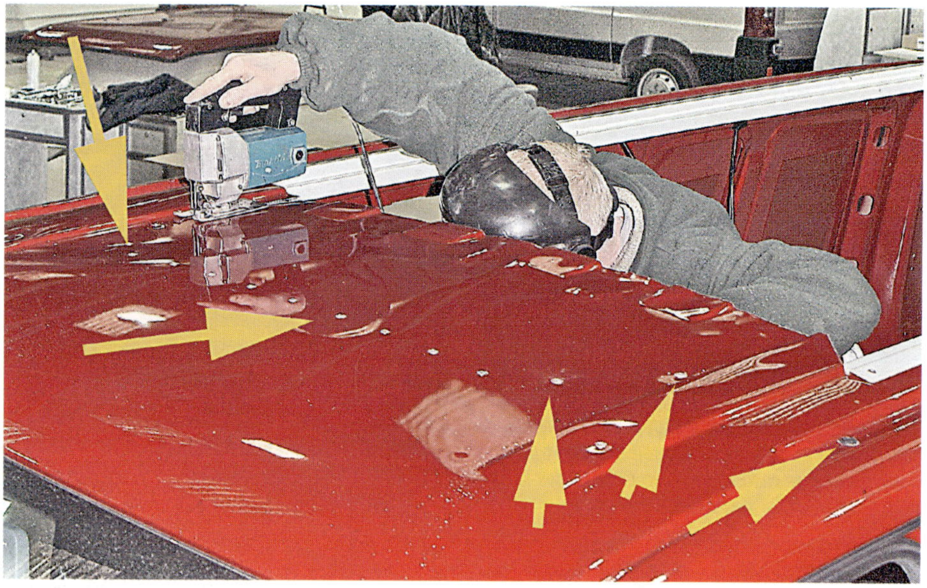

2-5-A73. Here you can see many of the pop rivets (arrowed). Barry is now carefully cutting ALONG the cut lines he made earlier, while stopping at regular intervals to have a look beneath to make sure that the jigsaw blade is reasonably close to the box sections, without cutting into them.

SAFETY FIRST!

Anyone carrying out this work is very strongly recommended to wear heavy duty industrial gloves to prevent any risk of cuts from the sharp edges being created.

2-5-A74. Barry continued to cut the roof away.

2-5-A75. The redundant section of steel was removed from the vehicle.

2-5-A76. Later, Barry went back and trimmed off any surplus material, up against the edge of the box sections. Obviously, it's best to leave on too much and trim it off later than to risk cutting into the reinforcing sections.

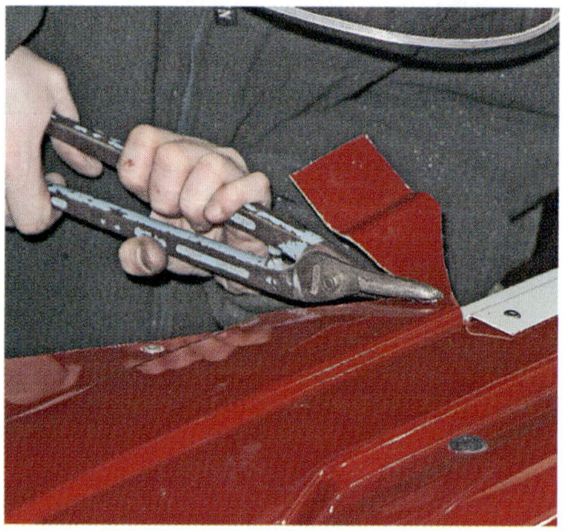

2-5-A77. Where there are problems with access or there is a risk of cutting into the wiring loom, it may be best to use tin snips in certain locations.

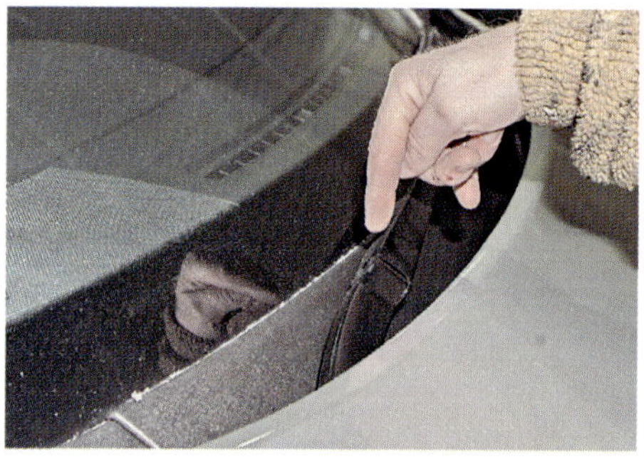

2-5-A78. After all the cutting has been finished, it is most important that the vehicle is checked all over for filings. In particular, the area around the front screen tends to trap filings and, rather than blowing them away when they can get lodged elsewhere, it is best to remove them with a vacuum cleaner or a magnet.

2-5-A79. Barry refitted the side curtain airbags to our vehicle as described in detail earlier.

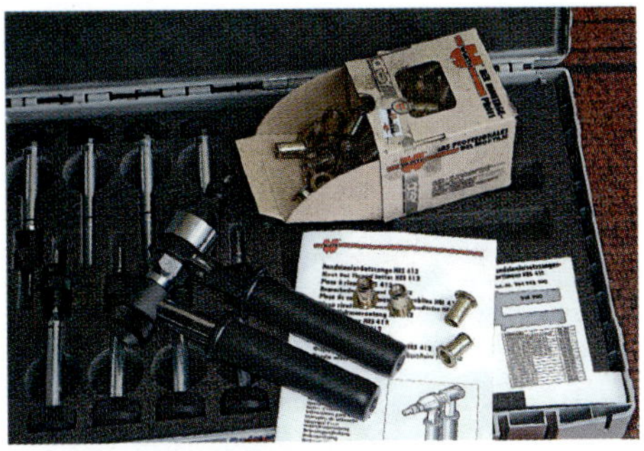

2-5-B1. The main strength in the fittings for the Reimo roof requires the use of rivet nuts. These are captive nuts that are fitted to enclosed panels and are held in place with a spreadable collar, not dissimilar to the way in which pop rivets are fitted. As the bolt in a rivet nut is tightened, the nut should become even more secure in its seat. Anyone who needs to fit a number of these rivet nuts and in particular anyone who wants to fit the larger and therefore stronger sizes is recommended to invest in a Würth Rivet Nut Thread Setter (HES412).

2-5-B2. The mounting blocks, seen in later shots, and the instructions from Reimo were used to locate the positions of the fixing holes. They were primed with paint after being drilled.

2-5-B3. Unfortunately, the rivet nuts supplied with the kit couldn't be tightened by Leisuredrive and new ones were obtained. The first step is to screw the rivet nut onto the mandrill on the fixing tool.

2-5-B4. The tool is tightened, compressing the sleeve on the nut and fixing it inside the hollow box section.

2-5-B5. Nothing 'snaps' as with a pop rivet; instead, the tool is unscrewed from the rivet nut, leaving it in the vehicle.

2-5-B6. The plastic mounting strips which are bolted down to the roof come with their own sealing adhesive on the back but both Barry and I felt that, at least in the winter temperatures in which we were working, this sealant was too stiff and so more was added with the applicator gun.

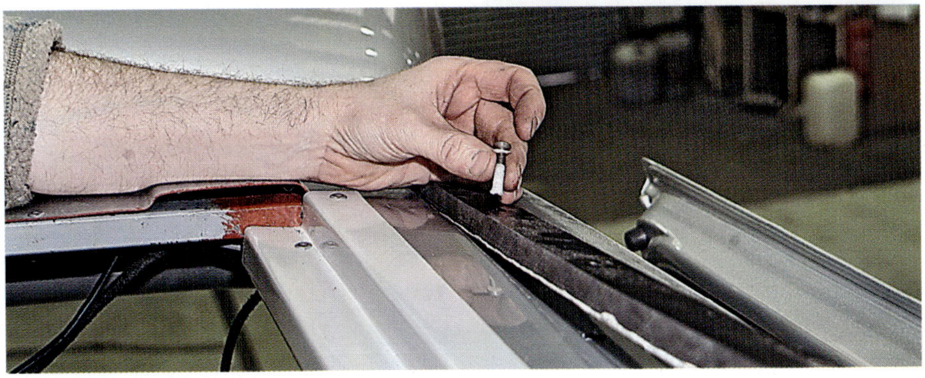

2-5-B7. The holes in the strips had to be lined up with the rivet nuts and the screws holding them down were aligned with their threads ...

PART B. FITTING THE REIMO ROOF

The point made at the start of Part A with regard to the need for anyone doing this work to be properly qualified, also applies here. An incorrectly fitted roof could conceivably come adrift as the vehicle was being driven with potentially very dangerous results.

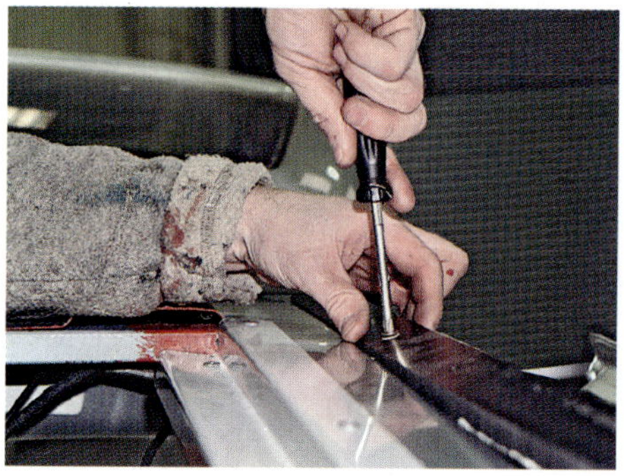

2-5-B8. ... and then tightened.

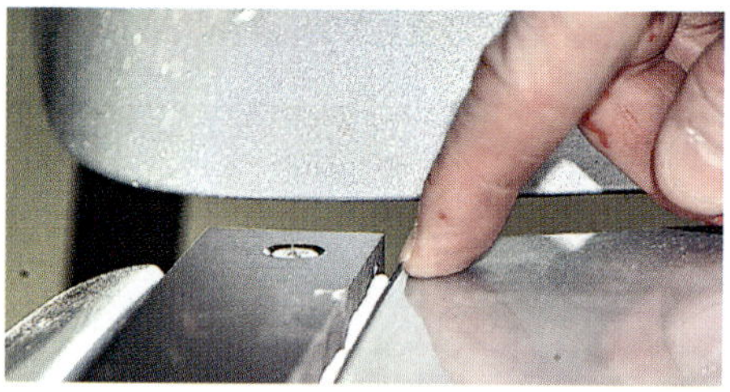

2-5-B9. There must be no risk of any leaks and therefore it was encouraging to see excess filler oozing all the way along the sides of both strips. Such excess should be wiped away while the sealer is still wet.

2-5-B10. Separately, mounting points for the struts are fitted to the body and again, rivet nuts will have been fitted first. Barry applied a liberal amount of sealer to the mounting plate.

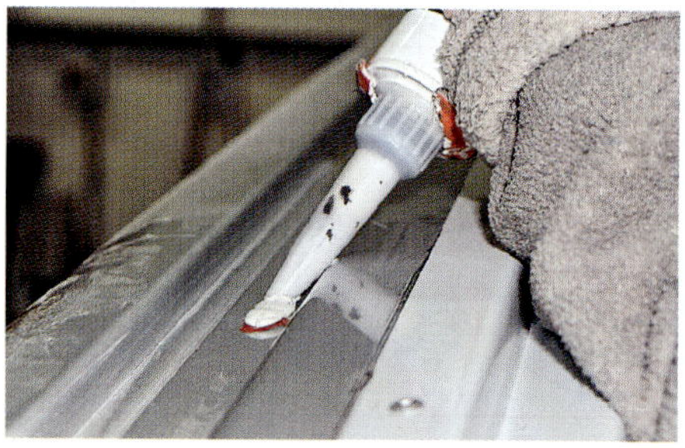

2-5-B11. He applied a little more to the hole in the body, just to be on the safe side.

2-5-B12. The multi-point socket-head screws are best tightened down with a ratchet wrench.

2-5-B13. With all of the bracketry in place, it was all hands to the roof as the lid was lifted into place.

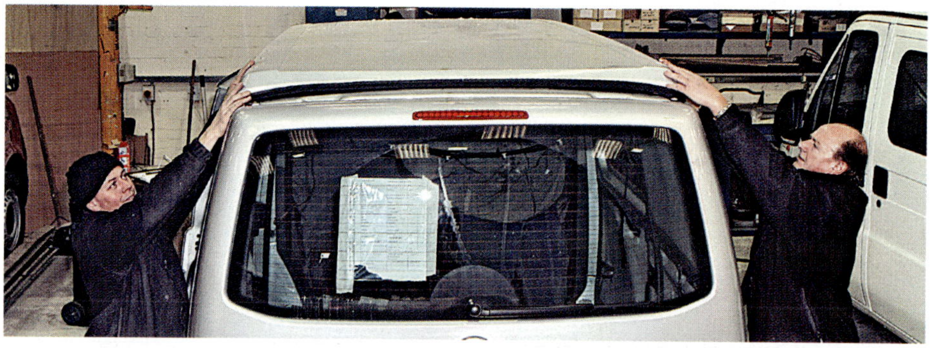

2-5-B14. Obviously, it is essential that the roof is correctly aligned at this stage.

2-5-B15. The roof was lifted up by the team of willing helpers, while Barry lined up the bolts holding the hinge mechanism to the plastic strips we saw being fitted earlier.

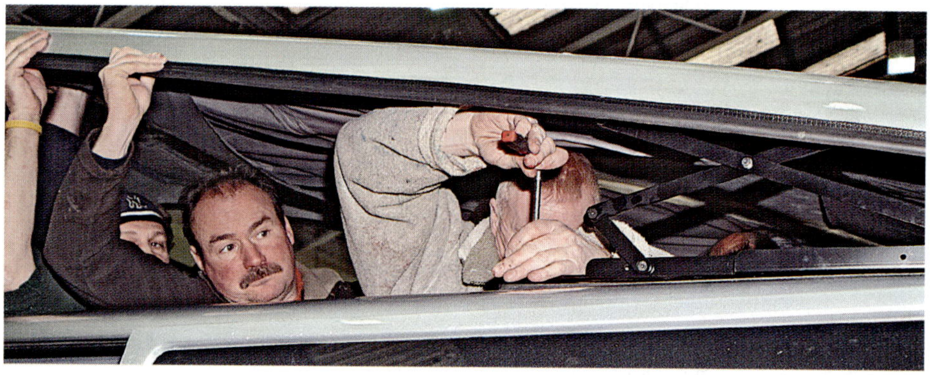

2-5-B16. The hinges are screwed through the plastic strips and into the rivet nuts in the bodywork beneath.

2-5-B17. It may have been an idea to have fitted the struts first because that would have held the weight of the roof while the hinge bolts were aligned – a tricky task.

2-5-B18. The struts themselves clip onto the balls on the brackets fitted to the roof and are then located with these spring clips (arrowed).

2-5-B19. The same principle is used for holding the top end of the strut to the bracket already fitted by the manufacturers to the roof.

2-5-B20. With the roof fitted and in its elevated position, there was obviously a gap between the roof and the body and this was filled by the fabric taped up inside the new roof.

2-5-B21. Each new roof comes with a bundle of fixings for the side curtains. Barry opened them up on his bench before starting work.

2-5-B22. Plastic strips used for holding the fabric down. The strips come pre-cut …

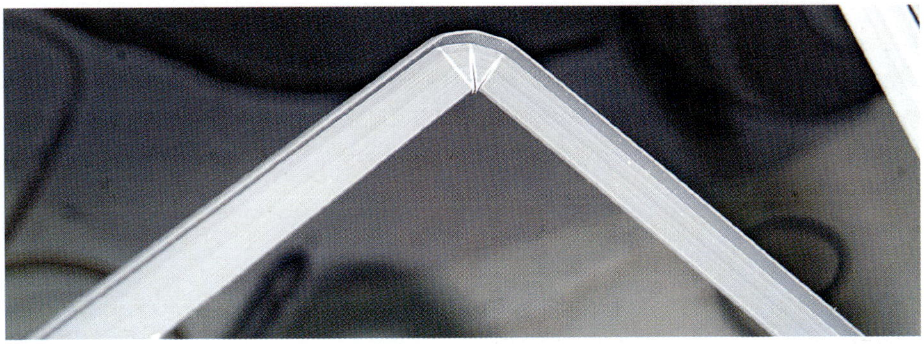

2-5-B23. … so that they can be folded at the corners to make perfect right angles.

2-5-B24. Barry marked the centre line on the bodywork of the vehicle and measured the width required for the first hole.

2-5-B25. This he transferred to the first piece of strip to be fitted.

2-5-B29. Self-tapping screws were used to fix the strips down to the roof panel beneath.

2-5-B26. This was then offered up to the fabric to check its location.

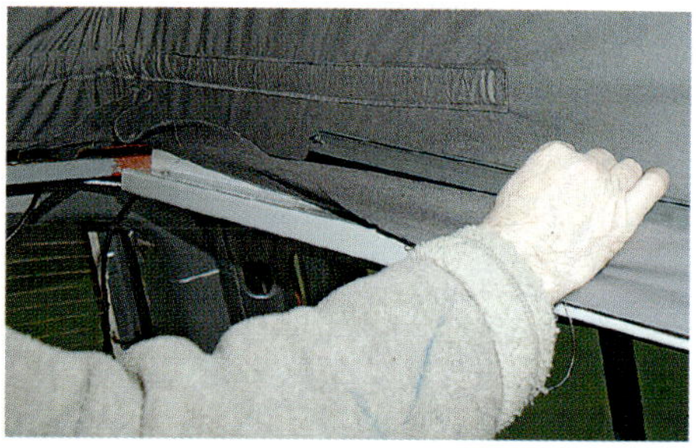

2-5-B30. It is important that the tensioning of the fabric is maintained evenly all the way round as each strip is fitted.

2-5-B27. Barry always uses a Clarke angle drill but has added his own protective shroud in the form of a piece of carpet taped around the chuck so that it can't damage the fabric as he drills it.

2-5-B28. Barry demonstrated how the chuck shield works.

2-5-B31. Where strips called for it, Barry overlapped them and screwed them both down together.

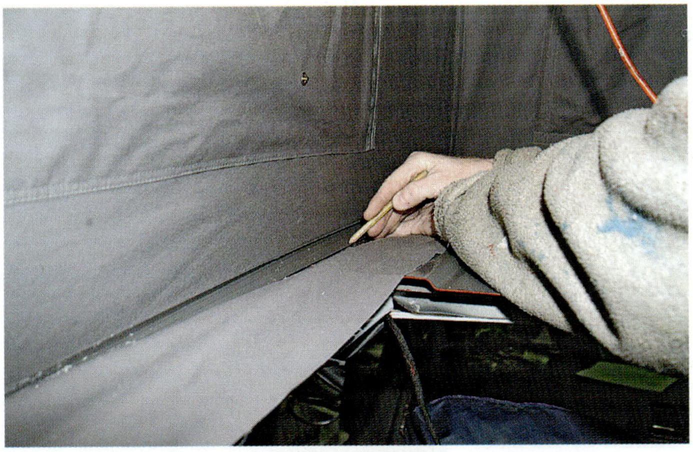

2-5-B32. In some instances, strips had to be measured …

2-5-B33. … but were easily cut to length in situ using a hacksaw and taking care not to damage the fabric.

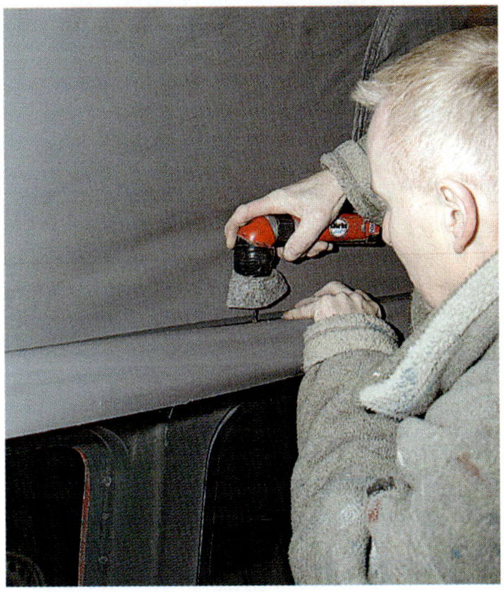

2-5-B34. After the first screws have been put in, holding the strips in position, the remaining screws can all have their pilot holes drilled and can then be fitted.

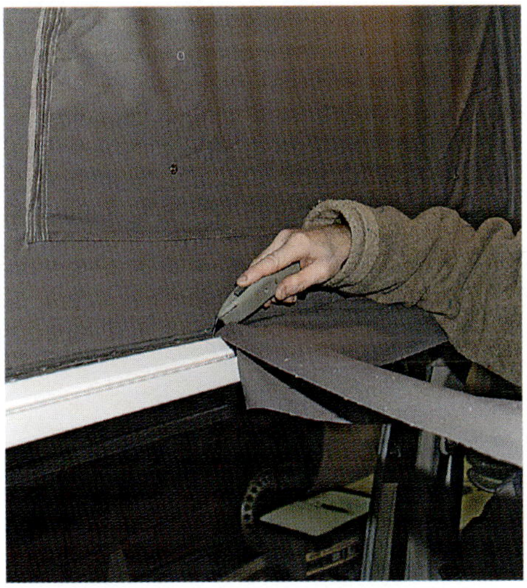

2-5-B35. Barry cut the surplus cloth away using a craft knife, up against the edge of the fixing strip. He pointed out that it's most important that you don't, in an absent minded moment, cut the wrong side of the strip!

2-5-B36. Swarf from the drill and plastic cuttings were blown away with an air line. Bear in mind that there is no interior at this stage except for the front seats which have been carefully covered up.

2-5-B37. The next work needed to be carried out on the outside of the vehicle. Barry wiped the paintwork with panel wipe to remove any grease or other substances that may prevent sealer from doing its job.

2-5-B38. The aim is to seal the joint between fabric and bodywork.

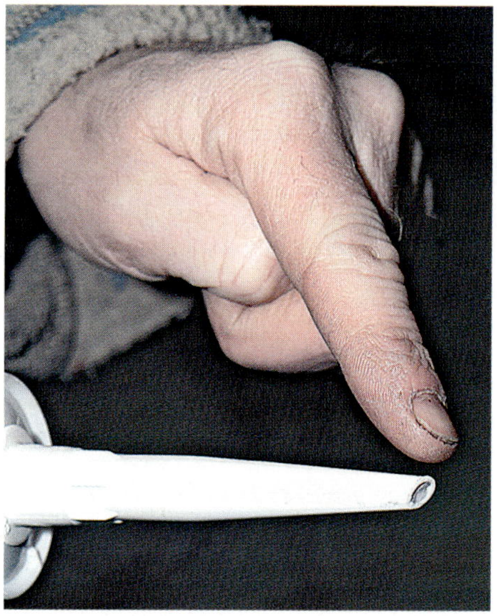

2-5-B39. Barry cut the nozzle on the end of his applicator at the angle shown.

2-5-B40. He gunned sealer into the gap, starting at one end …

2-5-B41. … and then moving his steps a stage at a time and sealing the fabric all the way around.

PART C. REIMO ROOF WIND DEFLECTOR

2-5-C1. The wind deflector is fitted to the roof in such a way that when the roof is lowered and the vehicle is travelling along, air is not forced underneath the front edge of the roof. Its positioning is therefore quite critical.

2-5-C2. This is the wind deflector at Leisuredrive. It is held down with double-sided tape which is simply peeled off the back of the deflector and the deflector is stuck down to the roof. Unfortunately, it doesn't last!

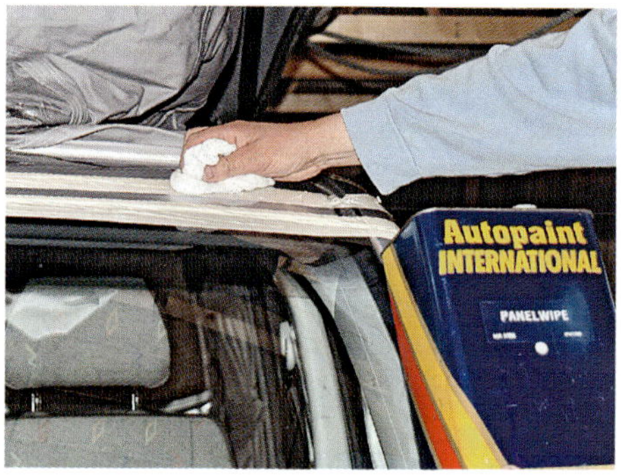

2-5-C3. It is always essential that the area to which the draft excluder is being fitted is cleaned off with panel wipe so that no traces of silicones or other contaminants prevent the tape from sticking down. Even so, I doubt if double-sided tape is strong enough by itself to do the job and that's why I carried out the work as shown here. The area to which the wind deflector is being fitted has been masked off on each side, leaving a clear strip.

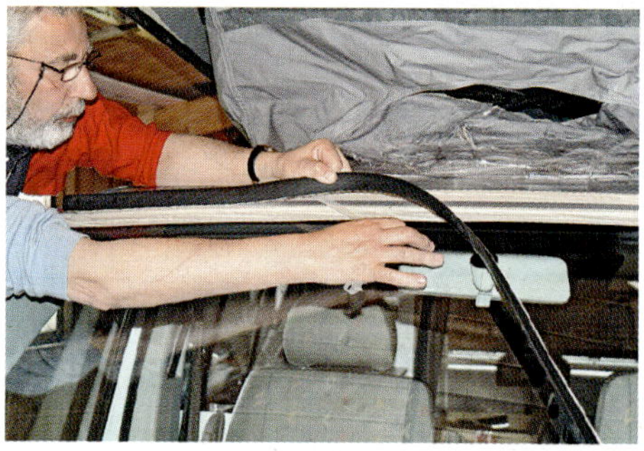

2-5-C4. I have removed all of the old double-sided tape and have replaced it with a fresh strip of commercial grade double-sided tape available from paint factors. You can see that I am peeling off the backing strip as the wind deflector is stuck down.

2-5-C5. As my wife, Shan, continued to take the photographs, I ensured that the wind deflector was pushed down hard against the double-sided tape all the way along.

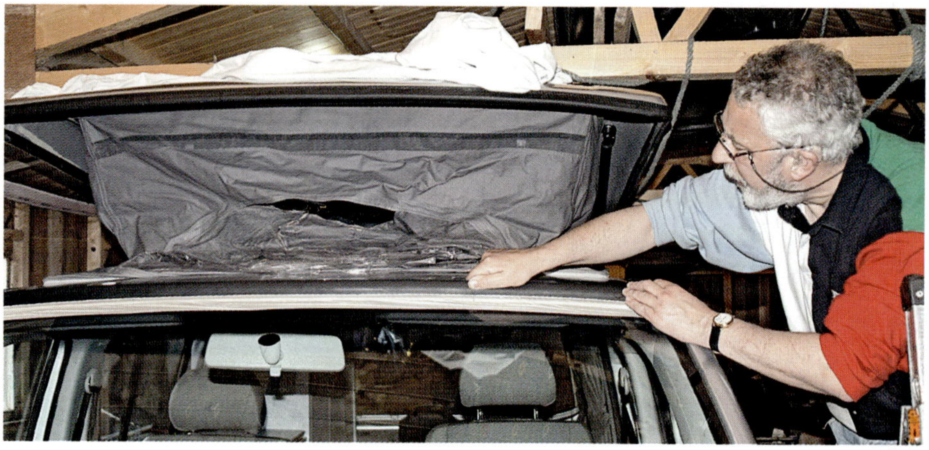

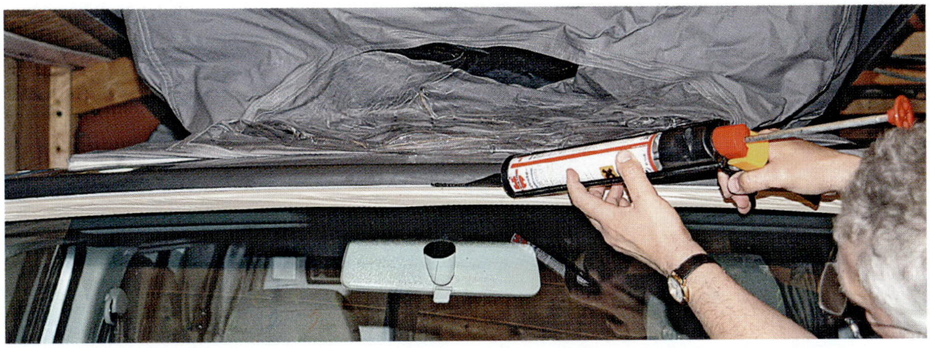

2-5-C6. I then added a bead of Würth Bond & Seal to both the front and the back edges of the wind deflector, with the aim of bonding it down to the bodywork and preventing water or wind from getting to the double-sided tape.

2-5-C7. While the Bond & Seal was still wet, I peeled off the masking tape and smoothed out the bead of sealant.

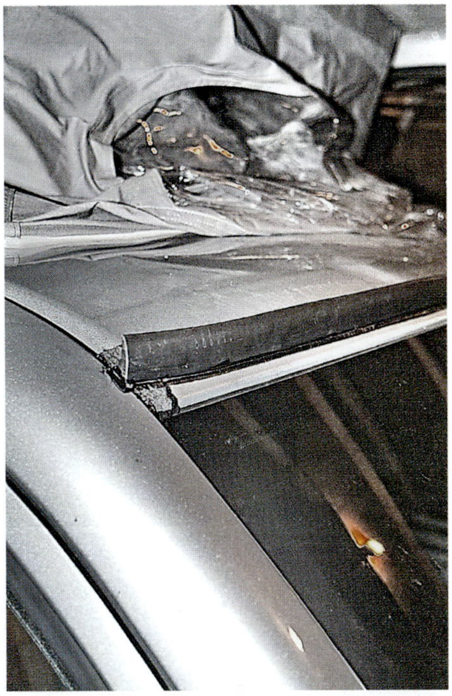

2-5-C8. Reimo also supply a piece of foam to fill the channel at the outer edges of the roof and I had also previously fitted this using Bond & Seal before the wind deflector had been fitted.

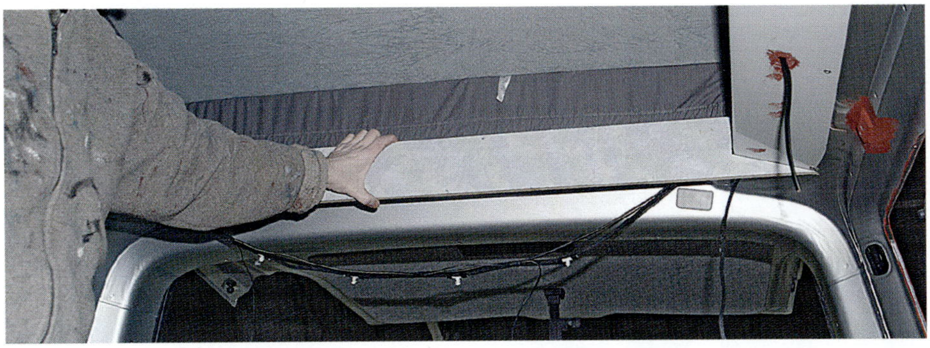

2-5-D1. As Leisuredrive, Barry has a template which he uses for marking out the panel that finishes off the rear end of the roof. Anyone doing this work for themselves would be strongly advised to start by making a template, similar to the one shown here, before cutting out the final section.

2-5-D3. ... and then cut out the shape with his jigsaw.

PART D. INTERIOR FINISHING

This section deals with finishing off the interior of the elevating roof and as such, is only relevant to the area around the elevating roof itself.

2-5-D2. Barry drew around the template ...

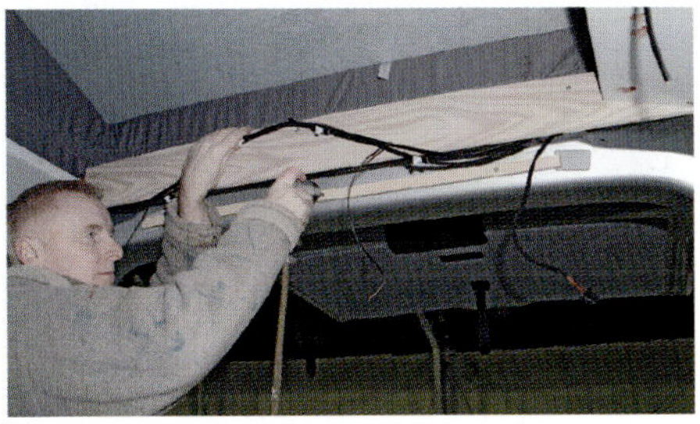

2-5-D4. Barry screwed a wooden strip to the rear door aperture against which the horizontal trim section could be fitted.

2-5-D5. This is the panel he made earlier for that horizontal section, along with a template that he also constructed to allow for the interior light, which will later be fitted into this panel.

2-5-D6. He cut out the apertures for the interior light at his work bench.

2-5-D7. New cable clips were used to hold the existing cables and the new ones for the interior light in position.

2-5-D8. Before closing the panel off, a 'belts-and-braces' job of treating any cut areas with Würth Cavity Protection Spray was carried out.

2-5-D9. The wires for the interior light were passed through the apertures in the plywood …

2-5-D10. … which was then stapled into position. You can see that the cable for the interior light and the two wires for the speakers have been pushed through their relevant holes before fitting the plywood panel.

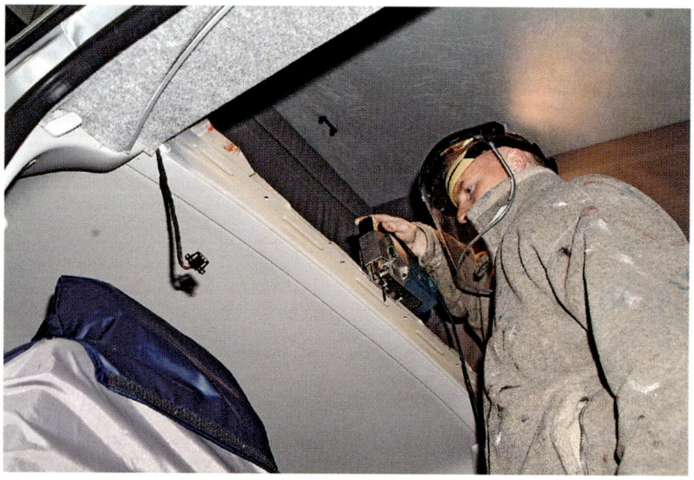

2-5-D11. At the front end of our vehicle, where the cab ceiling had not been removed, Barry trimmed the steel back to the line of the crossmember.

2-5-D12. He then screwed a finishing strip beneath the crossmember …

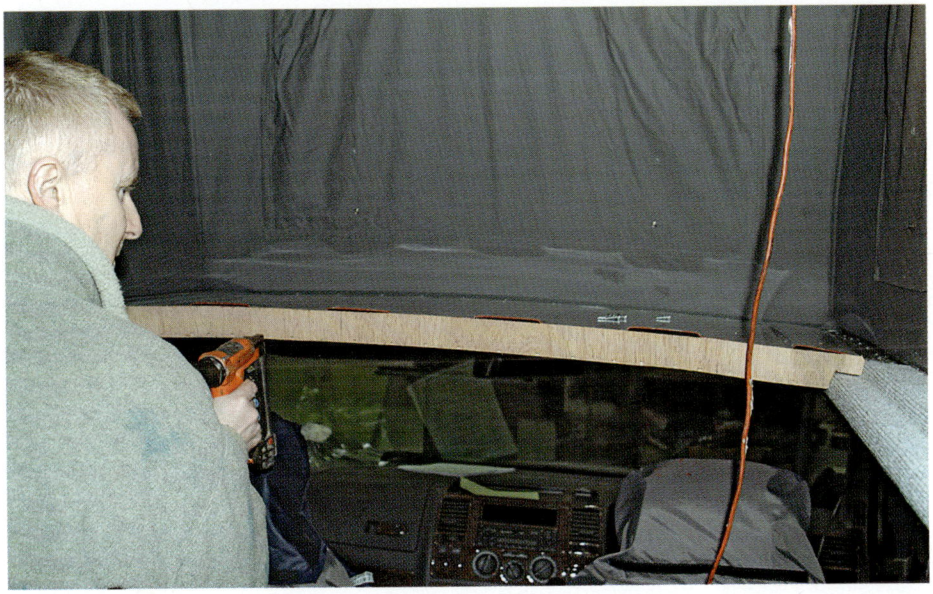

2-5-D13. … and another on the rear edge.

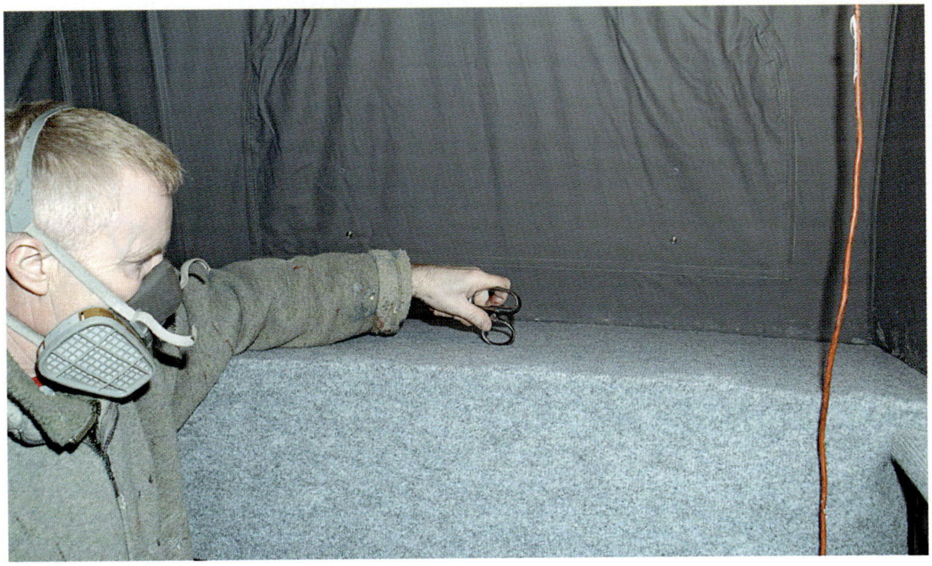

2-5-D14. He then finished off using trim material that you will see used in later parts of the manual.

2-5-D15. With the more conventional type of roof, where the front cab ceiling has been removed, the headlining has to be cut to match.

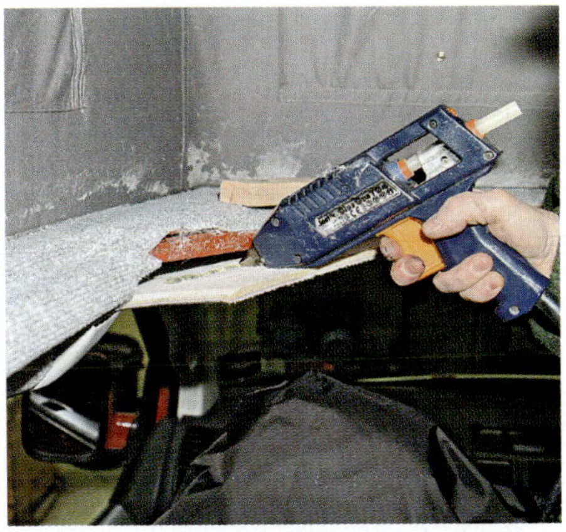

2-5-D16. Barry used a glue gun to apply adhesive between the edge of the headlining and the strengthening frame.

2-5-D17. He then pressed the headlining up against the frame until the adhesive had set. Note that the upper surface has been trimmed off in the same way as described in picture 2-5-D14.

2-5-D18. This allowed him to trim the headlining tightly back to the edge of the frame.

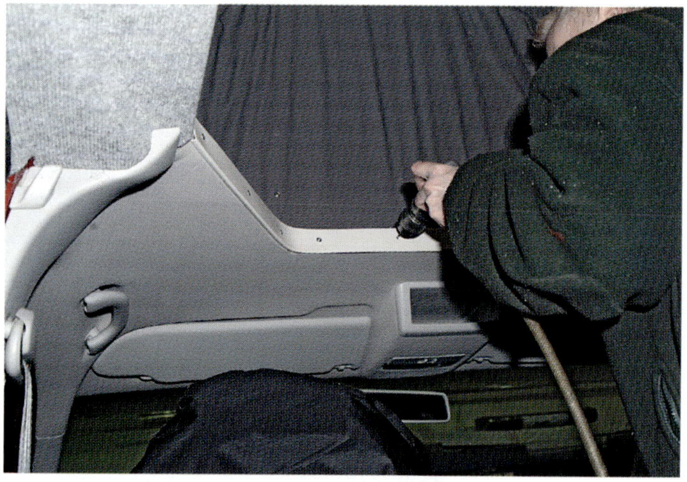

2-5-D19. This edge finishing strip which comes with the Reimo kit was pushed into place and the fixing screw holes drilled.

2-5-D20. This shows the strip fitted all the way along with all of the screws in place.

2-5-D21. Barry then fitted the rubber cover strip over the white plastic.

2-5-D22. The location of the two hooks for holding the top down, when in the lowered position, were carefully marked out. The trim and steel behind were drilled through and the hooks securely fixed with strong self-tapping screws.

2-5-D23. This is an over-centre catch that could possibly be used as an additional means of holding down the front of the roof. It is one of a wide range of Southco catches, available from Zygology.com in the UK. There's an optional lock available. It would be necessary to make brackets to fit to the roof structure in order to use these catches.

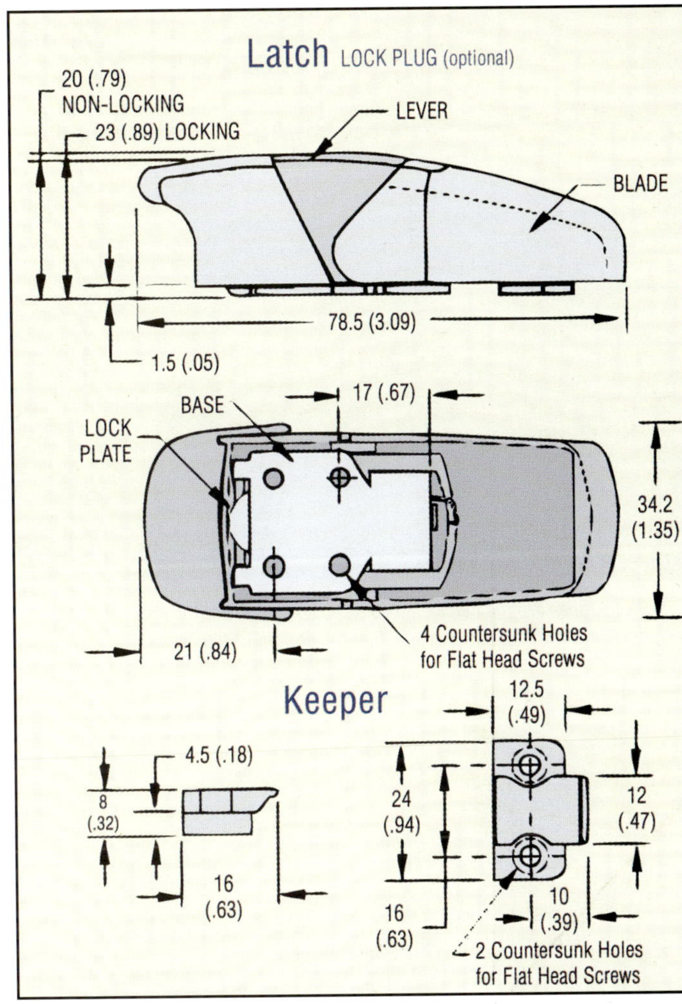

2-5-D24. These are the dimensions of the catch and the keeper onto which it hooks. The 'Average Ultimate Load' quoted for these catches is 2183 N (491 lbs.) and it would be necessary to continue to use the original straps as an additional safety measure to ensure that the roof cannot fly open when driving.

PART E. FITTING LEISUREDRIVE ELEVATING ROOF

Leisuredrive also developed its own in-house elevating roof using a different design to that of the Reimo roof. The following photographs were kindly supplied by Derek Andrews, MD of Leisuredrive.

2-5-E1. The Leisuredrive roof has echoes of the Volkswagen California in that the front panel is fixed to the roof, just above the windscreen.

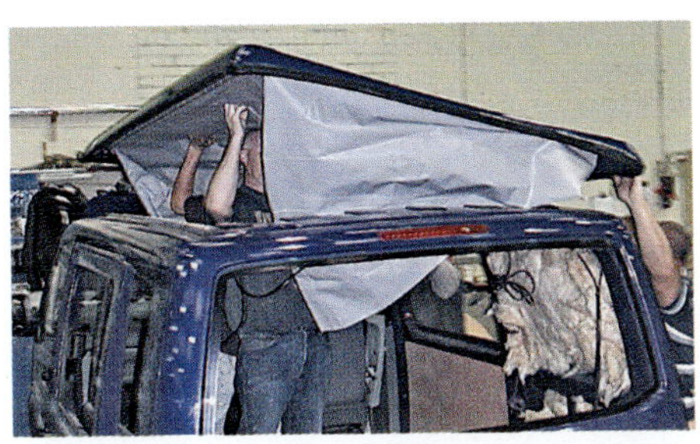

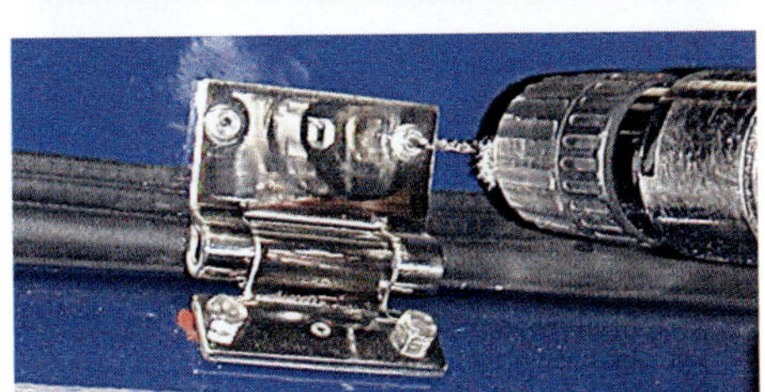

2-5-E3. After carefully checking and then double-checking the position of the roof on the body, the hinges can be offered up and holes drilled for the pop rivets used on the elevating roof and the bolts used on the vehicle's bodywork.

2-5-E2. After fitting the frame as described in Section B, the Leisuredrive roof was lifted into place in a similar fashion to that shown for the Reimo roof.

2-5-E4. In this installation, Leisuredrive used bolts top and bottom so there is obviously no hard and fast rule about which should be used.

2-5-E5. These are the two locations selected by Leisuredrive for fixing the hinges. The front one is just ahead of the upright of the front door frame, while the rear one is just in front of the upright in the pressing for the rear side window.

2-5-E6. Here, the roof has been raised and supported with two wooden props.

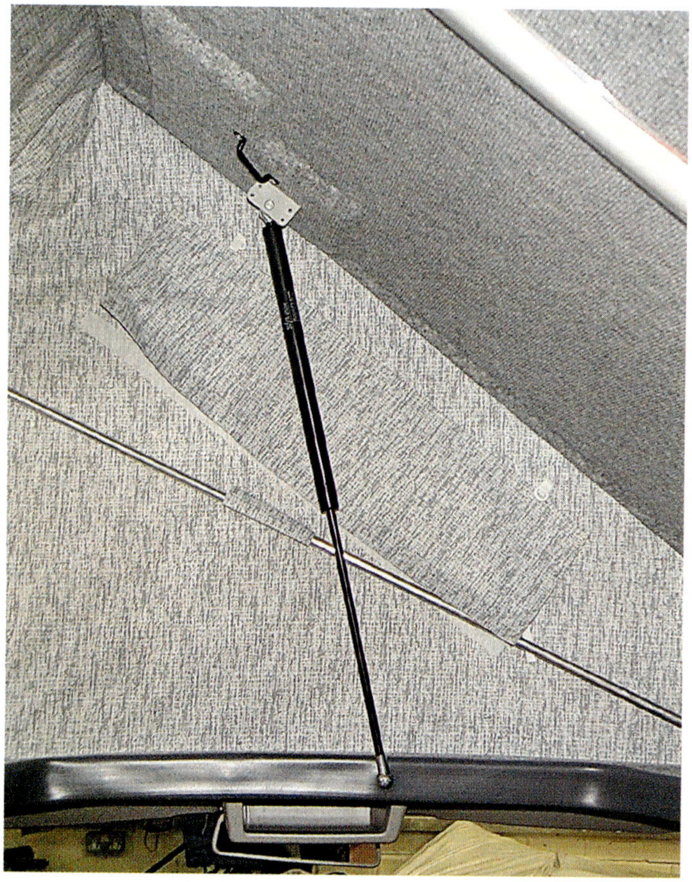

2-5-E7. This enables the hydraulic struts to be fitted, front and rear. This is the location of the front strut and the rear one will obviously have to match. Leisuredrive have welded the bottom of the strut to the frame, though this can't be seen underneath the cover trim which has already been fitted here.

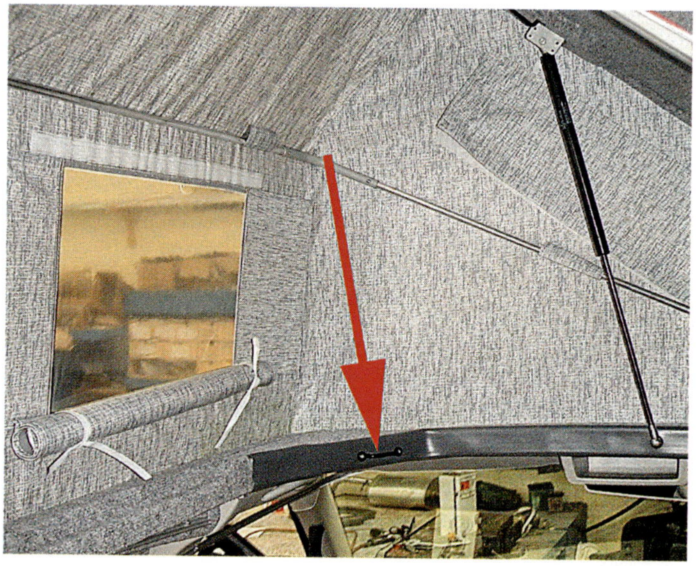

2-5-E8. As well as the strut and the roof window, this shot shows the bracket (arrowed) screwed to the edge of the frame. It has a matching partner fitted to the roof itself and these are used with strong straps to hold the roof in its lowered position.

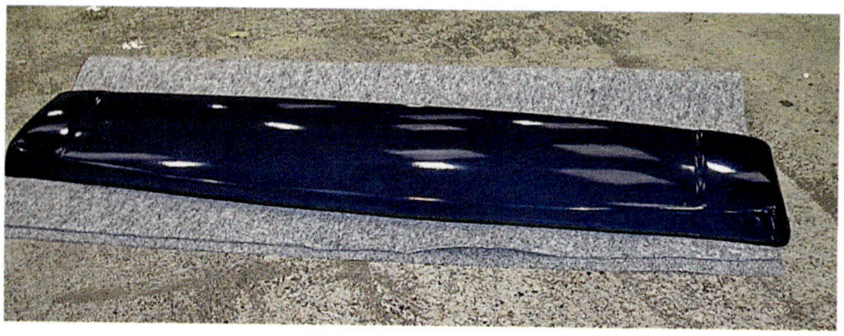

2-5-E9. This is the GRP front section ready to be fitted.

2-5-E10. On another vehicle, the front section is offered up into position.

2-5-E11. It has to be carefully located so that it runs parallel with the front of the screen.

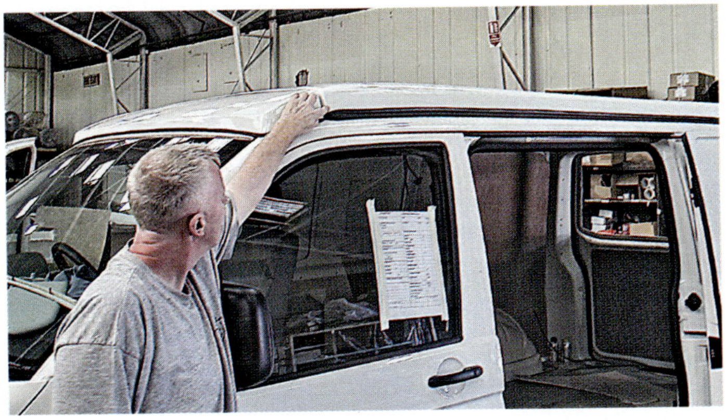

2-5-E12. It also has to have a narrow gap between itself and the main section of the roof to allow the main roof, complete with its sealing rubber, to raise and lower without fouling.

2-5-E13. The front panel is held down to the roof with bolts fitted from inside the vehicle.

2-5-E14. This is the completed Leisuredrive elevating roof in its raised position. Trimming instructions are similar to those for the Reimo roof described earlier.

Chapter 3

Interior structure

Important note: Don't carry out the work shown in this chapter or in any individual section without reading the rest of this manual. There are many jobs that are associated with other work. This manual has been divided up into logical sections of the vehicle but these are not necessarily the order in which you will carry out the work. Please study the whole of the manual before commencing work.

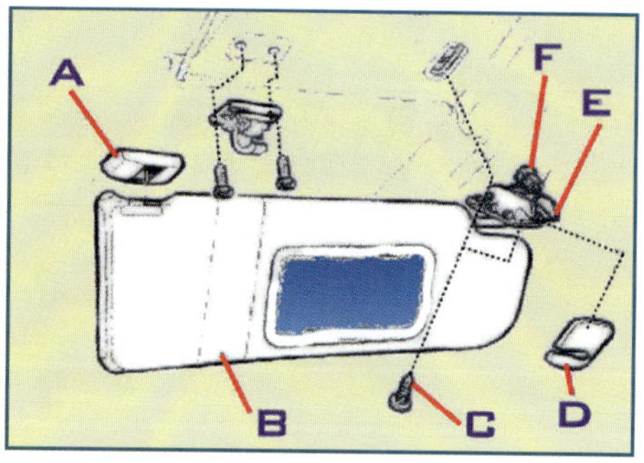

3-1-1. REMOVING SUN VISOR:
1. Switch off the ignition.
2. Pull the sun visor (B) out of its retainer clip.
3. Lever out cap (D) and remove the two screws (C) found beneath it. (Retighten to 2Nm)
4. Pull the sun visor bearing (E) out of its mounting bracket and separate the electrical connector (F) when fitted.
5. Lever off the cap (A), remove the two screws from beneath it (retighten to 2Nm) and remove the retainer clip.

SECTION 1. REMOVING CAB TRIM

Please see Chapter 2, Section 1 for further information on removing interior light and trim panels.

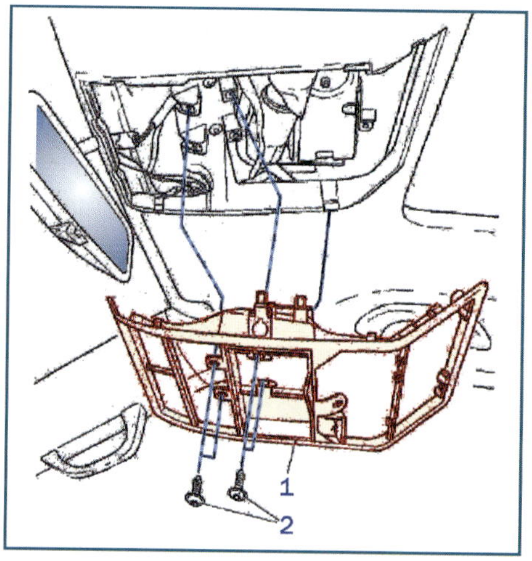

3-1-2. REMOVING ROOF CONSOLE (MULTIVAN):
1. Switch off the ignition.
2. Remove the fronty interior light and the switches for the interior and reading lights and, if fitted, remove the sunroof operating unit.
3. Remove the four screws (2) (retighten to 2Nm) and pull out the console (1) downwards from the moulded headlining, starting from the front.
4. NOTE: If fitted, unclip the anti-theft and tilt system control unit from the console.

3-1-3. On the standard van, the fittings in the roof panel are carefully levered out and then the roof panel itself can be removed. If necessary, unscrew and unclip any surrounding trim holding it in place.

3-1-4. The stripped out headlining reveals the vulnerable wiring and this must be carefully protected when the roof is cut away as described in the relevant section.

3-1-5. The tie-down D-rings are simply removed after unscrewing the retaining bolts with a multi-point socket.

SECTION 2. FIT REAR SEAT BELTS

SAFETY FIRST!

It is strongly recommended that this work is not carried out by a DIY mechanic. It must be entrusted to an engineer who has the skills to construct seat belts that are safe for use. If this is not possible, rear passengers should not be carried in the vehicle.

3-2-1. This is how Leisuredrive go about fitting rear seat belts to the standard van. First, a frame is welded together out of box section tubing …

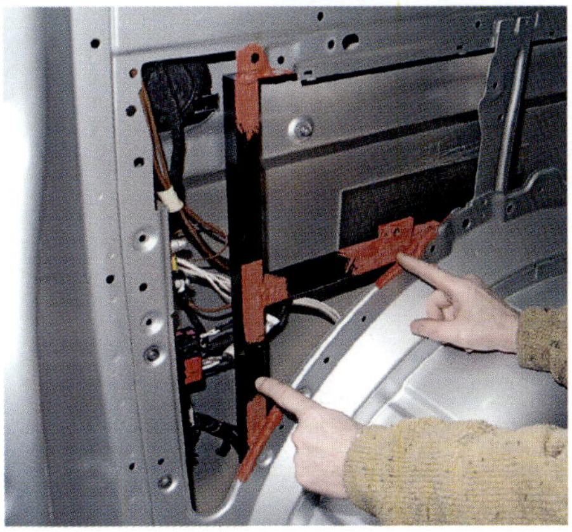

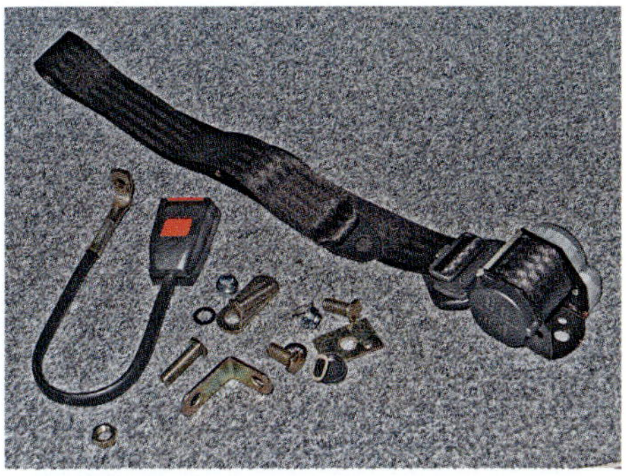

3-2-3. This is one of the Securon automatic retracting seat belts being fitted to the rear. Note that different stalk lengths are available from Securon to take account of the differing distances between the seat and the floor. At the time of writing, Securon's website, at www.securon.co.uk, supplies a full range of information on the various seat belt products available.

3-2-4. Just for reference, Barry holds up the inertia reel unit and shows how it will be fitted into the recessed space behind the trim.

3-2-2. … and this is welded in place at the rear before all bare metal is painted with red oxide primer. Note that the battery must be disconnected before carrying out any welding on the vehicle although, as stated earlier, this is emphatically not a DIY job.

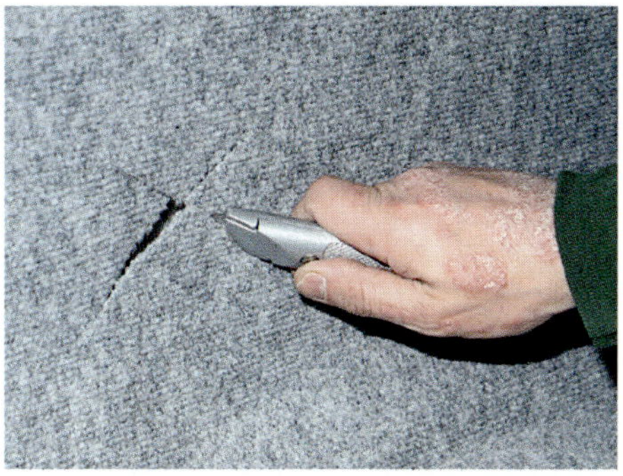

3-2-5. After the trim has been fitted (see relevant section of this manual), Barry cuts through at the relevant point and tidies up the edge of the trim …

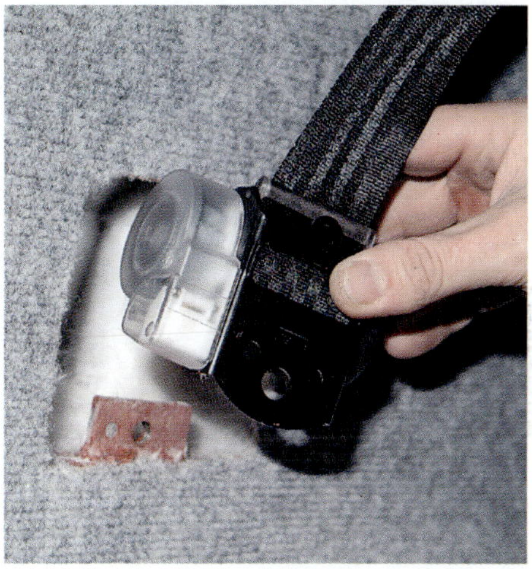

3-2-6. … before offering up the inertia reel seat belt to the threaded hole on the mounting frame.

3-2-7. The seat belt was tightened according to Securon's specifications.

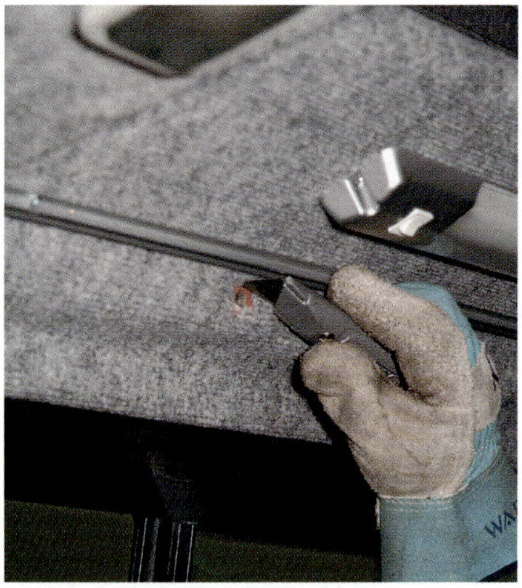

3-2-8. The upper mounting is already there on the passenger side and here Barry cut through the trim to expose it.

3-2-9. The fitting kit supplied with the seat belts was laid out before fitting. Later, as you will see in the section of this manual on fitting blinds, this mounting bracket had to be adapted so that the seat belt would miss the roller blinds. Note that the wavy anti-rattle washer is fitted on the spacer with shoulder, as shown here on the left of the bracket. The top bolt is fitted with a lock washer and the lower seat belt mounting is allowed to swivel on the spacer while being prevented from rattling by the wavy washer.

3-2-10. Barry bolted the top mounting in place on the body.

3-2-11. The third mounting point for the passenger-side rear passenger is also already in place and Barry found it just at the top of the rear wheel arch, as shown here. This shot emphasises the position of the shoulder spacer and the wavy washer. A spring washer can not be fitted in this location because if it was, the belt mounting would not be able to swivel.

3-2-12. The centre, lap-diagonal belt has to be bolted through the floor. This is the seat belt mounting (arrowed) being passed through the space under the seat box after the interior has been fitted – see relevant section of this manual.

3-2-13. Where there is an existing seat belt mounting such as in this location above the spare wheel on this particular vehicle, it must be used. If there is no mounting point at the position where you need it, a new one should only be created by a qualified engineer who is able to give it the necessary structural integrity.

3-2-14. To gain access to the underfloor area, after removing the spare wheel, the heat shield above the exhaust has to be unscrewed and removed.

3-2-15. The plastic covers are also removed in a similar way, after undoing the hexagonal nut-washers holding them in place.

3-2-16. A section of the underfloor covering is shown here being removed.

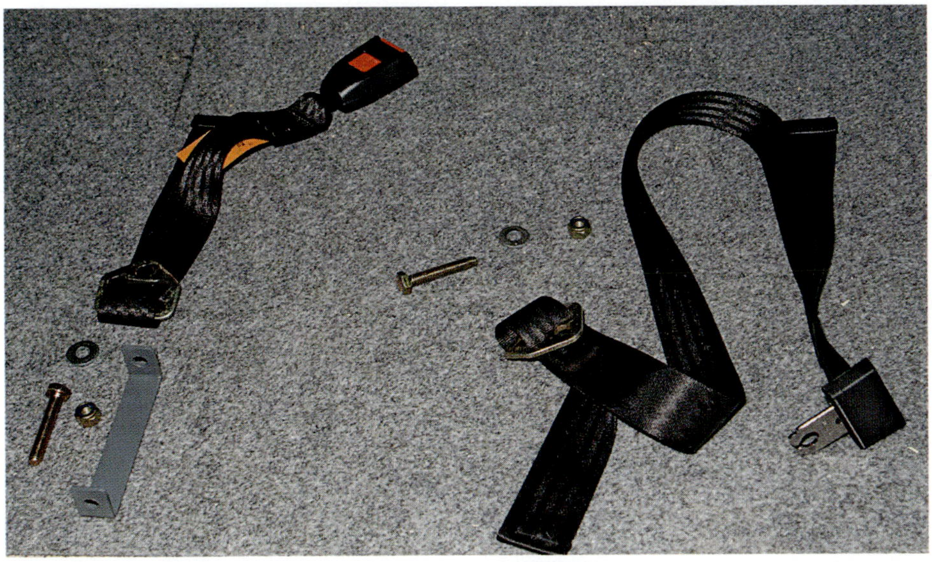

3-2-17. These are the Securon lap-diagonal belts that Leisuredrive fit …

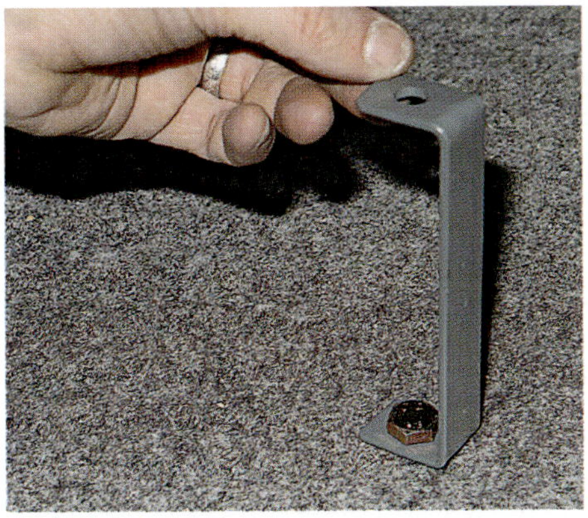

3-2-18. … and this is the extension bracket which is constructed to provide an extension for the seat buckle. It cannot be over-emphasised that this work is not suitable for DIY and must only be carried out by a qualified engineer.

3-2-19. Here, the floor has been reinforced and the seat belt mounting is being screwed into position.

3-2-20. On this particular conversion, the location of the seat belt differs and its position can be seen here on the C-post at the back of the sliding door.

SECTION 3. FLOOR AND HOLES

Because Leisuredrive is carrying out this work on a regular basis, it's easy for the company to know exactly where cupboards and other fitted units will be placed and thus work out the correct location of holes for gas and water supplies. If you are carrying out this work at home, you would be strongly recommended to fit the wooden floorboards, though only temporarily, without gluing them down as shown here. Then fit the bed and other cupboard units, once again as a temporary measure. This will enable you to calculate the exact positions of the kitchen equipment and heater and the position of the table, if you are fitting a recess for a centre post. You can then transfer those measurements to the wooden floor, drill the holes required and then refit floor and units on a permanent basis.

Important note: Before drilling holes through the floor, ensure the following:

- Do not drill into any wires, cables or pipes on either side of the floor panel.
- Take care not to drill into any flanges, hollow box sections or any other structural areas.
- Try to site holes so that no water or forced air can come up through them.
- Gas drop-out holes must be sited well away from any heat, such as a heater or the vehicle's exhaust.
- If fitting a gas drop-out point, make sure that gas cannot gather in an undertray fitted beneath the vehicle.

3-3-3. Andy goes in and out of the vehicle several times until he gets the main section of 12mm plywood to the exact shape.

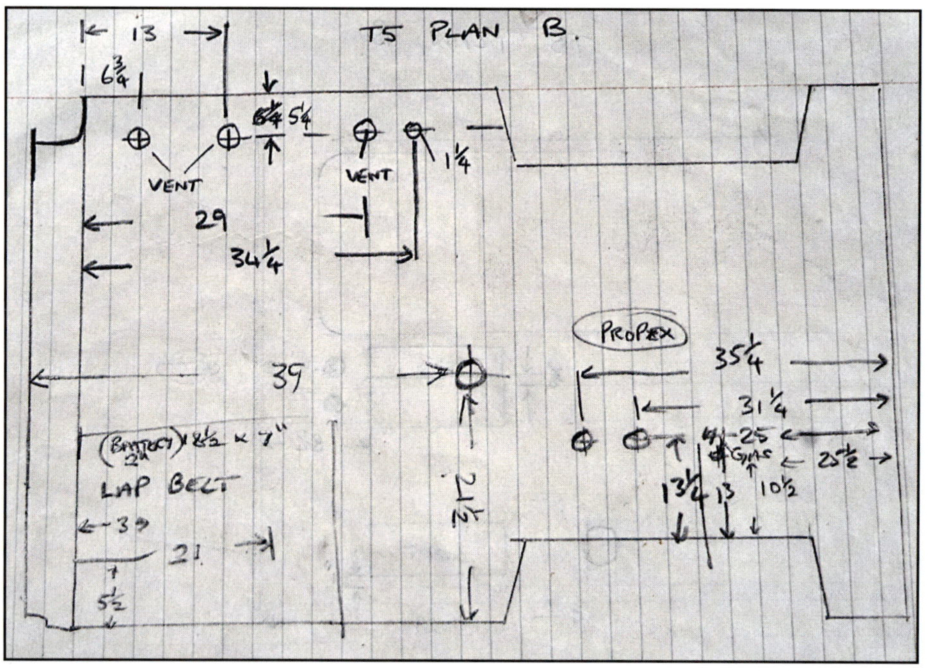

3-3-1. Before starting on the floor, make yourself a plan showing all of the items that require holes to be drilled in the floor and the correct positions for those holes. This is the sketch plan first made by Leisuredrive when it carried out its initial T5 conversions. You are strongly recommended to produce a similar plan of your own. Note that the bottom-right of the picture shows the location of a Propex LPG heater unit. Top-left shows the locations of four drop-vents, so called because they are simply holes in the floor through which any leaking LPG gas can 'drop' out of the vehicle. LPG is heavier than air. Leisuredrive place drop vents in the cupboard where the LPG cylinder or cylinders will be stored and also beneath the rear of the fridge. There are two more drop vents in the space where the Propex LPG heater is fitted.

3-3-4. Neil, helping out, cuts the narrower fill-in section to fit around the wheel arch on that side of the vehicle.

3-3-2. Depending on the layout, it might be necessary to run a gas pipe beneath the floor. If so, it will need to be made up now. You can see how this pipe will be fitted so that it runs beneath the level of the raised corrugations and is not pressed down by the wooden floorboards.

3-3-5. Meanwhile, Andy applies polyurethane adhesive to the high spots on the floor.

3-3-6. Only the area under which the larger sheet will be fitted had the PU bond applied to it. Andy makes sure he treads on the narrower section on the other side of the van while Neil helps him to manoeuvre the main floor section into position.

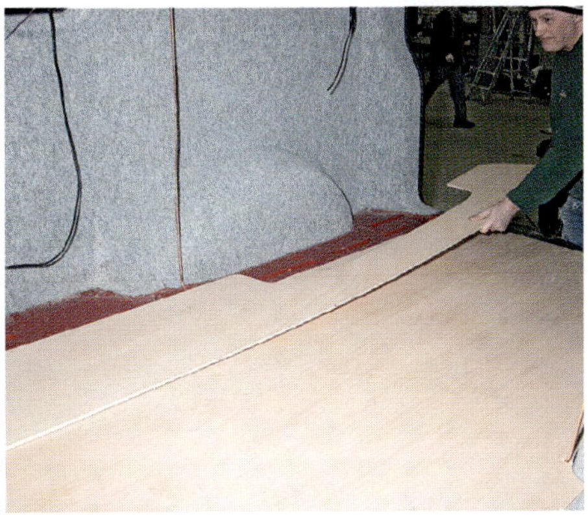

3-3-7. You can see Neil manoeuvring the narrower section into position and you can also see the gas pipe fitted beneath the floor before it goes in.

3-3-8. Neil uses a staple gun to apply half-a-dozen staples, close together at intervals of about 75mm. It would have been messier but optional to have applied PU bond along the edge of the larger floor panel before offering up the narrower one.

3-3-9. The sight of the smooth wooden floor indicates another step away from the vehicle's van origins.

3-3-10. Neil has drilled the four holes in the floor where the fridge and gas cylinders will be located and also for the drain pipe and the water feed pipe for the sink.

3-3-11. With the holes cut, Neil started to lay the carpet in place.

3-3-12. Once the position was correctly established, Neil sprayed impact adhesive onto the floor ...

3-3-13. ... and onto the carpet where it would touch the floor, before sticking the centre of the carpet in place. Note that you must always follow the safety instructions on the can when using volatile materials of this type.

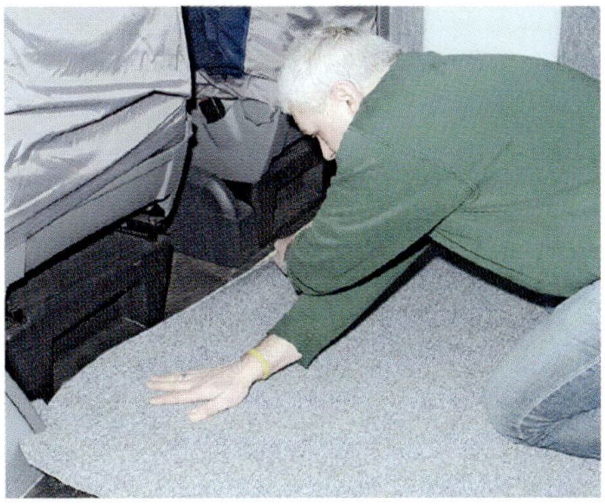

3-3-14. The trick is to cut the carpet roughly to shape but always to leave an overlap. This enables the carpet to be laid in position and then the final cut to be made later.

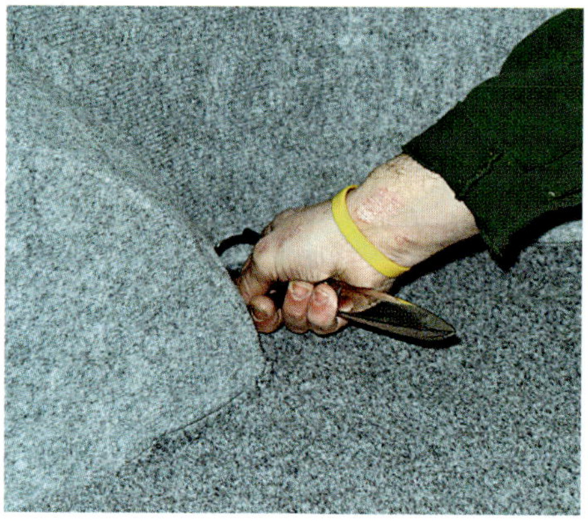

3-3-15. As an example, Neil presses the carpet down to the edge of the wheel arch and trims the final surplus off so that it fits perfectly.

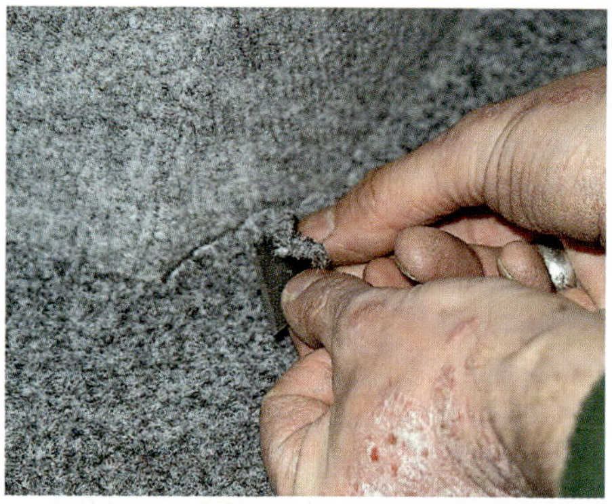

3-3-16. He chooses to use a knife blade without a holder but, for safety reasons, you are strongly recommended to only use a blade with its proprietary holder fitted.

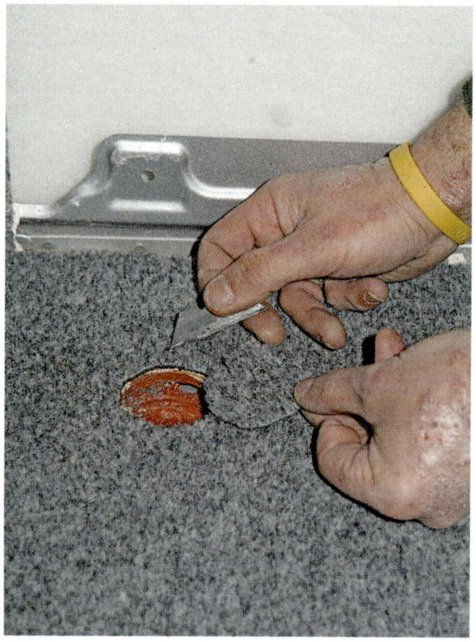

3-3-17. The same applies to the cutouts which have to be made where the carpet covers vent and other access holes.

3-3-18. Leisuredrive can supply these vent covers which allow gas out if necessary without allowing any of our little furry friends into the vehicle.

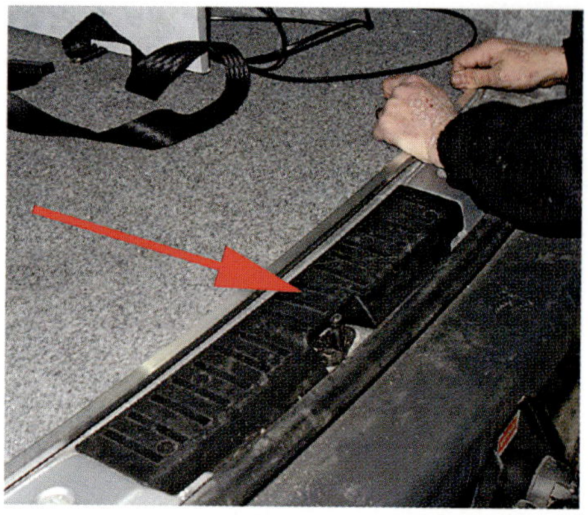

3-3-19. At the back, Leisuredrive fit an aluminium trim strip over the edge of the carpet. The black plastic cover you can see here (arrowed) is also unscrewed and removed.

3-3-20. Here you can see that another piece of carpet has also been fitted beneath the aluminium strip. It has then been folded back and glued down to the bare metal. A cutout has been made for the catch and Neil is cutting the edge of the carpet …

3-3-21. … before refitting the plastic trim cover …

3-3-22. … and the rubber seal that goes all the way around the door aperture.

3-3-23. Leisuredrive cut out carpet for the front cab, if you want to fit it. It is glued down to the existing rubber mats …

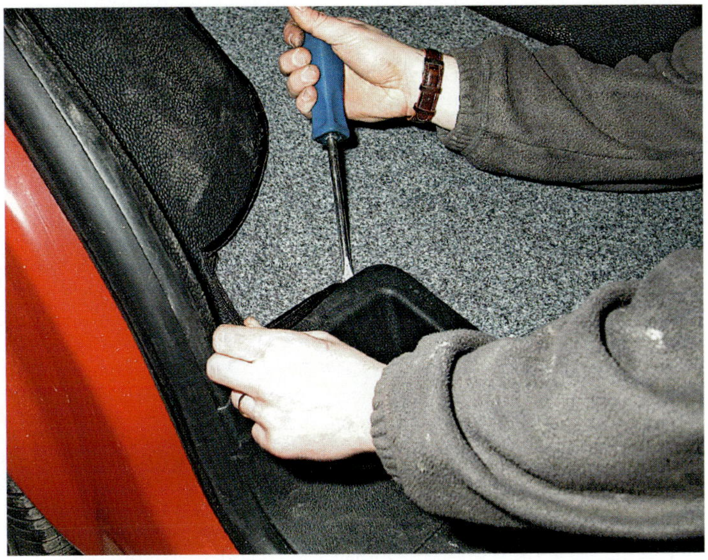

3-3-24. … and carefully tucked underneath the edges of the footwell trims.

SECTION 4. WALL PANELS AND INSULATION

Leisuredrive uses fibreglass insulation and it must be admitted that this is less expensive and far easier to fit than the type of insulation shown here. However, it is important that you wear the correct protective gear when handling fibreglass insulation – see the manufacturer's specification sheet for details. The insulation I chose is made by the Hodgson & Hodgson Group which makes insulation for a vast range of purposes, including railways and buildings as well as specialist vehicles. The material used here is called FiberForm and is manufactured from a mix of non-irritating, water repellent polyester fibres. The material we used is 50mm thick and has both thermal and acoustic insulation properties.

3-4-1. I found the best way of cutting the FiberForm insulation so that it fitted well was to make a paper template of each aperture first. The template didn't have to be exact but the FiberForm had to be fitted so that there were no gaps otherwise it would lose its effectiveness.

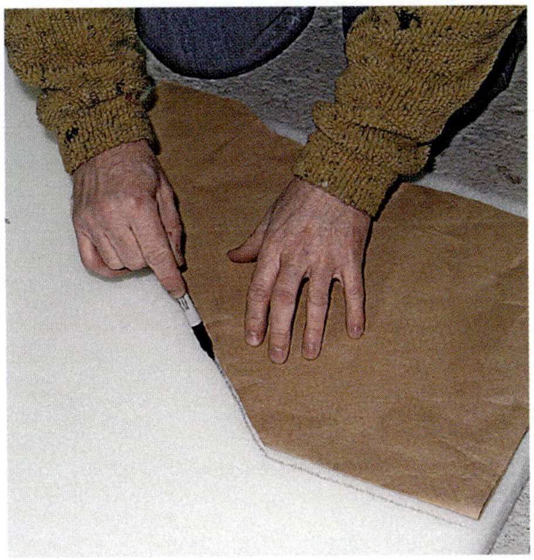

3-4-2. The shape of the template was then transferred to the insulating material with a felt pen …

3-4-3. … and the insulating sections cut out. This was initially the hardest part until I hit upon the idea of using sharp hedge cutting shears which did the job really well.

3-4-4. The insulating material in this instance was checked for fit …

3-4-5. … and then sprayed with contact adhesive before being glued in place. Fitting the insulation was fairly time consuming because there were a lot of small shapes to be cut out as well as several long, thin strips pushed down into hollow box sections in the doors and side walls. You only get one chance to do this job however so I didn't resent spending the extra time on it.

3-4-6. With the rear door fully insulated, Barry screwed the covered door panel into place on the inside of the door. On his left, you will see how large areas of insulation have already been fitted to the side of the vehicle.

3-4-7. These two push-in clips hold the base of the rear wiper cover in place …

3-4-8. … while this hook holds the top in position.

3-4-9. The cover is introduced top first and then the bottom clips are pushed into the holes in the door (positions arrowed) from which any overlapping trim material must be cut.

3-4-10. The rear door pull strap is simply fitted to the door as shown.

3-4-11. On the sliding door, the insulation and trim panel are fitted in a similar way. This is the stop buffer being screwed to the door with the trim in place.

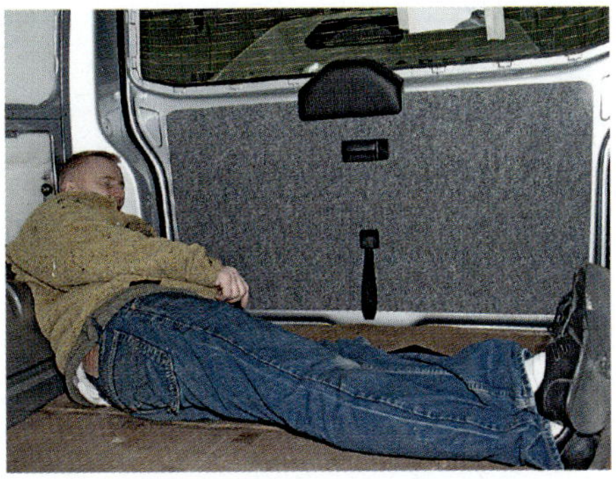

3-4-12. Barry thought he'd done so well, he'd take a break at this point. (He didn't really; you've got to have a smile, haven't you!)

3-4-13. Fully refreshed, Barry used a template to mark out the shape on this side panel …

3-4-14. … before offering it up to the vehicle. Don't worry if panels like this don't fit right first time; it's best to trim off too little and then cut them back so that they fit correctly.

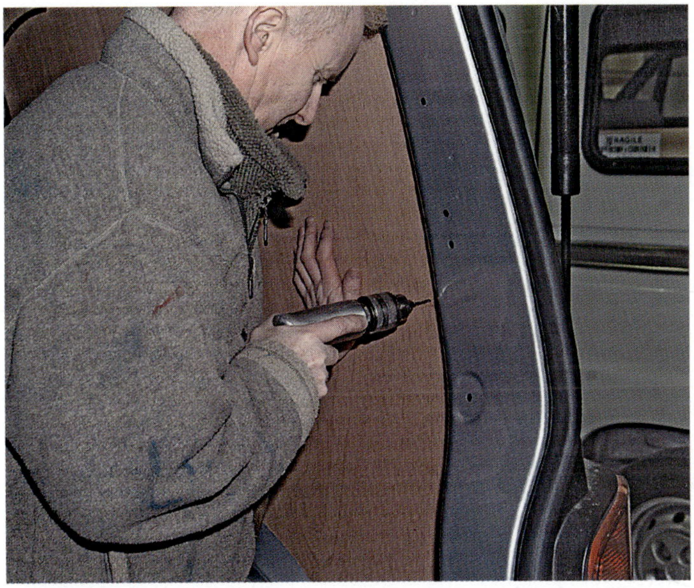

3-4-15. Barry drilled pilot holes into the steel and screwed the wall panels in place.

3-4-16. This is another panel for the rear of the vehicle and Barry is cutting an aperture for the seat belt inertia reel mechanism.

3-4-17. He also needed to cut some of the insulation away where the inertia reel device would be recessed.

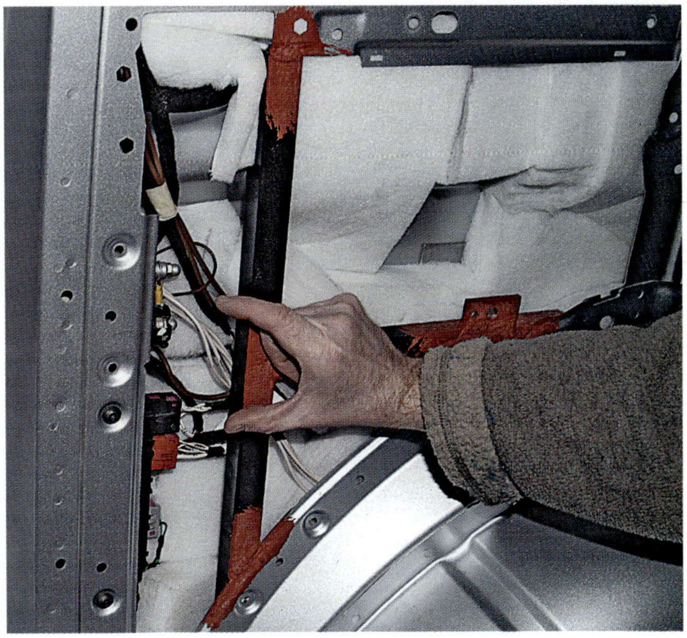

3-4-18. He pointed out that it was necessary to take great care to not damage any of the wiring found in some of the body side sections.

3-4-19. Another of his panels was cut, marked, adjusted as necessary and screwed into position.

3-4-20. Once all the side panels were in place, Barry started to glue the elasticated material, used for the wall coverings, into position.

3-4-21. Again, it is important to note that when contact adhesive is being sprayed, the user must follow the safety instructions provided by the manufacturer. Among the most important of those instructions will include the necessity for wearing breathing equipment, for working in a ventilated area and for keeping away from flames, sparks or any other sources of ignition.

3-4-22. Just as when fitting the floor carpet, Barry cuts out the wall covering oversize, gluing, stretching and fitting it into place, starting at the top …

3-4-23. … then moving down the side wall, gluing as he went.

3-4-24. Note that the wheel arches were not covered at this stage. Barry cut the surplus material from around the wheel arch …

3-4-25. … so that it could be fitted correctly into position.

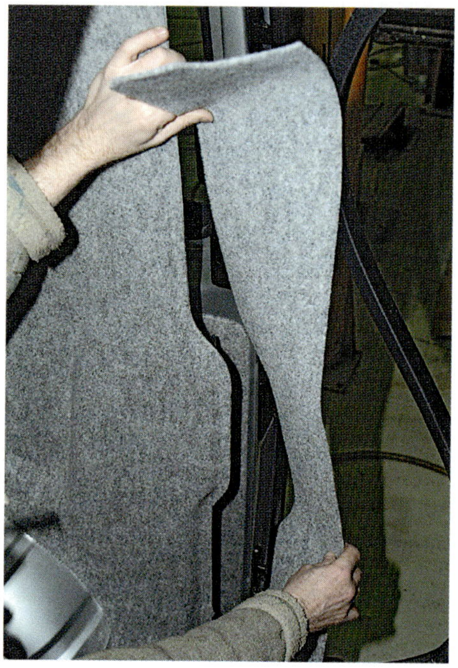

3-4-26. At the front of the side panel, Barry finally cut off the surplus material.

3-4-27. This allowed him to refit the trim seal over the edge of the wall covering. He used a rubber mallet to tap it fully home.

3-4-28. Note that where the two ends of the seal meet, there is a kind of rubber 'peg' projecting from one end of the seal. The other end of the seal has to be pushed over this 'peg' before being fitted to the bodywork.

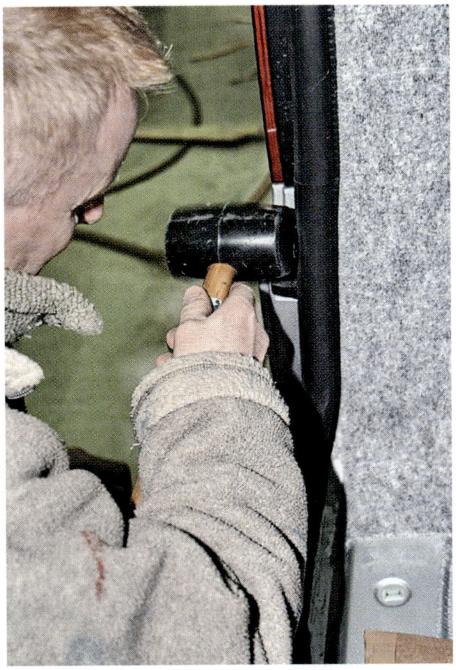

3-4-29. Barry taps the remainder of the seal, including the joined area, into place.

3-4-30. Before the left-hand rear wheel arch can be covered, the bracket for holding the jack in place has to be removed. It is best if you can remember to do this before fitting the trim but if, as can happen to anyone, you forget, make sure that the trim is protected against the hot angle grinder sparks and that none get on the side windows, windscreen or rear door glass. If sparks hit the trim, they will ruin it and the trim will need recovering. If they hit the glass, they bury themselves into it while red hot and can never be removed. Note that the bracket can be rescued and used again beneath the seat box for storing the jack in future.

3-4-31. Leisuredrive's trimmer makes up these wheel arch covers on the sewing machine.

3-4-32. Turned inside out, the cover is placed on the wheel arch and glue applied to fabric and painted steel.

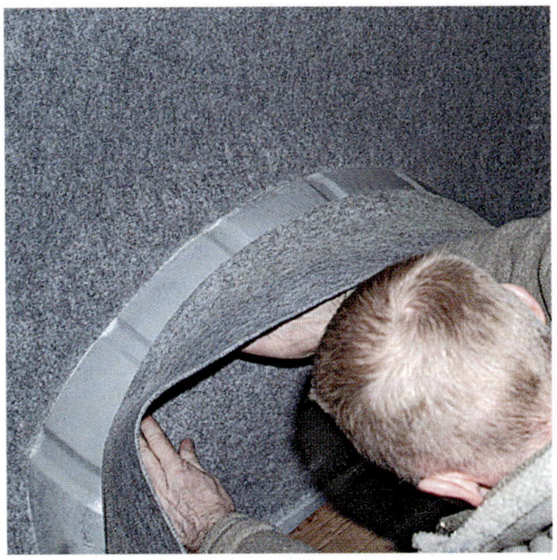

3-4-33. Barry then eased the cover into position …

3-4-34. … cutting the surplus material (not the good stuff) into sections so that it would fold into place.

3-4-35. He pushed the material tightly back into the corner …

3-4-37. There was then enough stretch to push the edge of the surplus material into place and then to cut it out with a sharp craft knife.

3-4-38. The tops of the side walls, where the roof strengthening panels are fitted, can also be covered with the same trim material.

Important note: You must always protect the fabric of the elevating roof so that you don't get glue overspray on it. The only way you will be able to remove glue overspray will be with a solvent which will also take out the waterproof properties of the fabric. This will then need to be reapplied.

3-4-39. As before, Barry used the handle of his scissors to push the material firmly down into position.

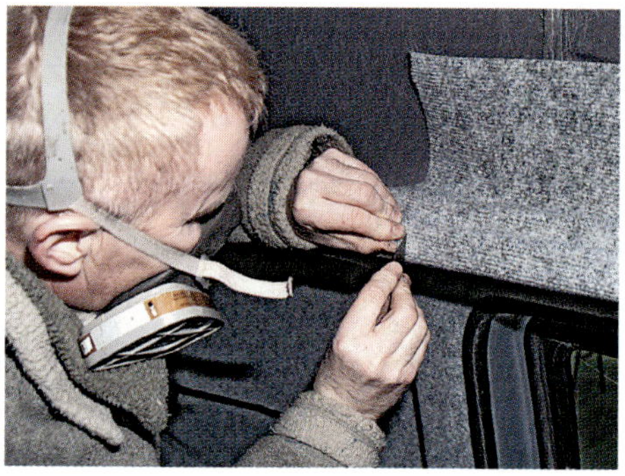

3-4-40. First, he cut the end, butt jointing the material together …

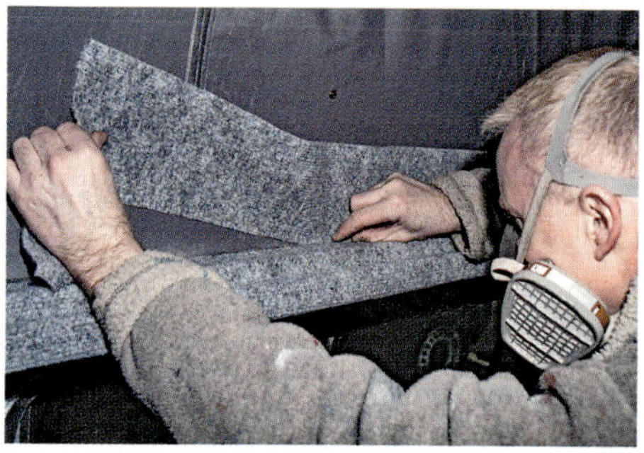

3-4-41. … and then cut just inside the line of the material of the elevating roof.

3-4-36. … then folded and glued the material down onto the wheel arch itself.

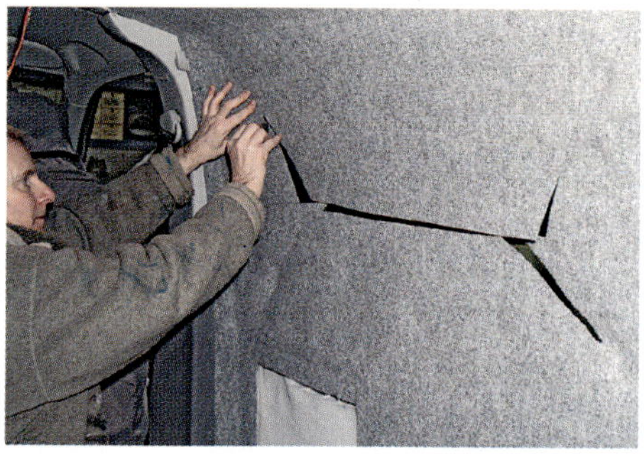

3-4-42. The way in which the windows are treated is really quite interesting! Note that this fabric has to be fitted after the window apertures have been cut out but before the glass is fitted. Barry 'finds' the edges of the window opening from the inside and makes the cuts shown here with his craft knife.

3-4-43. On the outside, he applied contact adhesive …

3-4-44. … and then proceeded to glue a narrow edge of the interior trim material around the edge of the steel panel.

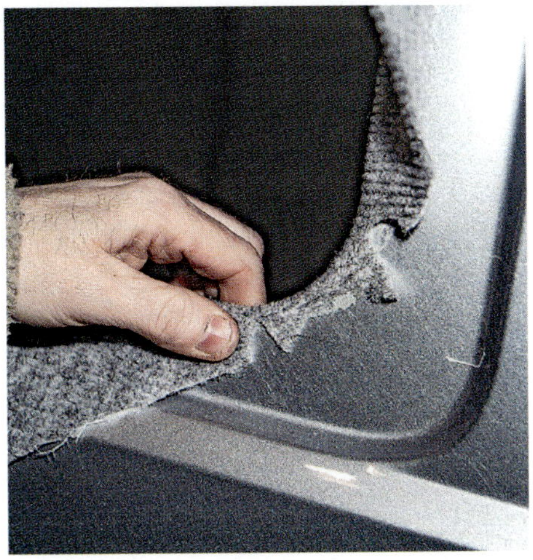

3-4-45. Here, you can see how he trimmed the surplus from the corners to enable the material to lie flat.

3-4-46. He followed this up by trimming surplus material all the way around, leaving the amount of trim material shown here. He then used solvent to wipe away any overspray from the glue.

3-4-47. On every vehicle, the back of the fridge has to be cut away so that it pushes as far as possible into the side wall of the van. Neil uses a template, ready made up at Leisuredrive, to mark out the material.

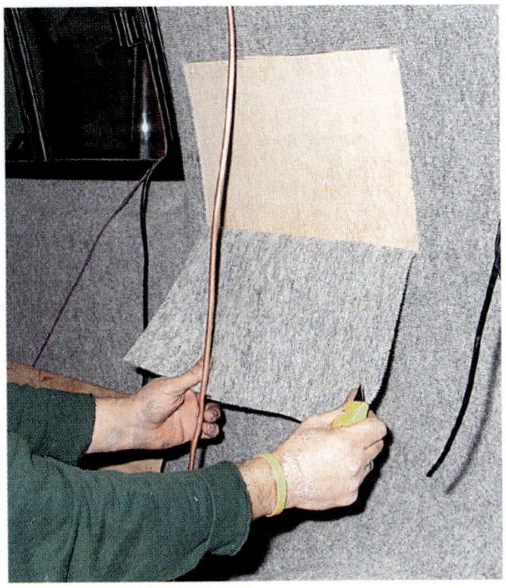

3-4-48. The fabric was peeled away …

3-4-49. … and then Neil cut again, removing the plywood panel from beneath. Here you can see the fibreglass insulation applied by Leisuredrive to the top part of the sidewall.

SECTION 5. BUILDING FURNITURE

If you buy a Leisuredrive kit for you to install into your own van, this furniture comes ready built, but if you want to build your own from scratch, this section may give you more than a few clues.

3-5-1. This is the furniture kit supplied by Leisuredrive for its Plan B conversion and this provides the traditional VW camper layout.

3-5-2. The later design of furniture, with smooth fronted units but slightly less bed width, was retro-fitted to our Camper, as you will see later. This is a slightly darker wood option with grey edging. It still has the original wooden bed box.

BED BOX SAFETY

The bed box is also the rear seat base and therefore is an important part of the strength of the vehicle when rear passengers are being carried. The earlier design, with wooden bed box has to have a steel reinforcing frame added to increase strength. If your vehicle was in an accident, you would want your rear seat passengers to be as safe as reasonably possible and the steel frame will help in this regard.

However, an alternative is to fit a steel folding frame rear seat and bed and this is strongly recommended for reasons of safety. See later in this Chapter.

Making the flats

3-5-3. Roy uses a template to mark out the shape of one of the flat panels.

3-5-4. He cuts out by hand, with a jigsaw, this particular internal shape …

3-5-5. … then finishes off with a router.

3-5-6. This bench-mounted machine puts a groove …

3-5-7. … all the way around this panel and inside the door openings.

3-5-8. T-section finishing strip is used to complete the door openings.

3-5-9. Roy taps it into the slots in the panel using a suitably shaped piece of wood.

3-5-10. These doors are framed with plastic extrusions and cut to length at the right angle with a radial saw. Other, later-style doors have different edging – see later.

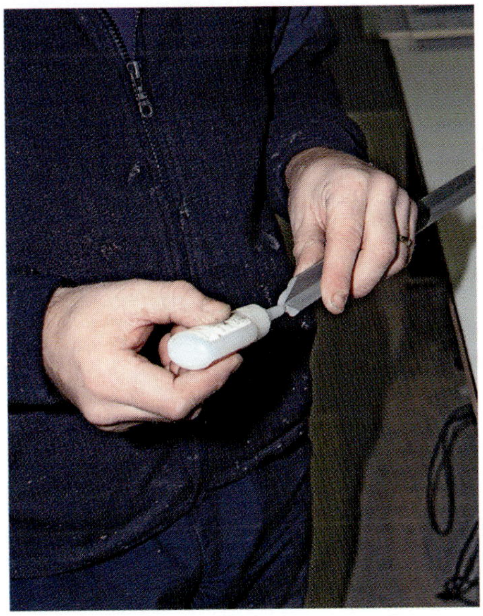

3-5-11. Super Glue-type adhesive is used on the corners.

3-5-12. It sets more quickly and strongly by using activator which is sprayed onto the opposite side of the joint.

3-5-13. The framing is fitted in place around the outsides of the door …

3-5-14. … and Roy nails the corners firmly into place.

3-5-15. These are all the flat sections completed, ready for assembly into furniture panels.

Constructing units

3-5-16. Roy uses 25mm timber battens to screw together some of the various sections …

3-5-17. … building them up into complete units.

3-5-18. Meanwhile, Steve sets up the machine used for creating dovetail joints.

3-5-19. This is a cutlery drawer side and back ready to be jointed together.

3-5-20. The washing-up liquid bottle contains PVA adhesive and this is used to glue the joints together …

3-5-21. … continuing the process all the way around the drawer unit.

3-5-22. Mechanically created dovetail joints in plywood make joints that are just about as strong as you can get.

3-5-25. The angle section is pushed onto the biscuits …

3-5-26. … and screwed to its supports on the rear panel.

3-5-23. Steve builds the kitchen units, screwing the grille door in place with the special hinges used to enable it to fold flat, rather like those used in domestic kitchen units.

3-5-27. Steve uses a pair of templates to mark the cutouts to be made in the sink and cooker top.

3-5-24. The front end of the cabinet has to be angled back otherwise there will not be enough legroom for the driver. The two sections to be joined together at an angle are both slotted and these 'biscuit' sections fit in the slats to provide a joint between the two edges.

3-5-28. Before fitting the top, gas pipes and connections have to be run inside the unit.

3-5-29. This shows the top being offered up into place ...

3-5-30. ... and screwed down to the base unit.

3-5-31. The Spinflo hob unit is fitted to the shape cut out earlier ...

3-5-32. ... and connected up underneath. This is one of those jobs that must be carried out by a registered gas fitter rather than on a DIY basis.

3-5-33. For no reason other that it just happened to be done now, Steve fitted the final plastic trim to the slotted edge of the cooker end panel. It could have been done at any stage, of course.

3-5-34. Where a cupboard fits against an upholstered wall, a doubled-up strip of trim is pinned to the back of the cupboard making a soft joint between cupboard and wall.

3-5-35. The excess material is cut away so that it doesn't show on the inside of the cupboard after fitting. This is a later style storage box to be fitted to the top of the wardrobe and shows an alternative location for the 13 amp socket.

3-5-36. Earlier, I mentioned the later type of door with curved shape. Steve cuts each of the door corners into steady curves.

3-5-37. Next, he grooves the outer edge of the door ...

3-5-38. ... before hammering in the T-section finishing strip.

3-5-39. Obviously, this style can only be used for doors which fit on top of the surface of the unit.

3-5-40. Our finished, retro-fitted interior shows the doors that have the rounded shape and also those that still have to be sharp-cornered, where they fit into the carcass of the unit.

3-5-41. This is another version with a steel-framed bed but also with square-cornered doors throughout.

SECTION 6. FIT WARDROBE AND CUPBOARDS

With elevating-roof models in particular, Leisuredrive fit the wardrobe first, followed by the kitchen units. When fitting the wardrobe, you have to make sure that it is positioned as far back as possible to allow the correct amount of room for all of the other units.

PART A. ELEVATING ROOF MODELS

3-6-A1. Andy puts the final touches to the construction of the units.

3-6-A2. The unit can be seen here receiving its first fit. You can expect to have to have the unit in and out a couple of times before you get it right.

3-6-A3. The unit is held firmly in position …

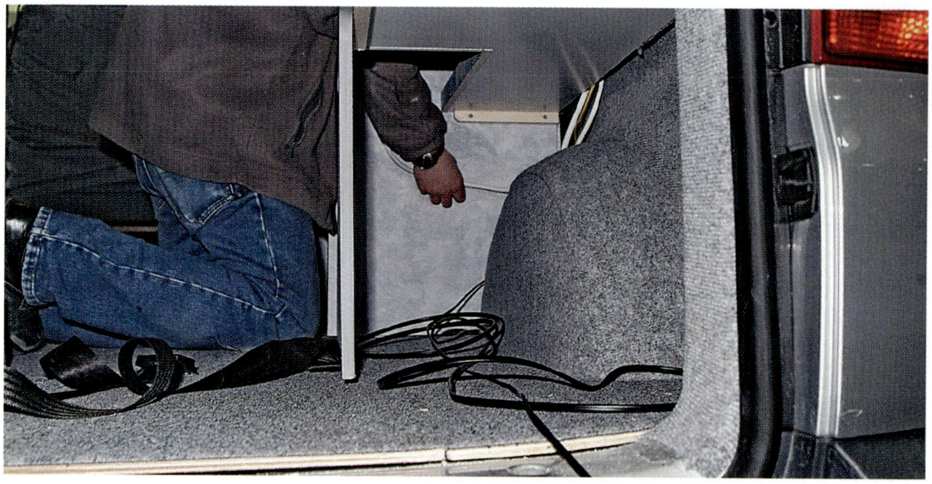

3-6-A4. … and getting the position right can involve making sure there are no wires trapped so that the unit fits against the bodywork.

3-6-A5. After final adjustment, the unit is reintroduced into the vehicle's body.

3-6-A6. This is the later-style wardrobe being retro-fitted to our Camper, by Roy. It is important that all adjustments have been completed and that the unit fits as well as possible …

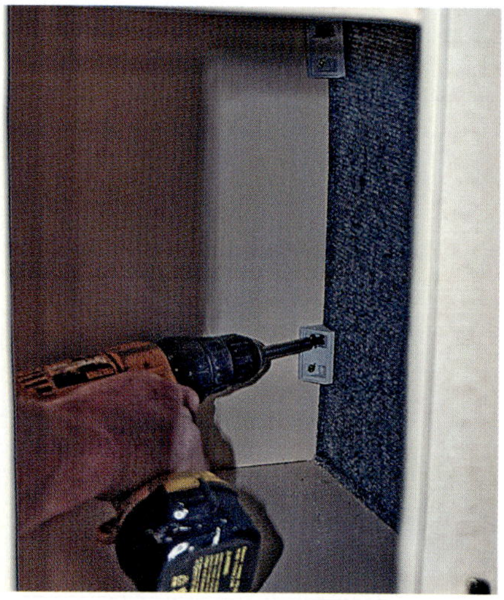

3-6-A7. … before using more angle brackets to screw the unit to the back wall …

3-6-A8. … in a number of locations, firmly fixing it in place.

3-6-A10. Steve fits the doors, as one of the last jobs, after all the units are in place.

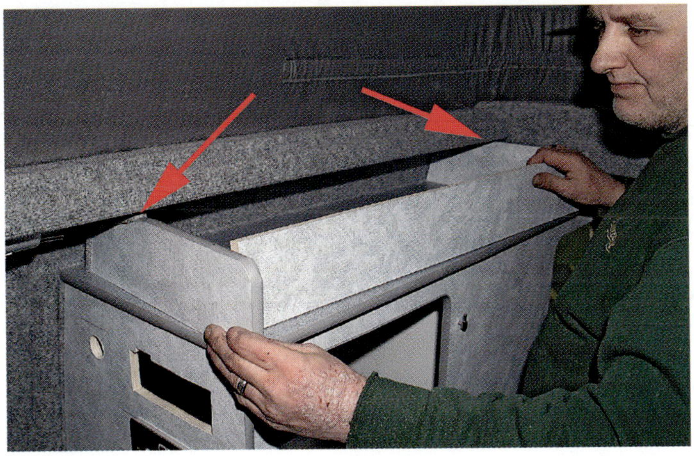

3-6-A9. The oddments tray that sits on top of the wardrobe is unusual in that it is made and fitted when the rest of the unit is in place. Note the trim material (arrowed) that has been stapled to the edges of the tray where they push up against the vehicle side-walls.

3-6-A11. The doors have to be adjusted at the catches to reduce rattling to a minimum. If necessary, you can fit felt pads – available from DIY stores – to the doors where they touch the carcass.

PART B. HIGH-TOP ROOF MODELS

3-6-B1. The wardrobe in the high-top version is naturally much taller than in the elevating roof version. Andy marks out the shape of the wardrobe using the Leisuredrive template …

3-6-B2. … before cutting out the shape required.

3-6-B3. The complex upright panel has to fit around the strengthening sections in the roof, as well as follow the shape of the van sides.

3-6-B4. This upright is screwed into place with the usual plastic angle bracket, both to the floor …

3-6-B5. …and to the wall. As you can see, the two main upright sections, one each side of the fridge, are now in place.

3-6-B6. This cupboard opening panel had previously established the distance between these two uprights and you can see the markings on the floor to which Andy is constructing the wardrobe.

3-6-B7. The door frame panel was next screwed in place, by Andy, to the two uprights.

3-6-B8. Here you can see the plethora of electrical cables for the fridge and other electrical equipment that have been let through the trim when it was fitted. They are now lined up inside the wardrobe, ready for the main electrical units which will also be fitted there.

3-6-B9. The Dometic fridge is obviously an important item in that it establishes the correct positioning of the major panels. Andy decides that he will check at this stage that everything is fitting correctly by offering up the fridge – a good practice for those carrying out their own DIY conversions.

3-6-B10. This panel is the template used by Leisuredrive for the end of the toilet compartment. As will soon become clear, there are a number of holes that need to be drilled in the panel after it has been cut out.

3-6-B11. Andy drills access holes for his jigsaw blade.

3-6-B12. The holes to be cut out have been marked onto the board and masking tape has been placed all around them so that the jigsaw will not cause any damage to the laminate. Andy 'joins-the-dots', having drilled a hole in each corner of the shapes to be cut out.

3-6-B13. The back edges of the upright can be seen here being trimmed, with folded-over trim stapled in place.

3-6-B14. The excess is cut off …

3-6-B15. … and the end panel offered up into place. Note the spacer board (arrowed) which is only fitted temporarily to establish the correct distance between the wardrobe panel and the toilet panel that Andy is holding here.

3-6-B16. Once he has established that everything is in its correct location, Andy fits more of those ubiquitous angle brackets to the back of the panel so that it can be screwed in place on the vehicle.

3-6-B17. Before the toilet compartment top can be fitted, Andy cuts out a small corner so that it fits neatly around the door pillar at the back of the van.

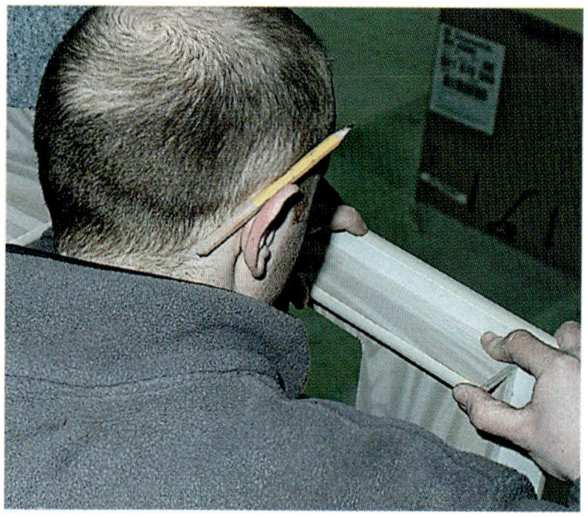

3-6-B18. On the inside of the end panel, Andy has built up a second thickness and this allows him to seat the top against the edge of this inner thickness …

3-6-B21. Next comes the front of the toilet compartment and this is the Leisuredrive template being offered up as an extra check that everything is lining up correctly.

3-6-B22. The door hinge panel is being clamped into place here before Andy screws it firmly from the back with angle brackets.

3-6-B19. …before drilling it down into the extra panel. The extra panel itself has been screwed to the inside of the end panel and the result is that from the back of the van, no screws are visible.

3-6-B23. The lift-up lid with long piano hinge is offered up. As you can see, it fits on the top that was previously fitted.

3-6-B20. Andy establishes that the back end of this panel is correctly lined up before screwing it into position.

3-6-B24. It will slot down snugly into the space between the wardrobe and the toilet end panel.

3-6-B25. Here you can see the angle brackets used to secure the top that was fitted earlier. More screws are now used to fix the hinged top in place.

3-6-B26. Leisuredrive fits a Thetford cassette toilet.

3-6-B27. Here you can see how it fits into the space created earlier. The bowl swivels through 90° when the toilet is in use. This is the waste tank being fitted through the access door that was cut out earlier. Above it is the access door for the flushing water.

3-6-B28. These are the Thetford doors ready to be built up before being fitted to the end panel.

3-6-B29. The door requires that these spring clips are first tapped into position ...

3-6-B30. ... and after the trim panel has been fitted ...

3-6-B31. ... Andy uses a scrap of wood so as not to cause damage, tapping the door and frame holding the trim panel together.

3-6-B32. The completed Thetford toilet doors have now been fitted and also the hinged access door can be seen on the left. This is simply placed on the pin hinges which are used throughout the motor caravan for cupboard doors.

3-6-B33. Not strictly a part of the wardrobe but storage space nonetheless. This is the Leisuredrive template being used to mark out a cupboard front ...

3-6-B34. ... which is constructed as described elsewhere in this chapter and can be fitted to the roof space providing more invaluable storage space.

SECTION 7. FIT KITCHEN UNIT

This section in particular needs to be followed in connection with Section 3, Floor & Holes.

3-7-1. Leisuredrive is so familiar with fitting out these vehicles that it drills the holes in the floor before fitting the kitchen units. See Section 3 for further advice on positioning the holes. This is a pilot hole being drilled …

3-7-2. … before a larger hole is put in the floor for one of the service pipes.

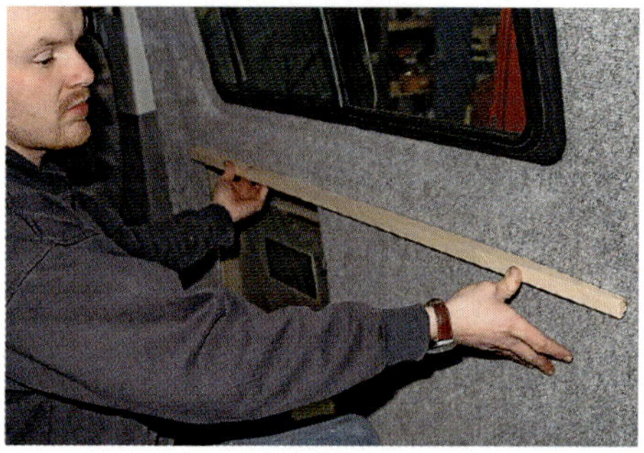

3-7-3. Andy offers up the batten to which the rear of the kitchen unit will be fitted. On its right-hand end, the batten has had to be tapered to follow the shape of the van's body. Also, note the way in which the cutout for the fridge has been made in the wall trim, as described elsewhere.

3-7-4. After drilling pilot holes, Andy uses self-tapping screws to fix the batten to the wall.

3-7-5. With the positions established, he takes it off again and covers the batten in trim material, fixing it in place with a staple gun …

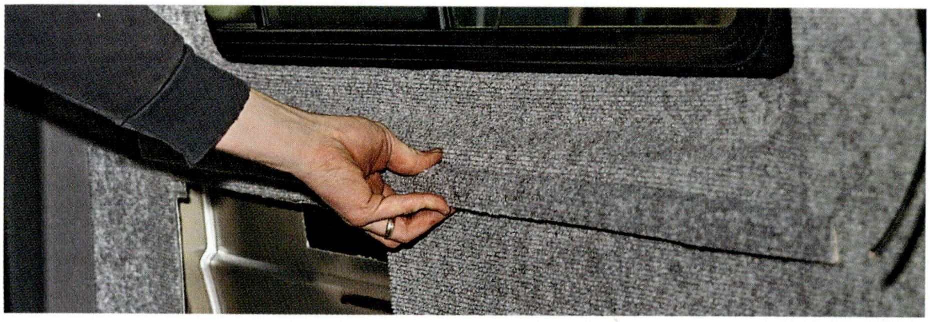

3-7-6. … before fitting the trimmed batten permanently in position.

3-7-7. This is the kitchen unit being 'delivered' into a Plan A conversion.

3-7-8. The unit is accurately positioned against the wall.

3-7-9. On all types of unit, plastic angle brackets are used to screw the sides down to the floor.

3-7-10. Several of these brackets are used so that the unit is securely held down.

3-7-11. More screws are applied through the rear frame and into the vehicle's bodywork. The frame uprights have been positioned by Leisuredrive in such a way that they allow fitting to the vehicle's body.

3-7-12. Back to our Plan B conversion, Steve drills pilot holes for the hinges used on the back of the sink cover.

3-7-13. He then screws the hinges down to the worktop ...

3-7-14. ... making sure that the cover is located in such a way that it clears the electrical fixings on the sidewall ...

3-7-15. ... and can be folded up against the wall. A turnbuckle clip is fitted to the wall in order to hold the cover up when the sink is in use.

Later design units

3-7-16. The principle of fitting these later-design units is very similar indeed. Steve (left) and Roy prepare to lift the sink unit – note the correct posture to avoid back damage, bending knees as far as possible.

3-7-19. He makes sure that the fronts line up. Here you can see how the units form a much smoother line than on earlier versions.

3-7-17. Note the service pipes and cables, as many of them as possible have been pre-fitted.

3-7-20. Roy screws the units together and secures the sink unit to the body of the van ...

3-7-21. ... before fitting the fridge, as described earlier.

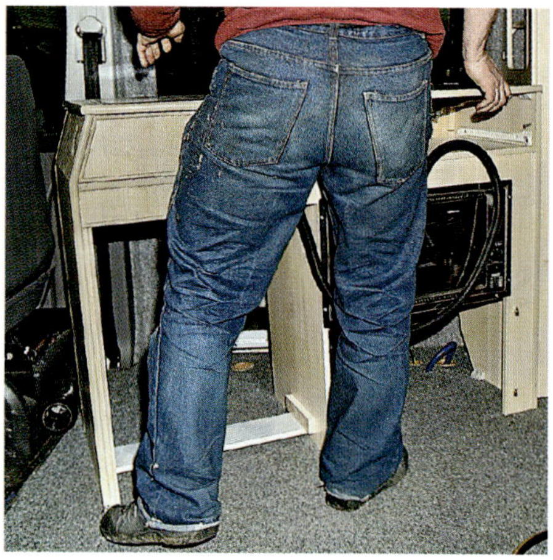

3-7-18. Roy eases the unit into position, against the wardrobe unit.

3-7-22. The table is supported by this neat rail which screws to the front of the sink unit.

3-7-23. When the spring-loaded leg is folded down the table simply clips into position.

Top tip!
- The table is stored down the edge of the rear seat, next to the wardrobe. If the table is made from the same material as the units, with the grain running in the same direction, it won't look as intrusive as if you use the same material as the work surfaces. All a matter of preference, of course, but in which position will the table be located for 99 per cent of its life?

SECTION 8. FIT BED

I very strongly recommend the use of the steel-frame folding bed and rear seat produced for Leisuredrive by its trimmer, NC Interiors, for the Plan B conversion. The alternative wooden structure may not be sufficiently strong in the event of a road accident.

Part A. Plan A

This section largely shows how Leisuredrive fit the kit of parts that is available for purchase at the time of writing to the Plan A variation with high-top.

3-8-A1. The basic bed box and cupboard unit fits behind the driver's seat and is screwed in position to the floor and wall.

3-8-A2. This is the pull-out steel support for when the bed is being made up.

3-8-A3. Andy drills pilot holes and then uses self-tapping screws to fix the seat/bed base to the pull-out unit.

3-8-A4. This is the fold-up base which comes complete with long piano hinge.

3-8-A5. The narrow strip at the back is screwed down to the batten which was previously screwed to the wall.

3-8-A6. This explains how the fold-up panel is raised, allowing the pull-out section to be slid into position.

3-8-A7. Opposite it and across part of the doorway is another cupboard base unit.

3-8-A8. *More of those plastic angle brackets are used to screw it down to the floor.*

3-8-A10. *Once again, there is a fold-and-slide top …*

3-8-A9. *This is the steel slide-out unit that provides the support for this side of the bed.*

3-8-A11. *… which is screwed down to the steel frame after first drilling pilot holes for the self-tapping screws.*

Part B. Plan B

This is the layout most often found on VW Campers. It probably descends from the days when Volkswagen Transporters had a rear engine which stuck up into the load bay and the bed was constructed upon the engine cover. The layout remains highly practical by utilising the space underneath the bed box as useful storage capacity.

This is the wooden seat base and bed structure which may only be suitable for static use rather than for carrying passengers because of its unknown strength in the event of a traffic accident.

When installing the bed box, make sure that it goes as far forward as possible while ensuring that the door under the sink or the oven door (according to fittings used) can open properly. On the other hand, if the bed box/seat base is fitted too far back, there will be a problem with upholstery fouling on the rear tailgate.

3-8-B1. *This is the bed base being lifted into the rear of the vehicle.*

3-8-B2. *Leisuredrive's Roy demonstrates the reason why the rear cupboard has a sloping angle on its opening. This is because the back of the seat comprises two cushions for the bed and this is the angle at which they stand when the seat is erected.*

3-8-B3. The bed box itself has to be fitted equidistant between the wheel arch and the wardrobe. It is important before fixing the bed box down to make sure that it is perfectly parallel and in the correct position. The position can be established by fitting the seat unit as shown later but, having established the correct position, it makes sense to measure the fitting positions, write them down and then reuse them later when the seat box is finally fitted.

3-8-B4. This is the reinforcing frame that Leisuredrive introduced after the first batch of photographs had been taken, as a means of strengthening the bed box. It fits inside the specially prepared bed box with the highest part of the frame at the front of the bed box.

SAFETY FIRST!

It is important to note that the bed and seat box shown here are not constructed to Manufacturers Construction & Use Standards and the safety and integrity of the rear seat cannot possibly be equal to those of a Volkswagen California, for instance, which is manufactured by Volkswagen.

3-8-B5. More angle brackets are used to screw the bed box down to the floor.

3-8-B6. Andy steps out of the vehicle with the bed and seat base units, having tried them for fit and marked where they need to be trimmed so that they fit properly.

3-8-B8. Neil makes sure that all of the hinge screws are fitted.

3-8-B7. After final trimming, the seat and bed base panels are laid in position on the bed box.

3-8-B9. The base units are then folded so that they are in the correct position for placing the rear seats.

3-8-B10. As well as checking the fit at the front, it is important to check that the bed base fits correctly at the back as well. This may look like it's going to be a rear seat, but it's not!

3-8-B15. Roy makes sure that the front part of the seat base is correctly located …

3-8-B11. It's best to fit objects that will go inside the bed box before finally fitting the bed and seat base. Note that the battery should be strapped down with secure supports which pass through the floor and into structurally sound material beneath. This is a job for an engineer to carry out. Otherwise, the risk of a heavy lead-acid battery flying around in the event of an accident doesn't bear thinking about!

3-8-B13. Once the steel frame is in place, the seat and bed base panels can be fitted for the last time.

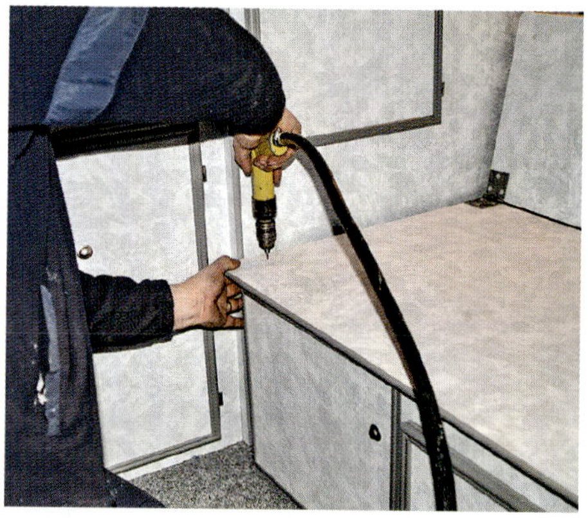

3-8-B16. … then drills a pilot hole through the seat base and into the steel frame which we saw earlier and which is now located alongside the wooden seat box.

3-8-B12. Andy prepares to refit the steel slid-out frame that provides the bed support.

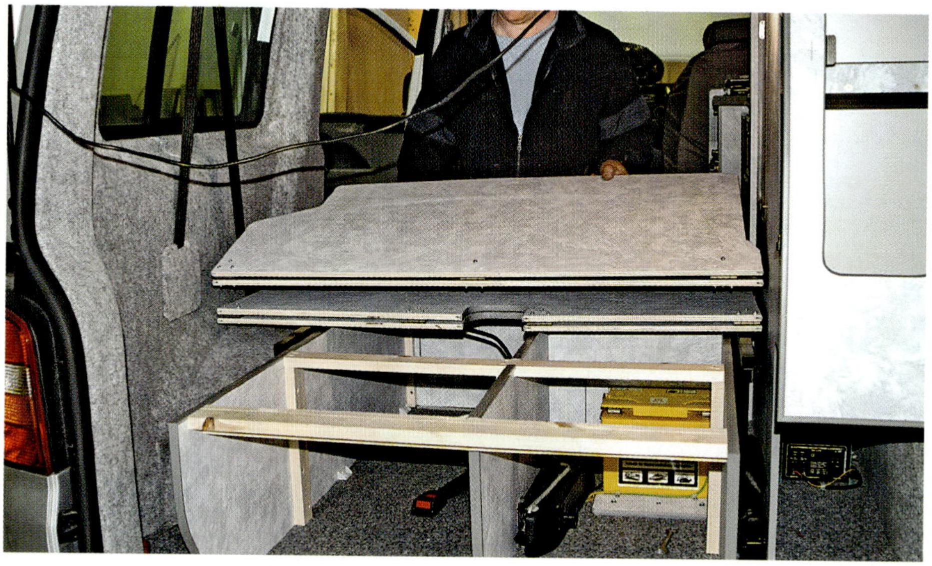

3-8-B14. Note, that next to the battery, the jack has been fitted using the bracket that was removed from the rear-left wheel arch, as shown in Section 4 of this chapter.

3-8-B17. The base is screwed down ...

3-8-B20. ... and then angle brackets are used to secure the cosmetic trim panels that give the front of the seat base an attractive appearance.

3-8-B21. These trim panels are also screwed to the bottom of the seat base itself.

3-8-B18. ... and the two halves of the seat/bed base finally fitted together with their hinges.

3-8-B22. The angle brackets used by Leisuredrive have small finisher plates which are clipped in place, concealing the screws beneath.

3-8-B19. The fronts of the steel supports are drilled with a pilot hole ...

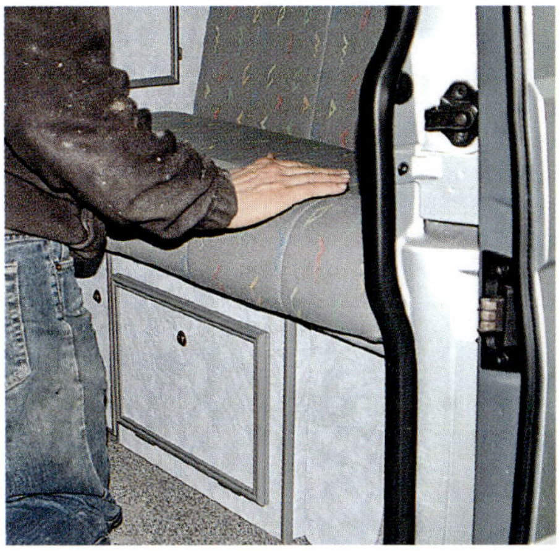

Important note: These hinges should first be fitted with the bed lying flat. If you don't do so, there is a risk that the two wooden boards will be too close together which will prevent the bed base from lying completely flat when it has been made up into a bed.

3-8-B23. The final job is to fix the Velcro strips to the seat bases using a staple gun, in accordance with the location of the Velcro sewn to the backs of the seats. The seat cushions can then be put in place.

Part C. Steel-framed folding rear seat and bed base

3-8-C1. Leisuredrive's proprietor, Derek Andrews, demonstrated to me the prototype of the then-new steel-framed folding bed and rear seat produced for Leisuredrive by NC Interiors.

3-8-C4. Leisuredrive's Paul began by fitting the nuts and bolts holding the hinges to the folding seat mechanism. The four tubes you can see on the front face of the seat back were carefully ground off because they were found to be intrusive. Instead, Leisuredrive drilled vertical holes through the box sections into which the headrest legs can be slotted.

3-8-C5. Your local branch of Autopaint International can mix you some paint to match the colour of the seat frame, should you need it. This is synthetic paint which is suitable for brushing and won't react against the paint that's already on the frame.

3-8-C2. Beneath the front of the seat you'll find this lever which, when operated, releases the catches …

3-8-C6. Paul also drilled holes in the frame for attaching the seat belt strap, though one can expect these holes to be ready-drilled in future, this being only the second such seat frame that had been made and, as always with new things, some tinkering was necessary.

3-8-C3. … enabling the seat frame to fold down flat and become the bed support.

3-8-C7. The seat belt strap was then bolted to the frame, one on each side.

3-8-C8. The four boards that are supplied with this seat base were cut to size and lipped by Paul.

3-8-C9. It was decided not to fit them at this stage because doing so with the seat base in the vehicle would allow some latitude for adjustment.

3-8-C12. It's best to mount the left-hand seat belt strap onto the manufacturer's seat belt mounting point in the sidewall. This was originally put there for an inertia reel unit but it doesn't have to be used for that, of course.

3-8-C10. Roy introduced the seat base into the vehicle, marked the positions for drilling the holes, and then went underneath the vehicle to remove the spare wheel and undertray – a fairly time-consuming operation. INERTIA REEL SEAT BELTS: Note that the inertia reel seat belts have already been bolted to the seat frames (arrowed).

3-8-C13. While other things were going on, Steve fitted drawer runners beneath the front half of the seat and installed the large drawer unit.

3-8-C11. In order to beef up the mounting points, I had three 4mm thick steel plates made to fit the spaces between box sections, with the plates resting on the flanges of the top-hat sections. The seat base was bolted down through both the floor and these reinforcing plates. Before finally fitting them, they were coated with wax protective aerosol spray.

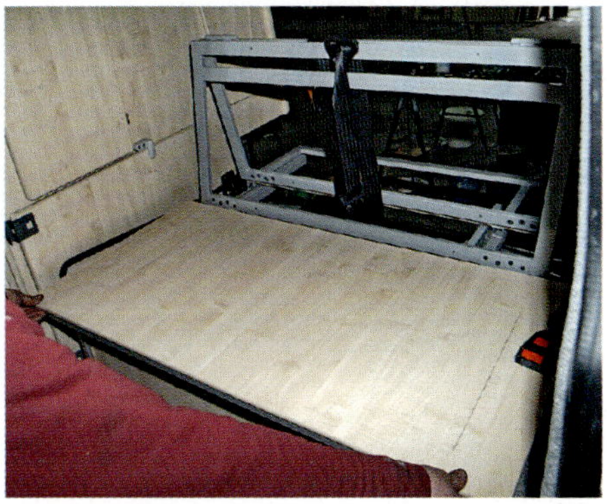

3-8-C14. Now Roy felt it was time to offer up the four panels fitted to the seat base. Incidentally, to the left you can see that the table has been clipped into place (see how the grain of the wood finish matches that of its surroundings) so that the clearances between the table and the seat base can be correctly judged.

3-8-C15. Roy drilled pilot holes ...

3-8-C16. ... and screwed each board into position on the frame.

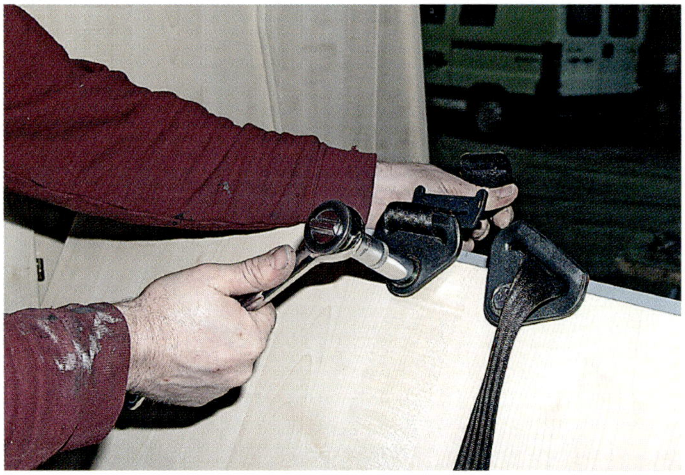

3-8-C17. Roy drilled holes in the laminate to match those in the steel frame and bolted the seat belt guides in place ...

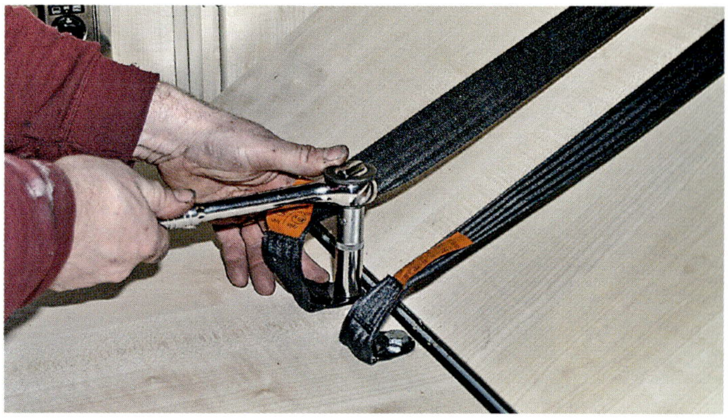

3-8-C18. ... the ends of the seat belt straps were bolted to the seat base at the rear.

3-8-C19. You can see that when the bed is folded down, the seat belt straps run through the guides and lie flat beneath the mattress.

3-8-C20. To fill the gap between the edge of the drawer and the side of the vehicle, these small filler panels are made and screwed into place.

3-8-C21. Roy prepares to fix the Velcro to the seat backs to match that on the trim.

3-8-C22. He uses a staple gun to attach the Velcro to the laminate …

3-8-C23. … leaving the final job that of placing the luxurious upholstery in position.

3-8-C24. The drawer unit is of an extremely useful size and makes the storage space beneath the bed far more usable than simply stuffing things in from the front!

3-8-C25. Viewed from the rear you can see that the fitted headrests look very elegant, as well as being of practical safety value. This is another of Leisuredrive's many trim options.

Chapter 4

Gas, water & electricity

Most important – read this first!
Before attempting any of the work described in this chapter, you must read and fully understand what it's okay to do and – more importantly, what it's **not** okay to do yourself. Please read this first! →

This is the most safety-critical chapter of this manual. That's not to say that you shouldn't carry out any of the work yourself, but you will certainly need to bring in the professionals to carry out final installation and checking of safety-critical areas. Read the SAFETY FIRST! notes on this page for further information. I can do no worse than quote verbatim from the website of the excellent Self-Build Motor Caravan Club (sbmcc.co.uk) on the subject of safety.

"Safety should never be compromised for the sake of speed, money, or just apathy. If personal safety is not enough to make people 'do things right', what about insurance claims, should it come to it. [Insurance companies may be] perfectly within their rights to not honour a claim when something like badly installed wiring leads to a fire. Even if it [the wiring] is not the cause of the fire, the claims assessor could and will use it as a reason not to pay!"

However, having made these important safety points, there's nothing to stop you working on the water system and the structural installations yourself. The illustrations showing Leisuredrive staff connecting up electrical and gas fittings are to give you an idea of what your chosen professionals will be doing for you and allow you to prepare the vehicle for them, saving yourself as much of its labour charges as possible.

SAFETY FIRST!

- **Gas safety:** It is essential that the installation of gas fittings and appliances are only carried out by a qualified professional – a CORGI registered LPG fitter, in the UK.
- **Electrical safety:** It is equally essential that all electrical wiring, appliances and equipment are installed by a qualified electrician – typically NICEIC qualified in the UK. Even though the installation of 12 volt wiring is nowhere near as dangerous as that of 230 volt mains equipment, it can still cause a fire or gas explosion if incorrectly installed.
- **DIY installation:** The work in this chapter is all shown being carried out by qualified staff at Leisuredrive. We very strongly recommend that you have the relevant work carried out by qualified professionals. However, there is no reason why you shouldn't carry out the preparatory work yourself. For instance, you could fit the electrical power unit to the wall, run the wiring in position (though leaving it accessible so that it can be professionally checked) but don't make any of the connections. Similarly, gas appliances such as <u>**a**</u> cooker or water heater can be fitted into position but not connected.
- **Final fitting and checking:** Have connections made by appropriately qualified professionals. Pay to have a thorough check carried out and a certificate to state that the installation is complete and safe, ready to present to your insurance company.
- **Second-hand appliances:** From 2003 in the UK, new appliances and regulators are fitted to all new caravans and motor caravans, running a different pressure to that of all older appliances. **Do not** mix-and-match appliances and/or regulators from the different eras!

Gas regulations

All caravans and campers built after 1st September 2003 have to conform to the EU standard known as EN1949, which specifies that the regulator will be a fixed part of the gas supply. Therefore, in place of the earlier and potentially dangerous piece of push-on rubber hose with a hose-clip, is a pipe with fitted ends from the fixed regulator to gas bottle. Push-on hoses are not allowed under these regulations. All new hoses must have threaded connectors, and must have excess-flow and non-return safety valves.

The advice for self-build installers in the UK is simple: You should strongly consider using the EN1949 standard for the following reasons: the system is standard in the UK and in Continental Europe, and it will, therefore, be much more convenient to use; all new appliances are designed to run at the new, higher pressure, so the regulators must match the requirements of the appliances being fitted.

Installing gas equipment

Section 8 of this chapter deals with the fitting and application of gas cylinders and equipment and it is important that the information given in that section is read and fully understood.

Order of working

There can be no hard and fast rules about which bits to fit first and which to leave until last. But there will certainly be some jobs that are best carried out before the furniture is fitted, some that can only be carried out after it's fitted, and some, no matter how hard you try, you'll wish you'd done before fitting something else in place! One important point relates to the fitting of gas and electrical components mentioned at some length in the rest of the introduction to this chapter. You may wish to route pipes and cables so that they can be seen (from inside cupboards of course – not across the interior of the motorhome!) so that the professionals who check, connect and certificate gas and electrical installations can see exactly what's there and where it all goes.

Don't forget, of course, that there's nothing to stop you fitting furniture and then taking it out again later if you need to. For that reason, it's sometimes best to use round-head coach-bolts and nuts rather than screws. Screws will only go into wood a limited number of times before their grip weakens and they become useless. If you're using chipboard screws, you should not expect to be able to remove and replace them once fitted.

Much of the furniture shown here has been constructed from laminated material screwed to 25mm x 25mm battens, or screwed-and-glued where no dismantling can possibly be necessary in future. In a few cases, such as the bed box mountings to the structure of the van, I have, on a previous conversion with a gas heater inside the enclosed bed box, replaced fixing screws with nuts and bolts. It's surprising how many times that bed box had to come out so that the components inside it could be maintained! Needless to say, this would be much more difficult with the much safer steel-framed rear seat and bed featured here, so the principle of making everything as accessible as possible becomes even more relevant.

You should also bear in mind the possible need to access components such as a Belling Malaga water heater, if fitted. One such heater was originally built into the units on our first van. The heater was fitted and the sink unit fitted over it. Then, when it needed maintenance, there was the threat of having to remove the whole sink unit. Instead, I cut out a panel from the sink unit and refitted it with a neat trim strip to cover the join, but how much better it would have been if an access panel had been built in from the first. Hindsight is a wonderful thing – but forward planning is the next best ...

Important note: Don't carry out the work shown in this chapter or in any individual section without reading the rest of this manual. There are many jobs that are associated with other work. This manual has been divided up into logical sections of the vehicle but these are not necessarily the order in which you will carry out the work. Please study the whole of the manual before commencing work.

SECTION 1. COOKER AND SINK

The cooker and sink fitted to most Leisuredrive conversions are made by Spinflo. CAK Tanks can also offer a range of sinks and cookers from Smev as well as all the plumbing requirements you may need. We fitted a CAK Tanks faucet to the 'early' type of layout and a CAK folding hot-and-cold tap to the 'later' type of layout.

4-1-1. For the earlier-type installation, we wanted a faucet that would fold away inside the sink when the lid was down, having had experience of knocking off and breaking externally fitted taps before! This meant having to drill a hole in the side of the sink and Leisuredrive's Steve selected the correct size on the stepped cutter and made a mark with his pencil.

4-1-2. Steve marked and centre-punched the position for the hole and drilled a pilot hole.

4-1-3. The stepped cutter was then used to open out the hole to the appropriate size.

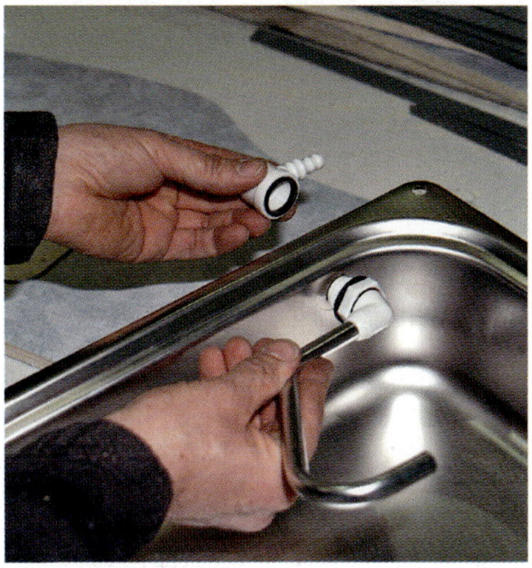

4-1-4. The CAK Tanks faucet being offered up to the hole in the sink. Note that this is known as a 'faucet' rather than a 'tap' because it is operated directly from the pump switch and doesn't have an on-off valve built into it.

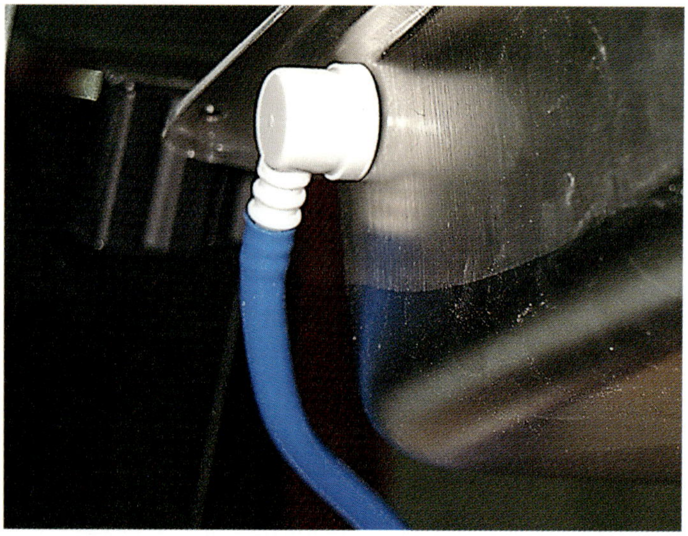

4-1-5. Seen from the underside of the sink, the faucet has been fitted and the water supply pipe pushed onto the connector. Obviously, it's far easier to do it before the sink is fitted.

4-1-6. Steve accurately placed the sink in position after having gunned a bead of sealant all the way around the edge. Some sinks will come with their own neoprene rubber seal which has to be fitted first.

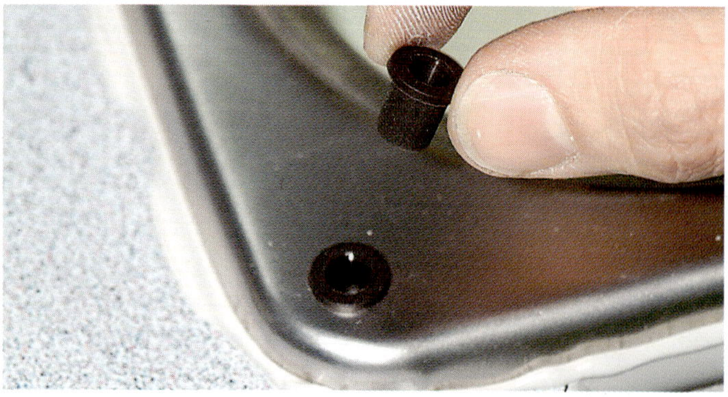

4-1-7. This sink is screwed down via a plastic clip which pushes into the pre-drilled hole in the sink.

4-1-8. The fixing screw then presses the clip down against the work surface and the clip holds the sink in position.

4-1-9. The clip is finished off with a simple plastic cap.

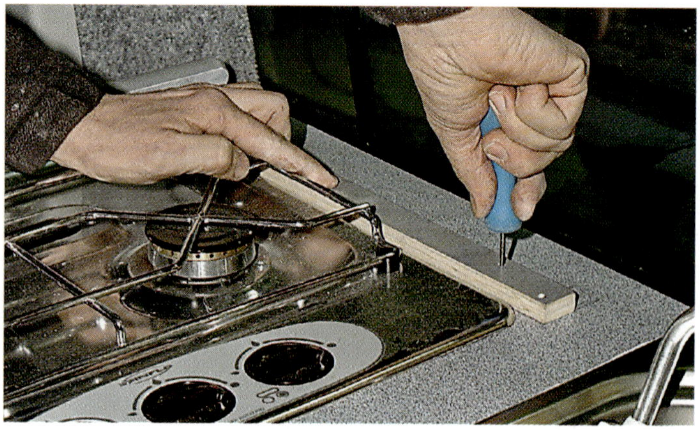

4-1-10. The hob unit has been fixed down as shown elsewhere and connected to the gas supply by Leisuredrive. These connections need to be carried out by a qualified CORGI fitter, of course. Steve uses a template made from scrap wood to mark out the positions for the hob cover. It's a good idea to make such a template yourself rather than try to guestimate the positions on the worktop.

4-1-11. The cover was offered up and the screws driven in …

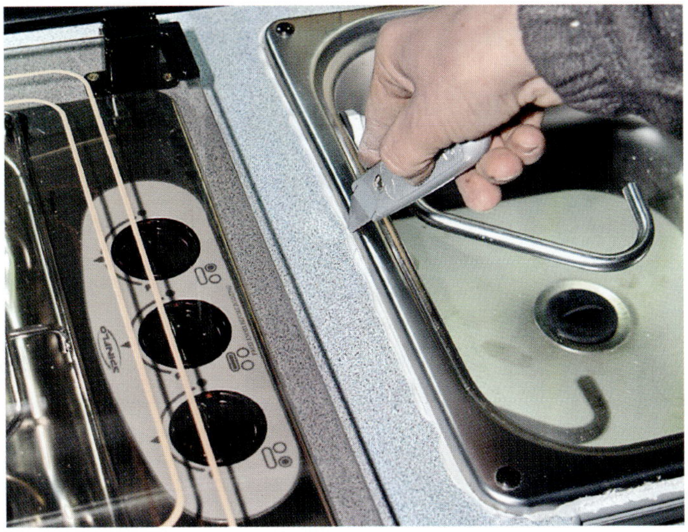

4-1-14. Once the sealant had gone off underneath the sink, Steve ran a craft knife blade carefully around the edge, only pressing down lightly so that he didn't cut into the laminate beneath.

4-1-12. … on both sides of the cover.

4-1-15. He then used an old wood chisel to lift the sealant from the laminate.

4-1-13. The cover is spring-loaded which holds it in either the lowered or the fully raised position. Some owners may wish to fit a folding aluminium flap which opens up and protects the back of the seat. It all depends how much cooking you envisage doing and how close to the seat the rings are situated.

4-1-16. The 'later' type unit was fitted with a Smev sink from CAK. These units have clips on their undersides which makes it easy to hold them in place when the units are being assembled.

4-1-17. It is complemented by the matching hob unit. CAK can supply black or grey folding glass tops, according to choice.

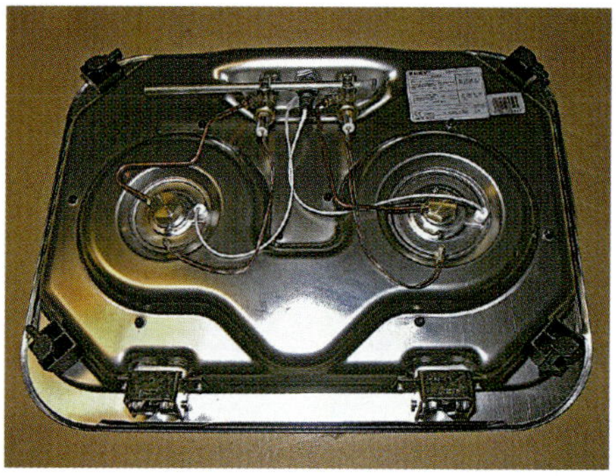

4-1-18. This Smev hob has auto-igniters. Viewed from beneath, you can see the gas pipe to which the supply is connected (top-left) and the plastic fitting clips, one in each corner.

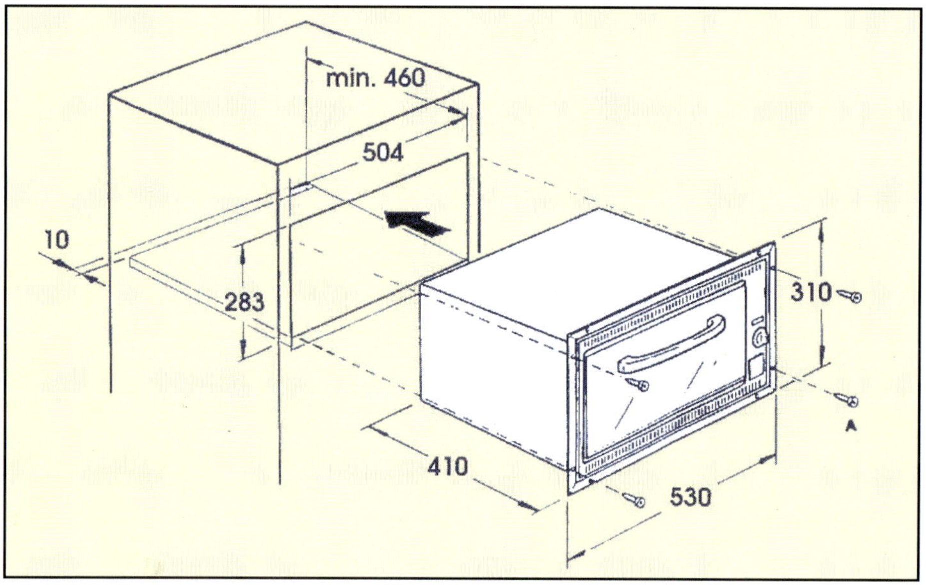

4-1-19. Although, at the time of writing, no Smev hobs come with grilles, a superb alternative from CAK is this Smev grille and mini-oven which slots into the dimensions shown.

4-1-20. With all of the trim in place, the oven is close to the rear seat but you could either lift the cushion out of the way when using grille or oven or place a cover over the seat fabric. It's a compromise (and all such positions in a compact camper are compromises) but we greatly prefer this layout over the earlier one with the hob unit right behind the driver's seat.

4-1-21. When I went to a place near Warwick to collect our taps from CAK, I was met by the hugely knowledgeable and enthusiastic proprietor, Jonathan Frost. He introduced me to these screw-on 'tails' which are fitted to the taps before they are fitted to the sink. The push-fit connectors on the ends of the tails are easily connected to the water pipes.

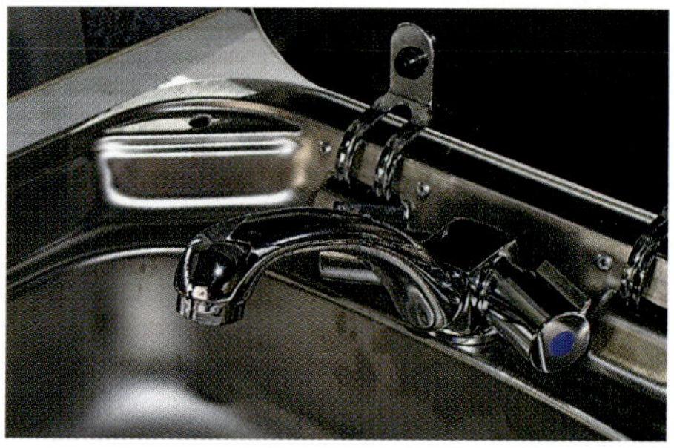

4-1-22. After fitting the CAK taps, the Leisuredrive fitters remarked on their good, 'domestic' quality unlike many camper taps which are rather flimsy. There are no internal switches. the Sureflo pump supplies water 'on demand' when the taps are opened.

4-1-23. Before closing the lid, the CAK tap is simply folded away first.

SECTION 2. FRESH WATER STORAGE

CAK Tanks has made a huge investment in manufacturing water storage and waste water tanks for the Volkswagen T5. It worked with Volkswagen GB before the launch of the vehicle and some of the photographs that it took to help CAK develop the tank from scratch are reproduced here, partly out of interest but mainly so that they will assist when it comes to fitting a tank to your own vehicle.

Thanks to Jonathan Frost of CAK Tanks for several of the pictures used in this section.

4-2-1. Jonathan Frost of CAK Tanks demonstrates the two water storage tanks that will be fitted to our project vehicle. There are two tanks because Jonathan wanted to maximise the amount of water storage available and the only way of doing it was to manufacturer two separate tanks with a connecting pipe.

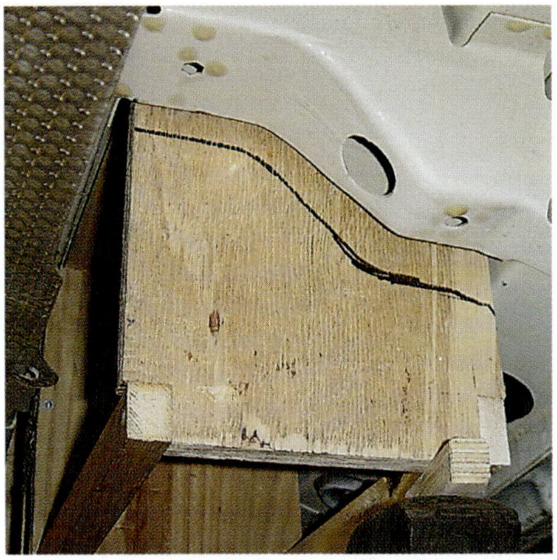

4-2-5. This is another mock-up of part of the tank and shows how the very first stage in the development work is simply to make shapes that will fit the complex underbody of the vehicle.

4-2-2. These are the pipes, fittings, water filter and at the top, lockable filler for the cold water system.

4-2-3. When working on a Volkswagen T5 prototype, CAK made a wooden frame to give it an idea of the dimensions of the tank it would need to make. You can also see the beginning of the strap mountings.

4-2-4. Viewed from the side, this is the narrow tank mounting point.

4-2-6. This particular strap hanger has to be fitted through a hole drilled in the underbody at the point shown here.

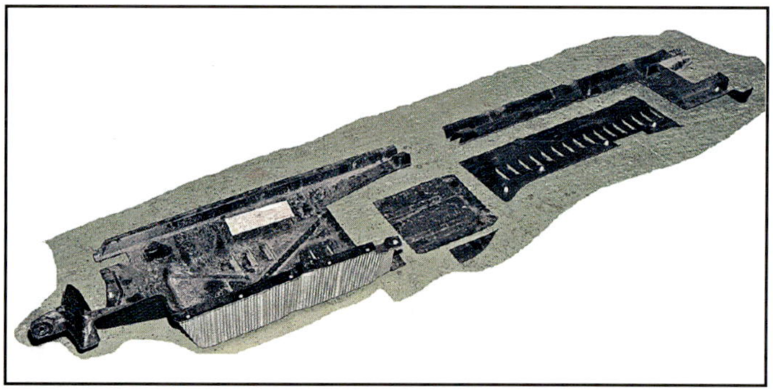

4-2-7. Jonathan also worked on the necessary cutouts that have to be made from the undertray.

4-2-8. You can see how the steel straps (arrowed) fit around the tank and come up inside the cutaway undertray.

4-2-9. The narrow tank has to be fitted with this special elongated hook which is supplied by CAK as part of the kit.

4-2-10. CAK also supply a water level gauge. This is the sender unit.

4-2-11. A hole has to be cut in the top of the tank with a tank cutter (this work is now being carried out by Leisuredrive). The correct seal, supplied with the sender unit, has to be positioned between the top of the tank and the sender.

4-2-12. Pilot holes are drilled and then the stainless steel screws provided are used to screw the sender unit onto the top of the tank. Before fitting the tank, make sure that the wiring has already been fitted to the sender unit.

4-2-13. At this stage, Leisuredrive were cutting the holes in the side of the van and so cut the appropriate hole for the water filler neck.

4-2-14. The main hose to the tank and the overflow pipe must be fitted at this stage.

4-2-15. The hoses are pushed through the bodywork and the relevant hole which has also been cut in the bottom of the van. The filler neck is temporarily pushed tightly into position.

4-2-16. Beneath the van, the one hole that needed to be drilled has its strap hanger fitted into position and, once the primer paint has dried, Würth Cavity Protection Spray was sprayed into and around the hole.

4-2-17. It makes sense to fit as much to the tank as possible before it is pushed underneath the vehicle. This is the drain tap on a short length of extension hose being fitted in place. In the top left is the entry for the filler pipe and beneath it is the main outlet stub.

4-2-18. Leisuredrive's Roy is seen offering up the main tank, having removed all of the relevant undertray sections.

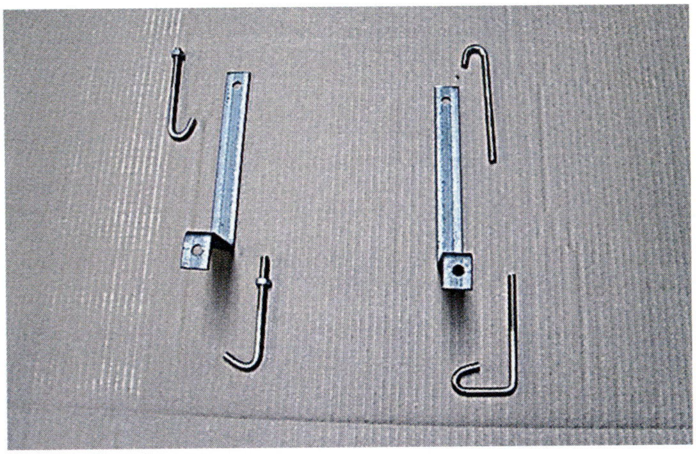

4-2-19. It's worth pointing out that I decided to have the tank straps galvanised, otherwise they will inevitably rust and look ugly beneath the vehicle. This was carried out by a company called Edward Howell, which will take on small jobs.

4-2-20. With the strap hangers in place and one end of each strap loosely fitted, Roy offered up the tank once again …

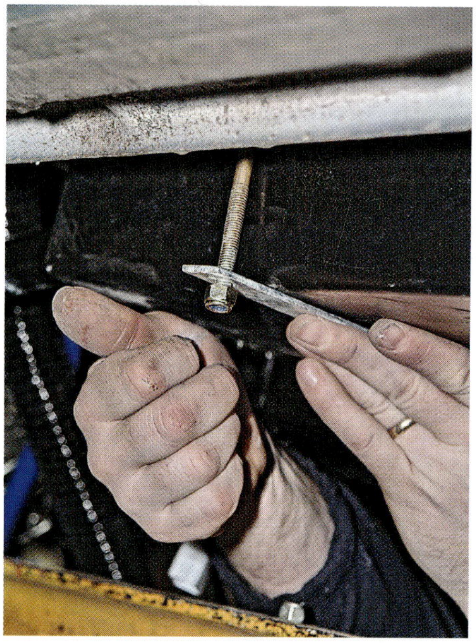

4-2-21. … and fitted the remaining locknuts.

4-2-22. He then used the air wrench to tighten the locknuts, both on the inside of the tank and the lower ones on the outside. It is essential to use locknuts for this installation because these straps must not be overtightened against the tank and there will also be no pressure to hold ordinary nuts and/or spring washers in place.

4-2-23. With the tank in place, the filler hose was connected. The outlet hose at the bottom was blanked off for now, to be connected later.

4-2-24. The wiring for the tank sender had been fitted by now and it was a simple matter to push together the male and female connectors.

4-2-25. Roy measured and marked out the undertray ready for cutting …

4-2-26. … and used a jigsaw to cut away the redundant material.

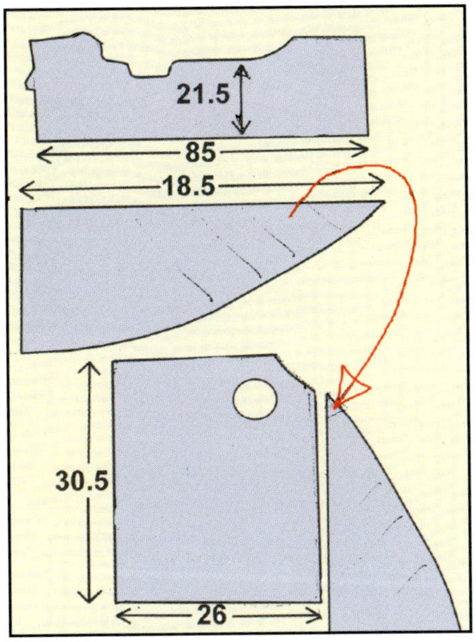

4-2-27. This is a sketch I made – NOT to scale! – indicating some of the dimensions of the cutouts made at CAK tanks.

4-2-28. Roy fitted the undertray temporarily at first and then trimmed it to its final shape.

4-2-29. When he'd finished, the undertray and insulation panels were refitted.

4-2-30. Here you can see the way in which the undertray fits around the end of the tank. The lengthened hose enables the drain tap to be accessed; the water feed pipe can be seen disappearing up behind the undertray in the background; the sink drain hose has also been inserted through the gap in the undertray, in the foreground.

4-2-31. Now that pulling on it won't risk causing any damage, the filler neck could be sealed …

The eagle-eyed among you may have spotted that we fitted only one freshwater tank to the project vehicle. The other tank can easily be added later if required but, initially at least, the vehicle was intended to be used for shorter rather than longer trips. For the same reason, the waste water tank, shown in Section 4, was offered up but has not yet been fitted.

4-2-32. … and screwed into place using the stainless steel self-tapping screws provided by CAK Tanks.

SECTION 3. WATER PUMP AND PIPEWORK

Give some thought to where the water pump will go at the design stage. The pump is not something that will need to be accessed on a regular basis, but when you need to get at it, you don't want to have to dismantle furniture. The pump is a mechanical object and prone to failure, and it may need servicing from time to time. Bear in mind the following important points:

- Don't fit the pump on the outside of the vehicle where it may be damaged by water or debris thrown up by the wheels.
- It's best to mount the pump in a relatively well-insulated area, such as inside a cupboard, and not fixed directly to the exterior of the van because of the risk of frost damage.
- You must take note of the manufacturer's instructions regarding the correct orientation of the pump. For instance, the Whale Clearstream 700 pump can be mounted either horizontally or vertically (although Whale recommends mounting the pump horizontally for best results), but must not be mounted upside down.

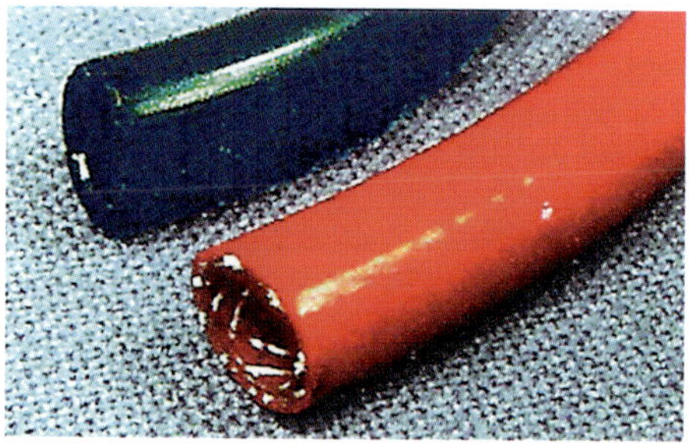

4-3-1. You'll need quite a number of fittings and all are available from a company with memorable name of CAK Tanks Ltd (it actually stood originally for Caravan Accessories, Kenilworth...). You'll need blue or black non-toxic water hose for the cold water supply and red for the hot water, if fitted.

4-3-2. Most flexible hose is fitted with hose clips and those sold by CAK are made from stainless steel – a much better idea.

- Leave room for a water filter between pump and tap if you want to fit one.
- You will need to fit a non-return valve when there is none integral to the pump – see the pump manufacturer's instructions.

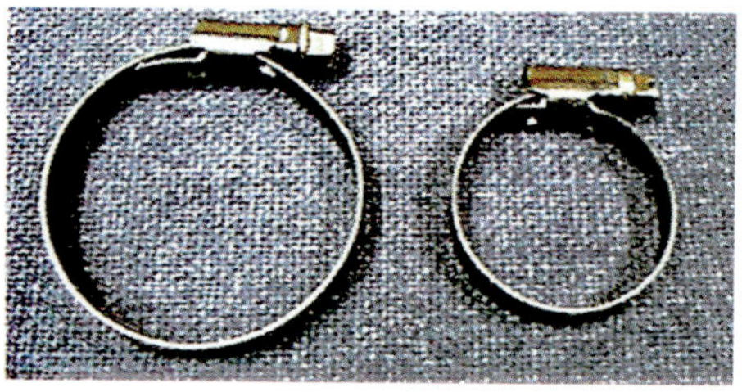

4-3-3. A superior alternative is the self-ratcheting push-shut type of hose.

4-3-4. A collection of 'P'-clips to suit the size of hose(s) you use will be essential.

4-3-5. Jonathan Frost, MD of CAK, advised me on what water-system fittings he recommended. CAK was established by Jonathan's late father when Jonathan was a small child, so he's well versed by now!

4-3-6. Jonathan recommended the Shurflo, American-made 'RV' pump for its high quality and low noise levels.

General information

The Shurflo RV pump operates when water pressure within outlet plumbing drops below a predetermined pressure. A drop in pressure occurs when a tap is opened. Taps with integral switches are not used with the Surflo pump.

Included in the Shurflo pump package is an in-line strainer, which will prevent debris and foreign particles from entering the pump. The clear housing allows inspection at a glance. The strainer is opened by a simple twist, and the screen can be removed for cleaning.

The following guidelines from Shurflo should be followed in order to achieve optimum pump operation.

Mounting

The Shurflo RV pump can be below or at the same level as the water tank, or up to 6ft (1.8m) above.

Consider a location that allows easy access when maintenance is required. The pump should not be located in an area less than a 300mm^3 unless adequate ventilation is provided. Excessive heat may trigger the integral thermal breaker and interrupt operation. When the temperature drops the breaker will automatically reset.

The pump may be mounted in any orientation. However, if mounting the pump vertically the pump head should be in the down position so that in the unlikely event of a leak, water will not enter the motor.

The motor cradle mounting pads should be fastened to a solid surface (thick plywood) that will not amplify pump operation. The mounting pads are intended to isolate the pump from the mounting surface. Over-tightening, flattening, or use of screws other than those provided will reduce the mounting pads ability to isolate vibration/noise.

Electrical

- The pump should be on a dedicated (individual) circuit protected by the specified 'slow blow' fuse indicated on the motor label.

- A switch rated at or above 15 amps is recommended, and must interrupt current flow on the positive (+ red) lead.
- The total current draw on the circuit must not exceed 15 amps. If the pump is used in conjunction with other components, over-load current protection (fuse or circuit breaker) and wire size must be for the total amp requirement of all devices on the circuit.
- Wire size (mm^2) is based on the distance from the power source to the pump. For wire lengths up to 20ft (6m), the minimum wire size is (2.5 mm^2). Use (4 mm^2) for lengths of 20-50 ft(6-15m).
- The pump must be earthed (grounded) to a known earth point of the vehicle's bodywork. The earth wire must be the same size as the positive wire.

Installation

CAUTION: All electrical devices in the vicinity should be turned OFF to avoid the possibility of electrical shock if water is spilled.

Note: Shurflo recommends at least 300mm (1ft) of 12mm flexible high-pressure tubing to plumb both ports. Ideally, the connections at the pump's ports and strainer should **not** be to rigid plastic pipe. The pump's normal oscillation may transmit through rigid plumbing causing noise, and possibly loosening or cracking components.

The strainer and fittings are designed with a taper-seal on the thread, creating a watertight connection. Always secure tubing connections with properly sized stainless steel clamps to prevent leaks.

Never use Teflon tape or sealing compounds on threads. Sealer may enter the pump causing a failure not covered under warranty.

Fitting

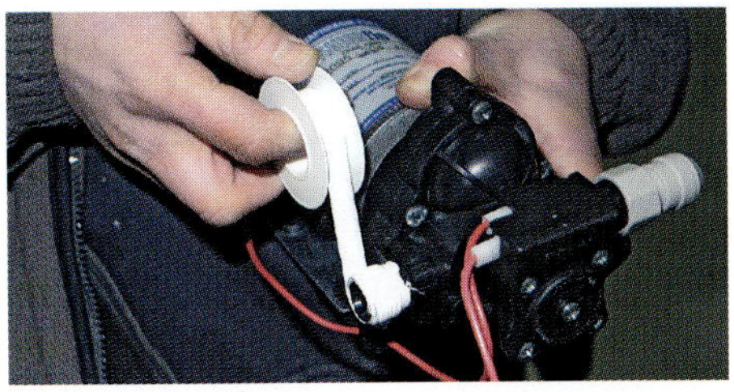

4-3-7. In spite of Shurflo's recommendation that no PTFE tape or sealer is used on the connections in case they get into the body of the pump, I agreed with Jonathan that we would stretch PTFE tape onto the threaded unions of my pump. It goes on clockwise – the same way as the thread – and Jonathan took GREAT care not to have any tape go over the opening or be allowed to pass into the body of the pump.

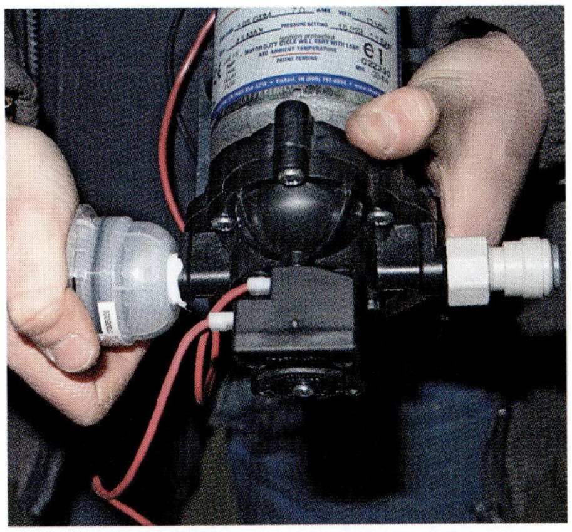

4-3-8. Jonathan hand-tightened the strainer to the inlet port until snug, (max. torque 3Nm).

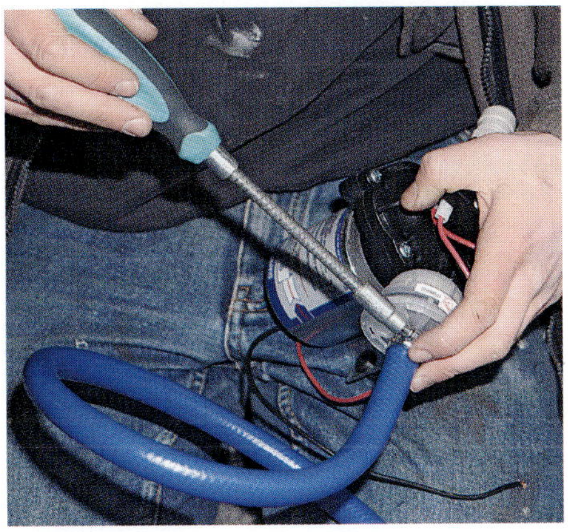

4-3-9. Using CAK's stainless steel clips, the inlet and outlet hoses were connected to the pump before fitting to the vehicle.

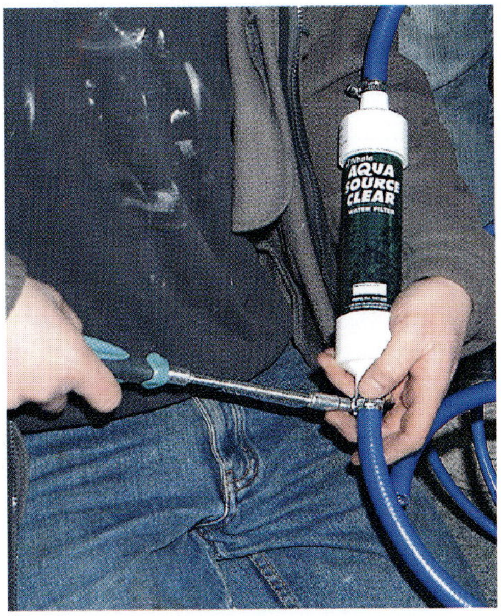

4-3-10. CAK also supplied a disposable Aqua-Source water filter cartridge which was also connected to the hoses by Leisuredrive before fitting it to the vehicle.

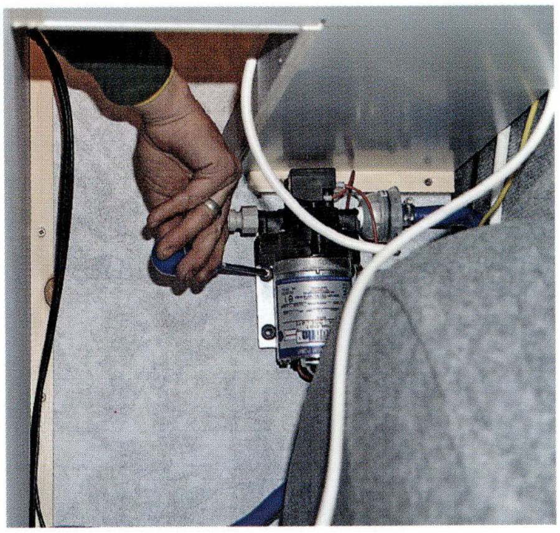

4-3-11. Leisuredrive positioned the pump in its mounting location, fitting it to a solid surface with the screws provided. Note: Over-tightening, flattening the rubber mounts, or (possibly) use of screws other than those provided will reduce the mounting pad's ability to isolate vibration/noise.

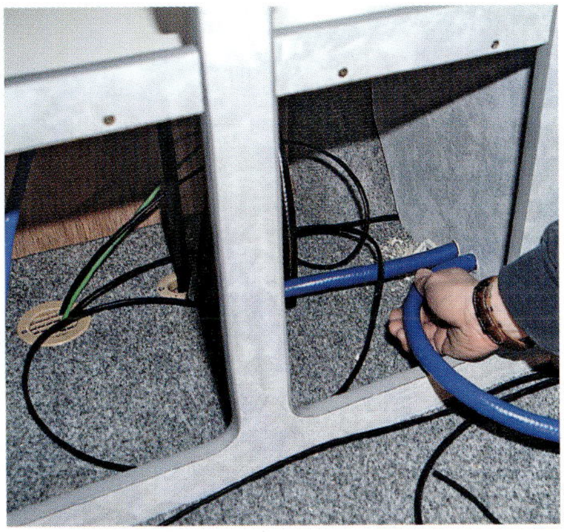

4-3-12. On this, the earlier installation, before push-fit hoses were used, the hoses were routed through holes drilled in the cupboard. Do remember, when positioning hoses, that there may be other appliances or gas cylinders to be fitted later.

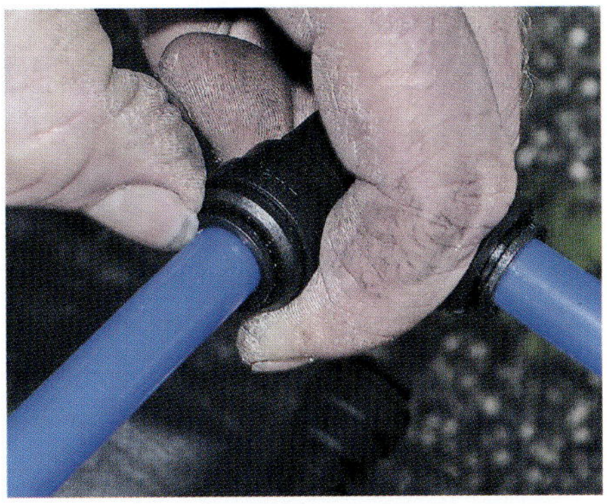

4-3-13. This is an installation with hot water and shows the hoses being connected to the taps. Note that these taps have integral switches and are used for operating the more common type of Whale pump shown in the following illustrations.

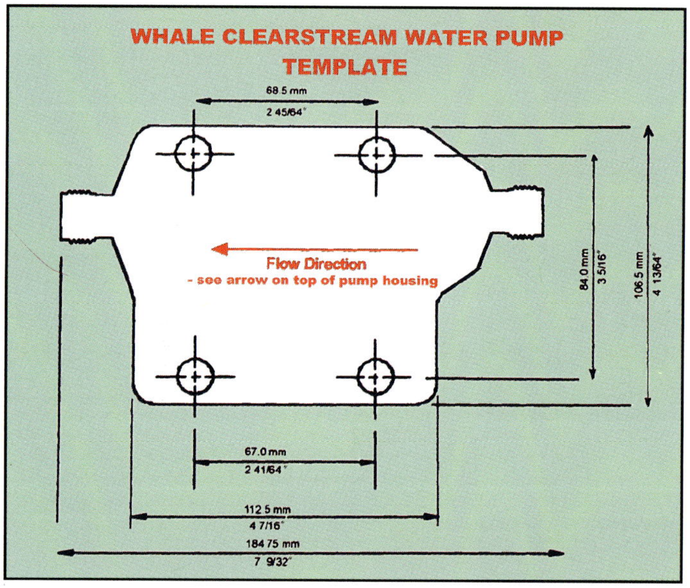

4-3-14. Included with this Whale pump is a template to enable you to drill the mounting holes in the correct positions. If you draw lines linking together the centres of the holes, it will be easy to measure the positions of the lines to make sure that they are parallel with the edges of the cupboard. The pump will look odd if it's at an angle. The orientation of the Whale pump should be as shown here.

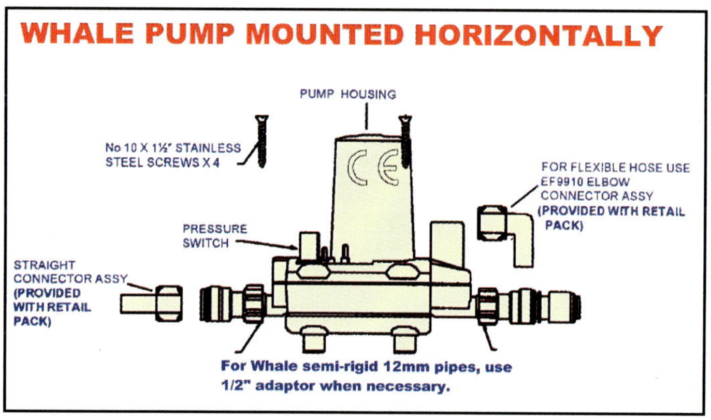

4-3-15. These are the components of the Whale Clearstream 700 kit and show the alternative pipe fittings for use with different locations and different types of pipe.

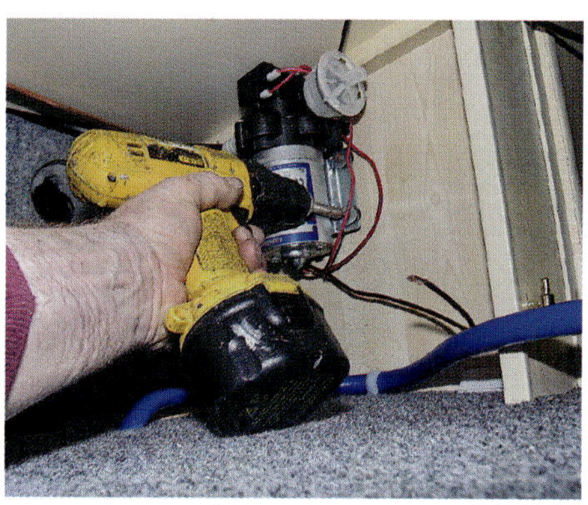

4-3-16. Before it can be fitted into the vehicle, the correct pipe adaptors need to be fitted to the pump.

4-3-17. The approximate positions of the pipe runs have already been established, and the location of the Whale pump is now being sorted out. It has to be far enough away from shelves and other fittings so that the pipes can be fitted to it, but it is best towards the top of the cupboard area so that heavy objects placed on the floor of the cupboard won't knock against it.

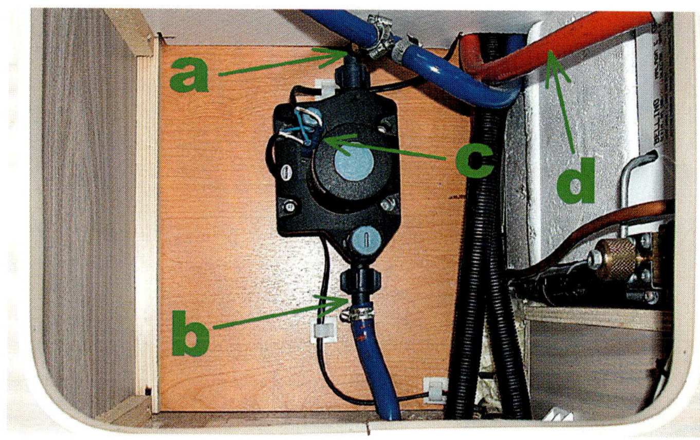

4-3-18. Note that in this instance, with a hot-and-cold connection, the outlet to the Whale pump (A) has to go off in two directions – one to the cold tap and one to the hot water heater. The inlet (B) comes from the storage tank. The feed to the hot tap (D) comes from the hot water heater, when fitted. The wiring (C) giving a power feed and a switch operated from the taps is connected in accordance with the wiring instructions that come with the pump.

4-3-19. When all the connections to a Shurflo pump have been made, Shurflo recommend that you:

- *Determine if the electrical circuit is properly fused and adequate for a 15 amp load. (Check manufacturer's instructions for different makes and models of pump.)*
- *Connect the positive (+ red) and negative (- black) wires to the pump. The connection should be water resistant and made in an area that is not subject to moisture.*
- *Fill the tank with enough water to perform a check of the system (or open shut-off valve).*
- *With all taps open, run the pump, allowing the air to purge from the plumbing. (If a water heater is fitted, it will have to fill before the pump will shut-off.)*
- *Close all taps and check the plumbing and pump for leaks.*

SEMI-RIGID PUSH-FIT PLASTIC PIPEWORK

In place of the flexible food-quality plastic hose used here, you may wish to consider using the more rigid, though still flexible, push-fit pipework. Much will depend on the layout you have chosen and the amount of pipework needed.

Advantages of semi-rigid push-fit plastic plumbing:

- The ends to be joined need to be clean and moderately square, but that's all.
- Push-fit joints can be dismantled and reassembled at will. If you cut a length of pipe too short to reach between two couplings, just dismantle the coupling and cut a longer piece of pipe.
- The pipe is less likely to kink if something is pushed against it inside a cupboard.
- You don't need access for a screwdriver or spanner when tightening joints; they just push together.
- Plastic pipe is flexible, though different pipe brands have different levels of flexibility.

Disadvantages of push-fit plastic plumbing:

- Not as flexible as fully flexible hose and will need a special collar to hold it in place when bent into a (slow) 90° bend.

MAKING A CONNECTION WITH JOHN GUEST PUSH-FIT PLASTIC PIPE FITTINGS

Step 1. Prepare the connection

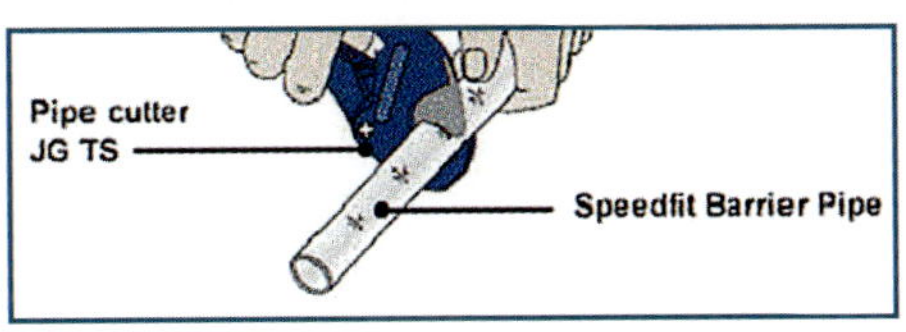

4-3-20. • We recommend the use of one of the special pipe cutters, such as the one shown here from John Guest.
• Cut the pipe square ensuring it is free of score marks.
• When using Speedfit BPEX barrier pipe, cut along an insertion mark.
• For soft or thin-walled plastic pipe we recommend the use of a tube insert or pipe insert.

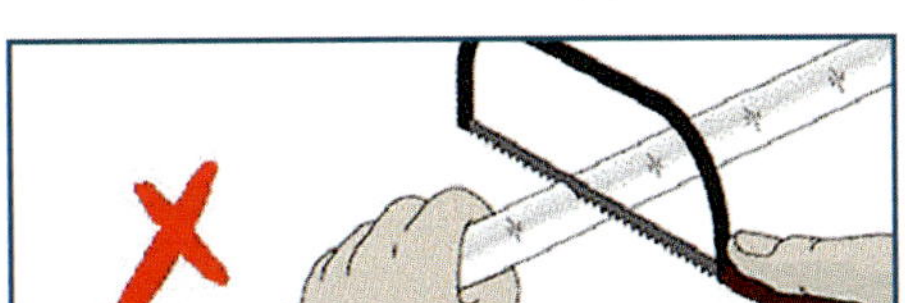

4-3-21. IMPORTANT NOTES:
• Do NOT use a hacksaw.
• To avoid damage to the 'O' Ring, make sure burrs and sharp edges are removed.
• With the fitting clean and undamaged and the pipe cut square, you are now ready to make the connection.

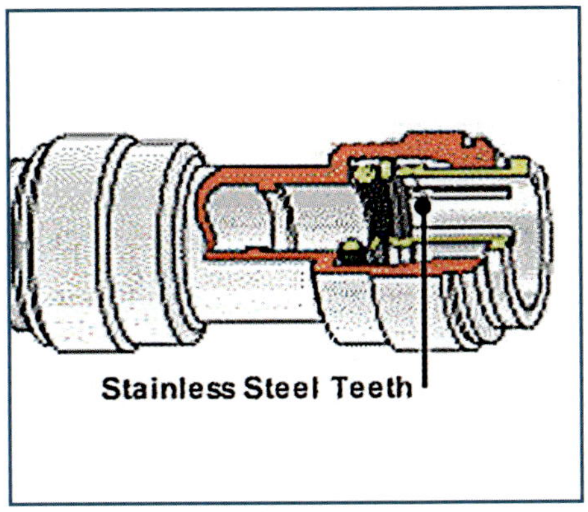

SAFETY FIRST!

4-3-22. Do not insert fingers into the fitting as the stainless steel teeth may cause injury.

Step 2. Assemble the connection using standard Speedfit plumbing fittings.

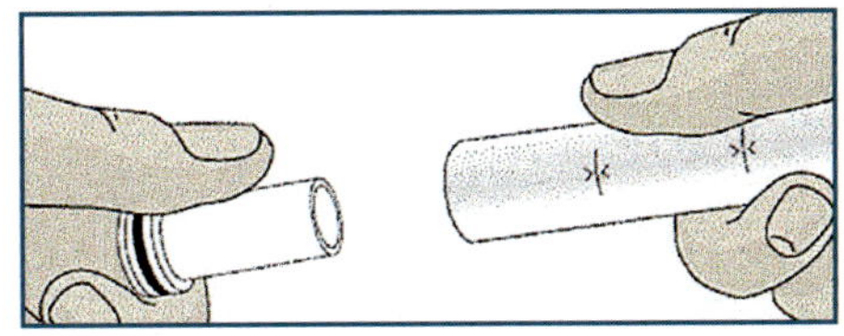

4-3-23. Use a John Guest pipe insert when connecting to Speedfit pipe. Enhanced sealing security is available by using the new 'STS' Superseal Pipe Insert. John Guest pipe inserts should only be used with Speedfit pipe. Different types of pipe may require different inserts – buy them all at the same time.

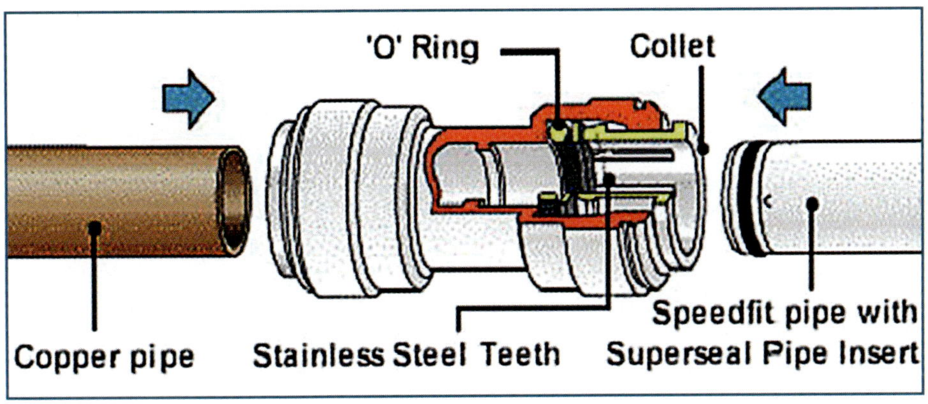

4-3-24. Push the pipe into the fitting, up to the pipe stop. When using correctly cut Speedfit pipe, the insertion mark on the pipe should be level with the collet head.

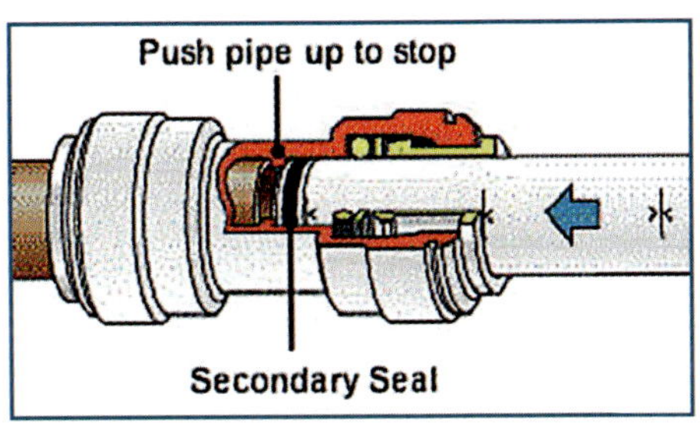

4-3-25. An 'O' ring on the head of the Superseal Pipe insert and the shape of the stem provide a secondary seal against the bore of the fitting. A combination of this and the main 'O' ring ensure a good connection.

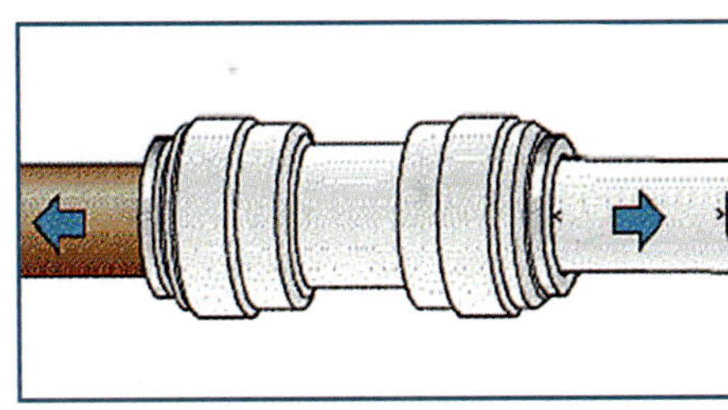

4-3-26. Pull on the pipe to check it is secure. It is good practice to test the system after completing the installation and before going away in the vehicle. The stem of the insert gives greater rigidity to the length of pipe within the fitting, reducing the chance of leaks if a side load is applied.

DISCONNECTING STANDARD SPEEDFIT PLUMBING FITTINGS

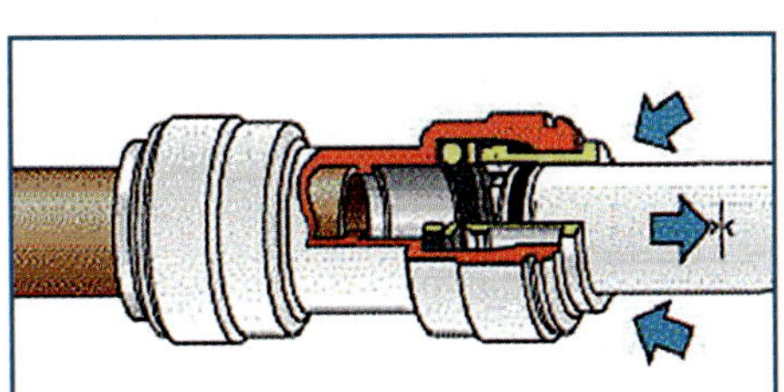

4-3-27. The fitting can be removed by using fingers or with the help of the collet release tool. Push the collet squarely against the face of the fitting. With the collet held in this position, the pipe can be removed. The fitting can then be re-used without the need for replacement parts.

SECTION 4. WASTE WATER

4-4-1. This is the CAK Tank's waste water tank showing the welded, one-piece strap and its hangers (arrowed).

4-4-2. As with the freshwater tanks, the waste water tank was developed on a T5 prototype vehicle and this shows the mock-up of the tank mounting. Note that the fixing straps have since been changed.

4-4-3. These are the locating points for the rear end of the waste tank. Note that the strap hangers have been fitted to holes in the body by easing up the bottoms of the plugs in those holes. They can be sealed later with suitable sealant, if required.

4-4-4. At Leisuredrive, Roy demonstrates the way in which they can fit this tank when required, just ahead of the spare wheel.

4-4-5. 'Supaflex' drain hose from CAK should be the type used. It has a smooth internal bore to prevent food particles from sticking in the pipe and causing smells. This is actually water filler pipe but the principle remains the same.

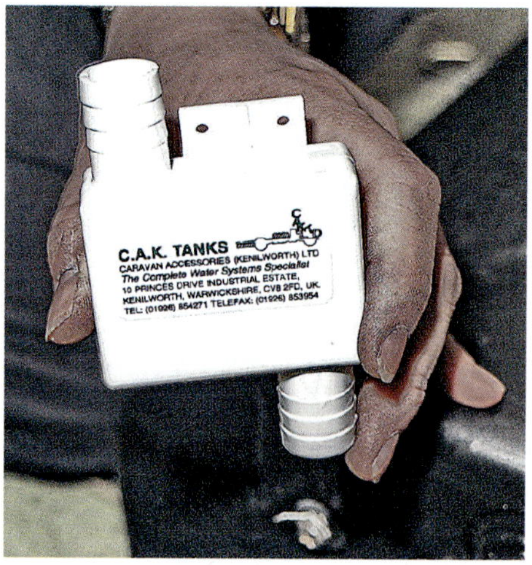

4-4-6. CAK Tanks have produced this nifty little U-bend trap which fits in the waste water line and prevents smells from coming back up from the tank, just like the traps in the sinks at home.

4-4-7. The Supaflex waste pipe has been fitted to the waste outlet on the sink …

4-4-8. … and fed through the cupboard, through a hole in the floor (arrowed) and takes its place with the panoply of hoses and wiring found in this location.

SECTION 5. ELECTRICS

When a new house is built, you don't put in the cooker, the light fittings and the wall sockets before the wiring. You put the cables in first, having established where all the electrical components are going to go, and leaving enough spare wire to connect them later. In this instance, the analogy with a motor caravan is a good one because you'll first need to establish where everything is going to go, run the wiring in place while the structure of the motor caravan is being built, and leave enough spare wire at each end to make the connections when the electrical components are fitted.

Do bear in mind the point made at the start of this chapter with regard to electrical safety, and the need for having your electrician make all the electrical connections and check the safe location and security of electrical cables and components when they are in place.

For that reason, you may wish to run cables inside cupboards where they can still be seen by the electrician who will be checking the job over. In the instance shown here, the qualified personnel at Leisuredrive ran cables behind wall and roof coverings before they were fitted into place. If you decide to run cables inside cupboards, you may wish to purchase plastic channelling from a DIY store. This comes with a clip-on cover so it can easily be accessed for checking or for adding more cables later.

SAFETY FIRST!

- Before being used, have the installation checked and tested by a qualified electrician. Pay to have a dated and signed certificate confirming that your motor caravan complies with the relevant IEE Regulations.
- Contact the National Inspection Council for Electrical Installation (www.niceic.org.uk) or the Electrical Contractors Association (www.eca.co.uk) for details of approved contractors in your area.
- Each electrical component will need to have the correct grade of cable.
- **Do not** under any circumstances use mains electricity cable for 12 volt wiring. Its characteristics are completely different and it can readily overheat and catch fire on a 12 volt system.
- **Do not** under any circumstances use household mains electricity cable for the 230 volt wiring in the motor caravan. Use the correct rating of multi-strand cable. Single-strand screwed-tight cable connections are prone to shaking loose and the cable itself could conceivably work-harden and break, both because of the movement of the vehicle on the road.
- Find out from the instruction book with each appliance the rating of cable that will be needed. If this isn't clear, contact the manufacturer or have the electrician who will be carrying out the check advise on the grade of cable to be used.
- Suitable 12 volt cable is manufactured by companies such as Ring (see the suppliers list in the back of this book), and can be purchased from most automotive DIY stores. Suitable 230 volt multi-strand cable can be purchased from DIY 'sheds' or electrical retailers.

There are three main elements to a motor caravan's electrical systems:

- The 230 volt mains system is supplied via an approved hook-up cable, no more than 25m long.
- The 12 volt system supplied from the leisure battery.
- The 12 volt supply connected to the vehicle's battery.

All three are connected to their fellows under various circumstances: For example: The 230 volt mains system should be able to charge both leisure and vehicle batteries and, when connected on site, will keep the leisure battery charged while 12 volt appliances are in use. When the engine is running (and only then), the vehicle's battery should charge the leisure battery and, if required, power the fridge.

INTRODUCTION TO MOTORCARAVAN ELECTRICS

- A mains consumer unit is a vitally important part of your electrical system.
- It protects your vehicle and occupants from electric shock hazards when connected to the site hook-up.
- The CBE DS120-S has an RCD main switch and a (strongly recommended) double-pole 13 amp MCB. Double-pole circuit breakers are essential in mainland Europe where positive and negative feeds are frequently interchangeable because double pole switches are the norm there.

In the following, the part numbers in brackets and italics are from CAK Tanks' catalogue for ease of reference. Jonathan says, "The electrical system is a very important part of your conversion. It is important to ensure it is installed in a correct manner by a competent person and inspected for safety regularly."

"To use mains 220-240 volt electric site hook-up in your vehicle you will need to obtain and install the following items:

- To connect between the site's electric post and your vehicle you will need a 10 metre mains input lead with blue CE connectors (ML10).
- If you are in Europe some sites will have a different plug so you will need the Continental adaptor (MCLE).
- To plug your vehicle into a domestic 3-pin socket at home, top up the battery or chill down the fridge, you will need a UK adapter (MCLUK).

"To connect the mains input lead into your vehicle you need a flush-fit external mains inlet socket with lid (MIFFB, colour black; MIFFW, colour white). This is fitted through the sidewall of your vehicle in a suitable place. You connect this with 3-core cable to the Mains Consumer Unit (DS120-S) which provides the safely of the RCD (Residual Current Device), ELCB (Earth

4-5-1. This Introduction is by Jonathan Frost of CAK Tanks who selected his recommended range of electrical components for our project vehicle. This is the CBE DS120-S mains Consumer Unit from CAK Tanks.

Leakage Circuit Breaker), 15 amp main switch and double-pole, 13 amp MCB (Miniature Circuit Breakers) to protect the mains electrical circuits in your vehicle.

"The charger-and-voltage transformer unit provides the link between the mains and the 12 volt system. It is fed from the 230 volt Consumer Unit, which is normally fitted in the base of the wardrobe or bedbox and which must be earthed to the chassis to provide the correct protection.

"The 12 volt system is the heart of the vehicle's conversion. The connections for the vehicles existing battery, the one it uses for starting the engine, will be referred to as 'AUTO' or 'B1' on the control panel. It is best not to connect any 'caravan' items to this battery because if you drain it, you will be unable to start your engine.

"You must install a second battery which will be referred to as 'LEISURE' or 'B2' on the control panel. This can be one battery of between 75 and 110 A/hr or for bigger electrical needs, a pair of 110 A/hr batteries in parallel, which means connecting positive terminal to positive terminal and negative to negative. By joining them this way you double up the batteries' capacity (such as 2 x 110 A/hr) but retain the voltage at 12 volts. (If you join them in series positive to negative you will get 24 volts!).

"You will "split charge" your leisure battery by connecting a relay (R228) between B1-and-B2 and the relay signal wire to the D+ terminal on your alternator. When the engine is started and the alternator is charging, both the vehicle battery (B1) and the leisure (B2) battery will be charged up via the relay but the vehicle battery will not be drawn down for appliances in the caravan-section of the vehicle.

"The main 12 volt system needs to be monitored and controlled from a control panel and distribution system (C860, PC100 or PC200). The system has control switches and built-in circuit protection fuses to protect key equipment. All items and their cable runs **must be fused** to the correct rating. Additional fused circuits can be provided using the blade fuse holders (BFH4, 6, 8 and R420/421). This system also has a charger to charge the leisure battery from the mains 240v connection – see above.

"To ensure the auto battery remains topped up when stationary for long periods or when using cab fitted equipment such as radio, DVD player or Sat. Nav. unit, use a CAK Battery Charge Manager (BCM12) which trickle charges excess charge from the leisure battery back to the auto battery when the leisure battery is being charged. For 'wild camping' the most effective way maintain charge in your batteries is by fitting a solar panel on your roof."

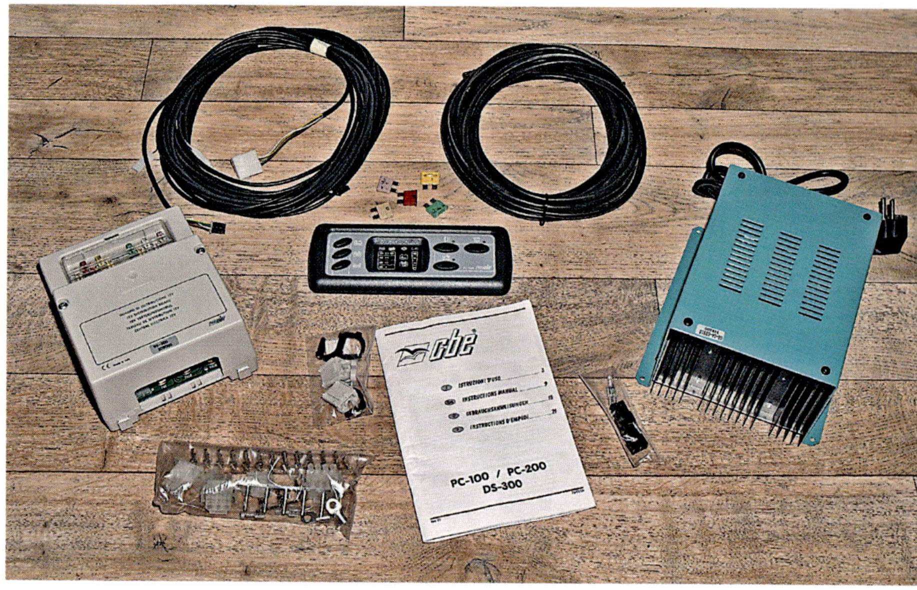

4-5-2. This is the kit of parts supplied by CAK Tanks. On the left is the Consumer Unit seen earlier; in the centre, the Control System and on the right a CBE battery charger, especially designed for lead-acid and gel-type leisure batteries. The beauty of the CBE system is that it is microprocessor based and electrically integrated – the supplied cables with ready-fitted plugs on their ends providing simple connections between the units and saving a lot of an electrician's time and expertise. Better still, the system is integrated with the water level gauge which is also simply plugged in.

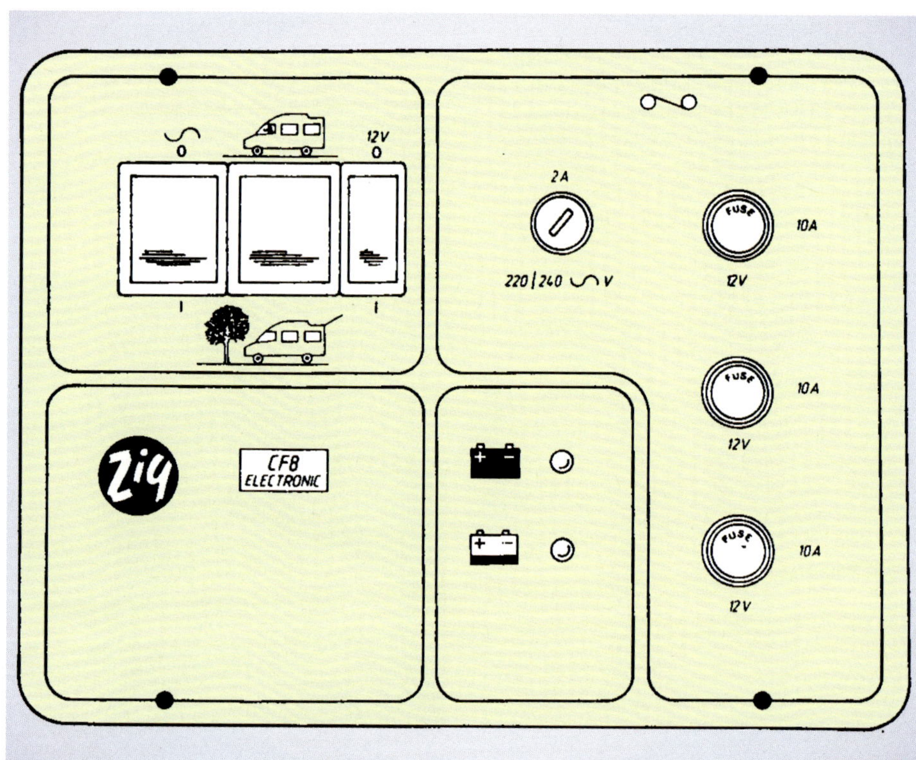

4-5-3. This is one of the units made by Zig Electronics Ltd. which manufactures a well established range of electricity units for all types of caravan and motor caravan. This is the CF8 battery charging and distribution system. The charger is built-in and can certainly become rather warm – though not dangerously so, we are assured – at the back of the cupboard where it is fitted. Zig recommends that the inside of the cupboard to which the unit is fitted must allow a free space of at least 25mm all the way around the unit, and that includes a space from the back of the unit to any cover that may be fitted.

4-5-4. At Leisuredrive, the CBE PC100 Control Unit's location on the wardrobe panel is determined before the wardrobe is fitted to the vehicle's interior.

Features of the PC100 are:

- Microprocessor control panel with LED display showing, on illuminated scales:
- Voltage levels for batteries 1 and 2.
- Fresh and waste water tank levels.
- Switches for pump, lighting and fridge.
- Battery recharge control.
- Low voltage remote control of functions at panel which are switched at the distribution board. This reduces the spaghetti of wiring normally going all the way to the control panel. Now only the control wire runs from the panel to the distribution box.

In addition, the more expensive PC200 unit features:

- Battery voltages in volts; power consumption if activated.
- Tank levels as a percentage.
- Internal and external temperatures.

YOU CAN DO THE FOLLOWING JOBS YOURSELF:

4-5-5. It's always best to make a template before cutting into the real thing. This has the benefit of your being able to test the unit to make sure it fits the template and then, if it does, to use the template as a guide for marking out the position of the hole.

4-5-6. A 3mm drill was then used to make a hole in each of the four corners and a slot within the shape of the hole so that a jigsaw could be started there.

4-5-7. On the later-style of layout, the consumer unit is moved to the side of the wardrobe, away from the cooker. This is the CAK 12v auxiliary supply (cigarette lighter) socket and water heater switch, matching the PC100's control unit, being fitted to the wardrobe.

4-5-8. Here, a hole is being drilled in the 'old-style' wardrobe. A cigarette lighter socket purchased from an auto-accessory store would later be installed to provide a source of power at the rear of the camper for a mobile phone, laptop or other accessories.

4-5-9. With masking tape on the bottom of the jigsaw foot to prevent it from damaging the laminate, the hole was cut out …

4-5-10. … and the control unit checked for fit.

4-5-11. A 13 amp socket was due to be fitted in the same area and so another hole was marked out and cut …

4-5-12. … allowing the backplate to be fitted to the unit.

4-5-13. When the wiring plug was test-fitted (and bear in mind that none of the electrical connections have been made at this stage so there is no electricity 'flowing' around the system), it was found that the unit fouled on the edges of the hole and so a slightly larger cutout (arrowed) had to be made.

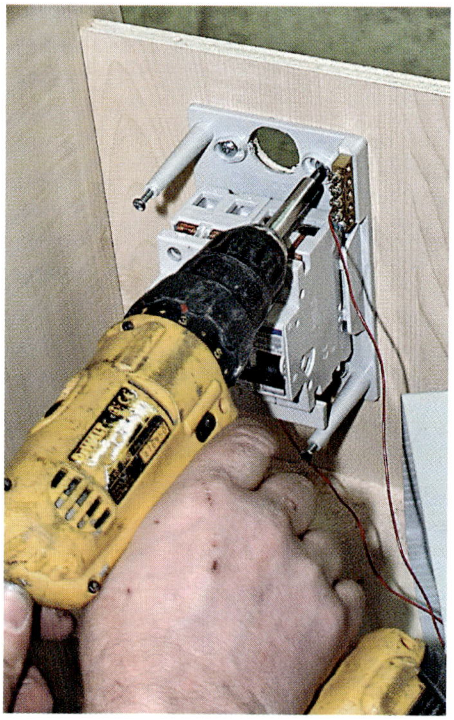

4-5-14. If you were doing the installation yourself, the units themselves could be installed as shown here, before the units are installed, but the wiring connections would have to be made by a qualified, certified electrician.

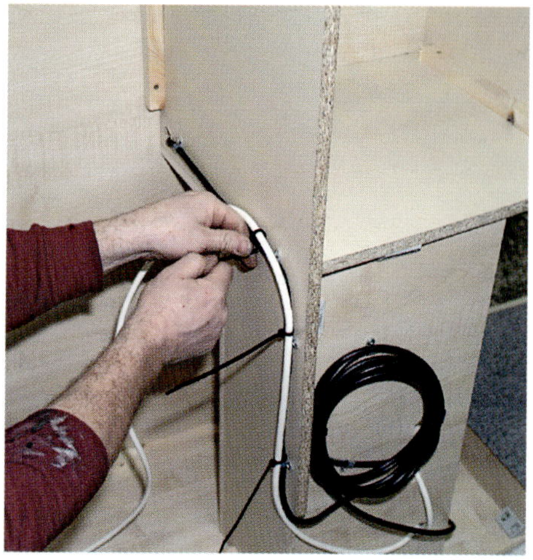

4-5-15. If you are able to follow the basic principles of a wiring diagram, you may be able to run the wiring into place, both inside the units and as you build up the interior of the motor caravan.

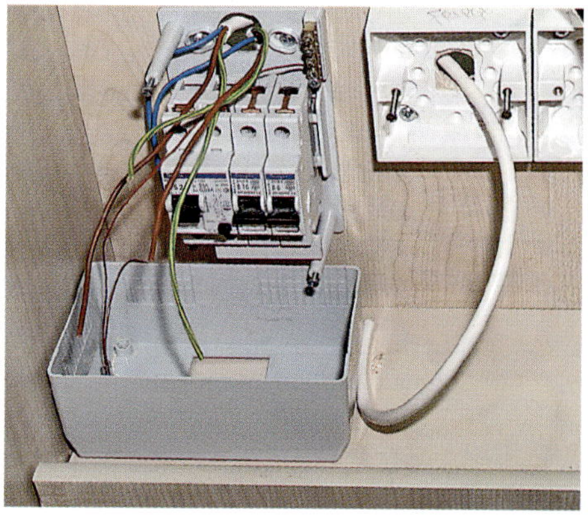

4-5-16. The idea will be to leave ends of cables ready for your electrician to connect up the relevant components.

4-5-17. The backing plate for the 12 volt distribution unit can certainly be fitted to the vehicle.

4-5-18. In addition, the mains consumer unit can be screwed into position. All of these units are being fitted to the wardrobe while it is still out of the vehicle and while access is so much easier.

4-5-19. Dramatically different but also coming under the category of work that can be carried out by someone who is not an electrician, is the cutout in the side wall for the mains input socket.

4-5-20. It's always best to cut slightly undersize and then to trim the hole later so that the unit fits snugly. Note that by this time, the transfers have been added to the side of the vehicle. This is the time to do them: after cutting the holes but before fitting any of the units.

4-5-21. The bare edges of the steel had been painted with primer but I added a good squirt of Würth Cavity Protection Spray to protect the edges and the inside of the steel.

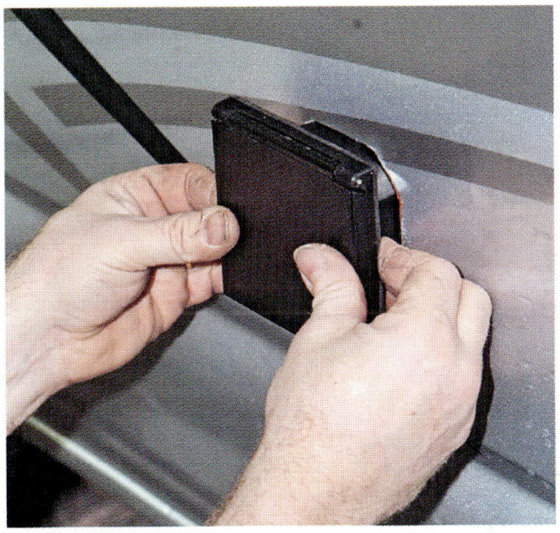

4-5-22. Although it was obvious that the unit would have to be removed again for the auto electrician to do his job, it was fitted once more …

4-5-23. … and, after drilling pilot holes, screwed to the body with the stainless steel screws provided with the CAK kit. None of the wires have been fitted at this stage, nor has any sealer been used around the edge of the unit.

4-5-24. The heavy-duty voltage transformer and battery charger was found a home in the base of the wardrobe. In some ways, this unit might be better placed towards the top of a side wall inside one of the cupboards or bed boxes because then the flow of cooling air around it would be less likely to be impeded. The four holes in the flanges on the base of the unit make it easy to screw into position.

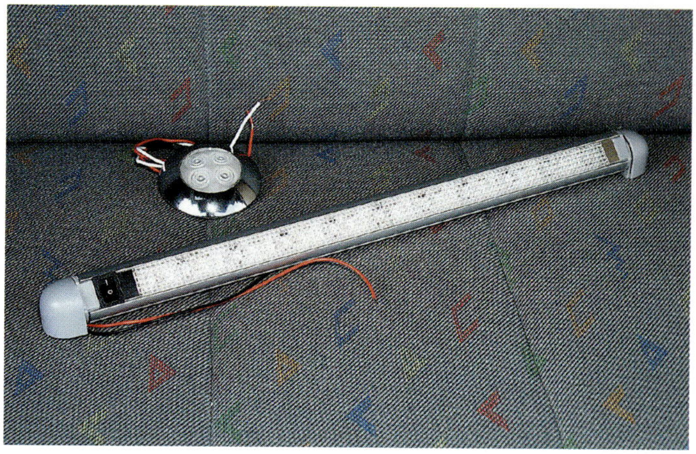

4-5-25. An electrician should connect wiring to the lights though you can fit them yourself. These are some of the LED units available from Mobile Centre. They require only ⅕th the power, so your leisure battery will last far longer, and provide a brighter, whiter light. LED units can be expected, it's said, to outlast the vehicle to which they're fitted and are water- and vibration-proof.

YOU SHOULD NOT DO THE FOLLOWING ELECTRICAL JOBS YOURSELF UNLESS YOU ARE A QUALIFIED ELECTRICIAN

4-5-26. Auto Tec supply and fit Mobile Centre's LED units. Julian, the man behind Auto Tec, fitted a smaller LED light in place of the door-operated unit above the sliding door. It can be angled to illuminate the area you choose.

4-5-27. Julian also fitted the larger units to run from the leisure battery in the living compartment. The swivelling head is a real boon when you're working in the kitchen area and you don't want to be dazzled.

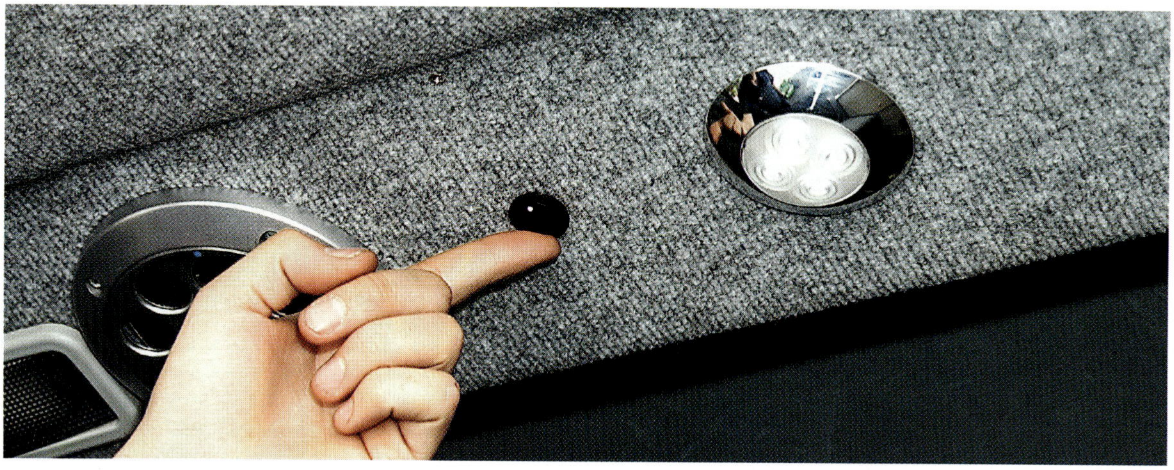

4-5-28. In the hollow section over the rear door, Auto Tec installed one of Mobile Centre's smaller, round LED units and a switch, to act as a reading light and for extra illumination into the load area.

4-5-29. These are the electrical connections at the rear of the 'cigarette lighter' power point and you can also see the exposed printed circuit board on the back of the PC100 control unit. But don't worry; both will be covered and protected later! These connections have to be made by a qualified electrician so you won't be putting the cover in place yet awhile.

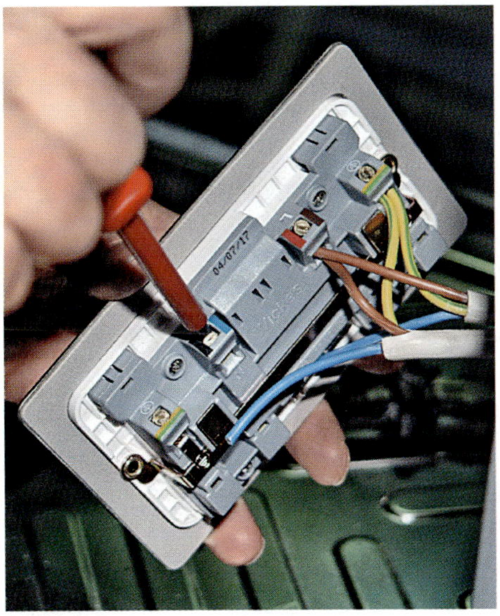

4-5-30. Your electrician will also connect up the 13 amp socket.

4-5-32. Leisuredrive bring the relevant 12 volt wiring through to the vehicle's battery under the bonnet. The cables have been neatly looped and strapped together and fixed to a proprietary eye which is bolted onto the battery clamp.

4-5-31. These are the mains connections on the back of the input socket on the side wall; another job for the auto electrician.

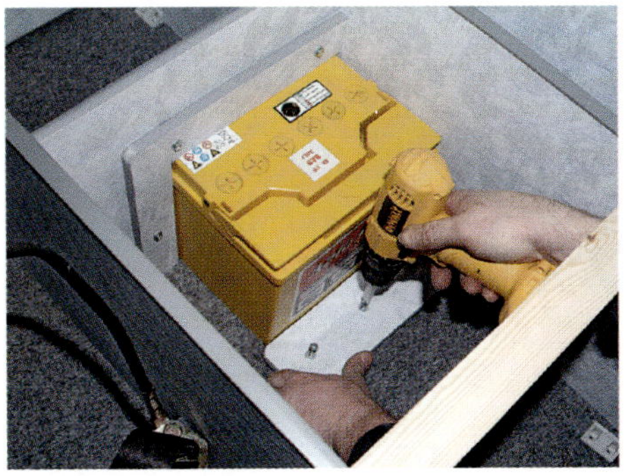

4-5-33. You could certainly make your own leisure battery retainer and though I strongly recommend that yours incorporates steel fixings that pass through the floor of the vehicle. Do bear in mind the usual warnings about drilling into the floor – see Section 8 of this chapter. Your auto electrician should make sure that all of the feed wires from the battery are fused.

4-5-34. With all of the connections safely made, Leisuredrive connected the mains power to the input socket so that it could start to carry out the necessary checks. Bear in mind that, after fitting the electrical connections to the back of this socket, your electrician will need to seal it thoroughly as he screws it back to the vehicle side wall.

4-5-35. Once he could see that the units were connected up correctly, Leisuredrive's electrician snapped the control unit into position …

4-5-36. … and clipped the fascia cover into place.

4-5-37. He then carried out the full range of tests to make sure that everything was working correctly.

4-5-38. When he was happy that all the connections were finally okay, Paul fitted the protective board to the inside of the wardrobe; the one behind which the electrical connections we saw earlier are located.

4-5-39. This is the Zig CF8 unit we referred to earlier. Beneath it is the separate water tank level gauge. These units have been faithful servants for many years but I have to say it does look a little clunky by modern standards.

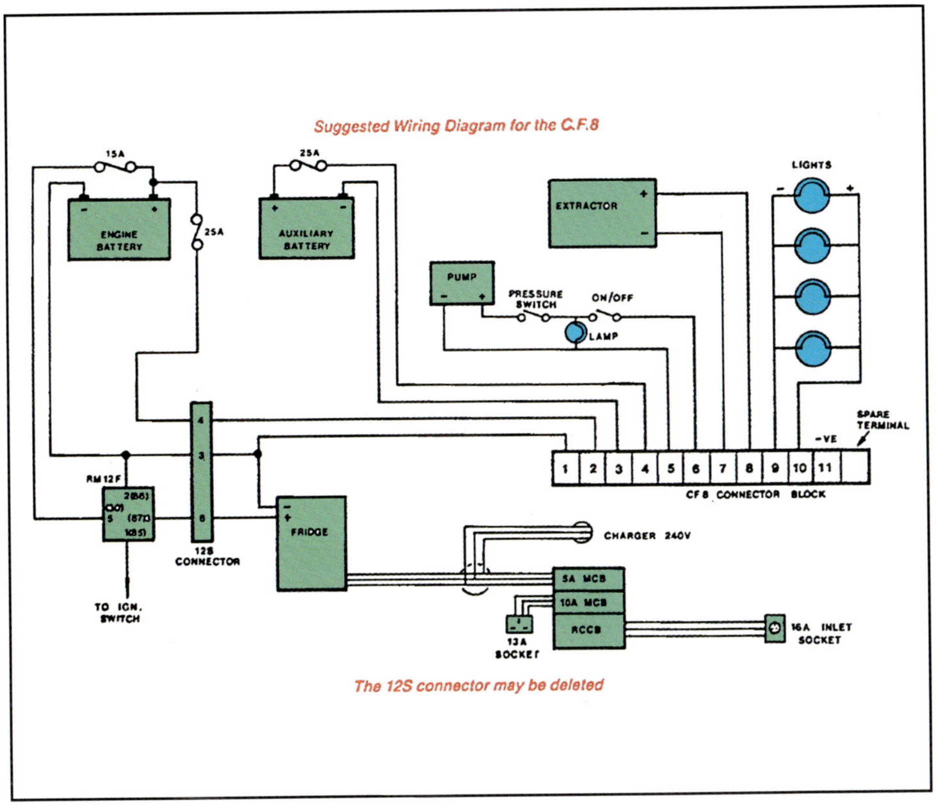

4-5-40. *In addition, there don't appear to be any integrated wiring harnesses with these units and it would take an electrician quite a lot longer to connect up compared to the CBE unit from CAK Tanks that we saw earlier.*

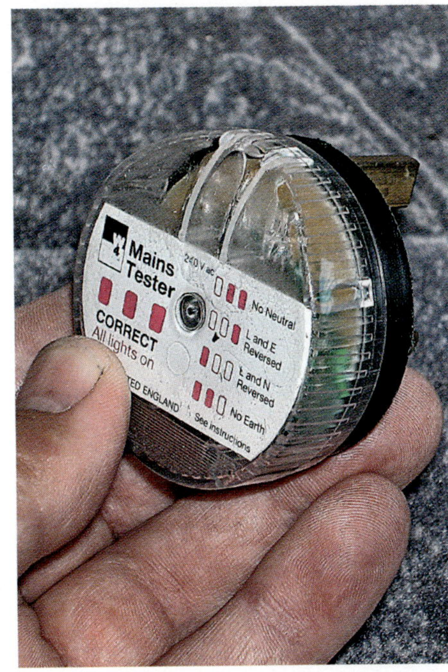

4-5-41. *This is not strictly part of the vehicle's wiring and double-pole switches may make them less essential for some purposes. However, a mains tester should still be considered essential, especially for continental touring. It checks that the earth is present and correct on 13 amp sockets and it also detects if live and earth polarities have been reversed.*

SECTION 6. FRIDGE DOOR ADAPT

The Dometic fridge comes with a door that can be hinged on either side and a front panel that can be removed for one that matches the décor of the motor caravan's interior.

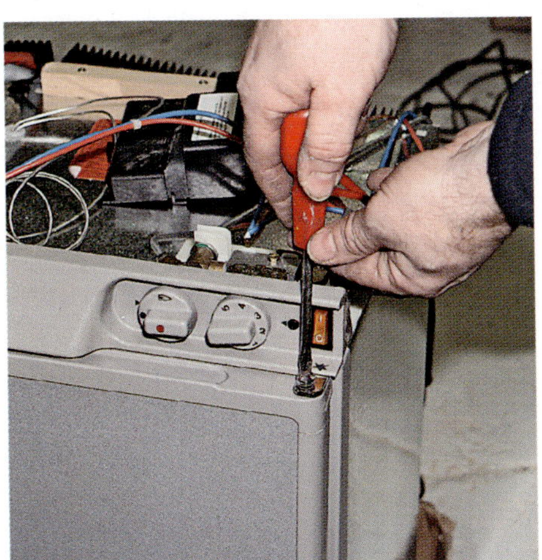

4-6-1. *Unscrew the top hinge pin using a screwdriver with a straight blade and taking care not to lose the set of washers and bushes.*

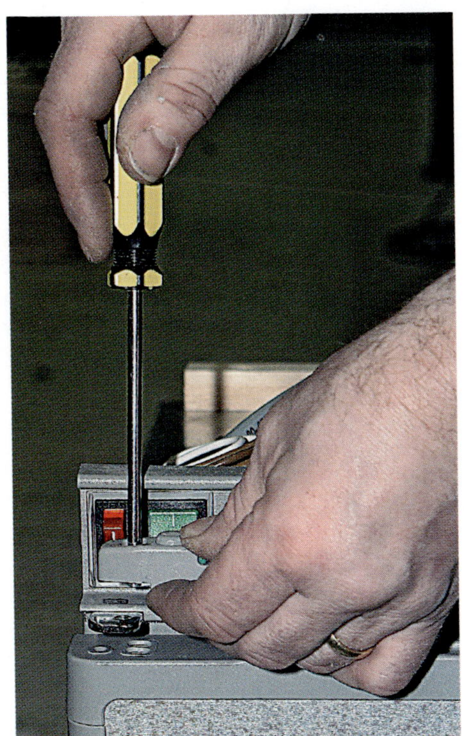

4-6-2. *From the other side, you can remove the catch.*

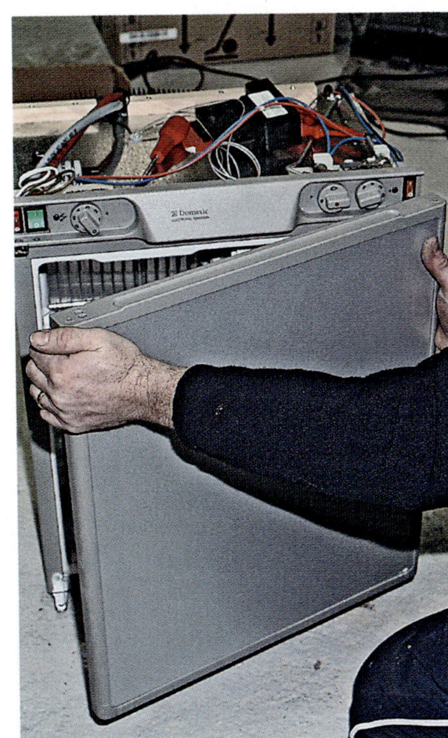

4-6-3. *The door is lifted up off the bottom hinge pin.*

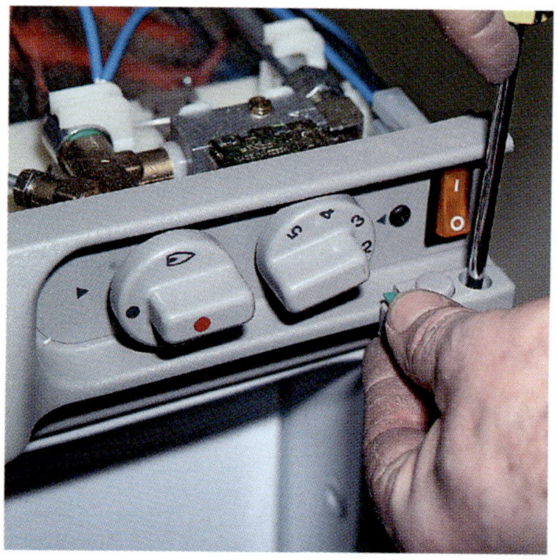

4-6-4. The door catch will be transferred over to the other side later.

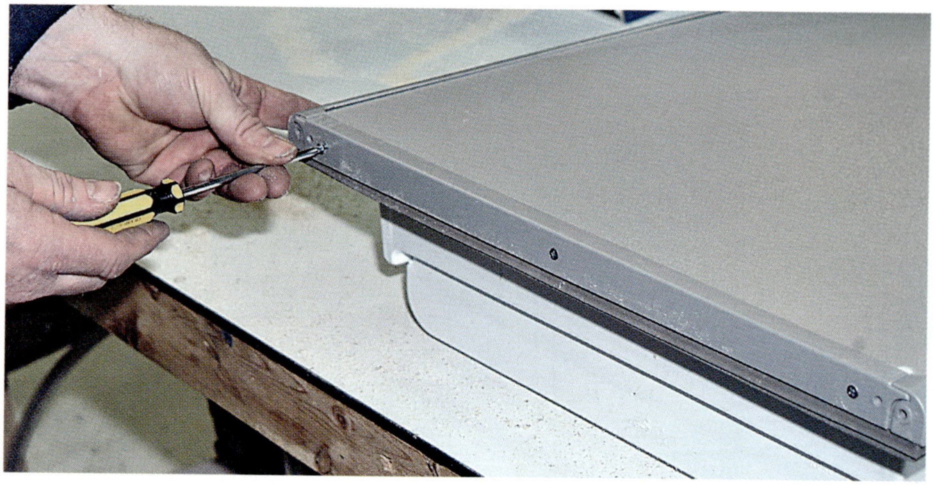

4-6-5. To remove the door trim panel, take out the three screws from the bottom of the door.

4-6-6. You can now remove the lower trim moulding.

4-6-7. Slide out the trim panel.

4-6-8. The new trim panel must have dimensions of:
Height: 532mm
Width: 453mm
Thickness: 3.8mm max

4-6-9. Fit the lower trim moulding back in place.

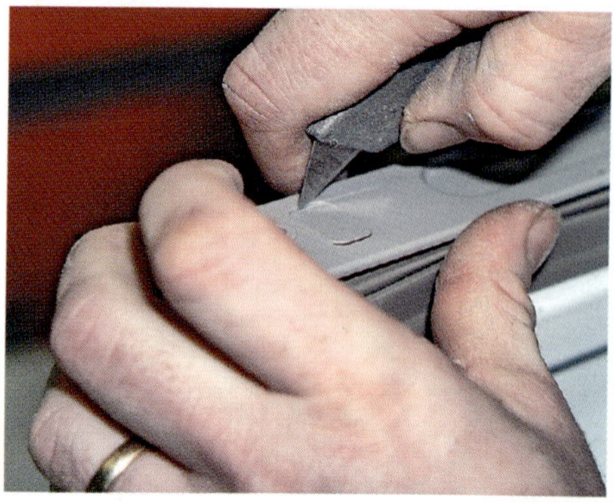

4-6-10. Lever out the trim insert. Leisuredrive's Roy used a craft knife but note that the trim insert is not cut out but is simply levered.

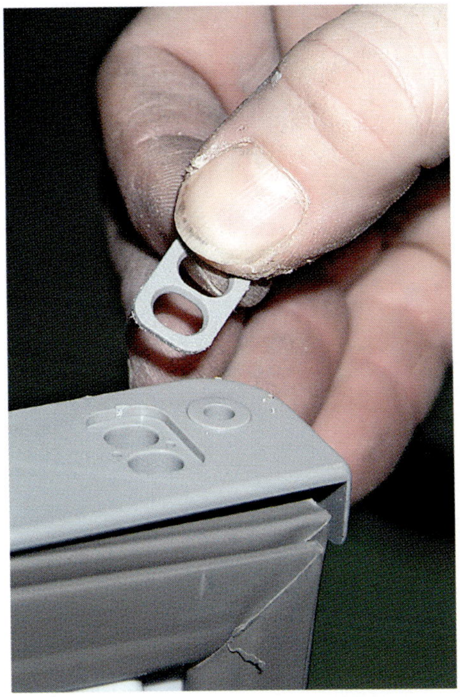

4-6-11. From the side where the catch was previously located, lever out the plastic insert with two holes for the alternative catch positions.

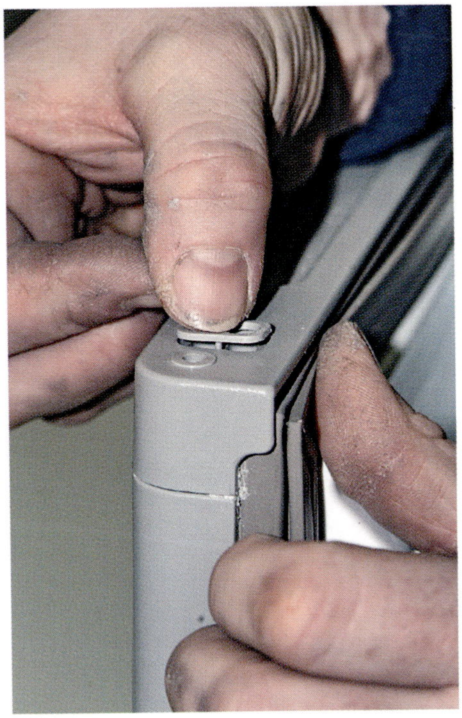

4-6-12. Swap the two inserts over, clipping each one back into position.

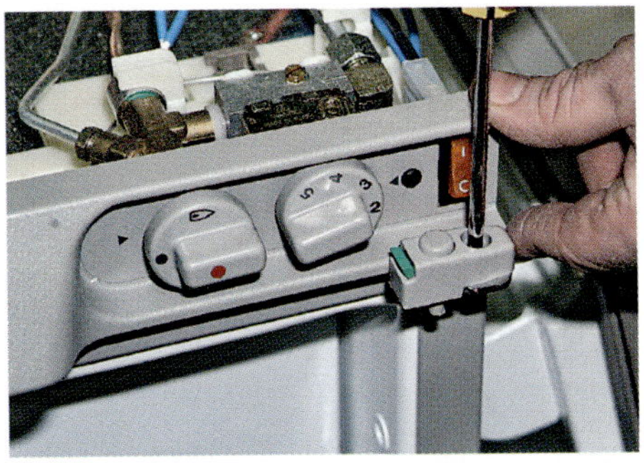

4-6-13. The catch is screwed down to the threaded hole previously used by the hinge pin.

4-6-14. You now have to unscrew the bottom hinge pin.

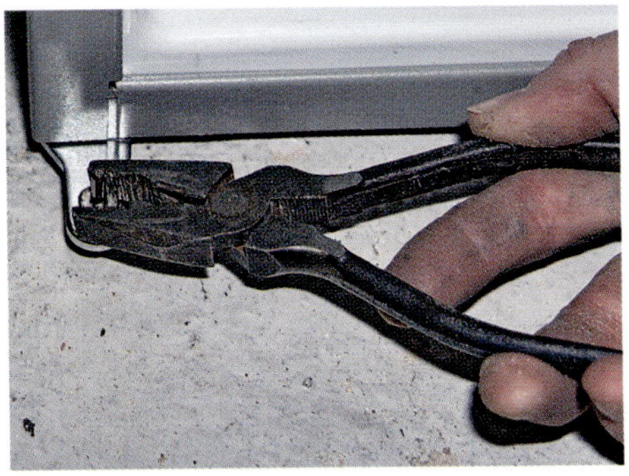

4-6-15. You will probably need a pair of pliers to free it and also to fully tighten it into its new location on the other side of the fridge.

4-6-16. Roy re-hangs the door by fitting it first to the lower hinge pin.

4-6-17. The top of the door is lined up, the washers and bushes refitted as they were before …

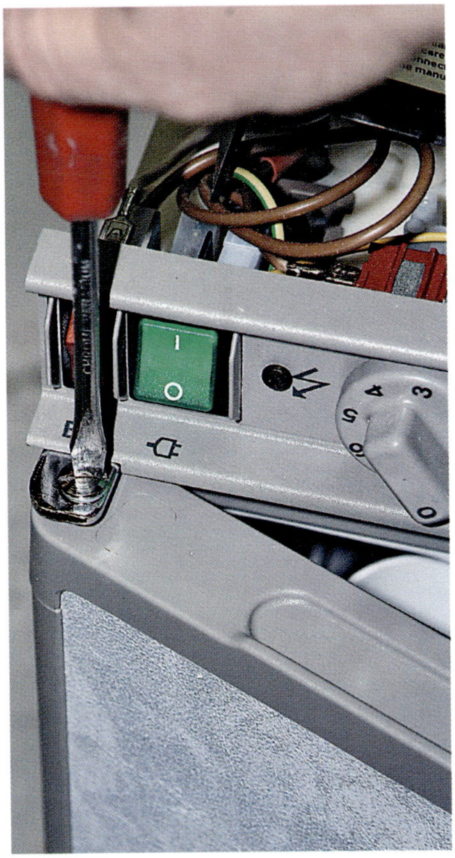

4-6-18. … and the top hinge pin is screwed back into position.

SECTION 7. FIT FRIDGE

4-7-1. Here's how the excellent Dometic fridge will look when it's fitted and finished.

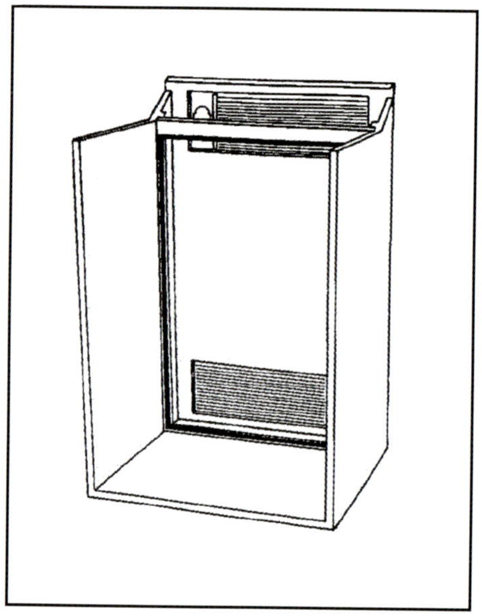

4-7-2. This is illustrative of the kind of structure into which the Dometic fridge should be fitted. The sides and the top will need to be sealed between the fridge and the interior of the motor caravan. The rear of the fridge must have open access to a pair of vents, one at the top and one at the bottom.

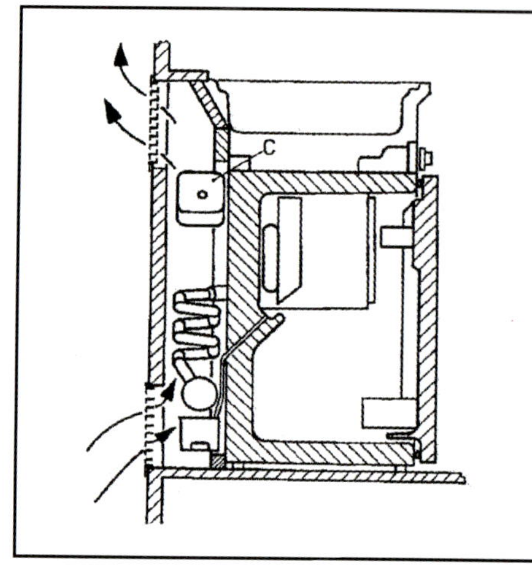

4-7-3. This is so that cool air can be drawn in through the bottom vent at the rear of the fridge and pass over the heating element on the back of the fridge, before being expelled by convection through the vent towards the top of the fridge. If the fridge is not sealed between its sides, top and base, and the inside of the motor caravan, the essential air which is used to pass over the elements on the rear of the fridge and allow it to work will create a draught inside the vehicle.

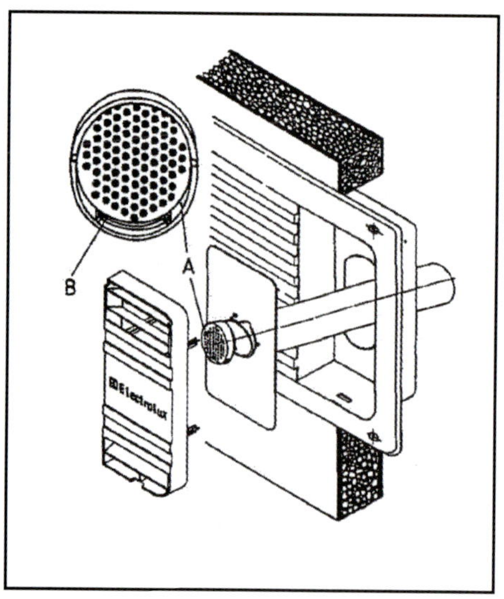

4-7-4. When the fridge is working on gas, combustion takes place and carbon monoxide, among other gases, is produced. The exhaust from the combustion process would be potentially toxic were it not for the fact that the exhaust is vented directly out of the motor caravan as shown here. This part of the installation is also something that will have to be checked by your qualified gas fitter. It will have to be disconnected in order to gain access to the rear of the fridge when he connects the gas pipes, so he will also check the connection of the exhaust when he refits the fridge to the vehicle. Preparing the vents, and the exhaust through the wall of the motor caravan, is another part of the work that you may be able to carry out yourself.

4-7-5. After placing masking tape around the spot, Neil uses the Leisuredrive template to mark out the precise cutting lines for the fridge vents.

4-7-6. He drills a 3mm hole in each corner and then makes a slot by drilling several holes close together, a little way inboard of the cutting line.

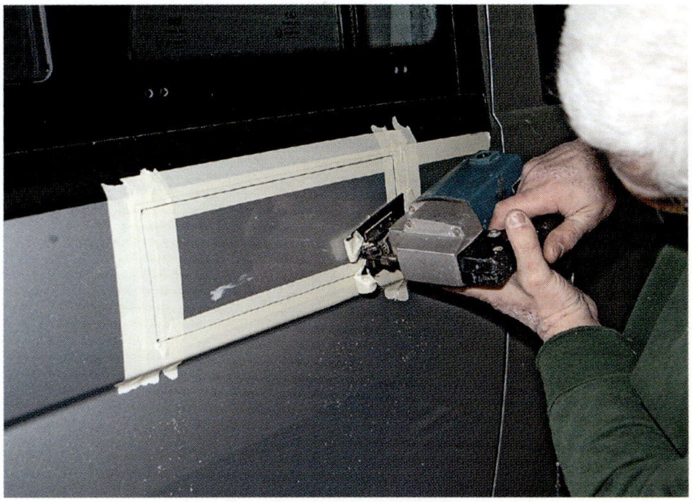

4-7-7. This enables him to insert the jigsaw blade and make a gentle curve down to the bottom line and into the bottom left-hand corner.

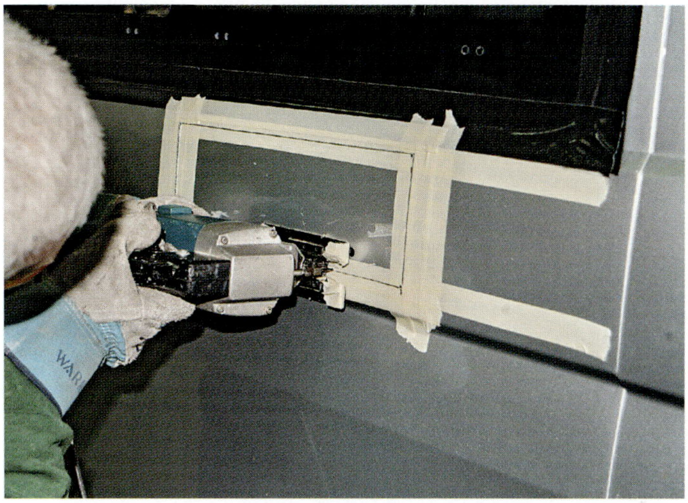

4-7-8. With the saw turned off, he then removes it, re-inserts it and cuts back to the bottom right-hand corner.

4-7-9. The procedure when cutting into the corner is to go right up to the drilled hole (arrowed) ...

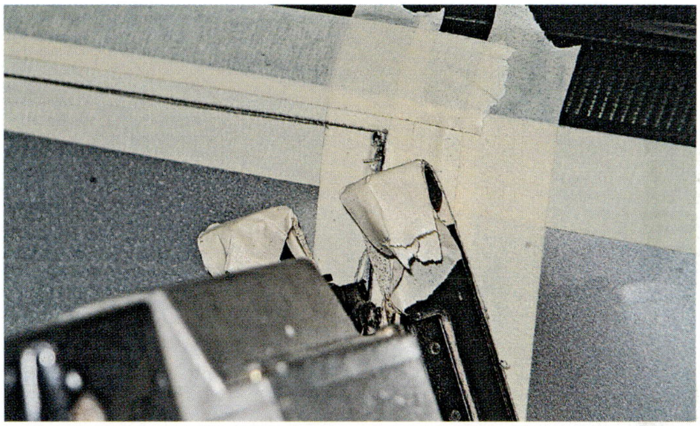

4-7-10. ... then come a little way back from the corner and make a curving cut to the next line, coming back later to complete a straight line into the corner as described previously.

4-7-11. With the hole cut out, Neil painted all of the metal edges with metal primer.

4-7-12. He next turned his attention to the inside of the vehicle because the fridge had to be pushed further back than the edge of the interior trim. On the T5, there is a small reinforcing piece which Leisuredrive find needs to be cut into in order that the fridge can go sufficiently far back. Neil cuts into it with his jigsaw ...

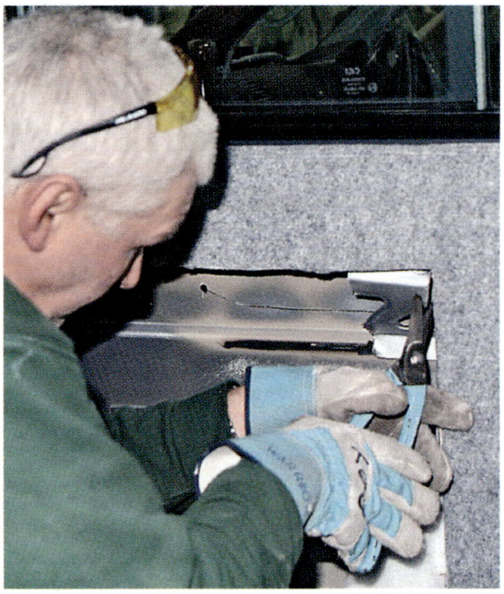

4-7-13. …then finishes off the cut with tin snips, taking very great care not to damage the outer bodywork.

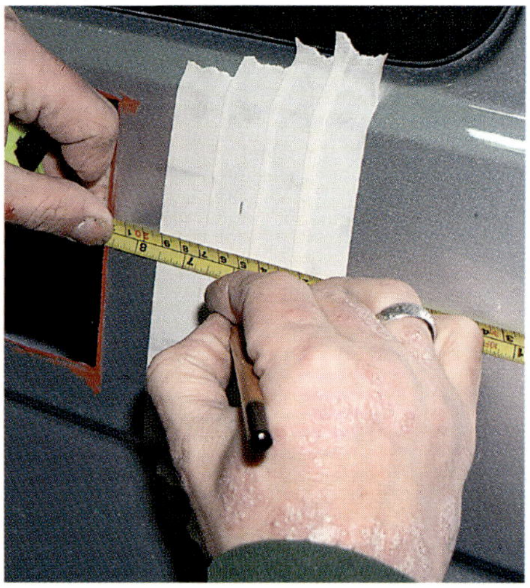

4-7-14. The template we saw earlier was used to mark the position of the flue pipe and the exact measurement was double-checked with the tape measure.

4-7-17. Over we go now to a fridge that Andy is fitting to another Leisuredrive conversion, this time a high-top. It is important to follow the instructions with the particular fridge you are fitting. Here, Andy drills a tapping hole into the extension piece on the flue …

4-7-15. Neil drilled a small pilot hole in the centre of the access point for the flue pipe…

Top tip!

- Hole cutters will last a lot longer if the cut is lubricated with cutting oil or, in the absence of any cutting oil, ordinary lubricating oil.

4-7-16. …then used a hole cutter to cut out the hole to the size described in the fitting instructions.

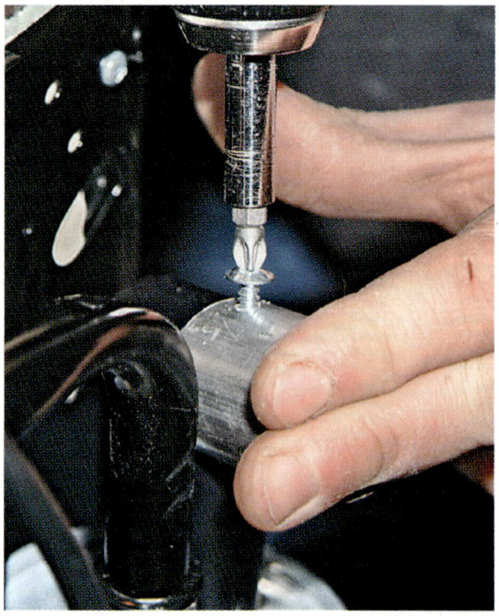

4-7-18. … before driving in the screw that holds it in place.

4-7-19. He demonstrates how this piece of flexible pipe links up with the outlet on this particular conversion.

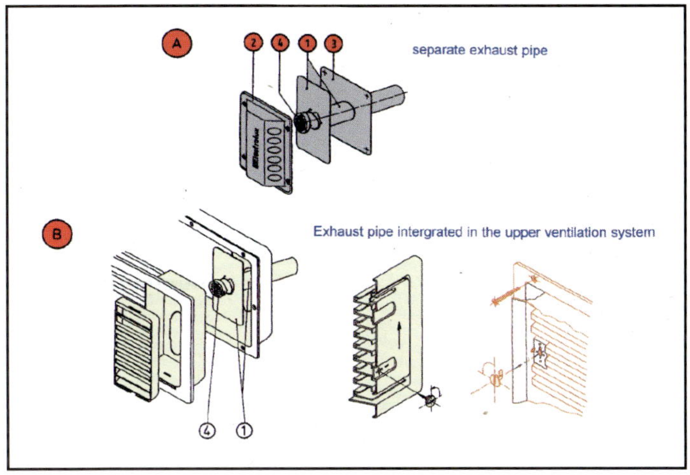

4-7-20. Dometic fridges use one of two types of exhaust system. One of them (A) has a separate exhaust outlet. The other (B) has an exhaust integrated with the upper vent.

SAFETY FIRST!

When you have your gas installation finally assembled and checked by a CORGI-approved engineer, he will need to carefully check these gas outlets. If you are in any doubt, leave this part of the work to him. He will, in any case, need to dismantle it, if necessary, in order to check that the job has been done properly.

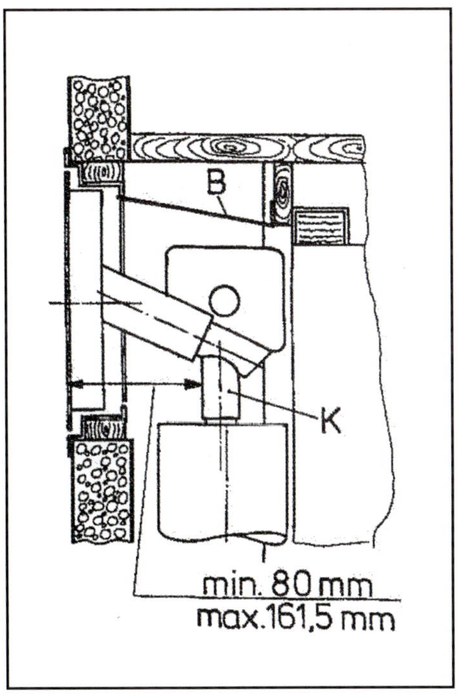

4-7-21. The rear of the fridge must not be pushed against the rear of its enclosure. As this Dometic drawing shows, there must be a gap of at least 110mm between the back of the fridge and its enclosure and the top vent must be suitably located at the height shown.

4-7-22. Back on our project vehicle, the flue pipe extension has a different shape but the principle of drilling the tapping hole …

4-7-23. … then driving the screw is the same.

4-7-24. The layout of the flue pipes is somewhat different in this instance and again, it must be emphasised that the instructions with the particular fridge you are fitting must be followed.

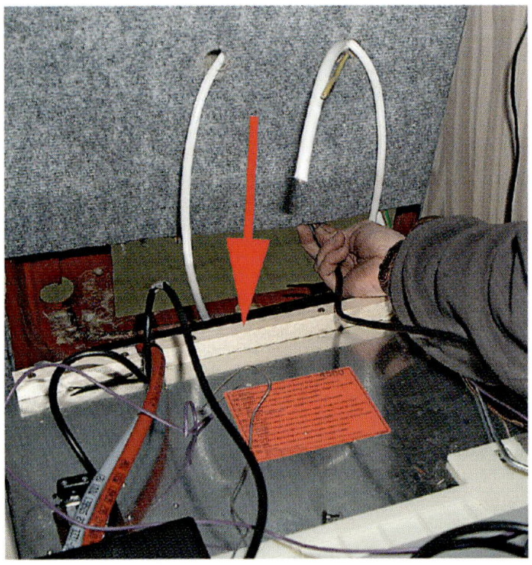

4-7-25. On the high-top conversion, a wooden batten (arrowed) has been screwed to the back of the fridge with slots in it to enable cables to pass through. Andy feeds all of the relevant electrical cables into position.

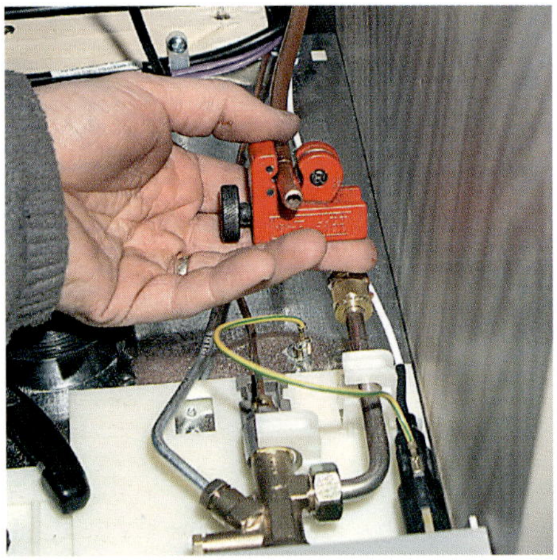

4-7-26. Stressing once again that none of these gas connections must be made by anyone other than a qualified CORGI engineer, Andy cuts the gas pipe off to length with a pipe cutter.

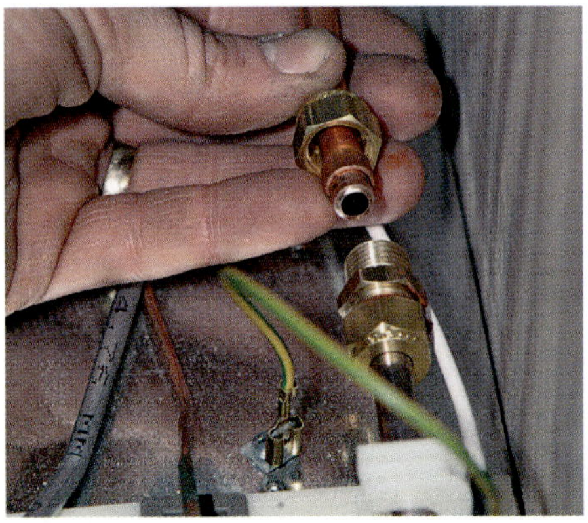

4-7-27. He assembles the connections 'dry' – that is to say, it is now strongly recommended that sealant is not used.

4-7-28. There is some skill involved in tightening gas compression units by the correct amount. Too much and they'll leak; too little and they'll leak! It's more difficult to get it right, I'm told, than with water pipes and the risks of getting it wrong are, of course, far more serious.

4-7-29. The fridge in the high-top conversion is finally pushed fully into position …

4-7-30. … and the top shelf screwed down.

4-7-31. On our elevating roof version, wooden floor battens are screwed down so that the fridge fits snugly.

4-7-32. More battens are screwed to the uprights.

4-7-34. The electrical cables were gathered into position and fitted to the fridge and the gas pipes also connected up. In both cases, of course, only qualified engineers must carry out this work.

Important note: Before the fridge was fitted, extra insulation was pushed into the gaps between the furniture and the body at the rear so that the sides of the fridge became, as much as practicable, sealed from the outside. The only air you want coming in and out of the vehicle is across the back of the fridge itself and not into the passenger compartment.

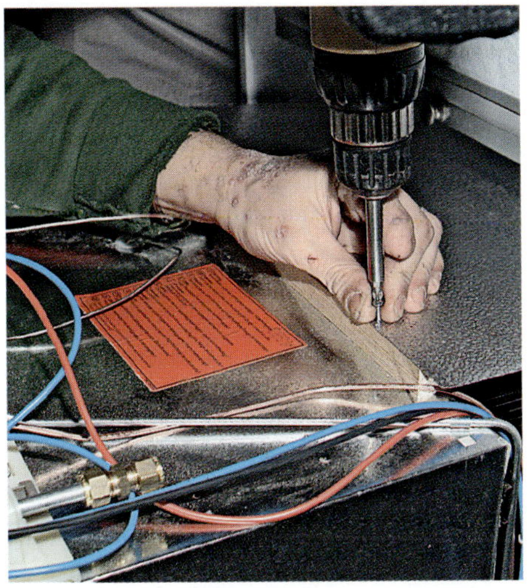

4-7-33. The wooden batten shown being screwed down to the back of the earlier fridge has also been fitted to the back of this one. On to it goes an aluminium baffle plate.

4-7-35. Neil began to manoeuvre the fridge into its slot.

4-7-36. As it got close, the gas pipe was connected as before.

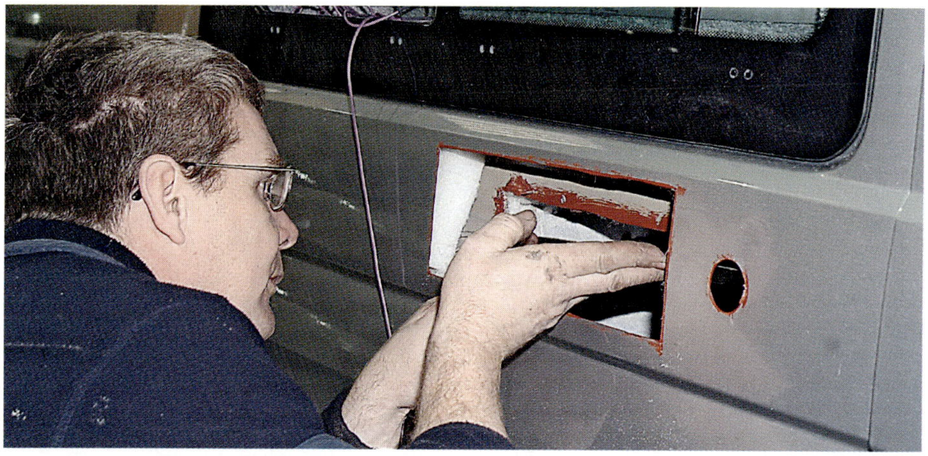

4-7-37. Outside the vehicle, Roy waited to receive the aluminium baffle plate …

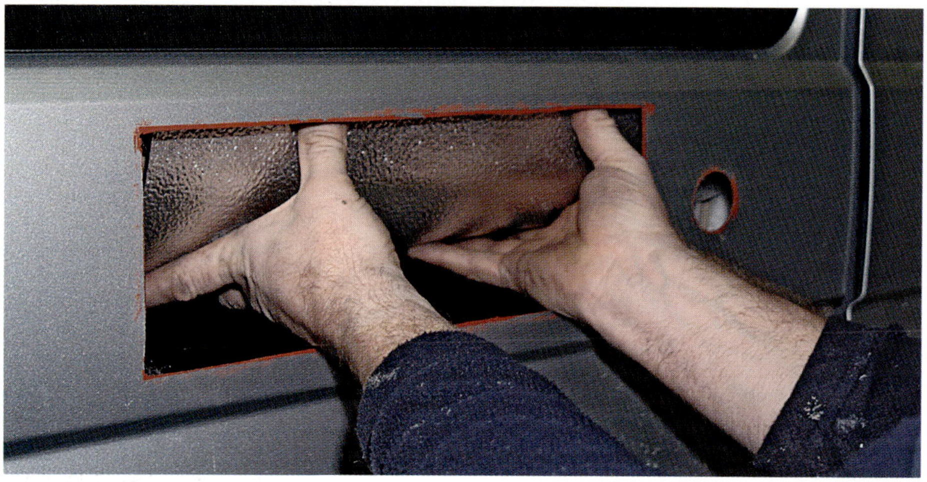

4-7-38. … and bend it up at an angle so that it is resting against the outside of the van's body. The joint between the aluminium and the van's body should now be sealed with silicone sealer. This will prevent any rattling but won't be so strong as to prevent the fridge from being removed when it needs servicing.

4-7-39. The flue pipe outlet is fitted from outside, while the inlet is held on to it with a jubilee-type clip.

4-7-40. Roy checked the vent cover for fit …

4-7-41. … and marked the positions of the holes for fixing it in place. After removing the vent cover again, the holes were drilled to a tapping size for the stainless steel screws to be fitted.

4-7-42. PU sealer was applied around the perimeter of the cover …

4-7-43. … which was then refitted and the screws driven home.

4-7-44. I decided that I disliked the white flue cover so we set about painting it. First, it was rubbed over with plastic pre-paint primer.

4-7-47. The flue cover now matched the vent covers.

4-7-45. Then aerosol primer was sprayed on and when that was fully dry …

4-7-48. Quite some time later, I decided that I would like to fit covers for the vents for the winter – they can be supplied as an extra by Leisuredrive – and that I wanted them body colour coded. I used Autopaint International's colour-matched aerosol paint and lacquer.

4-7-46. … a coat of satin black was applied.

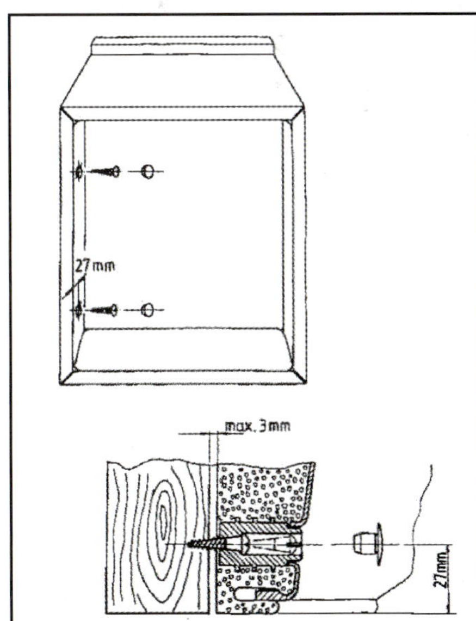

4-7-49. Holes are provided in the sides of the fridge to enable you to screw it firmly to the furniture surround. Lever out the plug (bottom) …

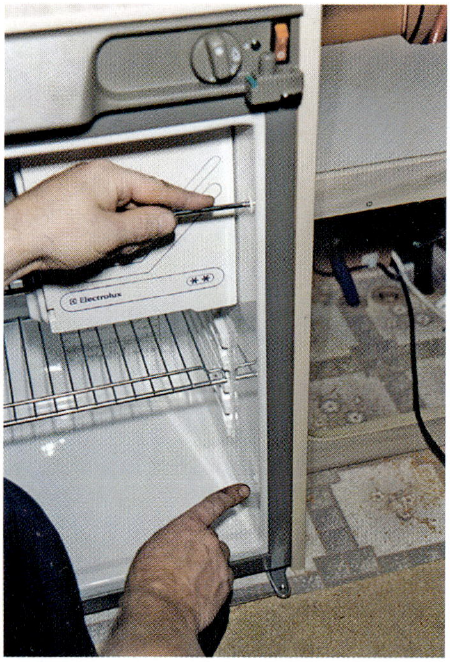

4-7-50. … before screwing the fridge into place and refitting the plugs.

4-7-51. There is another similar but narrower fridge available from Dometic, the RM 4181 M with a capacity of 40 litres and width of 401mm. This compares with the 55 litres (inc. freezer compartment) of the larger RM 4210 shown being fitted here, which has a width of 486mm. Both are '3-way' (12v + 230v + gas) operation. The width saving of the narrower fridge might make a difference to the amount by which the driver's seat will slide back, which could be important for the tallest of drivers.

SECTION 8. WORK ON GAS SYSTEMS

Who is allowed to work on a motor caravan's gas system? Well, in the UK, The Gas Safety (Installation and Use) Regulations 1998 state that, "No person shall carry out any work in relation to a gas fitting or gas storage vessel unless he is competent to do so." Unfortunately, the word 'competent' is not defined but you can bet your bottom dollar – in fact you might have to – that an insurance company would claim it would not have to shell out if there was an accident caused by someone carrying out an installation who had not been trained by the proper authorities, such as Calor or CORGI. On the other hand, the same Regulations also specifically state:

"Nothing in these Regulations shall apply in relation to the supply of gas to, or anything done in respect of a gas fitting on –
(a) a self-propelled vehicle except when such a vehicle is –
(i) hired out in the course of a business; or
(ii) made available to members of the public in the course of a business carried on from that vehicle;
and (as well as other exemptions, such as for hovercraft!)
(e) a caravan used for touring otherwise than when hired out in the course of a business."
The full text can be seen, at the time of writing, at: www.opsi.gov.uk/si/si1998/19982451.htm

So it appears that you can still, legally and acceptably, carry out most of the work yourself though you'd be a mug not to have final connections made and checks carried out by qualified specialists, as described in the following sections. There is always the possibility that you would be personally liable for faults if you don't.

Important note: The Regulations specifically **don't** prevent you from changing cylinders yourself, of course.
In summary then, you can safely:
- Fit appliances provided that, if they have to be removed again for connecting up (such as the fridge) it would be daft to screw them fully in place at this stage.
- Run pipework in place.
- Make the mountings for the gas cylinder supports, fit the regulator, if you're using a body-mounted 30mbar type.
- Leave **all** pipe connections, including straight compression connections extending lengths of pipe, to a CORGI qualified engineer.

You can be sure of finding a properly trained and qualified engineer to make the final connections and carry out servicing and repairs by going to the CORGI (Council of Registered Gas Installers) website at www.trustcorgi.com. Then (at the time of writing) you click on the link shown as 'Find an installer'.

Additional points made by The Self-Build Motor Caravan Club (see, at the time of writing, www.sbmcc.co.uk) are to do with:
- GAS STORAGE:

The BS 1646 standards state (in simple terms) that gas cylinders must be stored in a purpose-built locker. This means accessible only from outside or in a completely sealed locker, if accessible to the interior. [The locker] must also be able to resist fire for a minimum of 20 minutes … It also must have a 'drop-out' [vent] hole at its lowest point. The gas cylinders must be connected with a flexible hose to a coupling outlet running to the outside of the box, sealed from the outside with a gas tight seal. The shut off valve must be outside the box. UNDER NO CIRCUMSTANCES MUST ANY ELECTRICAL EQUIPMENT BE STORED IN THE SAME BOX."
- GAS APPLIANCES:

[Each] must have a dropout hole [vent] at the lowest point and have a shut off valve to service each one independently."

There are three additional points worth making here:
- This advice applies to the UK. Those in other areas must check to make sure that they will comply with local regulations and laws.
- The information was correct in the UK at time of writing but may be changed at any time. You should check the latest regulations before carrying out any of the work.
- It would be best to liaise with your chosen gas or electrical fitter before starting the DIY part of the work, just to make sure that what you are doing is both legal and acceptable to your fitter.

INSTALLATION REGULATIONS

HEAVY LEGAL STUFF – BUT ESSENTIAL READING!

The following is my own view and reflects the available information as I understand it. I may be wrong and it is imperative that you do not rely finally on the advice given here.

British Standards (BS) and the later form of BS standards which known as BS EN (standards commonly agreed across Europe) appear to be aimed at manufacturers rather than DIYers. The legal status of British Standards with regard to manufacturers does not seem to be as clear as say, statute law (otherwise known as Acts of Parliament) and I have seen British Standards described as having a 'quasi-legal status'.

However, it seems to me that there are several main points here, as they affect the DIY converter:

- DIYers are not manufacturers (unless they start carrying out work as a trade, in which case further expert advice must be sought) **But:**
- It seems sensible, in general, to follow the relevant BS EN standards where applicable. As the Health & Safety Executive website says, "Standards, be they European or British, should reflect the state of the art at the time they are written."
- At the time of writing this manual, the type of regulator that fits directly to the top of the cylinder is still widely available as are appliances that run on the 'old' gas pressures. It seems likely that they are still safe enough to use, in spite of their being a new Standard. If in doubt, obtain confirmation from appliance and regulator manufacturers or suppliers.

REGULATORS

The job of the gas regulator, among other things, is to 'regulate' the pressure of the gas so that it remains constant, no matter what the pressure inside the cylinder and so that – provided the regulator matches the appliance it is supplying – the pressure is the correct one for the appliance in use.

There are several different designs of cylinder mounted regulator, depending on the country of origin and manufacturer of the gas cylinder.

'Old'-type regulators

Before September 2003, there were two broad classes of regulator:

- Blue ones for using with butane gas at 37mbar pressure.
- Red ones for use with propane at 28mbar.

There are several different fixing systems, dependant on manufacturer and country of origin.

With these 'old' system regulators, the gas regulator fits to the top of the cylinder and only low pressure gas comes out of regulator.

The hose from regulator to fixed gas pipe is usually low-pressure rubber tube. Bottled gas is a petroleum product and, as such, degrades rubber, which is why the tube has to be replaced regularly.

But, from September 2003, very few regulators on new motorhomes and caravans are cylinder mounted and here's why: All caravans and motorhomes factory built after 1 September 2003 should conform to the British Standards known as European Standard EN 1949: 2002, which deals largely with installations and European Standard EN 12864: 2001 which deals largely with regulators.

READING UP ON THE BRITISH STANDARDS

If you want to know the full story of what the Standards contain, you will have to fork out a fairly large sum of money to the BSI for printed copies (at an equivalent cost to about two weeks of decent quality site fees, at the time of writing) or see if you can find a set of the relevant regulations in a major public lending library near you.

'New'-type regulators

New gas installation British Standards came into effect in September 2003 for National Caravan Council certified (i.e. most British factory-built) caravans and motor homes. From that date, appliances and regulators fitted to all such caravans and motor caravans operate at a different gas pressure to that of all older appliances.

4-8-2. This is one of the Gaslow wall-mounted regulators.

Under the 'newer' standards:

- The regulator is almost always mounted to a fixed point adjacent to the cylinder.
- These regulators supply gas at a pressure of 30mbar and work with both propane and butane.
- There is a high-pressure flexible hose from the regulator to the cylinder.
- All flexible hoses have threaded connectors, and have excess-flow and non-return safety valves incorporated in them.

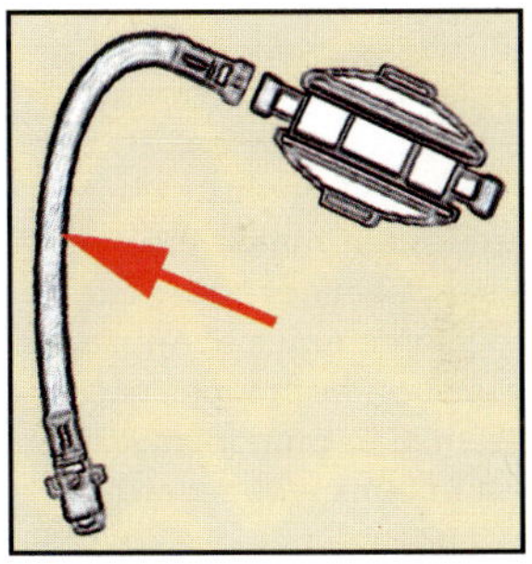

4-8-3. The screw-on high-pressure hose (pigtail) is all that needs replacing when switching to a different type of cylinder.

4-8-1. These are Gaslow's three main cylinder mounted regulators. Note that, unlike most other regulators, these come with a contents gauge which, needless to say, is extremely useful!
1. For Calor-type 4.5kg butane cylinders with a hexagonal fixing nut.
2. For Calor-type 3.9kg & 6kg propane cylinders.
3. For Campingaz cylinders with an M20 x M20 adapter.

EUROPEAN STANDARD EN 12864: 2001
Potential pros & cons

Advantages
- The system is standard in the UK and Continental Europe and it will, therefore, be more convenient to use if touring abroad.
- When you swap to a different type of cylinder, you keep the same regulator and only have to swap the high-pressure hose, sometimes known as 'pigtails'. (Previously, users required a regulator for each manufacturer of cylinder and type of gas they used: 28mbar for butane and 37mbar for propane.)

Fittings, being factory-fitted to the hoses and screwed on to the regulator and cylinder adaptor, are much less likely to leak.

Disadvantages
- The regulator has to be specially mounted.
- There is a length of flexible (and potentially slightly vulnerable) hose under high pressure between cylinder and regulator. If it should become damaged, there is nothing to prevent the escape of gas from the cylinder.

All the relevant authorities, such as Calor and CORGI currently strongly recommend:
- Do not mix-and-match appliances and/or regulators of different types.
- The regulator used **must** match the requirements of the appliances being fitted.

There may be some types of appliance that work equally well on both types of system but it is essential to **only** follow the manufacturer's instructions with regard to regulator and appliance matching.

Which gas?
If you plan to spend a lot of time in Continental Europe, you may want to stick with Campingaz. Cylinders are widely available on both sides of the Channel, and there will be no need to have a different pigtail for each country. For Campingaz, an M20 x M20 hose connection is required, plus a Campingaz adapter.

If you choose not to use the (often more expensive) Campingaz, you will need to obtain a pigtail connector to match the cylinders available in the country you are visiting. The new connector is used to replace the UK pigtail (attached to the bulkhead regulator), while you're using the European cylinder, and then switched back when in the UK.

Can the newer regulator system be retro-fitted?
Most British motor caravans built between the early 1990s and late 2003 will have appliances manufactured to comply with the Gas Appliance Directive. They were designed for an operating pressure of between 28 and 37mbar and so, on the face of it, should be able to run on the newer standard of 30mbar. However, gas suppliers insist that this is not the case and that only appliances that specifically match the 30mbar regulators should be used. It is essential that you check the appliance data plate, instructions, or contact the appliance manufacturer or local dealer. If you are not sure, don't have the later system retro-fitted!

Maintenance
Gas appliances must be installed in accordance with the safety requirements of British Standards and EU regulations, or other local laws. All gas appliances must be serviced annually to keep them in a safe and efficient condition. The service must be carried out by a qualified engineer and should include:
- Check gas cylinder storage, which should be in an area insulated from the interior of the motor caravan.
- Ventilation check. Air inlets and cylinder storage ventilation should be clear and adequate.
- Gas leak check, condition of pipework and hoses and compatibility of fittings.

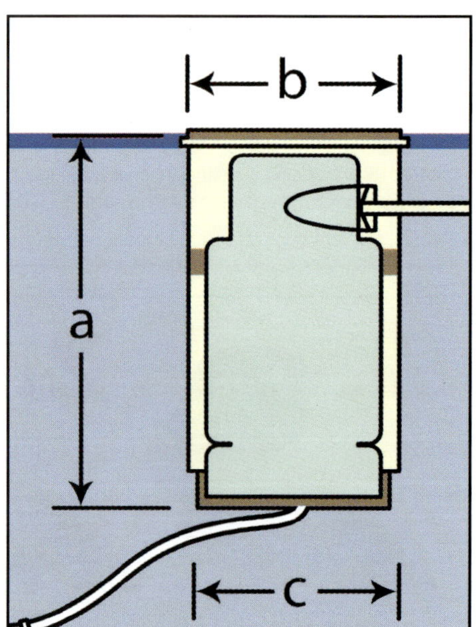

4-8-4. If you want to fit a sealed gas cylinder container, you could try using one of these marine-type housings, again from Gaslow. For the Campingaz cylinder, the housing measures: 295mm x 350mm x 310mm

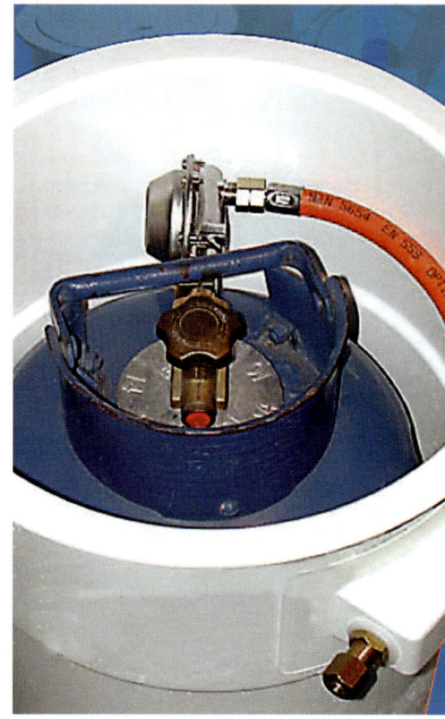

4-8-5. This shows a Calor-type cylinder and regulator but the principle is the same. The regulator and hose fit inside the sealed locker and there is an external union for connecting the low-pressure gas supply.

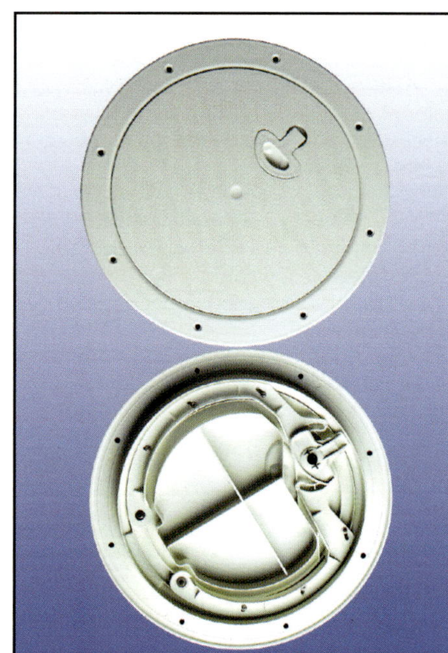

4-8-6. It might be possible to fit the locker inside the floor of the wardrobe although the access would have to be larger than with the standard Leisuredrive wardrobe rear door. The drop-out pipe would need to be routed to a safe place beneath the vehicle, away from heat or ingress of forced air or water.

- Flue check: Smoke spillage test.
- Appliance safety devices must work correctly.
- Appliances must be safe for further use.

Important note: Before drilling holes through the floor, ensure the following:

- Do not drill into any wires, cables or pipes on either side of the floor panel.
- Take care not to drill into any flanges, hollow box sections or any other structural areas.
- Try to site holes so that no water or forced air can come up through them.
- Gas drop-out holes must be sited well away from any heat, such as a heater or the vehicle's exhaust.
- If fitting a gas drop-out point, make sure that gas cannot gather in an undertray fitted beneath the vehicle.

4-8-7. Every separate appliance must be fitted with an isolator valve. Here, Leisuredrive's Steve fits the valve to a panel still to be fitted to the sink unit ...

4-8-8. ... before fitting the panel and isolator valve in place. It's far easier doing it this way round and is a good piece of Leisuredrive forward thinking!

4-8-9. This is a Gaslow bulkhead-mounted regulator and low pressure hose with cylinder connector.

4-8-10. The Leisuredrive Campingaz container is made of steel and can be located beneath the wardrobe floor, accessed through the tailgate. The base of the container is of open mesh and beneath it is a drop hole through the rear floor to allow escaping gas to flow away. The container is not sealed.

4-8-11. There is room between the box and the wardrobe floor for the regulator to be mounted. Note the tap on the regulator, allowing the supply to the regulator to be turned off when the low pressure hose has to be replaced.

4-8-12. Inside the box, the low-pressure hose and connector are screwed to the top of the gas cylinder in the normal way. It's a good idea to incorporate a nylon strap so that the cylinder can be held tight in its container.

Chapter 5
Interior trim

SECTION 1. MAKING UPHOLSTERY

Leisuredrive makes all of its own upholstery in-house and very good it is too. If you buy a kit from Leisuredrive, this is the upholstery you get.

5-1-1. Leisuredrive has its own trim shop 'upstairs', and here you can see the trim that has been made for our conversion using the original VW fabric to match the front seats.

Important note: Don't carry out the work shown in this chapter or in any individual section without reading the rest of this manual. There are many jobs that are associated with other work. This manual has been divided up into logical sections of the vehicle but these are not necessarily the order in which you will carry out the work. Please study the whole of the manual before commencing work.

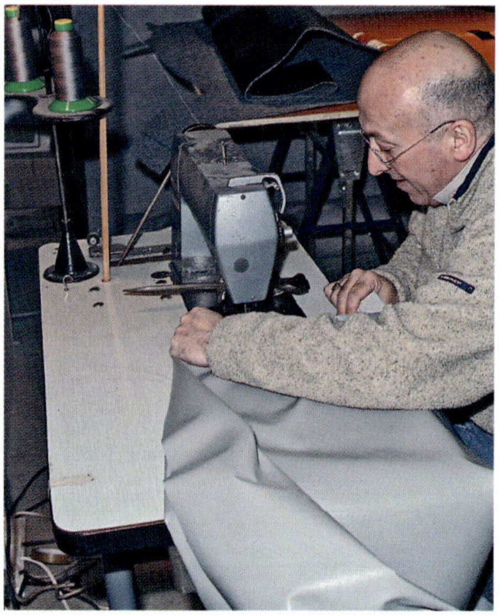

5-1-2. The first step in manufacturing trim is to cut out the sections to be sewn together.

5-1-3. All of the covers are sewn inside-out, as it were.

5-1-4. This is one of the curtain ties having been folded back-to-front.

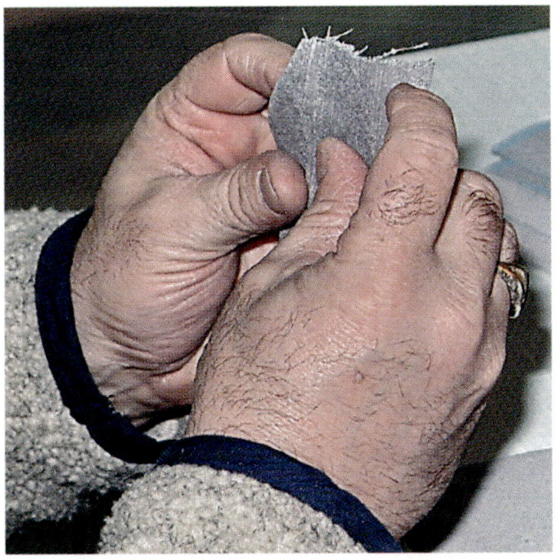

5-1-5. The sewn tube is then turned inside-out so that it becomes the right way round – if you see what I mean!

5-1-6. When the seat and bed foam covers are made, strong Velcro tape is sewn onto their backs and here you can see the matching strip being peeled away.

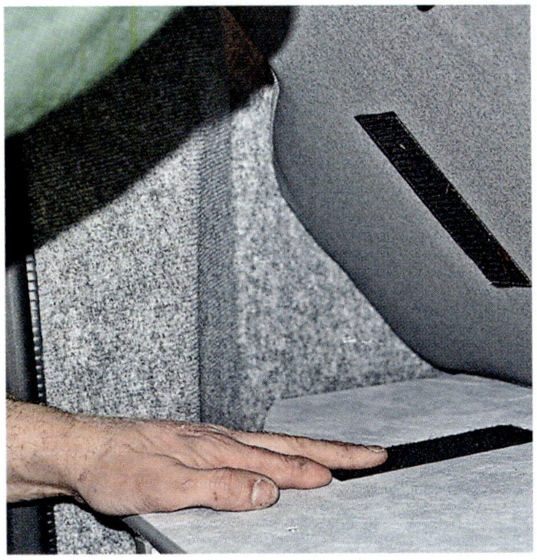

5-1-7. It has to be fitted on the seat and bed base boards so that it matches its positions on the seat upholstery.

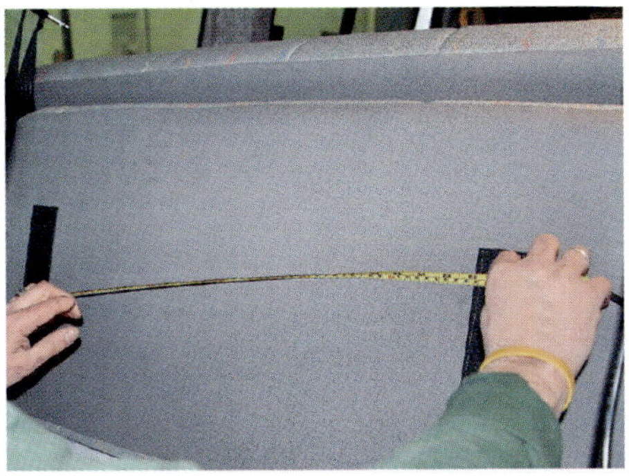

5-1-8. Be sure to measure the distance between the Velcro strips on the upholstery …

5-1-9. … and then to transfer those measurements to the boards. Incidentally, do make sure that the upholstery is fitted in its correct location with the backrests sitting on top of the seat bases, otherwise you will fit the Velcro in the wrong places.

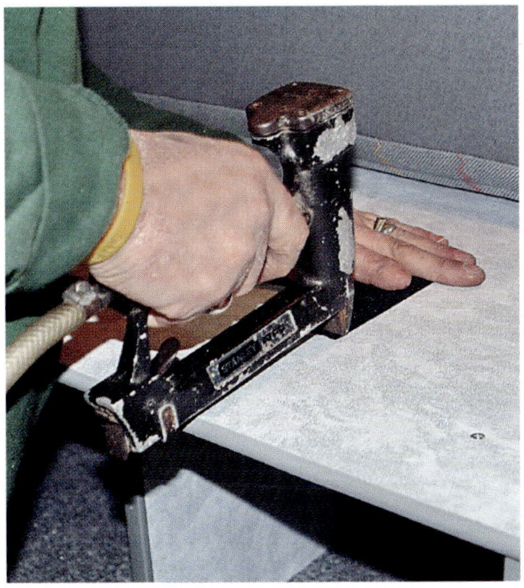

5-1-10. It's by far best to staple the Velcro down to the wooden board rather than try gluing it.

5-1-11. These are the similar strips on the rear side of the seat backrest. Glued-down Velcro will almost certainly peel off again in the future.

5-1-12. The cushions for the rear end of the bed are placed in position inside what is now the vehicle's luggage area. I always carry a cloth to drape over the upholstery to protect it when carrying anything on it.

5-1-13. Inside the vehicle, the seat upholstery is fitted in the same way. Note that the raised foam edge goes on the seat base and also that the seat belt buckles pass through the space between the seat base and backrest.

SECTION 2. SEAT REMOVAL AND STRIP

Much more information on seat stripping can be seen in Chapter 6: Extras and Accessories, Section 1 where we show how to fit a lumbar support and seat heater.

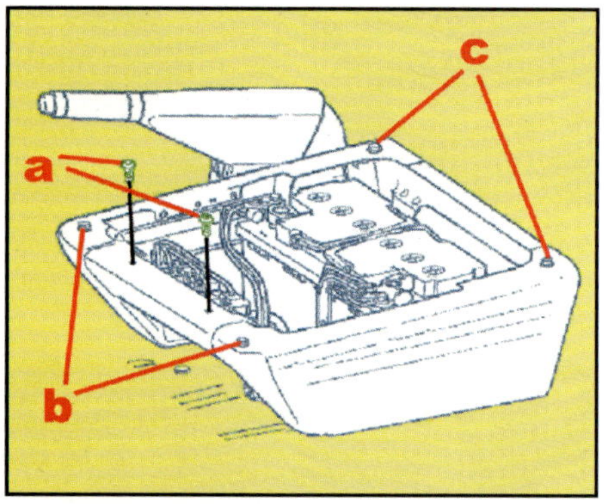

5-2-1. A typical T5 seat base may look like this. Note that the bolts (a) are only for holding a relay panel in place. The front studs (b) are fitted with nuts but in some installations, there are captive nuts fitted to the seat bases and bolts are used. The same may apply to the rear studs (c). In all cases, the correct high tensile bolts and nuts must always be used. This is one of the seat base types which includes the battery.

5-2-2. The front nuts or bolts are easily accessed by sliding the seat fully backward.

5-2-3. With the seat pushed fully forward, the rear bolts can be accessed. All have multi-point socket head studs. Note the plastic cover on the back of the seat base which is simply unclipped by pulling it backward.

5-2-4. With the four bolts undone, the seat can be removed.

Important notes:

- Many seats, including all of those with airbags, have electrical connections going into them. Be sure to disconnect any electrical connections and to make a note of how they should be reconnected before removing the seat.
- Read carefully the information in Chapter 2, Section 1 before disconnecting airbag wiring. If you simply disconnect the wiring without following the proper preparations, the vehicle will show an 'error' on the dashboard and you will have to have it reset by your VW main dealer.

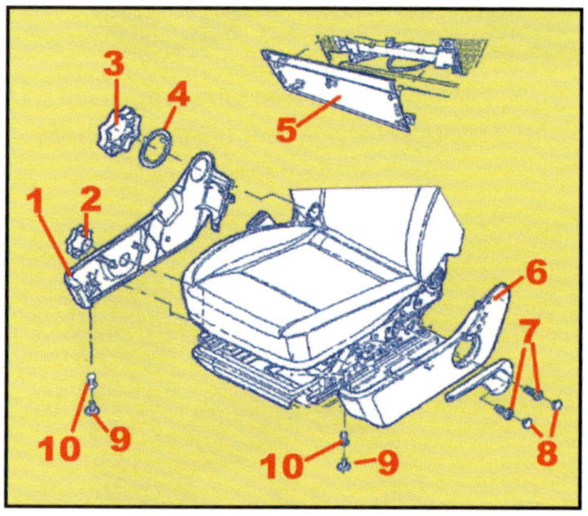

5-2-5. You may never need to remove the trim from the base of the seat but if you do, here's how it fits together:

- *The height adjuster is removed from the left-hand side of the seat by levering off the two caps (8) and unscrewing the two screws (7).*
- *Both left-and right-hand trims (1 and 6) are removed by levering the centre (9) out of the hollow spreader (10) to free the fronts of the trims. The rears are unclipped from the frame.*
- *The right-hand adjuster knobs are removed by levering. You should, when removing the adjuster wheel (3) for the backrest adjustment, use special pliers to unclip the retainer (4).*
- *This (5) is a slightly different rear trim to that seen earlier but it unclips in the same way.*

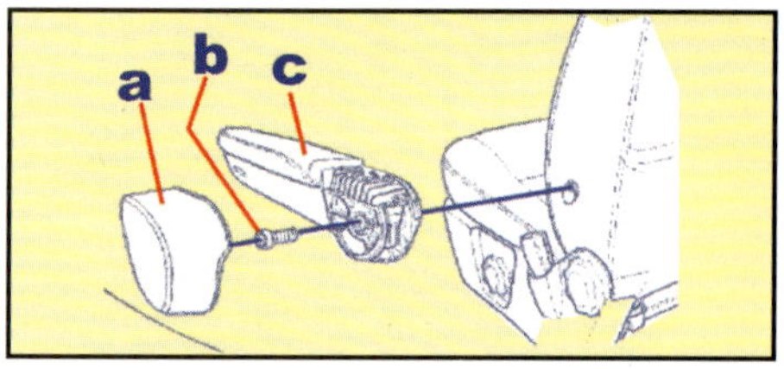

5-2-6. If the driver, for instance, does not use his/her armrest, you may consider removing it to improve access to the rear of the vehicle from the front. To do so, you carefully lever off the cover (a), take out the screw (b) and lever off the armrest (c). Volkswagen recommend always refitting by using a new bolt and after cleaning out the thread in the seat frame. It would be sufficient to clean both threads and apply a medium-strength thread lock, however.

SECTION 3. FITTING CURTAINS

You may or may not want rather old-fashioned looking curtains in your T5 motor caravan. This sequence shows how Leisuredrive fit curtain rails for those who want curtains to be fitted. It's worth pointing out that it doesn't seem possible to fit a roller blind to the tailgate window because of its shape. However, you could always fit an insulated screen to both the front windscreen and doors and also to the rear tailgate.

5-3-1. This shows the location of the curtain track at the front of a T5. It is screwed through the headlining in the position shown. The aluminium track can quite easily be bent between thumb and fingers but take care that the bend doesn't close in on itself and prevent the track from running. Note that there will need to be an overlap in the track near the middle so that the curtains can be properly closed at the front.

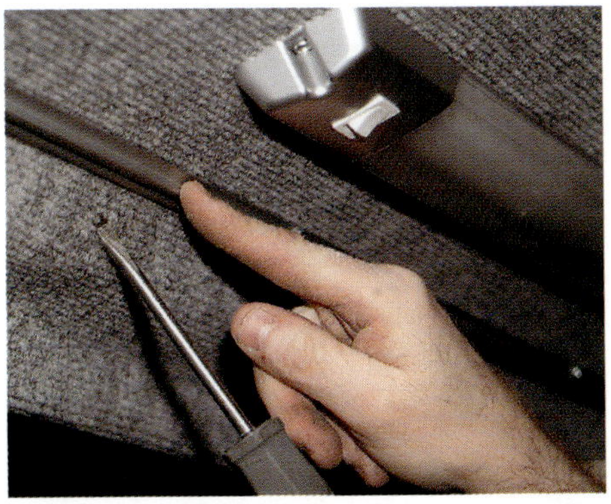

5-3-2. Along the sides of the vehicle, the curtain track has to be screwed to the box sections just beneath the strengthening panels. Fit them higher, as shown here, not in the lower position indicated by the screwdriver.

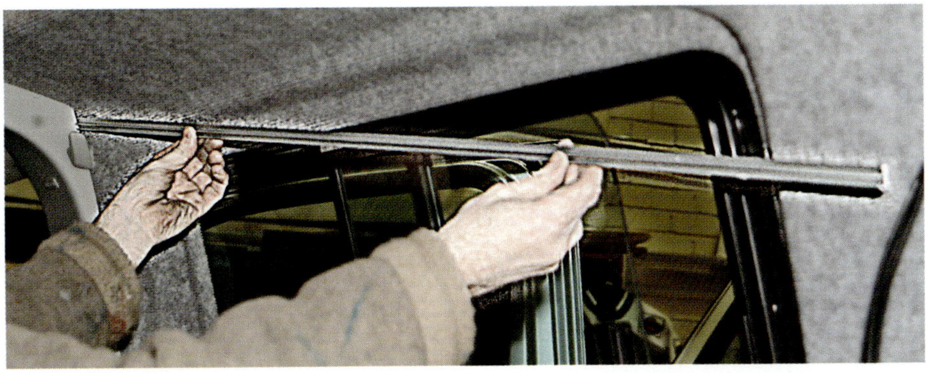

5-3-3. The track has to be cut to length and, where necessary, carefully bent to shape before fitting.

5-3-4. Start by fitting the centre of the track. Make a small mark with a pencil, drill a pilot hole and then screw the first pre-drilled hole in the track to the vehicle. You can now use the remaining pre-drilled holes to align the tapping holes that need drilling for the remaining screws. The reason for not drilling all of the holes first is because it is incredibly difficult to find a drilled hole; the pile in the trim tends to close itself up, hiding the hole.

5-3-5. After each hole is drilled, its corresponding screw is fitted in turn.

5-3-6. You will also need to allow an overlap where the curtain crosses at the B-post. You must take very great care not to interfere in any way with the airbags – leave the curtain track well back from this area if airbags are fitted – and also make certain that there are no sharp edges or corners where you could hit yourself or against which you could be flung in the case of an accident.

5-3-7. The curtain track for the rear window is simply screwed to the box section that runs across the vehicle beneath the hinges. The curtain can simply be tucked out of the way behind the line of the wardrobe. In our case, we had window tinting fitted and an especially dark patch installed behind which the curtain can not be seen from outside the vehicle.

SECTION 4: FITTING ROLLER BLINDS

Here's how you can fit a set of Dometic's Seitz roller blinds to your T5 camper.

Volkswagen's 'own-brand' camper, the California and the Auto-Sleepers version, provide everyone else with new targets to shoot at in terms of the quality of its fixtures and fittings. In particular, the integrated blinds are really nice! However, even they have their drawbacks and can't be fitted to front or rear (tailgate) glasses. Larger coachbuilt motor caravans usually have cassette blinds but they are not an option on many van conversions because of the peculiar shapes of the interiors of many vans. Coachbuilt conversions are, of course, much flatter inside like the inner walls of caravans, so cassette blinds can more easily be fitted.

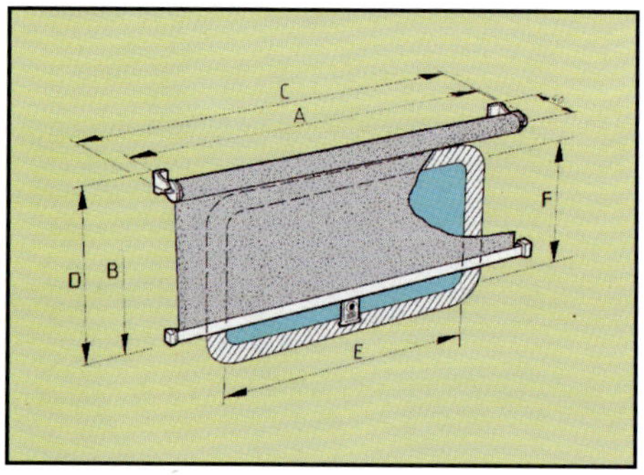

5-4-1. This is Dometic's diagram showing how to establish the size of blind you will need for your particular installation. The overlaps shown here are Dometic's recommended figures; you might disagree or they might be impractical in certain locations but this is a good starting point.
A = size of width to order (length of unit)
B = size of length to order (length fully extended)
C = width overall
D = height overall
E = width, window cutout
F = height, window cutout

Our Leisuredrive Volkswagen T5 conversion came fitted with side and rear curtains, though we eschewed the front curtains in favour of insulated stick-on panels from CAK. Shan, my wife, really dislikes motor caravan curtains however, so I looked at alternatives, with the help of Dometic. We agreed that the only practical alternative would be Dometic's Seitz roller blinds, which take a minimal amount of mounting space and can be tailored to fit. However, you will probably need to give a bit of careful thought as to where the roller blind mounting points will fit. Ours couldn't, mostly, be fitted in the conventional way, flat against the wall, so a bit of creative thinking was needed. The ways in which the brackets are adapted will vary according to the shape of the interior of your motor caravan. And they can also, of course, be fitted to the flat walls found on coachbuilt motor caravans as a lighter and less expensive alternative to cassette blinds.

Ordering size		Dimension over all		Window cut out		Weight
width = A	height = B	width = E	height = D	width = E	height = F	kg
770	700	785	685	700	650	0,45
920	700	935	685	850	650	0,51
970	700	985	685	900	650	0,53
1120	700	1135	685	1050	650	0,58
1270	800	1285	785	1200	750	0,65
1320	800	1335	785	1250	750	0,79
1370	800	1385	785	1300	750	0,81
1520	800	1535	785	1450	750	0,88
1620	800	1635	785	1550	750	0,93
1720	800	1735	785	1650	750	0,98
1820	800	1835	785	1750	750	1,03
1920	800	1935	785	1850	750	1,08

5-4-2. This chart shows the blind size options available. You order the next size up from the measurements you need, then cut it down to fit. Blinds can be ordered from caravan and motor caravan accessory shops.

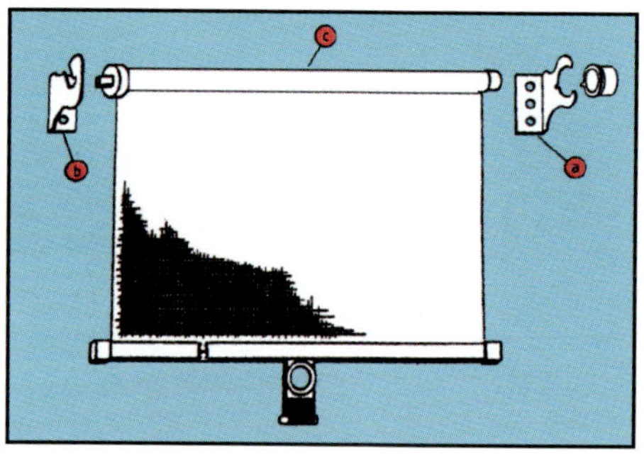

5-4-3. These are the major components that you will be dealing with. The two separate parts are the roller housing (a); the end retainer (b) has a slot into which the sprung bar at the end of the roller blind is clipped; the roller blind with internal spring (c) comprises the rest of the assembly.

5-4-4. The roller housing is best fixed in place first but you will need to spend some time establishing its correct location. In this particular case, the folded steel with the three holes in it, for fixing to the caravan sidewall, had to be straightened and then bent 90° the other way so that the housing would fit where I wanted, inside the window recess.

The first job is to work out what sizes of blinds you will need and, indeed, whether or not it will be possible to fit them at all. Sharply angled windows, such as the Volkswagen T5's tailgate window, just won't allow the fitting of a blind that, by its nature, can only work over a shape that is more or less rectangular.

5-4-5. The end retainer also needed a little modification as it was cut down in height so that it too would fit inside the window recess, while holding the blind sufficiently high to blank out the top of the window.

5-4-6. I used a felt pen to mark out the steel on the inside of the sliding door. Note that the angle on the end retainer is no longer 90° but has been opened out to match the curvature of the door frame.

5-4-7. You need to drill a pilot hole that will be small enough to give the self-tapping screws plenty of thread to grip on and yet not so small that you tend to shear off the screws as you tighten them up. It might be worth practising on some scrap steel before turning your attention to the interior of your motor caravan.

5-4-8. I used a rechargeable screwdriver on the screws but unfortunately, most of them haven't got enough 'bottle' to drive screws into steel for the first time.

5-4-9. This is the window behind the cooker on our Volkswagen camper. It was just possible to get the roller housing into the horizontal area of the recess while providing enough overlap at the edge of the blind. The red line added to this picture indicates the edge of the recess. It wasn't, I promise you, drawn on the trim of our motor caravan!

5-4-10. Where this bracket fitted onto the curved part of the sliding door window, the angle of the bracket (arrowed) had to be opened out.

5-4-12. Over to the dining room table and the bush is simply levered out of the end of the roller.

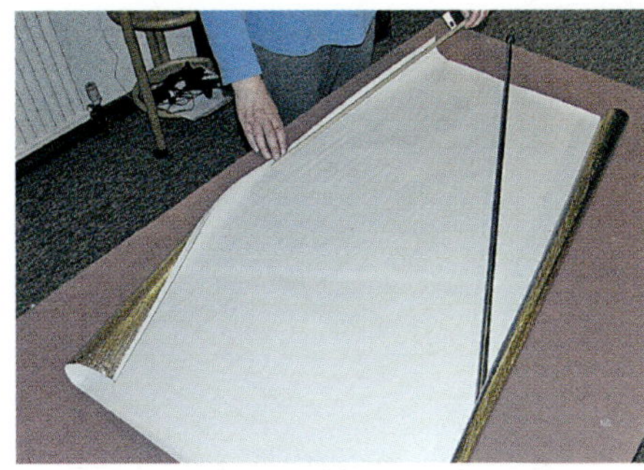

5-4-13. The end cap is rather more difficult to get out of the bottom rod without causing any damage. I found the best way was to insert a very thin-bladed screwdriver in the side of the clip, push it in a fair way and then lift the screwdriver carefully, easing off the clip.

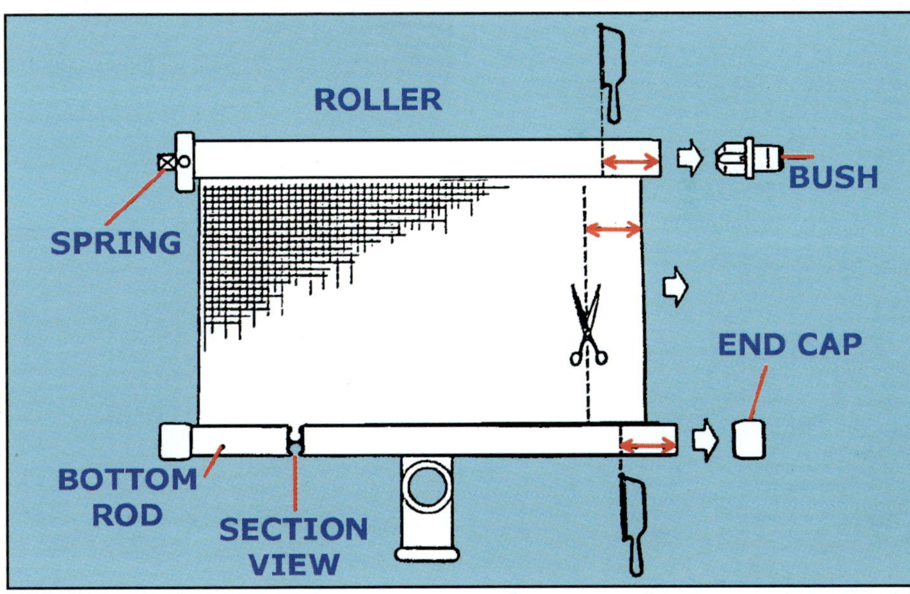

5-4-11. With all of the supports in place, you now have to turn your attention to cutting down the blinds so that they fit properly. There probably won't be any need to cut off the length of the blind because you will have chosen a blind which is only a little longer than your requirements but if you do, simply follow the instructions shown here for removing the bottom rod. The vertical dotted lines on the right of the drawing show that the amount cut off the roller and bottom rod have to equal the amount cut off the blind and that the edge of the blind is recessed from both of them. You should also note the eye hanging down from the bottom rod. This slides into the channel in the rod and is actually free to slide from side to side. Just don't forget to refit it before pushing the end cap back on again!

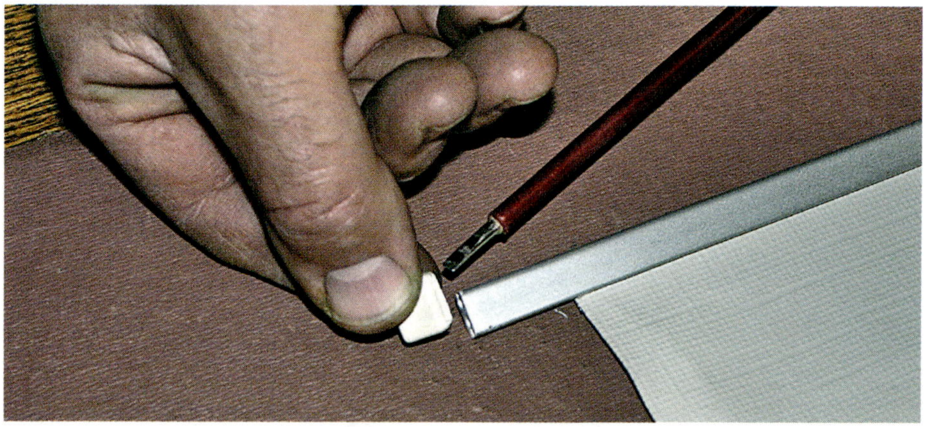

5-4-14. The roller and the bottom rod can now both be slid off the fabric of the blind.

5-4-15. It's probably best to mark out and cut the roller first using a junior hacksaw. You can then refit the bush, go back to the motor caravan and make sure that the roller is the correct length before going any further. You will know the amount cut off the end of the roller and this exact amount must be measured, marked and cut off the end of the roller blind fabric.

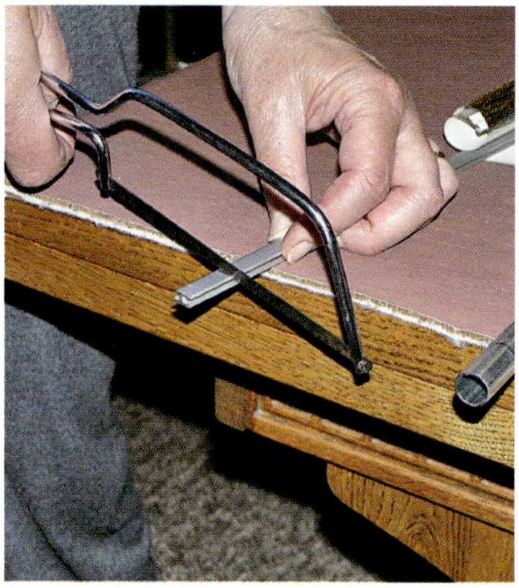

5-4-16. The same amount must be cut from the end of the bottom rod.

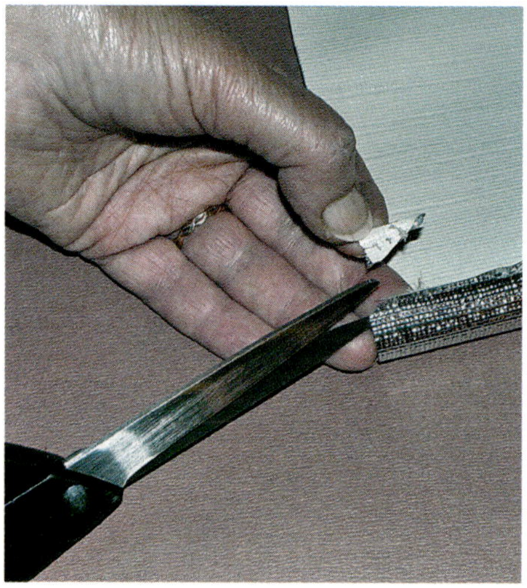

5-4-17. It's important to note that, when you slide the fabric back into the roller, you will need to cut off a corner of the fabric so that the bush can be pushed fully home.

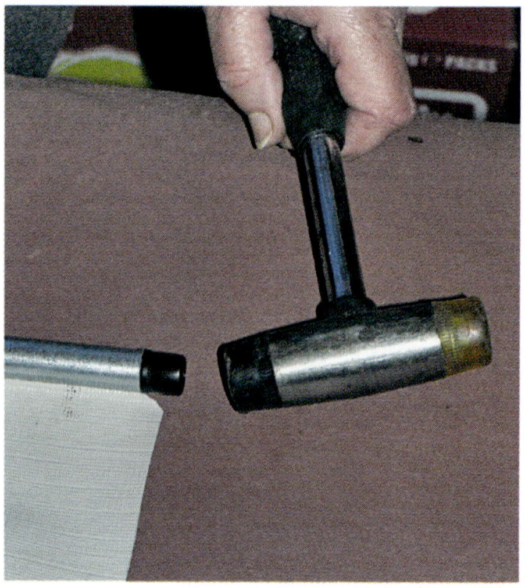

5-4-18. You will probably need to tap in the bush using a mallet and you must make sure that the slot in the bush lines up with the fabric.

5-4-19. This white plastic clip is screwed into place and the eye on the plastic clip on the bottom rod hooks over it, holding the blind down. Normally, the blind stays in the 'down' position by itself but it can leap up if knocked and this extra clip may save your blushes. In this particular instance, the glass on the side wall of the motor caravan runs behind the steel panel to which the clip would need to be fitted so I made a supplementary bracket, screwed the bracket down into a safe area and screwed the clip to the bracket.

5-5-20. As I said earlier, the neatly made CAK insulated stick-on screens are used in place of blinds for the windscreen and front door glasses.

5-4-21. The finished result is neat and unobstrusive. There are no flapping curtains in the way and the blinds can be closed very quickly indeed. This is an inexpensive and effective way of adding lightweight blinds to your Volkswagen T5.

Chapter 6
Extras & accessories

SAFETY FIRST!

- Always disconnect the battery before carrying out work on the vehicle.
- Disconnect the earth (ground) lead first and reconnect it last.
- Work on electrical systems must only be carried out be a competent auto electrician.
- Disconnect the battery before starting work, making sure that you have the radio code (otherwise you may not be able to use it again) and that no other items, such as an aftermarket alarm, will be affected.

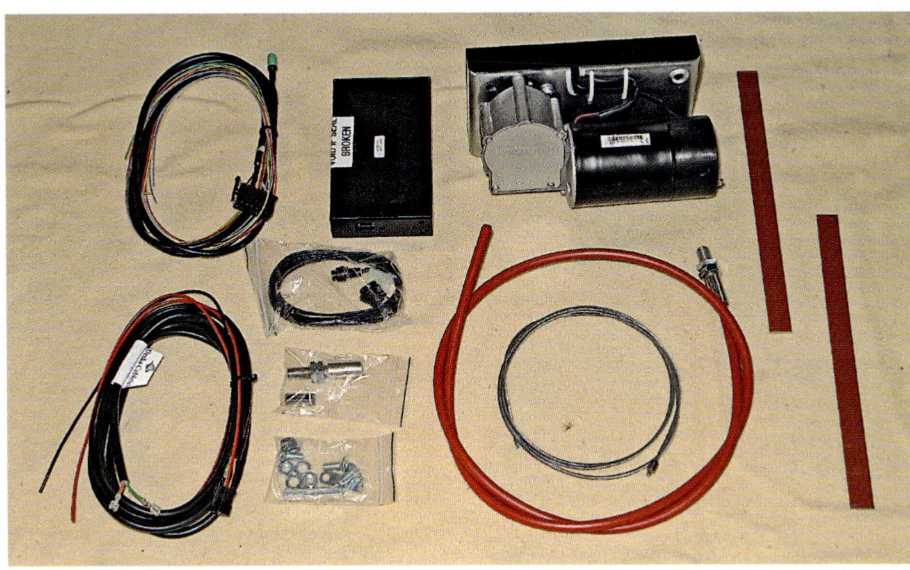

6-1-1. The entire AutoClutch kit weighs no more than a few kilos. By contrast, auto transmission might add, typically, around a couple of hundred kilograms to the kerb weight of a motor caravan's base vehicle.

SECTION 1. AUTOCLUTCH

AutoClutch – The third way?

Before we ordered our new VW T5 late in 2004, we thought long and hard about the gearchange. We both like driving autos but there are several penalties involved. One is that, if you want to tow (which we do), there is always the risk of over-stressing the torque converter – and I know 'cos I've done it! Another is that you're lugging a lot of extra weight around because automatic gearboxes are huge, heavy lumps. But the third – and worst, in my view – is that an auto transmission vehicle is always noticeably less economical. On paper, its performance will also be down but, because of the fact that autos shift-down more rapidly than you can do it manually, the loss of acceleration is not always apparent, certainly not with the more powerful engines. The drop in economy would certainly be noticed and I can't risk having ma wee Scottish grandmother spinning in her grave, now can I?

At first, we resigned ourselves to the old clutch-and-change routine of a manual gearbox. This was not too much of a hardship because the T5's gearchange is not just the best I've used on a van, it's one of the best gearshifts I've ever used, full stop. The VW clutch is light enough but using it can still be tiresome, not to say tiring, in heavy traffic. For anyone with even a minor disability that can be a real trial while for some, more heavily disabled people, it's just not possible. Then, we remembered a device called AutoClutch and wondered what it would be like.

AutoClutch (also known as 'Click 'n' Go' on the continent) is distributed in the UK solely by Vehvac Ltd, a company I have known for some years. I've been full of admiration of its high standards when it has fitted other devices for me in the past. So, I set out for Edenbridge, in Kent, in our T5 Camper with caravan hitched behind, to spend some time at Vehvac while it fitted the AutoClutch (and a couple of other items) for me. I camped in its quiet, secure car park; a facility that Vehvac can offer motor caravanning customers while they are having work carried out. What nice, thoughtful people they are!

The black box at the top of the picture is often called just that – the 'black box' – but is more properly known as the ECU (electronic control unit) and this controls the AutoClutch system. To its right, is the motor, which operates the clutch pedal in one of three modes, following the instructions of the ECU, according to a number of variables such as engine speed.

The remaining parts are the fixings, cables, switches and wiring. Vehvac point out that AutoClutch can only be fitted by an approved, trained supplier because it not only needs installing correctly, it also needs to be set up electronically so that it suits the characteristics of the vehicle to which it has been fitted.

6-1-4. Young Karl, one of Vehvac's engineers, starts by stripping off the trim panels in the engine bay and then unclipping the grille.

6-1-2. Whether AutoClutch is being fitted to the largest A-Class or the smallest van conversion, Vehvac's first job is to establish a suitable location for the motor unit. This powers the clutch when required.

6-1-5. With the lid taken off the motor unit, Karl works out a location on the front panel where brackets can be mounted for sitting the motor unit.

6-1-6. Karl uses Vehvac's portable cutting and folding tool for shaping the brackets, to make it possible to bolt them in place.

6-1-3. It's not just a matter of finding space in the engine bay for the motor unit; it's also a question of being able to run the electrical cables and (more importantly) the clutch operating cable in a smooth arc from its mounting on the bulkhead, adjacent to the clutch pedal, to the motor unit. If the operating cable has kinks or sharp bends in it, it could rapidly fail.

6-1-7. Keith, Vehvac's Workshop Manager, comes over to check Karl's handiwork. Once he's satisfied that everything fits as it should, Karl takes off the brackets once more, paints them and then fits the motor unit permanently to the engine bay front panel.

6-1-8. While Karl was working in the engine bay, Keith was inside the vehicle taking off the trim around the gearchange.

6-1-9. After easing off the finisher from the top of the gearchange knob, Keith took out the screw and simply lifted off the gearchange knob.

6-1-10. From underneath it, Keith removed the shroud, complete with the sleeve which operates the reverse gear lock. It's this that you raise with the first two fingers of your left hand when moving the gear stick into reverse.

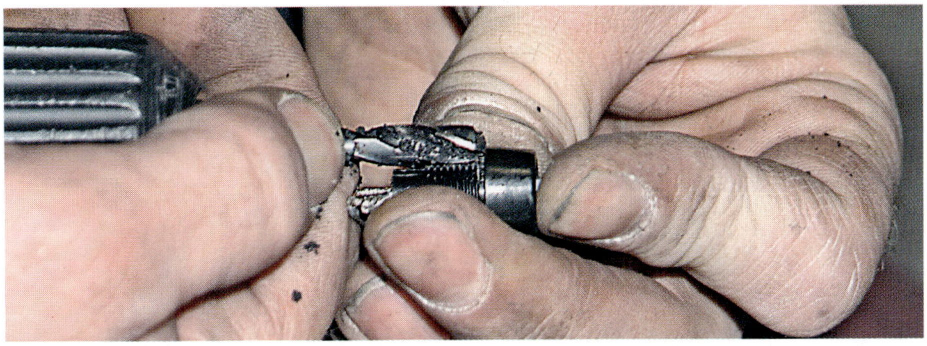

6-1-11. Keith has to fit a small push-button switch to the gear knob which means drilling a hole in the knob. He marks the drill to the depth of the threaded portion of the switch …

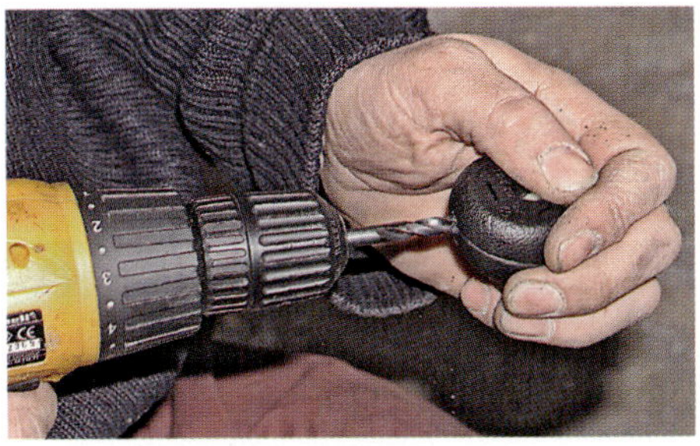

6-1-12. … and carefully drills, first a pilot hole, and then a full-sized hole in the knob where the switch is to be mounted.

6-1-13. The hole is not so large that the switch will drop out but is small enough so that the thread on the switch screws into and bites the plastic in the gear knob.

6-1-14. The cable from this switch has to pass down the inside of the gear knob and the only way of allowing it to do so is to cut a groove on the inside of the knob into which the cable will fit. I asked Keith what we did before the Dremel was invented and he just said, "struggled!".

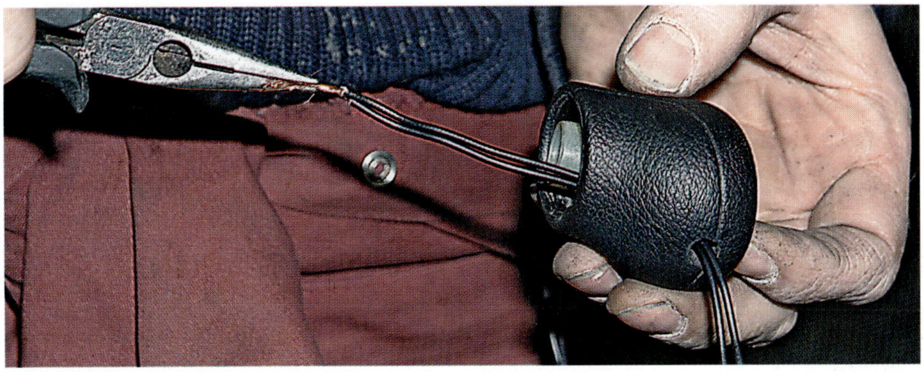

6-1-15. Keith connected his wiring to the switch and then passed the further end of the wire through the hole in the knob …

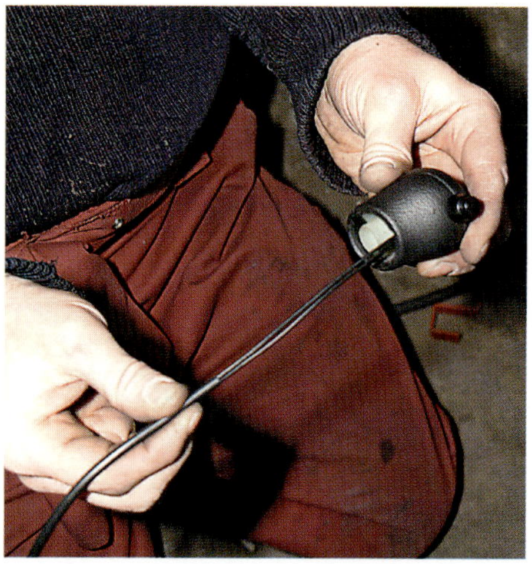

6-1-16. … and pulled it through making sure that the wire didn't twist as the push button was screwed into the knob.

6-1-19. Keith then eased the shroud back into place and fitted the whole assembly back onto the gearchange mechanism.

6-1-20. At this point, it all started getting a little complicated. The AutoClutch 'black box' needs to 'read' the speed of the engine at all times and the only way of doing so, on the T5, is to tap into the windings on the alternator. On some vehicles, it may be possible to tap into some other speed indicator but it's normal to have to go direct to the alternator itself. Karl removes the undertray from beneath the engine.

6-1-17. He now had to get the wire down the gear knob while still being able to operate the reverse lock. He had the bright idea of simply drilling the lock ring to allow the wire to pass through it.

6-1-21. Just to make life even more complicated, Karl found that the alternator couldn't be reached without moving the air conditioning pump which is sited beneath it. Fortunately, Vehvac's background is in air conditioning, so it was a simple matter for Karl to remove all of the gas from the air conditioning system, allowing him to break into it and move the air conditioning pump. This is something that absolutely must never be done other than by a specialist with the correct equipment and indeed, on older air conditioning systems, it is illegal to vent them to the atmosphere. This is because, on older systems in particular, the gas used is extremely harmful to the ozone layer.

6-1-18. This shows the gear knob and reverse gear operating mechanism assembled in place, with the AutoClutch switch and wire fitted.

6-1-22. If I had extreme difficulty in photographing this (which I did!) then imagine how difficult it was for Karl to carry out the work! He cut a small hole in the alternator casing and through it, adeptly soldered on the cable he needed. I thought this was rather clever of him!

6-1-23. Meanwhile, back in the cockpit, engineer Keith gets on with the next stage of the work. He has found that there is a suitable location on the bulkhead right next to the clutch pedal lever. On some vehicles, he has to fabricate a mounting bracket but on the T5, the bulkhead is handily flat at this point.

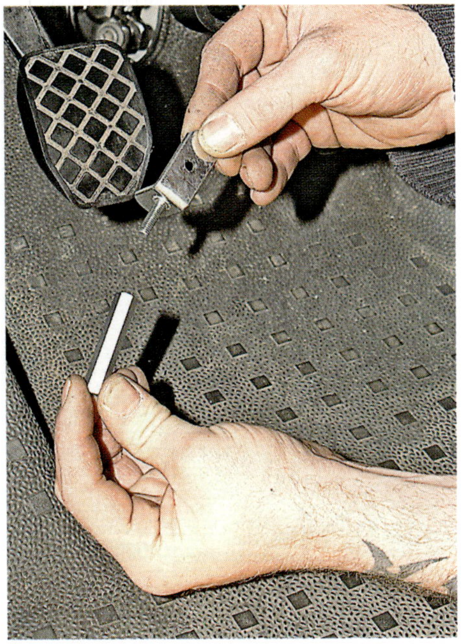

6-1-26. The cable mounting had to be fitted a few millimetres further over than would have been ideal because of the shape of the bulkhead, so Keith had to fit this extension to the clutch pedal lever.

6-1-27. With everything at the clutch pedal fully connected, you can see how the AutoClutch cable pulls down on the pedal to operate the clutch when needed.

6-1-24. This enables Keith to fit the mounting which he then screws permanently to the bulkhead.

6-1-25. Later, after pushing the cable inner through the mounting, he fits this connector (arrowed) to the end of the cable.

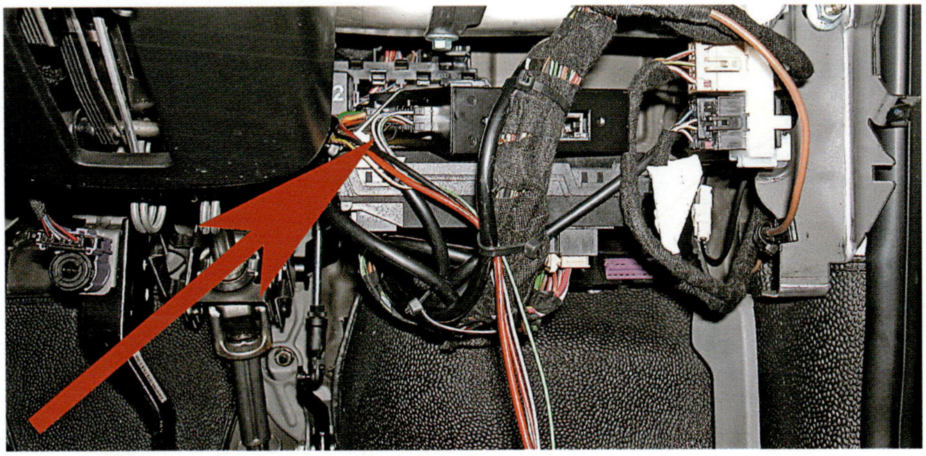

6-1-28. After removing some more dashboard trim panels, Keith found a suitable location (arrowed) for the 'black box', just to the right of the steering column. The wiring loom supplied with the kit was plugged into its relevant sockets in the back of the ECU.

6-1-29. Keith then needed to run connections from the ECU to the switch on the gear knob and the override switch on the dashboard, as well as to the motor unit in the engine bay.

6-1-30. With his right hand, Keith is pointing to the override switch, showing its chosen location on the dashboard. With the switch in the 'up' or 'off' position, you drive the vehicle as normal but when it is turned on, the AutoClutch operates as described later.

6-1-31. The main operating cable is supplied over-length so that the unit can be fitted to a wide range of vehicles. Keith trims of the surplus before connecting it to the motor unit.

6-1-32. He also brings the electrical cables through the bulkhead – he found a suitable blanking grommet and converted it to a wiring grommet – to connect the ECU with the motor unit.

6-1-33. Once everything was fitted, Keith connected up his electronic setting tool and sat in the vehicle to start adjusting the various settings available to him ...

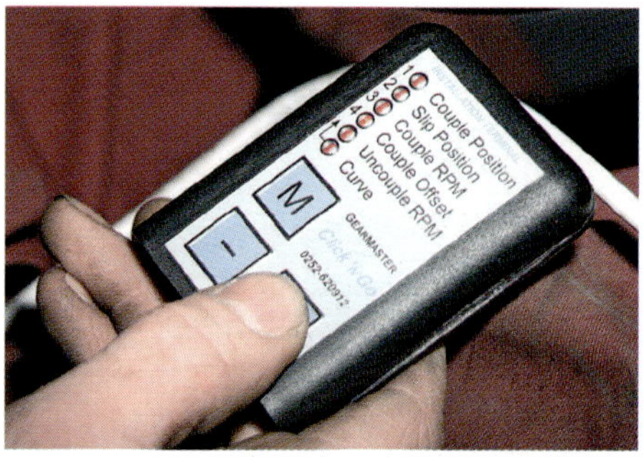

6-1-34. ... these include the clutch take up – which, in our case, he set to slightly slow so that it would also cope when we are towing – as well as engine speed points for the unit to cut in and out and a whole range of other settings to enable the unit to work smoothly.

6-1-35. When he was satisfied that everything was set up correctly, Keith disconnected the electronic setting tool and fitted the lid to the motor unit under the engine bay. Finally, he road tested the vehicle just to check that everything was working as it should.

6-1-36. Driving the vehicle with AutoClutch fitted isn't exactly like driving an auto and isn't exactly like driving a manual. It's like a driving a – well, an AutoClutch!

AUTOCLUTCH ON THE ROAD

With an automatic transmission, you just put the shift into 'Drive' and then forget about it. With a manual transmission, you also forget about what you're doing because you're so used to doing it. However, with AutoClutch, to start off with at least, you have to apply some thought to your driving again. This is because you're simply not used to declutching with the index finger (or thumb – the choice is yours) of your gear-changing hand. Once you get the hang of it, though, you come to see that it is so much easier to use, especially in heavy traffic with a lot of stop-start driving. Here's what you have to do.

1. With the gearbox in neutral, turn on the AutoClutch main switch. Nothing will happen until you depress the brake pedal and then, the clutch pedal depresses itself, as if by magic.
2. Slip the gearchange into first gear.
3. When you're ready to move off, take your foot off the brake pedal and the clutch will gently bite. If you need a fast getaway, just accelerate and the clutch will bite that much faster, just as if you were operating it with your left foot.
4. When you want to change gear, put your hand on the gearchange and press the button on the gearknob. Change gear, take your hand off the gearlever (or, at least, release the button) and the clutch takes care of itself.
5. When you want to stop, just brake to a halt in the normal way – except that, just like on an automatic, you only brake; you don't need to touch the clutch pedal. As the vehicle's speed drops, the clutch disengages and you come to a halt in the normal way.
6. If you're coming up to an traffic island and don't want to fully stop, just slip the gearchange into second, release the brake and away you go. If you stop, keep your foot on the brake, apply first gear and release the brake, as before, when you're ready to move off.
7. If you want to change to a lower gear when going downhill, I found that using the button on the gearknob caused a jerk as the clutch re-applied itself. There are two ways of overcoming this. One is to increase engine speed with the accelerator, so that the engine speed is close to the one it needs to be when it is in the lower gear – this is not always easy to judge. A simpler way is to apply the brake (which always depresses the clutch), shift down a gear or gears, then take your foot off the brake pedal and the clutch applies the lower gear perfectly smoothly.

If you don't want to use the AutoClutch facility or someone new is driving the vehicle, you can simply switch the unit off at the master switch on the dashboard and then the vehicle reverts to normal use. What's more, if you want to change gear conventionally (or if you forget and accidentally revert to 'normal' driving), AutoClutch doesn't mind; you just do it!

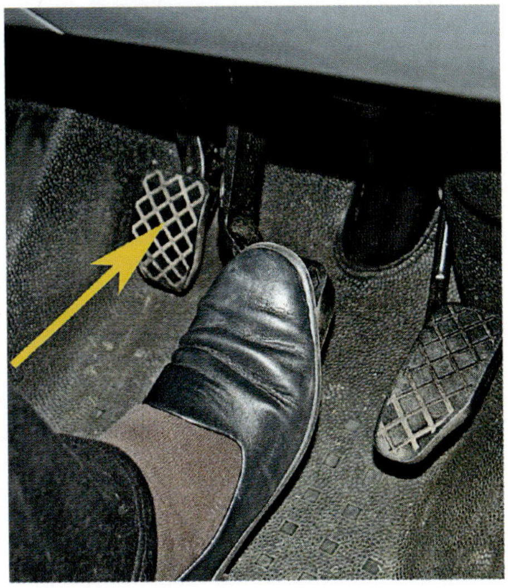

6-1-37. There are two important points in connection with using an AutoClutch.
• Firstly, there are two ways of making AutoClutch operate the clutch pedal. One is with the switch on the gearknob; the other is by applying the brake pedal. You use whichever is right for the circumstances. Normally, you use the brake pedal for stopping and starting plus changing down when going downhill, and the button for gearchanging. Whichever you use, the AutoClutch mechanism moves by 50mm, so the fitter will have set the height of the cable connection on the pedal lever so that the AutoClutch motor moves the pedal by the correct amount.
• The second point is that you need to familiarise yourself with AutoClutch – just as you would with an auto gearchange if you'd never driven one before. But once learned, you'll appreciate the benefits of easier gearchanging and starting away – and no more aching left leg in the rush-hour traffic – with no performance or fuel consumption losses to contend with.

Incidentally, it's worth pointing out that one major Vehvac customer is the AA. When its patrol men have to carry a full complement of passengers in one of its crew-cab service vehicles, there often isn't room for the driver to use the clutch without tying himself in knots. AutoClutch solves the problem! The device is also approved by the German TÜV testing organisation.

Vehvac also says that, if you change your vehicle, they can simply swap the AutoClutch system over to the new vehicle for you.

SECTION 2. REVERSING SENSORS

Reversing your camper can be a tricky business, and there's always a worrying risk of there being an unseen obstacle and the truly frightening thought of there being a child just out of your line of vision. Reversing sensors make sense in more ways than one! Here, Vehvac, the well-known supplier of electrical and electronic equipment for motor caravans, fits Rostra ParkPilot reversing sensors to the Volkswagen T5 Transporter.

Rostra is an American manufacturer of OE-quality equipment. I've been using Rostra stuff for many years now and I've always been impressed by the quality of its equipment and the way in which it blends smoothly with the fixtures and fittings of most vehicles.

Stripdown

You have to remove one of the rear light clusters so that wires can be fed through into the vehicle's interior.

6-2-4. Karl was then able to pull away the trim then lift the panel, freeing the hooks on the leading edge seen here, before removing completely.

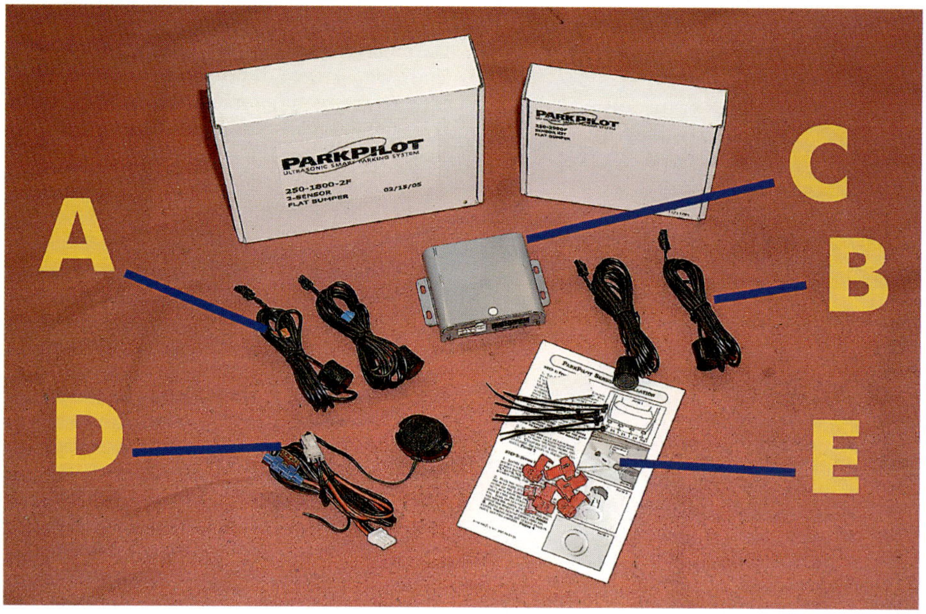

6-2-1. These are the components supplied as part of the Rostra ParkPilot kit:
A: Two sensors, supplied as standard.
B: Two extra sensors; optional extras and recommended for motor caravans.
C: Electronic Control Unit (ECU).
D: Warning buzzer.
E: Instructions, cable ties and Scotchlok wiring connectors – not suitable for use in exposed locations.

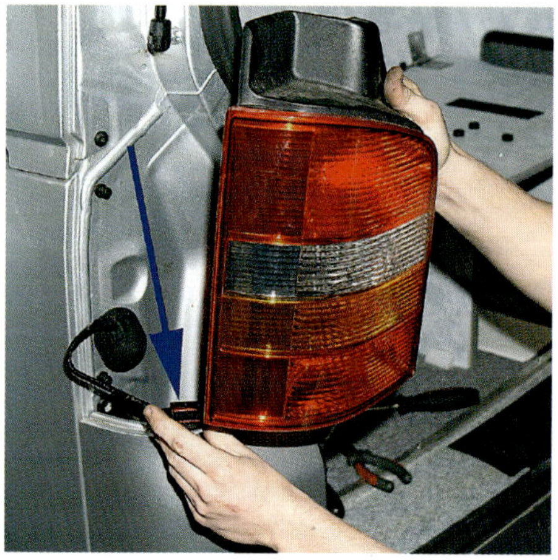

6-2-2. Vehvac's young engineer, Karl, started by taking out the screws, unclipping the light lens and disconnecting the electrical plug (arrowed).

6-2-3. These special plastic clips hold the rear quarter panels in place. Use an Allen key to unscrew the centre, which releases the tension on the outer section and allows it all to be removed.

6-2-5. There was more! The same technique as described in step 6-2-3 was used to remove the cover plate from behind the quarter panel. This gave access to behind the top of the bumper.

Sensor location

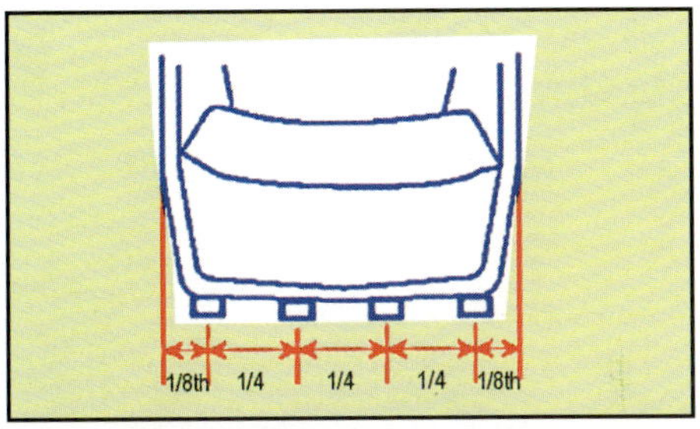

6-2-6. The ParkPilot sensors are designed to mount flush with the bumper. The positioning of the bumper-mounted sensors is important. The ideal location will be a flat surface that is perpendicular to the ground and 150mm to 550mm (18in to 22in) off the ground.
For steeply angled bumpers, where a perpendicular surface is unavailable, you would need to use the special angled-bezel sensors, part no. 250-2990a, available from Rostra.

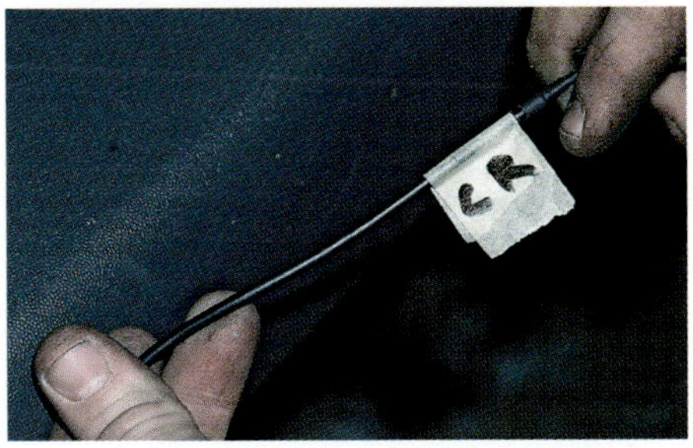

6-2-11. Using the wiring diagram supplied, he looked for tags on the sensor wires that correspond to their bumper location. They should be marked 'L' (left), 'CL' (centre left), 'CR' (centre right), and 'R' (right). Ours weren't, so he labelled each of the sensor wires with a tag of masking tape.

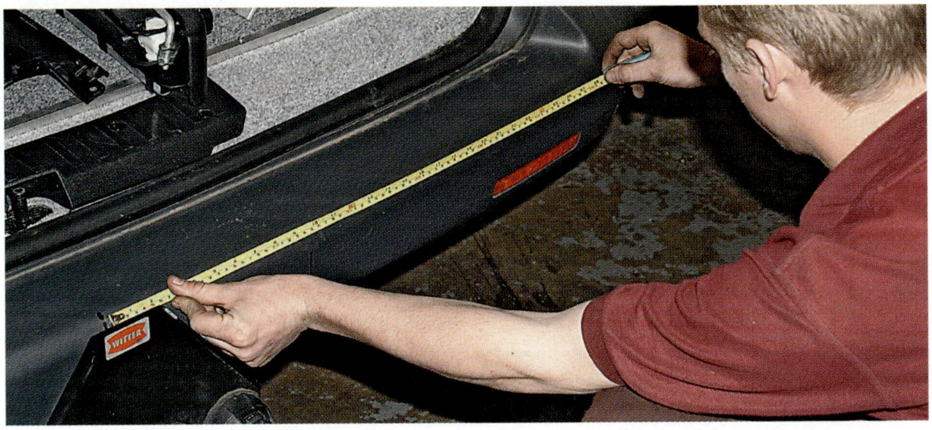

6-2-7. Make sure there is room behind the bumper, or panel to which they are being fitted, for the body of the sensor and its wire harness BEFORE drilling!
For two sensor systems, place each sensor ¼ of the distance from each end.
For four sensor systems, you measure the width of the bumper and mark locations at ⅛ and ⅜ distance in from each end as shown.

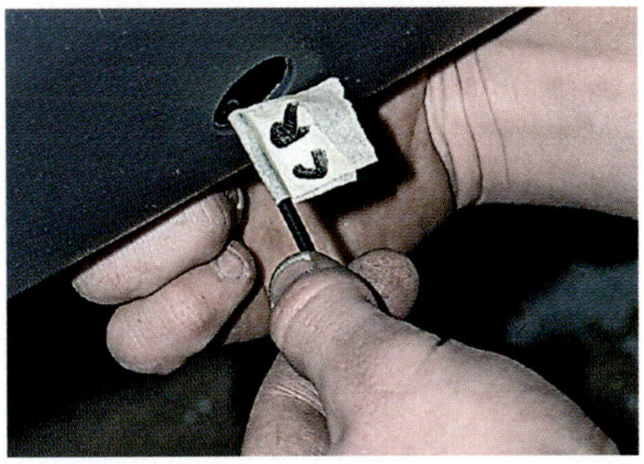

6-2-12. Each one was pushed through its relevant hole until it was accessible from the inside of the bumper. You have to route the harness away from any sharp edges and pull it until the sensor is at the level of the bumper fascia.

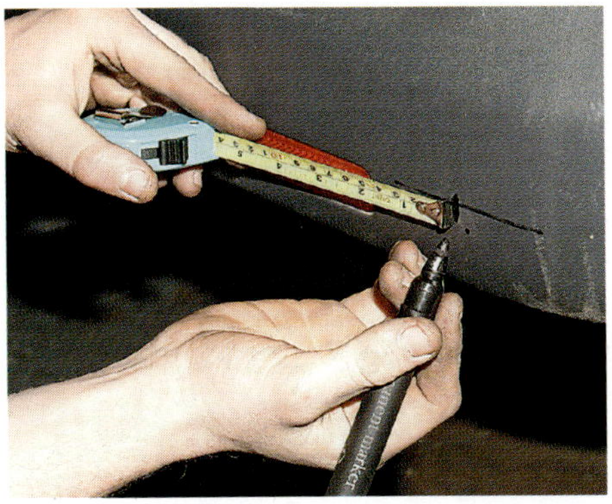

6-2-8. Karl marked the surface of the bumper with a non-indelible felt pen.

Mount sensors

6-2-9. Karl used a stepped hole cutter and marked the 22mm position required with the same felt pen so that he wouldn't accidentally drill too far.

6-2-10. He then drilled a hole at each mark, holding the drill steady and level. He had to carefully use a fine metal file to remove burrs of plastic from the backs of the holes so that the sensors would clip into place.

6-2-13. Next, he had to turn the sensor so that the mounting tab with the arrow on it is facing the top of the vehicle.

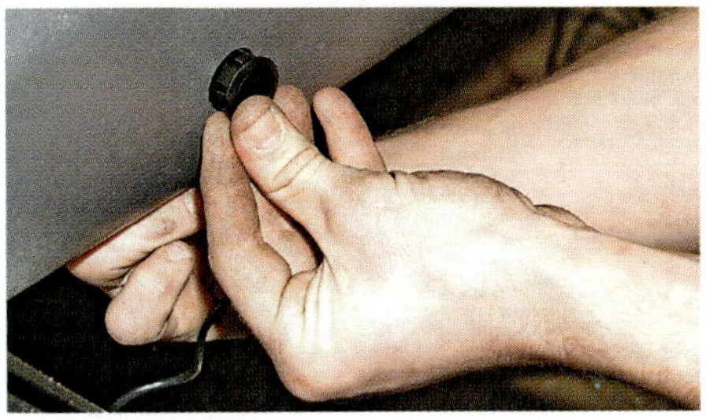

6-2-14. He pressed the sensor firmly into the fascia, making sure the sensor fitted with a 'click'.

Mount electronic control and buzzer units

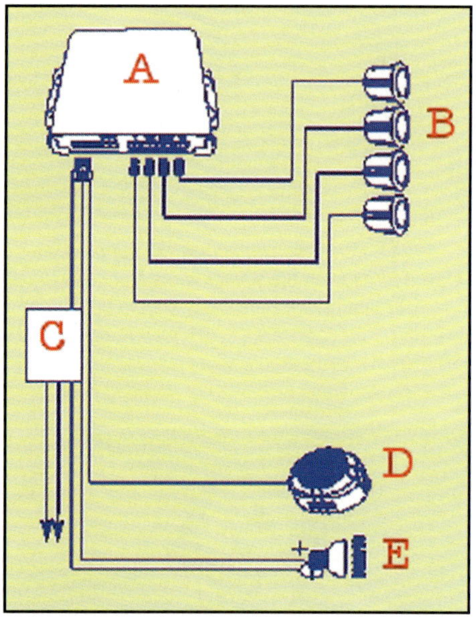

6-2-15. This wiring diagram shows how each part of the system has its own harness with a plug on the end. Each plug is simply plugged into its host component.
A = ECU
B = Sensors
C = Optional towing connections (so that reversing sensor does not sound when a towed trailer is detected by the sensors).
D = Buzzer
E = Reversing light on vehicle

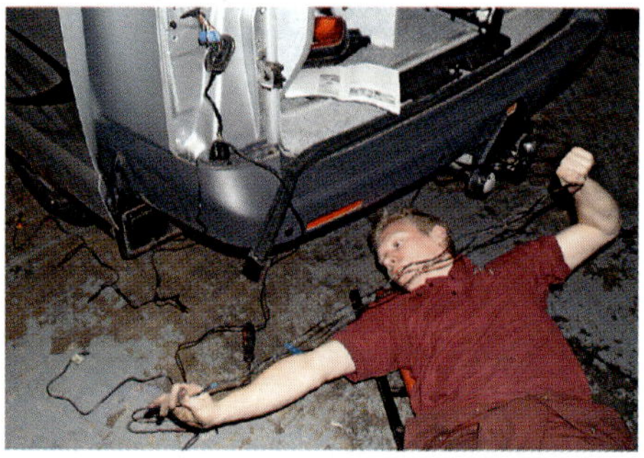

6-2-16. Karl next routed the various wires of the ParkPilot harnesses to the underside of the vehicle.

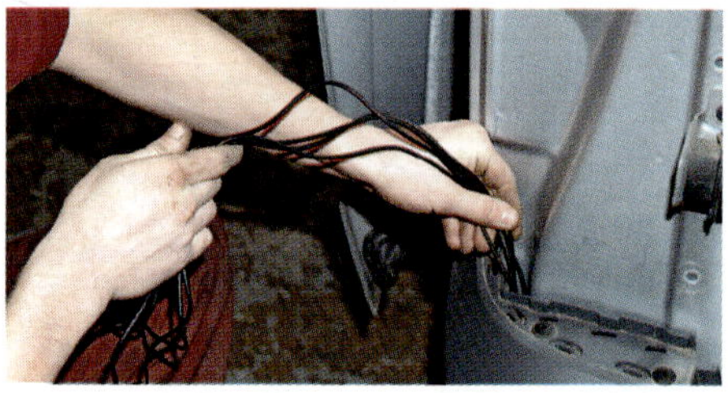

6-2-17. They then passed behind the bumper and up through the access hole gained by removing the components seen earlier.

6-2-18. A large grommet carrying the existing wiring loom was removed and the new wires passed through it before refitting it securely.

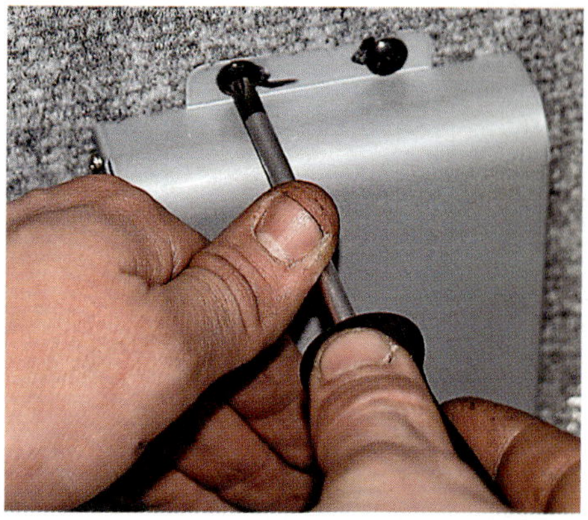

6-2-19. Using the supplied Velcro pad, you can mount the ECU on or behind a trim panel in the cargo area but there is also a mounting flange with holes so you can screw it down if you prefer.

The ECU must be mounted inside the vehicle away from areas prone to moisture. Also, make sure the in-line fuse holder is on the inside of the vehicle.
Secure excess wire with cable ties.

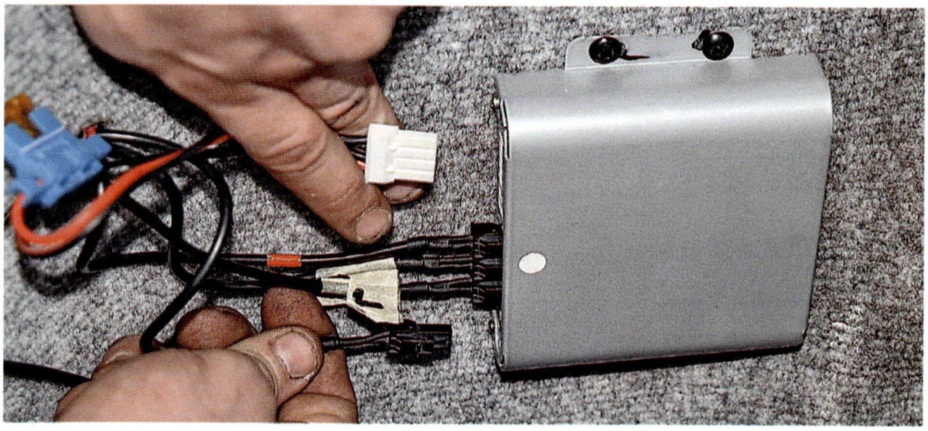

6-2-20. Karl next connected four sensor harness plugs to the corresponding sockets on the control module (ECU) and the plug for the buzzer unit. The 'HI/LO/OFF' switch on the buzzer unit is preset to the 'HI' setting. Verify this before mounting it.

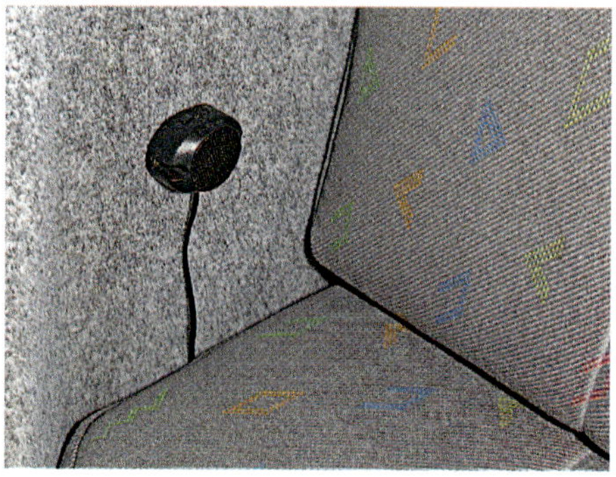

6-2-21. The buzzer can be mounted in an inconspicuous position away from potential damage, such as in the bed box but then, you might not be able to hear it. I compromised with a position on the side-wall.

6-2-22. The final workshop job was for Vehvac's senior engineer, Keith, to make the final power connections to the ECU and check the installation with his test meter.

Test the system

Here's how to make sure the unit is working correctly:

- Turn the ignition to the 'ON' position, engage the parking brake and put the vehicle into reverse. The alarm unit will alert two quick beeps to indicate that the system is active. Average distances are as follows:
- Zone 1 (slow beeping): From about 1.5m to 900mm (60in to 36in)
- Zone 2 (fast beeping): From about 900mm to 150mm (36in to 18in)
- Zone 3 (solid tone): About 150mm (18in) or less.

6-2-23. This installation looks similar to the one fitted by Volkswagen in the factory, and shows the location of the four sensors.

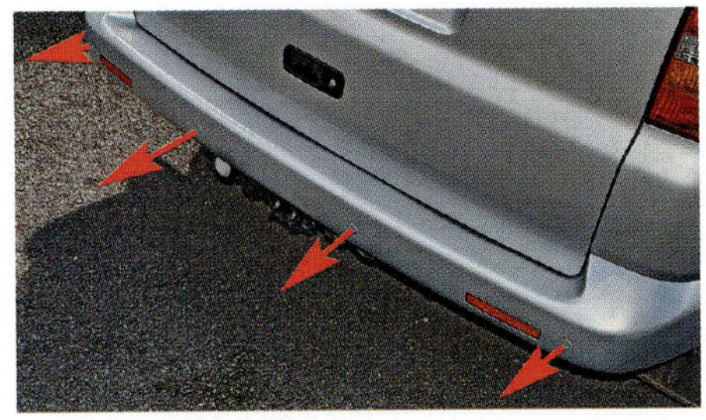

6-2-24. This also reminds you of the extent of that blind spot beneath the rear window and just why reversing sensors are next to essential for the safety-conscious driver.

SECTION 3. TOW BRACKET PART A. FITTING A FIXED WITTER TOWBRACKET

Fitting a tow bracket to a modern panel van tends to be more straightforward than to a coachbuilt because the manufacturers will have been able to build a towbracket that is fully compliant with the relevant EC regulations. This means that it has to have been tested and approved for safety and indicated load capacity.

The process is different for each manufacturer and there are even differences between models but there are many aspects of the work that will be common to all modern vehicles. We show leading towing equipment experts, Towcraft, in the West Midlands, first fitting a type-approved Witter tow bracket to our new Volkswagen T5 van and then, after its conversion, fitting a Brink removable-type in its place. In the first section, you're seeing it in its bare-van state, prior to conversion. It meant that there would be slightly less for the Towcraft fitters to remove beforehand but the job is essentially the same for a fully converted vehicle.

The point of all this is that dismantling modern vehicles is meant for main dealers who will have all of the special tools and equipment necessary. If you don't have it, you have to show a little bit of ingenuity and sometimes, quite a lot of head-scratching too!

6-3-A1. Martin, the main man in the workshop, sets out the Witter towbracket and accessories ready to fit to our new van. As you can see, he's already clipped the fitting instructions to his board so that he can refer to them as he goes along.

6-3-A2. Martin starts by unscrewing the rear light unit from the body. It's worth pointing out that these are special plastic screws which, as they are unscrewed, allow the plug beneath to come loose, freeing the component being held in place.

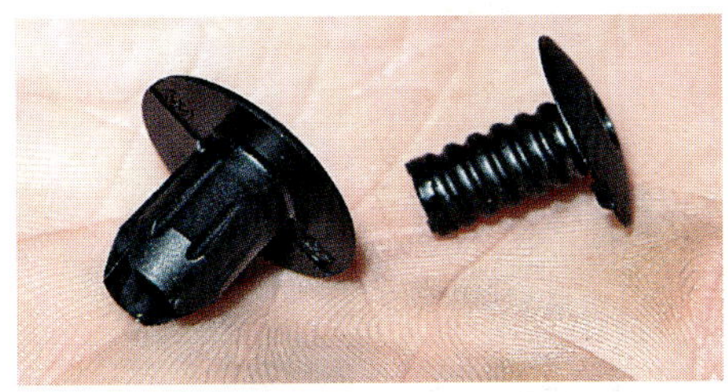

6-3-A3. These are the components of the special screws. It is highly likely that these are solely used by Volkswagen but each manufacturer seems to have its own variation on the theme and these days, it's very unusual to see ordinary steel screws in use. We found the best way of removing these was with a Torx bit, rather than the Allen key that they appeared to require because the plastic is soft and the Allen key is inclined to turn in the recessed hexagon.

6-3-A4. Martin lifts away the light unit …

6-3-A5. … far enough to be able to get at the clip holding the wiring plug and socket to the back of the light unit. While Martin held the unit, another pair of hands carefully levered the clip free to allow the wiring plug to be removed. Again, there are many different types of fixing, varying not only be manufacturer but by location and year. All you have to remember is that they ARE intended to come apart so you just have to think your way through the puzzle.

6-3-A6. Here's another example of a Chinese puzzle. The plastic body panel that fits beneath the light units is simply clipped into place. Until it's removed, there is no way you can see that this is the case but after spending time looking over it, it becomes obvious that there are no fitting screws and that it must therefore clip into place. The only question that remains is – how? Martin solved the problem by carefully pushing and sliding in the only two possible directions, which were upwards and to the right. When you think about it, the direction had to be upwards because the light unit was holding the panel in place, preventing it from sliding. It's all a bit Bletchley Park at times!

6-3-A7. Happily, the trim panel from beneath was held on with some more of those plastic screws and its removal was obvious.

6-3-A8. Paul got ready to remove the rear bumper by unscrewing some of the trim in the rear wheel arch. Note how a Torx bit (or in some cases, a screwdriver) used on a ratchet wrench can often enable you to get into a space where a screwdriver won't fit.

6-3-A9. On the other side of the van, you can see that the wheel arch liner could be eased back, exposing metal screws with a conventional Phillips head.

6-3-A10. Meanwhile, Martin was removing the spare wheel carrier …

6-3-A11. ... so that Paul could gain access to these bumper mounting brackets. He removed the hexagonal head bolts in the normal way.

6-3-A12. Paul removes another bracket holding the bumper in place, this one doubling up as an attachment point for the mud flap, as well as for the front-end of the undertray.

6-3-A13. With a little help from his colleague, Gavin, Paul lifts the detached rear bumper from the vehicle.

6-3-A14. Then it was Martin's turn again as he removed the bolts holding the bumper support panel in place ...

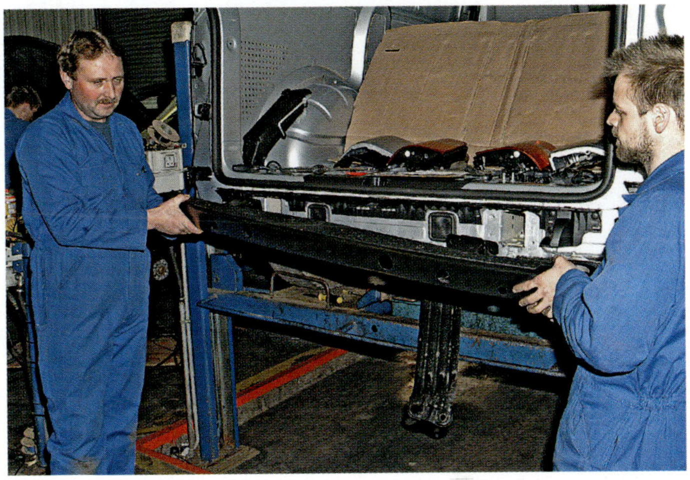

6-3-A15. ... allowing him and Paul to lift the panel away. It was not going to be reused.

6-3-A16. Back beneath the vehicle, Martin removes the remaining bolts – some of them also holding brackets in place such as this one – holding the undertray in place.

6-3-A17. Not all of the brackets had to be removed. Some of them could be slackened where they also pass through the undertray but left in place where they did not. There is a lot more ingenuity required when working on modern vehicles when compared with the classics!

6-3-A18. Martin and Paul now lift the undertray from beneath the rear of the van.

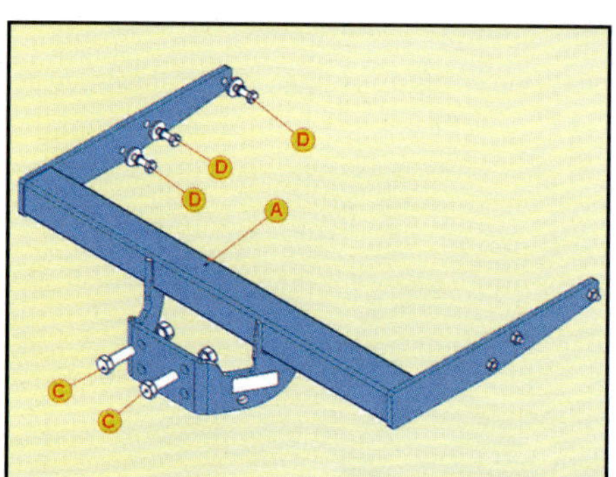

6-3-A19. These are the components of this particular Witter towbracket. Naturally, each vehicle requires a different shaped bracket and passenger-carrying vehicles (from S-registration onwards) must have an EC Type Approved towbar fitted.
A – Witter towbracket
C – towball mounting bolts
D – towbracket mounting bolts – three per side

Important note: There may be reinforcing components to remove from some models. See the notes associated with Part B of this section.

6-3-A20. Martin and Paul offer up the Witter towbracket, sliding the mounting arms into the open chassis rails. Apparently, some T5 vans are fitted with chassis rail end stiffeners and if this is the case, they must be removed and discarded.

6-3-A21. With the towbracket held lightly in position, Paul fits the three bolts per side, along with their flat washers and plain washers, passing them through the holes that are already found in the Volkswagen chassis rails.

6-3-A22. Going against the Witter instructions, Paul now tightens each of the six bolts to the recommended torque of 53Nm. You can see later why Witter don't recommend that the bolts are tightened at this stage but, in practice, it all worked out fine!

6-3-A23. With the easiest part of the job out of the way, the guys moved on to fitting up the electrical components. Paul removes the rear side panels from inside the van …

6-3-A24. … and Martin pushes a fish wire – a piece of moderately stiff but still bendable wire – through the holes in the rear panel, so that he can pass the electrical cabling through the body for wiring in the towbracket connections.

6-3-A26. The same process is used for passing cables from one side of the vehicle to the other, routing them through enclosed panels, both for aesthetic reasons and to protect the cables from damage.

6-3-A27. In the meantime, Paul fits the 12N and 12S sockets to the rear of the van. In our case, these sockets are fitted to a Witter bumper protector which is an essential accessory, in my view. It prevents the tow hitch on your trailer or caravan damaging the rear bumper if you misjudge things slightly when hitching up.

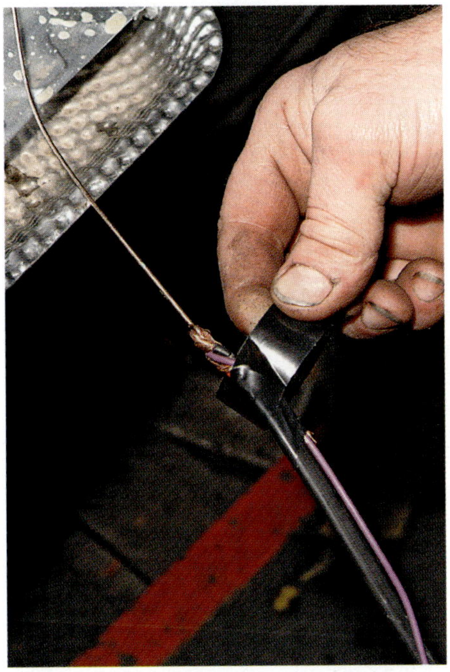

6-3-A25. He securely fixes the ends of the cables he's going to use to the end of the fish wire and wraps insulation tape round them for belts and braces effect and to prevent the ends of the cables from snagging as the fish wire is pulled through.

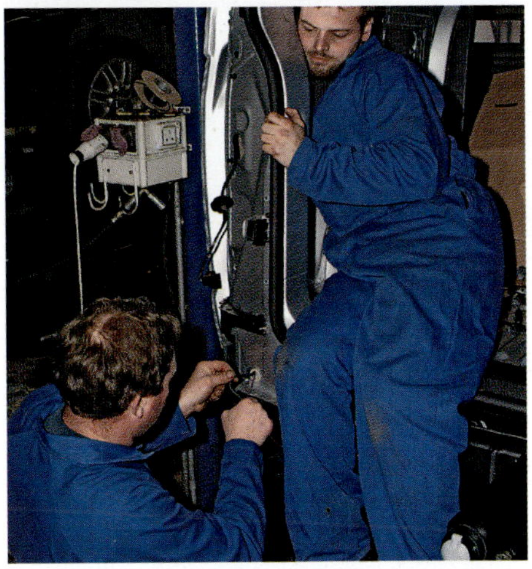

6-3-A28. Having the rear sockets in place enabled Paul and Martin to judge the correct lengths of the cables they were fitting as they installed them in the back of the vehicle.

6-3-A29. Martin then went to the front of the vehicle and took a main feed from the battery, which he protected with a fuse at the battery-end. This is the way that Towcraft install tow wiring. An alternative is to use the (expensive) dedicated VW wiring kit which plugs in to the vehicle's existing wiring. If you don't use this kit, it is essential that an entirely different process is followed. Towcraft uses electronics specifically designed to be compatible with modern vehicle electrical systems to overcome any potential problems and we'll come to that in a moment.

6-3-A30. It takes a couple of blokes and a fish wire to 'fish' the wiring along an under-vehicle route: one that avoids hot exhaust components while protecting the cable from the elements.

6-3-A31. This wiring is also passed through enclosed body panels until it reaches the rear of the vehicle …

6-3-A32. … where it is brought into alignment with the more complex wiring at the rear of the vehicle.

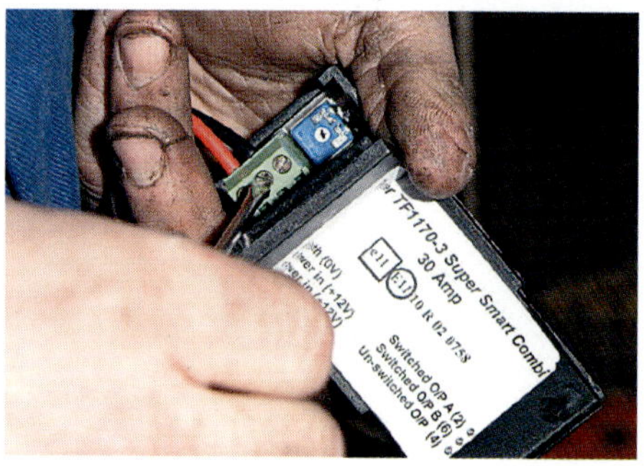

6-3-A33. This electronic box of tricks is designed to overcome any problem that you may have by tapping into the vehicle's existing wiring, as you would have done in the 'old days'. If you tap into a modern vehicle's wiring, you're likely to cause major problems with the vehicle's electrical circuitry. For that reason, this little lad takes its feed from the battery, judges when a particular lighting circuit is in use, without actually taking any detectable current from it, and supplies current to the relevant part of the towing circuitry direct from the battery.

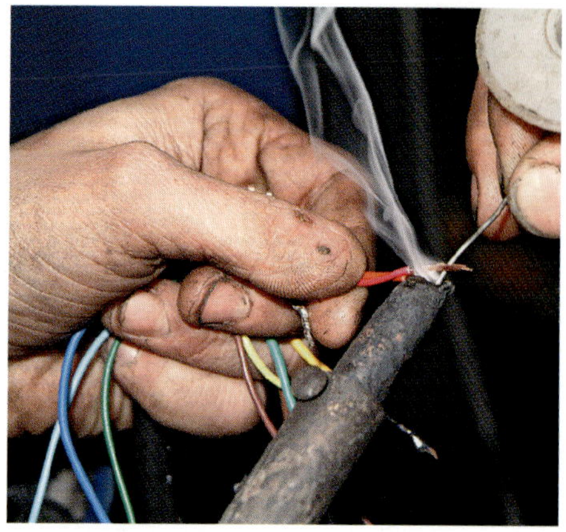

6-3-A34. This means that all of the cables for the rear sockets have to pass though the electronic gizmo. Martin 'tins' the cable ends with solder so that join cables are permanently fastened, and screwed-down connections are made more secure.

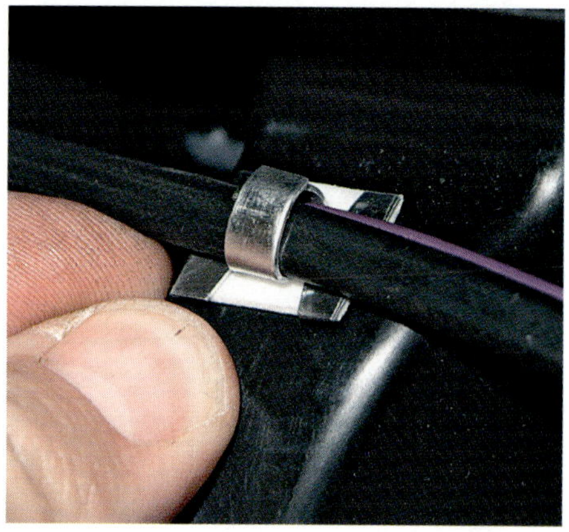

6-3-A35. On the subject of secure, any cables or groups of cables that are left visible are held in place with self-adhesive cable clips.

6-3-A36. Where holes have had to be drilled and grommets fitted, they are treated with underbody wax to prevent corrosion in future.

6-3-A37. Note that the rear sockets are fitted to the Witter protection plate which is still only temporarily mounted to the towbracket. Before reassembling any of the body components, Paul uses Towcraft's custom-built test rig, which replicates the electrical loading of a Caravan or Trailer, thereby testing the 12N/12S electrics under full operating conditions.

6-3-A38. With the top of the towbracket protected, it proved to be just possible to fit the bumper back onto the vehicle. This is what Witter's instructions were warning about, but in the event, turned out to be no problem. Witter were suggesting that the three bolts on each side, holding the bracket to the chassis, should be left loose so that the towbracket could be tilted down slightly while the bumper is fitted. That undoubtedly would have made things slightly easier.

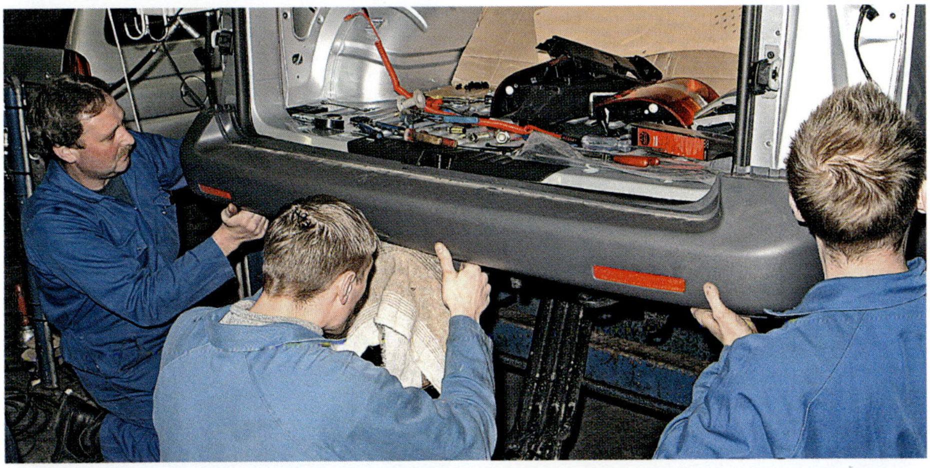

6-3-A39. Next, the undertray was refitted to the underside of the vehicle …

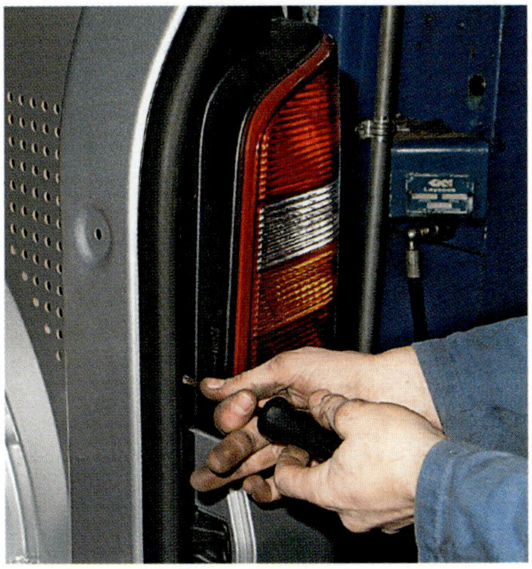

6-3-A40. … and the rear panels and rear lights fixed back into place.

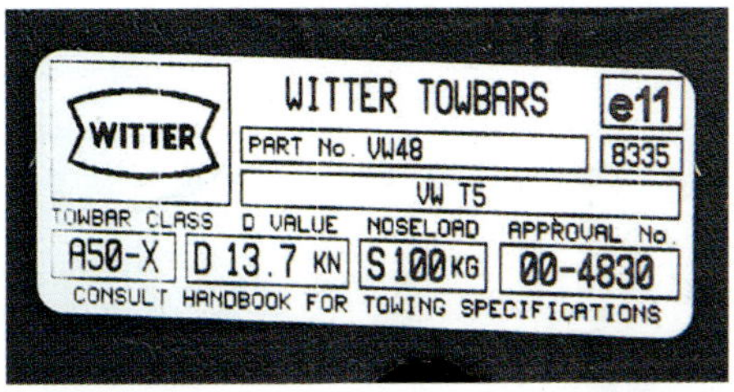

6-3-A41. At this point, it's worth pointing out that the tow vehicle will have its own towing limits which should be stated in your handbook, on the VIN plate or the information should be given to you by your local vehicle dealership. The towbracket also has its own tow limits and those will be shown on the plate mounted on the towbracket as shown here. The third item with its own limits will be the towball you fit to the vehicle.

6-3-A42. Witter supply their own brand of towballs but we will be towing a caravan fitted with an Al-Ko hitch. Al-Ko specify that their towballs have different dimensions to standard towballs to provide clearance for the Al-Ko hitch and so we fitted an Al-Ko towball. Towcraft, quite correctly, always remove any paint or plating from the ball because friction tow hitches, such as those fitted by Al-Ko, will be damaged unless they operate on clean, non-greasy metal.

6-3-A43. Towcraft can supply an attractive 'flipper' towball cover but unfortunately, it can't be fitted to the larger Al-Ko ball, so we fitted one of Al-Ko's own ball covers.

6-3-A44. The completed Witter towbracket looks as if it was made to fit – which of course it was! This is the second time that I've had Towcraft fit a towbracket to one of my vehicles and I must say that I'm very impressed by their high standards of workmanship – and I'm not easily pleased!

PART B. FITTING A DETACHABLE BRINK TOWBRACKET

This must be read in connection with Part A, where information on stripping rear lights and surrounds, removing the bumper reinforcement panel and connecting wiring are covered.

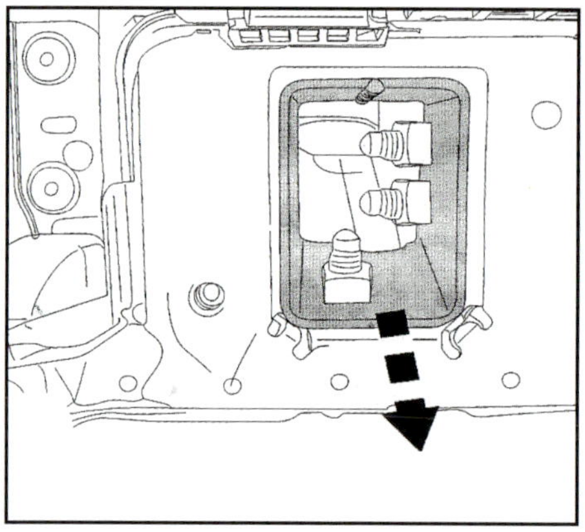

6-3-B1. The unit shown here is the 'OE' detachable towbracket, made by Brink and supplied to VW dealerships in the UK, at the time of writing. Again, the experts at Towcraft, who can supply all available towing equipment for your VW T5, showed how the job should be done.

6-3-B2. When fitted, you have to remove the reinforcement tube from the chassis members.

6-3-B3. From left-to-right, Towcraft's MD, Trevor, takes one end of the bumper while Martin prepares to insert the new Brink towbracket and Chris holds the other end of the bumper.

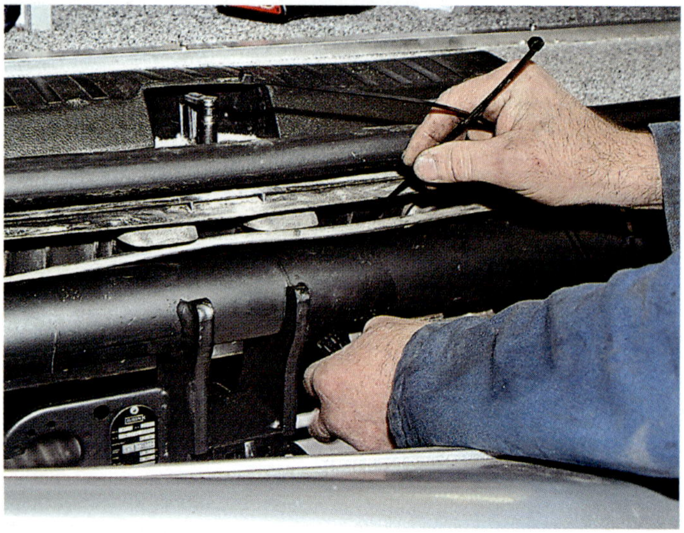

6-3-B4. Martin ensures that the bumper is fully home and that the bolt holes inside are lined up.

6-3-B5. Wiring that needs to pass from one side of the bumper to the other is held to the towbracket tube with cable ties.

6-3-B6. Martin makes certain that the bumper will fit and is not in any way impeded by the towbracket ...

6-3-B7. ... then loosely inserts the three mounting bolts on each side.

6-3-B8. These are then tightened to the recommended torque setting of 79Nm.

6-3-B9. The Brink towbracket only has a single electrical socket mounting, so Martin fits a double-adaptor. One side is split to allow it to pass over the cable without having to completely re-wire. Where a new installation is carried out, this would not be necessary.

6-3-B10. No modifications are required to the bumper but the undertray fouls on the towbracket here.

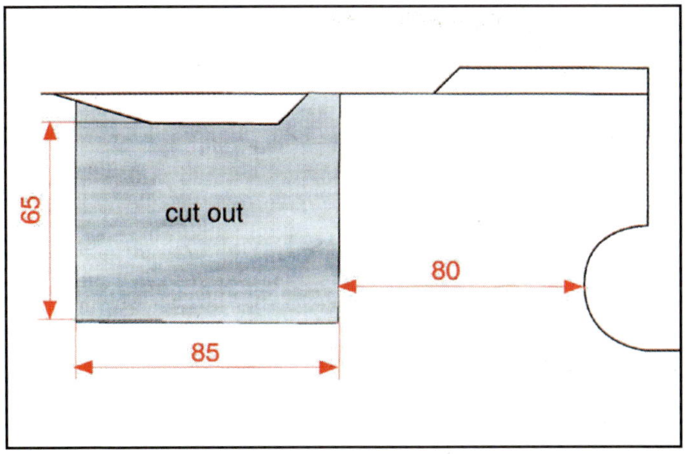

6-3-B11. These are the instructions given by Brink indicating the size of the cutaway required.

6-3-B12. Martin marked out the redundant material, cut where he could with tin snips and then finished off with a jigsaw.

6-3-B13. Martin refitted the 12N and 12S sockets using stainless steel screws and locknuts from Screwfix. Mild steel screws are notorious for rusting solid in this location.

How to use the Brink detachable towball

6-3-B14. Trevor Guest, Towcraft's MD, demonstrates how quick and easy it is to attach and remove this towbracket.

6-3-B16. Trevor introduces the towball into the housing in the towbracket.

6-3-B15. When the towball is not fitted, this clip-in filler plug is used. You simply pull it out with thumb and forefinger.

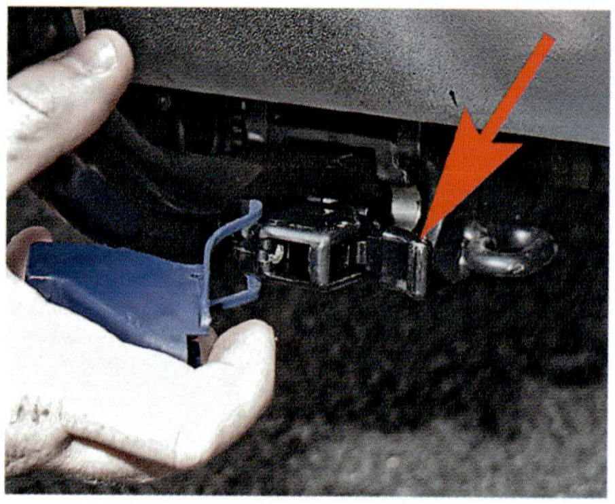

6-3-B17. Note that before the towball is located in its housing, the safety catch (arrowed) will be in the forward position, exposing a mouth or slot just to the left of it.

6-3-B18. As the towball is pushed fully home, it can be heard to locate with a snap as the safety catch (arrowed) clicks back into the position shown here.

6-3-B19. So that the towbracket can not easily be unhitched (which would make it rather easy to steal the caravan when connected), there is a small lock that can be inserted into the towbracket, preventing it from being removed without the key.

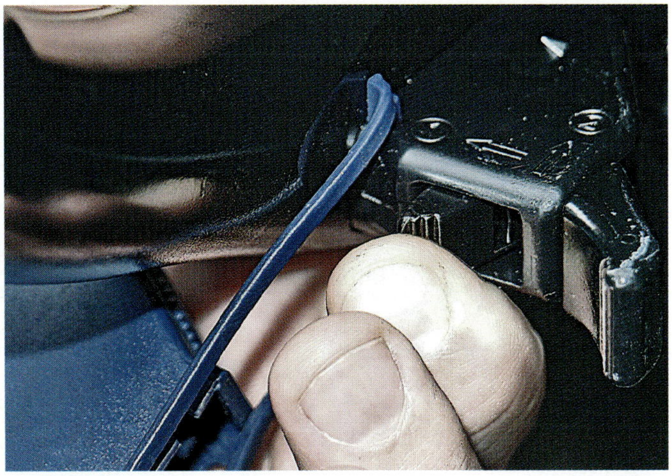

6-3-B20. To remove the towball, Trevor demonstrates how the lock catch has to be pressed to one side …

6-3-B21. … followed by the main safety catch …

6-3-B22. … after which, the towball assembly can be removed.

6-3-B23. With its protective rubber cover in place, the Brink detachable towball looks much like any other swan neck towbracket when in place but it's very discrete, as can be seen in picture 6-3-B14, when removed.

SECTION 4. BODY DECALS

Here's how to fit a set of body decals to your T5 – and how to remove old ones if you need to.

6-4-1. This is the decals set for the Leisuredrive Crusader, though the principles shown here apply to any other similar stick-on transfer set.

6-4-2. Roy started by using a degreasing agent over the whole area on which the decals were to be fixed. If your vehicle has been waxed or has gone through a carwash, you will need to use a proprietary brand of panel wipe such as that produced by Autopaint and featured elsewhere in this manual.

6-4-3. *It's essential that the decals are fitted both parallel to the pressings on the side of the vehicle and level so that they don't appear wavy. Roy used a soft pencil to mark the edge of where he wanted the decal to be positioned – it's difficult to know what else you could use apart from, perhaps, a china graph pencil. An indelible felt pen has the disadvantage that it's – uh, indelible! – a water-based felt pen will wash off, as you will see in the following steps and you can't use masking tape for the obvious reason that the decals have got to be stuck directly onto the paintwork.*

6-4-4. *The whole area to be covered with the decal had to be sprayed with a mixture of water and washing-up liquid. The adhesive on the back of the decal will stick immediately to dry paint but you need to be able to adjust its position. The washing-up liquid solution enables you to do this.*

6-4-5. *Roy started to peel the backing paper from the reverse side of the decal …*

6-4-6. *… and Andy, who had been standing by, helped to separate one from t'other.*

6-4-7. *Working off the marks made on the paintwork earlier, Andy and Roy positioned the decals all the way along the length of the body. This is the crucial time that establishes that the decals will not only be lined up correctly but will also be straight. You need to go and look down the length of the decal to make sure that it's not wavy. Looking at it from the side is often deceptive and when you come to look at it from one end, it can look like the waves on the sea – which isn't so good if it's not a nautical theme!*

6-4-8. *Andy and Roy pressed the decal down evenly, starting from the centre and working out towards both ends. There's no need to press down hard at this stage and in any case, the decal will still move around – or should do! The main objective is still to get the decal correctly positioned.*

6-4-9. Roy went back to the centre of the decal and used a plastic filler spreader as a squeegee to press the decal down onto the paintwork. In contradiction of what we saw in the previous picture, Roy lifted one end of the decal away again but it just goes to show that there are no hard and fast rules; only general principles. Especially when you are as experienced as Roy, you know when it's best to bend the rules a little. If the weather is particularly hot and the paintwork behind the decal is starting to dry out, now is the time to spray some more washing-up liquid solution onto it.

6-4-10. Now, working back towards the rear end of the sliding door, Roy carefully squeegeed the large expanse of the decal flat onto the paintwork.

6-4-11. He then had the tricky job of cutting the decal precisely in its correct locations. He's back at the front end of the decal now and used his spreader as a short straight edge ...

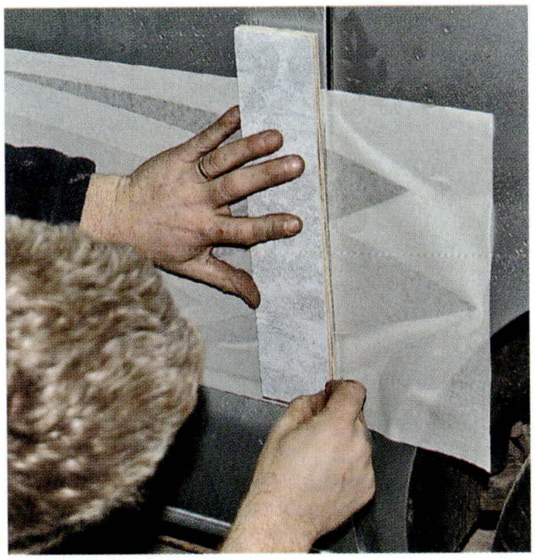

6-4-12. ... though for longer stretches, he used a piece of wood to make a pencil mark in line with the edge of the panel.

6-4-13. You can see that there are two pencil lines on the decal; one in line with the edge of each panel. Roy used a really sharp craft knife to cut right down the centre, between the two lines.

6-4-14. Roy lifted up one edge of the decal by as little as he could and used a pair of scissors to cut along the pencil line before doing the same to the other side of the decal.

6-4-15. Each cut length then has to be pressed down again with the squeegee to make sure that it is tight against the paintwork.

177

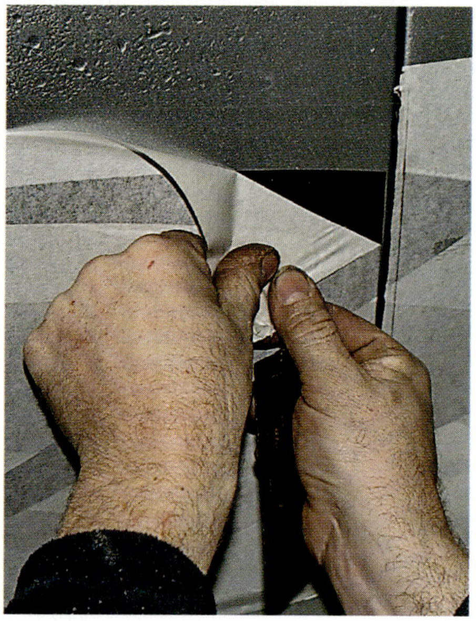

6-4-16. Now comes the slightly tricky part where you aim to get the backing paper off while leaving the decal on the body.

6-4-17. Roy eased the backing paper away, pressing very lightly with his fingertips on the decal itself if it looked like lifting. Note the angle at which he is pulling the backing paper; as near to parallel with the side of the body as possible. If he was to pull at 90° to the body, there would be a greater risk of pulling the decal back off again.

6-4-18. Here's a useful tip, especially if there seems to be a danger of the decal pulling off. Roy tore the backing paper so that he started to remove it from the middle rather than the end of the decal.

6-4-19. If the decal still looks like picking-up, there's nothing to stop you going back over it later, using a scrap piece of backing paper and pressing down the decal where necessary.

6-4-20. In an ideal world, you won't need to do that but, especially at the ends, it's a good idea to lightly press the decal down with the squeegee as the backing paper is removed.

6-4-21. Roy went carefully over the decal with the squeegee as all of the backing paper was removed, wiping it firmly but carefully over the decal to squeeze out any of the washing-up liquid solution and, just as importantly, any air bubbles that may have been left in there. If you don't do this now, before the water all dries off and the glue on the back of the decal sets, you may not be able to get out any little blisters that air or water may have left in the decal. This is also the reason why the panel had to be cleaned off scrupulously beforehand. Any small specs will leave a tiny dome in the decal out of all proportion to the size of the spec, it seems.

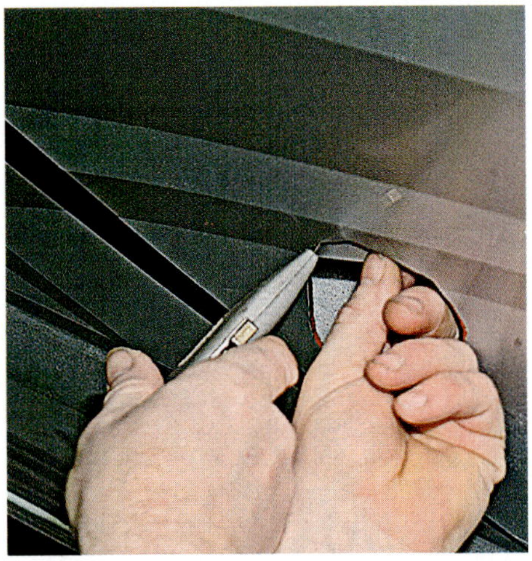

6-4-22. There should be no fixtures and fittings on the side of the van while the decals are being fitted. This is the hole where the water filler will later be fitted. The decal is cut with a craft knife around the edge of the hole so that the water filler neck will cover it completely when fitted.

6-4-25. If you have needed to remove old decals off before starting, you may have tried peeling them off by hand but if so, you'll have found it a thankless task. Even with the use of a hairdryer to soften the decal and the adhesive behind it, it can take ages and there is the risk of heat from the hairdryer damaging the paint on the vehicle. A much better tool is this Würth Decal Remover. It fits in the chuck of an electric drill and is passed up and down the decal with the drill running. The drill's speed should be no more than 2,000 rpm which makes something like this Bosch rechargeable drill ideal, especially when you bear in mind the extra safety benefits when working outside. The decal remover leaves a crumbly residue on the surface, rather like that left by a pencil eraser on paper although somewhat thicker. You have to be careful not to linger for too long in one place because of the small chance that an excess build up of heat could damage the paint. I have used panel wipe in the past for removing the last traces of adhesive off the surface. This is a magical tool and I wouldn't consider removing decals in any other way.

6-4-23. The Leisuredrive Crusader badge on the back fits in the same way – spray water and washing-up liquid solution on first.

6-4-24. The badge has to be lined up accurately as you squeegee it down because it will tend to slide but once it's on, it's on!

6-4-26. The decals fitted to our Leisuredrive Crusader give a cheerful appearance and have an attractive style that goes well with most colours of bodywork.

SECTION 5. MOTOR CARAVAN WHEELS & TYRES

It's easy to buy motor caravan wheels and tyres on price alone and to inadvertently end up with a motor caravan that is unsafe, as I discovered when I started looking.

When it comes to wheels and tyres, you can't go wrong, can you? If the wheels fit the vehicle and the tyres fit the wheels, everything will be hunky-dory, won't it? Well unfortunately, when it comes to motor caravans, there's a lot morze to it than that and I'm not talking the usual guff about items that cost more being generally better quality; I'm actually talking about the fact that you can easily go out and buy wheels and tyres for many motor caravans that will:

- Fit perfectly
- Look great
- Be downright dangerous!

This is a minefield that car drivers don't usually get into, for reasons that will become apparent in a moment but, if you're running a motor caravan, you need to look very carefully before you buy.

Each of the following three sections will look at a different aspect of what you need to know about buying and using motor caravan wheels and tyres.

PART A. CHOOSING ALLOY WHEELS FOR MOTOR CARAVANS

After its conversion by Leisuredrive, our Camper looked so good that my wife Shan and I decided to add more cosmetic improvements, such as alloy wheels. It was then that I discovered that you can buy alloys that fit your 'wagon but that are not safe for use on it!

I first became suspicious when I saw some really cheap alloy wheels on eBay being advertised as suitable for the VW T5. I couldn't figure out what the catch was, so I picked the brains of Duncan Clubbe of Tyresave which specialises in alloy wheels for motor caravans – it seems that my suspicions were well founded!

Tyresave's top tip

*• Duncan Clubbe says, "We get a lot of enquiries asking if it is possible to fit alloys on vehicles with twin rear wheels but it is **not** possible to supply alloy wheels for these vehicles. However, we can supply alloys for the Fiat Ducato Motorhome chassis with twin rear axles."*

Original equipment alloy wheels tend to be very expensive and a lower cost route to an upgrade is to choose from one of the increasing number of aftermarket suppliers. But as Duncan points out, just because a wheel will fit your van, it doesn't mean that it will be strong enough for use on a vehicle with a commercial chassis. For example, several wheels from VW's and Mercedes' passenger car ranges will also fit its vans in the sense that they can be bolted on to the hubs, but there's more to it than that. Car wheels are rarely strong enough to carry the weight of a motor caravan.

Another, though lesser problem is that ours is a relatively specialised market and there is less choice of styles and sizes for motor caravan alloys. Mostly, sizes are limited to 15in and 16in diameter, though there are some wheels available from Tyresave right up to 19in for Mercedes Vito and VW T5 Transporter. This means that it is often possible to upgrade to a larger-size wheel if you want to. Larger diameter wheels look better than smaller ones but they are more expensive and, of course, larger tyres cost more. If you fit larger wheels, you need to fit lower profile tyres so that the effective diameter of the wheel remains about the same. If you don't, you will change the vehicle's gearing and speedometer readings, possibly illegally.

It's important to note that lower profile tyres provide a firmer and more stable ride, something which Duncan says may appeal to owners of larger motor caravans, which can be susceptible to body roll when cornering. On the other hand, you might not want a firmer ride if 'firmer' translates into 'harsher', the tyres are noisier (which they are likely to be) and the steering becomes too sensitive – the choice is yours!

6-5-1. The Porter Volkswagen Leisuredrive T5, fitted with the superb Michelin Agilis tyres on Fox TOP alloy, heavy duty wheels, for commercial use and thus suitable for a motor caravan. They cost £440 inc. Vodka-And-Tonic (VAT) from Tyresave in the 16in size used on the T5 and £390 for the 15in diameter. Tyres are extra and their price tends to vary, so shop around.

FACT FILE: TYRE 'PROFILE'

- The 'profile' of a tyre is its height measured as a percentage of its width. So, a 215 65 R16 tyre is one that measures 215mm wide, with a wheel-to-tyre height of 65 per cent of its width (or 139.75mm) to fit a 16in diameter wheel.
- Inches and millimetres in the same breath? It's a wheel-and-tyre tradition that may gradually be phased out in favour of all-metric – but don't hold your breath!

If their existing tyres are in good condition, many people buy wheels to match the tyre size and then fit the original tyres to the new wheels. Most tyre depots can handle this work but, as Duncan advises, be sure to check they have modern tyre machines which will not scratch the new wheels. Also note, there can be a wide variation in charges for this work so get a quote first. To provide a benchmark, Tyresave normally charges £20 to swap over four tyres and balance the wheels if you buy from it, or £30-£40 if you buy them elsewhere.

Last but not least, the choice of wheels is down to the style that you like. Tyresave offers four different styles of 15in and 16in wheels that are rated for heavy duty use on motor caravans. They are all 5-spoke wheels but not all wheels will fit all vans. The full list with pictures can, at the time of writing, be seen at www.tyresave.co.uk along with a list of the vehicles it can fit. Duncan strongly recommends that anyone interested checks with him, supplying vehicle year and chassis details to find out whether your choice suits your particular motor caravan.

6-5-2. These are similarly heavy-duty Vantec wheels, as sold by Tyresave at an economy price, seen here on a coach-built motor caravan. In the 15in size, they cost £325, at the time of writing.

PART B. CHOOSING THE RIGHT TYRES AND CARING FOR THEM

I spoke at some length with Michelin about suitable tyres for motor caravans and it was quite clear in what it said. Just as with wheels, so with tyres: You can buy a tyre that will be absolutely the right size but won't be safe for use on your motor caravan. Tyre manufacturers, such as Michelin, design tyres for various types of use. Some tyres are particularly well suited for performance cars, with handling capabilities and the ability to shift water from the road's surface to match. These are often directional tyres, which must be fitted so they rotate in the direction shown on the tyre, or asymmetrical tyres, which must be fitted with the outer sidewall facing away from the vehicle. Motor caravans don't usually require such niceties (though Bürstner sometimes fits directional tyres, which makes the use of a single spare wheel awkward).

Our Volkswagen T5 was fitted with Michelin Agilis 51 tyres when new, and these will also be used when replacement time comes around. This is not only because of

LOAD INDICES

This is the full range of Load and Speed Indices shown on the tyre and what they mean: The Load Index figure imprinted on the sidewall of the tyre denotes the maximum load capacity of a tyre when driven at the maximum speed allowed by the tyre (see below).

Load Index (LI)	Max. kg per tyre	Load Index (LI)	Max. kg per tyre
65	290	93	650
66	300	94	670
68	315	95	690
69	325	96	710
70	335	97	730
71	345	98	750
72	355	99	775
73	365	100	800
74	375	101	825
75	387	102	850
76	400	103	875
77	412	104	900
78	425	105	925
79	237	106	950
80	450	107	975
81	462	108	1000
82	475	109	1030
83	487	110	1060
84	500	111	1090
85	515	112	1120
86	530	113	1150
87	545	114	1180
88	560	115	1215
89	580	116	1250
90	600	117	1285
91	615	118	1320
92	630	119	1360

Michelin's generally superb reputation for tyre quality but also because these particular tyres were designed to be suitable for our Volkswagen's commercial vehicle maximum gross weight, of 2.8 tonnes, as well as its semi-performance car top-speed of around 115 mph.

There are not many vehicles with the same requirements of both load and performance, though it would certainly be possible to find tyres designed for 4x4 models with suitable load and speed characteristics. In fact, there may be an argument for fitting 4x4-type tyres to a motor caravan if only to provide the extra grip that you might expect them to deliver on wet grass or mud. However, neither Michelin nor any of the other major tyre companies I spoke to would recommend doing so (though it didn't specifically warn against it, either), mainly on the grounds that this is not the use for which they have been tested.

6-5-3. Vantec2 wheels are sold by Tyresave and, being built in the 16in diameter size, are available to cover a wider range of vehicles than 15in wheels.

HOW TO TELL IF TYRES ARE UP TO THE JOB

Look for the speed and load ratings shown on the sidewall. The arrangement of the numbers and letters will always be the same.

In Part A, we looked at the tyre size marking, but in addition to the designation '215 65 R16' we referred to earlier, the tyre might also show '98', which indicates a load capacity of 750kg for each tyre (note: not the axle, or the whole vehicle) and 'S', which would indicate the tyre's maximum speed capability of 130mph.

SPEED RATINGS

All tyres carry a speed symbol in the form of a letter, indicating the maximum speed for which the tyre is intended. The table below shows which speed is represented by each letter.

Speed symbol	Max. speed mph	kph
N	87	140
P	93	150
Q	99	160
R	106	170
S	112	180
T	118	190
H	130	210
V	149	240
W	168	270
Y	186	300

WORSE FOR WEAR?

This isn't about basic tyre maintenance but here's a few extra tips likely to be of special use to VW Camper drivers:

- When undertaking a long tour, examine the tyres at intervals during the holiday – but only check pressures after the tyres have cooled down, which can take several hours after stopping.
- After driving over rough, uneven, unmade ground and especially if you have to drive over ground littered with debris, check the tyres soon afterwards to ensure that no foreign objects have become trapped in the tread patterns and examine the sidewalls for cuts or bulges.
- Overloading the vehicle, although easily done, is illegal and is likely to put excessive strain on the tyres. Tyre overheating leads

6-5-4. This selection box shows a number of different designs, grouped together for comparison. From top-left, clockwise, they are: Vantec; Fox TOP; Vantec2; RVS Strong.

to more rapid wear, greater susceptibility to impact damage and the greatly increased danger of a blow-out.

- RoSPA says, "Tyres that have been in storage (such as spare wheels) should not be used if over 6 years old, from their date of manufacture. When a tyre is in use, ageing effects are lessened, but such tyres should be replaced after 10 years, even if not worn out or visibly deteriorated."
- It's best not to wash tyres with detergents and you must never use solvents. They remove protective chemicals which are intended to migrate to the outer surface of the rubber. Some types of tyre paint may also be harmful.

PART C. POSITIVE SAFETY STEPS

This isn't to denigrate the usual safety tips to do with tyre pressures, tread wear and so on; in fact they are paramount, but there are several steps you can take to make the tyres on your motor caravan even safer than before. The main, unforeseeable risk is that of a tyre blowout. It happened to me once, back around 1970, when a Mini Van I was driving along a motorway contraflow section of the M5, blew out the front-right tyre at about 50mph. The van lurched uncontrollably through the cones, across the line of oncoming traffic and came to rest on the 'wrong' hard shoulder without touching a thing. Seconds later, while Shan and I were still sitting and in shock, a police patrolman pulled up and started to have a bit of a rant about stupid driving – until he saw what had happened to the tyre, hanging half-off the rim.

Most motor caravans are inherently less stable than most cars (or Mini Vans, for that matter) because of their bulky bodies and top-heavy payloads. If a front tyre was to blowout when on the motorway, the lack of directional control – and believe me, you can't do anything about it – could mean that the vehicle might roll over even if it doesn't hit anything else. The risk is slightly less with a rear tyre but if it happened when cornering on an ordinary road – or even in the Alps or the Pyrenees, if you want a really horrible thought – the vehicle would be just as dangerously out of control.

The main reasons for tyre blowouts include, though not necessarily in this order:

- A tyre defect from new, which is actually quite uncommon.
- Tyre under-inflation, which is by far the most common reason, either because the owner has forgotten to check or because a puncture has slowly let the air out of the tyre. An under-inflated tyre will flex its sidewalls excessively, stressing them beyond their design limits and overheat, leading to failure.
- Sidewall damage. The sidewall can be damaged when driving off-road, such as over a kerb or sharp stones. And if the tyres are the ones fitted when you bought the vehicle second-hand, you might not even know about it unless you check.
- Tyre ageing leading to sidewall deterioration.

It may be impossible to prevent any possibility of a blowout but you can do two things about it:

- Make the tyre less likely to blowout by dealing with some of the causes.
- Deal with the symptoms if it does

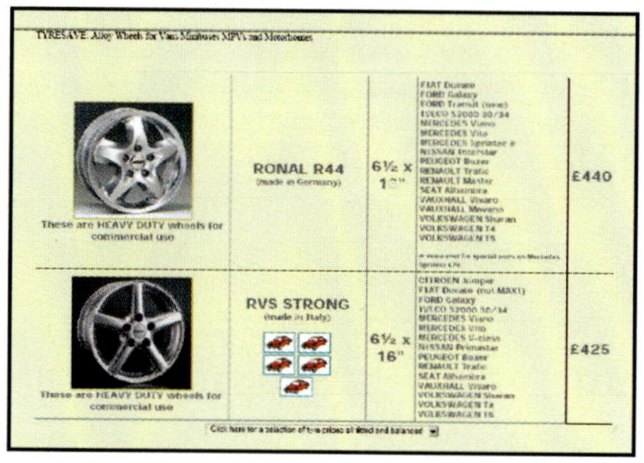

6-5-5. The Tyresave website is an essential source for anyone considering buying alloy wheels for a motor caravan. See ww.tyresave.co.uk/alloyvan.html for all the detailed information you may need, to allow you to choose what can be used on your vehicle.

Maintain tyre pressure

There are now sophisticated tyre pressure monitoring systems that check tyre pressures and/or tyre circumference electronically and inform the driver if anything is wrong. They are expensive and sometimes impossible to fit to an existing motor caravan.

A much more economical way of keeping an eye on things is to use Ultraseal Tyre Pressure Monitors, fitting one to each wheel of the motor caravan.

Another – and this might sound radical but it's actually the coming thing – is to fill the tyres with nitrogen gas instead of air. (Don't confuse it with the flammable Hydrogen used in the Hindenburg airship; nitrogen is quite inert.) ATS tyre centres are starting to make nitrogen 'fill-ups' available across its network and here's why:

- Better handling and road holding.
- Reduced tread wear and a claimed increased tyre life by up to 25 per cent.
- Reduced rolling resistance, said to improve miles per gallon by 2 per cent.
- Nitrogen is the largest constituent of air (around 79 per cent of it, in fact) but it doesn't assist corrosion, like oxygen. Corrosion on the inside of a wheel can cause leaks where the tyre bead is meant to seal against the wheel.
- It takes a lot longer for tyres to 'go down' than when filled with regular compressed air.
- For vehicles such as many motor caravans which stand for a lot of the time and then go off on long motorway trips, most of these attributes are priceless.
- A third way of protecting tyres is to use a puncture preventative such as that marketed, once again, by Ultraseal. The claim is that Ultraseal, having been injected into the tyre, will seal small, slow punctures without any of the adverse effects of traditional tyre sealants. There's more to it than we've got room for but you can see the rest on the Ultraseal website.

Keep the tyres in place

Some modern vehicles are being fitted with run-flat tyres. In theory, they can sometimes be fitted to existing vehicles but in reality, they shouldn't be. For one thing, the wheel rim may not be suitable, and for another, run-flat tyres are always fitted with an in-car pressure monitor to tell the driver when the air has gone. One driver carried on without any air in a run-flat tyre, oblivious to the dangerous change in his vehicle's handling for weeks, until an MoT check stopped him!

The best solution is to fit Tyron bands, as fitted by institutions as diverse as the MOD and the Saudi authorities responsible for running the vast fleet of buses across the desert to the annual Haj at Mecca. Here's how Tyron bands work.

Each vehicle wheel (apart from large commercials and a few others with split rims)

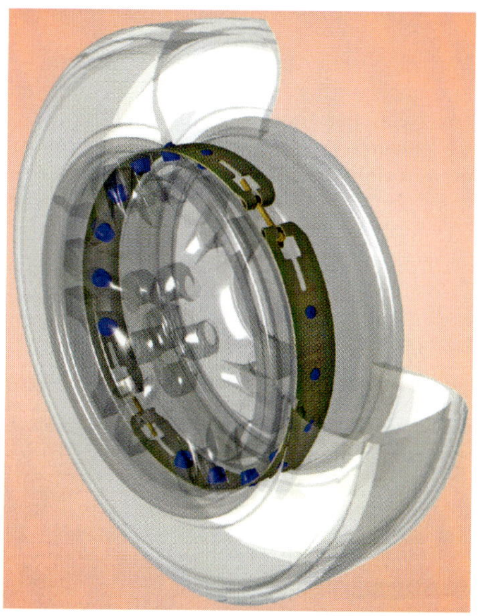

6-5-6. Tyron bands are an excellent safety accessory. Normally invisible, this is how they would look if you had some of those smutty X-ray specs they used to advertise in the News of the World when I was a nipper!

has a well in it to enable the tyre bead to be stretched over the rim when it is fitted. Normally, the tyre bead is pressed tight against the wheel rim when held in place by gas pressure. If a tyre loses its pressure through a blow-out, the tyre bead drops into the well, the tyre comes all or part-way off the wheel and the vehicle goes out of control.

Tyron bands are fitted after the tyre has been fitted to the wheel but before it is inflated. They close off the well so that, even if the tyre catastrophically loses its pressure, the tyre stays on the rim and allows you to control the vehicle while bringing it to a halt, even while driving slowly over a short distance to a place of safety.

For those of us with motor caravans, they are a 'must' in my opinion. But then, I have found myself shooting uncontrollably across the oncoming traffic on a motorway and that's a memory you never quite forget!

6-5-7. The ATS branch in Evesham fitted ours and started by snapping the spacer buttons into each band ...

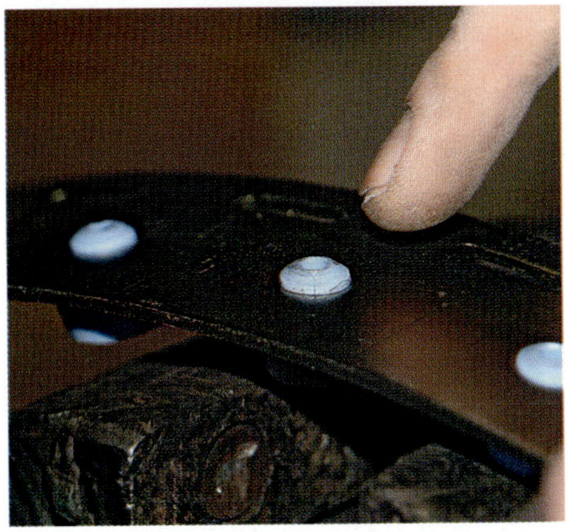

6-5-8. ... until the mushroom-shaped head on each on is seen correctly located.

6-5-9. Mick, who carried out most of the work, clamped an alloy wheel to the tyre fitting machine – protective rubber pads in place – and levered a new tyre valve into the wheel.

6-5-10. Next he fitted one of the new Michelins to the wheel. Some of the main advantages in using Michelin Agilis on a motor caravan are:

- *Car-like comfort and handling in a tyre built for light van usage.*
- *Silica-based rubber providing even tread wear and a commercial vehicle-type of reinforced casing.*
- *Comfortable and quiet as a result of the variable sized tread blocks.*

6-5-11. Some modern designs of alloy wheel, including mine, have spokes that protrude slightly from the outer edge of the wheel rim. Before entrusting a tyre fitter with the job of putting tyres on your nice, new alloys, ask the fitter if he will guarantee not to scratch them. I tried two tyre companies who wouldn't give such a guarantee, before approaching ATS! Mick explained that the trick is to set the machine, used for pushing the tyre bead over the edge of the wheel, so it does its job but without risk of contact, bearing in mind that some movement may take place. Mick carried out the work perfectly ...

6-5-12. He used the tyre fitting machine to push the tyre down sufficiently to insert one half of the Tyron band, ensuring that it was the correct way up, as described in the excellent instructions.

6-5-13. This tyre compression device is available from Tyron. Fitting and removal is a two-minute job, compared with the 15 minutes or more it can take when you have to struggle with the tyre fitting machine.

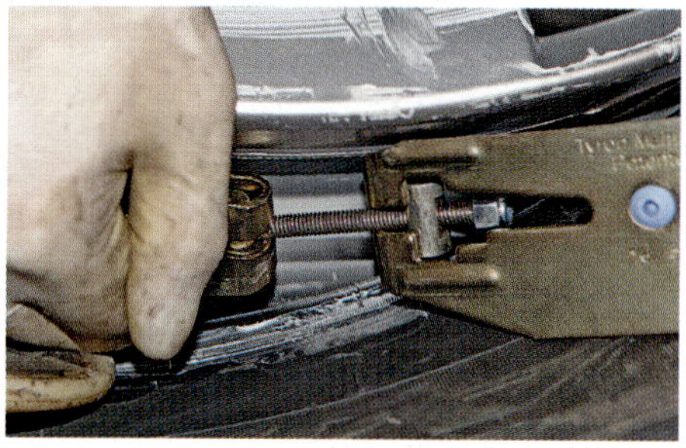

6-5-14. With both band-halves in place and the opposite joint symmetrically placed each side of the tyre valve, Mick fitted the screw-up clamp to each side.

6-5-15. After tightening evenly by hand, using the long-reach Allen key supplied by Tyron ...

6-5-16. ... he used this lovely little Britool torque wrench to tighten the screws to the specified low torque figure of 7.5Nm.

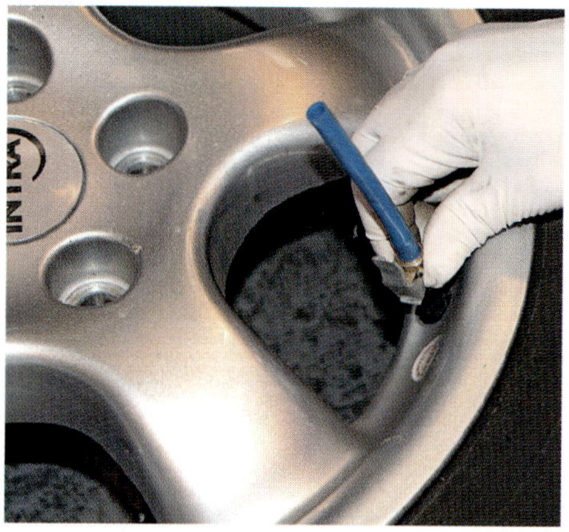

6-5-17. The tyres were to be inflated with Nitrogen, for reasons fully explained in the main text. If an already inflated tyre was being 'converted' to Nitrogen, ATS first jack up the vehicle, so there will be no weight on the tyres, then let all the compressed air out.

6-5-18. Mick inflated our new Michelins to the prescribed pressure using a gauge that looks identical to one used for compressed air but which is, in fact, attached to ATS's nitrogen pump and reservoir. (You will need to call ATS on the number given at the end of this manual to see where this service is offered.)

6-5-19. This special valve cap is fitted to show that nitrogen has been used. The relatively tiny amount of air used for topping-up in future won't, over a tyre's average life, noticeably compromise the performance of the nitrogen in the tyre.

6-5-20. Mick next took each wheel over to the ATS wheel balancing machine.

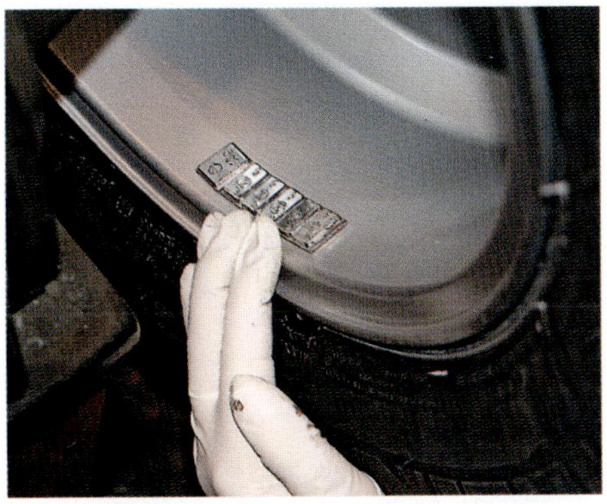

6-5-21. The machine cleverly told him how many stick-on weights to use and where to locate them in order to bring the wheel and tyre back into dynamic balance.

6-5-22. Steve lined up each wheel, fitted the wheel bolts ...

6-5-23. ... then tightened them with a torque wrench to the specified torque. It is especially important that the correct torque settings are used with alloy wheels, so you may wish to consider investing in one.

6-5-24. Ultraseal's Tyre Pressure Monitors are purchased to match the specific pressures of your tyres, as shown in the driver's handbook. They enable you to check tyre pressure status at a glance and at only a few quid per wheel – they're great value!

6-5-25. Before fitting, check that the O-ring is correctly seated (top) and make sure you fit the correct Monitors to the correct wheels, noting the pressure settings shown on the tops of the caps.

6-5-26. Here's how they work:

- The tyre pressure monitor is firmly screwed by hand onto the valve stem. If the tyre pressure is correct, the dome at the top turns green.
- If, when in use, the tyre pressure drops by 3 to 6psi, the yellow indicator starts to become visible – a strong recommendation that you top up this tyre with air. (When the tyre pressure drops more than 5psi, the red indicator starts to become visible.)
- At 6 to 10psi drop in pressure, the red is very visible, indicating a seriously under-inflated tyre.

6-6-1. This is the kit of parts and the brief instructions supplied with the kit. The arrows indicate the positions suggested on the instructions for adding the clips supplied – more on that later!

SECTION 6. SIDE WINDOW WIND DEFLECTORS

These wind deflectors from Parma Industries allow you to drive with the window a little way down and without a howling gale entering the cab. They also have the side-effect of looking rather stylish!

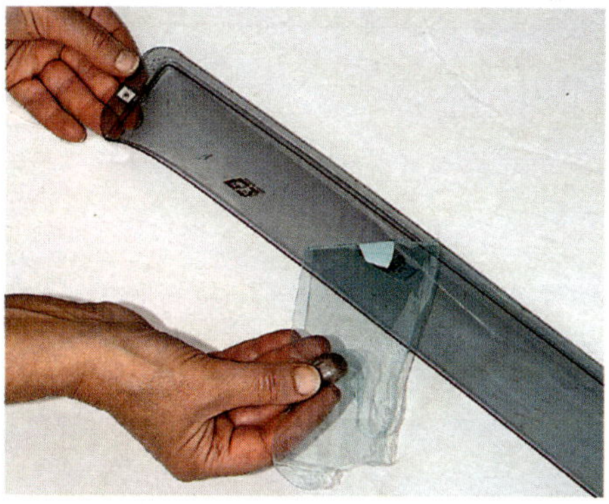

6-6-2. The first job is to peel the protective layer off the clear plastic deflectors.

6-6-3. There is a clip already fitted at the rear end and, with the window fully lowered, this is inserted first into the window channel.

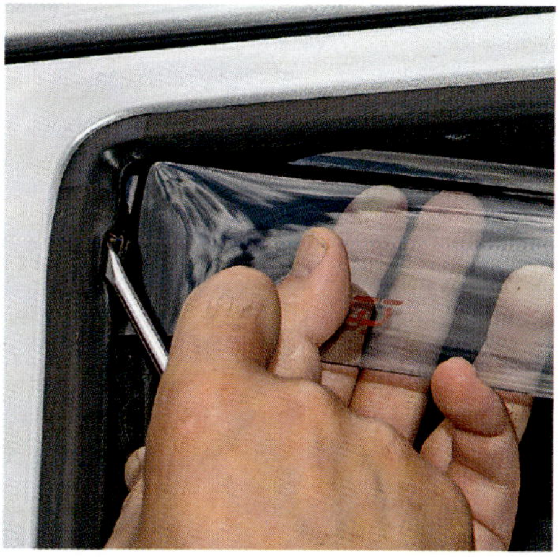

6-6-4. You need to carefully push the rubber to one side. Careful – it can tear!

6-6-5. The first of the clips has to be pushed into the channel ...

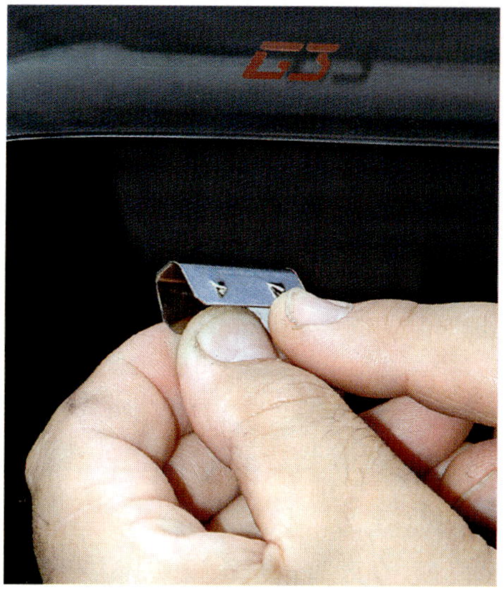

6-6-6. ... the claws facing the plastic deflector.

6-6-7. The other clips have to be carefully pushed into position with a screwdriver.

6-6-8. I found that the top-most clips caused the electric window's safety system to return the glass to the fully open position when it hit the clips. Two of them had to be removed and repositioned to overcome this problem.

6-6-9. The final result looks great and the wind deflectors, which seem well designed and made, stay firmly in position even at high motorway speeds.

SECTION 7. COLOUR CODING BODYWORK

Van-based motor caravans often wear their commercial origins for all to see, in the form of dull-looking bumpers and grilles while upmarket, MPV-versions of the same vehicles, are always better finished. Here's what's involved in making the bumpers match the bodywork.

All the van-based MPV, or 'people carrier' vehicles have colour-coded bumpers and it's a way of transforming a motor caravan's appearance, too. Having said that, you can't just buy a can of aerosol and slap a coat of paint over the grey plastic. Well you can, of course but, no matter how good your painting skills, you'll soon wish you hadn't!

6-7-1. When our VW T5 arrived back from being converted by Leisuredrive, it looked great but still had that van-like front-end, evident in the grey front bumper and grille.

6-7-2. This is Volkswagen's Caravelle version of the same vehicle and, although there are several minor styling differences in the front bumper style, the biggest change comes from having everything the same colour.

6-7-3. Rob Ebrey started early on a Saturday morning by removing the top panel and grille – easily done after removing fixing screws and unclipping the panel.

6-7-4 Rob started the numbers game by scrubbing the surface of all the plastic to be painted with ICI Autocolor's P273-1333, thinned 50 per cent with water.

PAINT QUALITY

PD Stevens refuse to use anything but ICI paint. They say that its quality has never let them down and colour matches are perfect. In fact, according to Rob, if you go back to ICI in several years time and quote to them the exact name and number of the paint used, you'll have a perfectly matching paint for touch-up or repair work.

6-7-5. The ICI surface cleaner is scrubbed into the surface with a medium-coarse Scotchbrite pad, ensuring that the outer layer of plastic mould release agent and other contaminants that have landed on the surface while the vehicle has been in use are all removed.

The problem is that the plastic material from which bumpers are made, hates being painted over and, unless skilfully and meticulously prepared, will shed the finish in ugly scabs of peeling paint.

I went to PD Stevens and Sons in North Shropshire to have the bumpers painted on our VW T5 Leisuredrive Camper. It is one of the finest commercial vehicle painters in the country and have been chosen by the likes of Michelin to paint exhibition vehicles. Of course, being equipped for the largest trucks on the road, PD Stevens have the facilities to paint even the largest American motorhomes and all to the same stunningly high standard. This was the second vehicle of mine it had worked on, the first being a 'show condition' Land Rover called 'OLO' that many Land Rover 'nuts' know about. Now, it was time for PD Stevens to go nuts on our Camper!

6-7-8. ... then dried off with an air line and cloth, chasing out every trapped droplet of water.

6-7-6. It's essential that every nook and cranny is scrubbed otherwise the paint won't stick. This is the mains electricity socket but the fridge vents have been removed from painting off the vehicle.

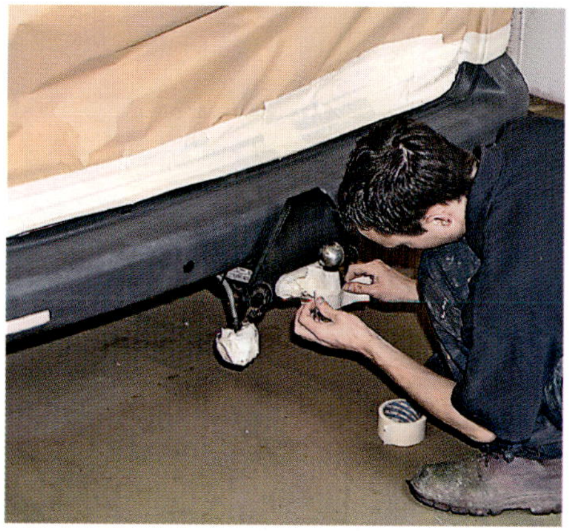

6-7-9. There's a huge amount of masking-off involved. Only small areas are being painted but the risk of paint overspray landing on the main bodywork has to be removed

6-7-11. Rob gave everything two coats, including the parts he'd removed from the vehicle.

6-7-7. Rob thoroughly washed the surface off with warm water ...

6-7-10. The next number out of the hat is ICI Autocolor's P572-2001, the special adhesion primer for plastic that makes all the difference between paint sticking or peeling away. It looks like water and dries almost instantly.

6-7-12. ICI's brand name for commercial vehicle paint is currently 'Nexa' and this is its High Build Primer, P565-1027. It doesn't have quite the catchiness of a bingo call but it's just the job for levelling out some of the dimples on the surface of the VW van's bumpers. Caravelle's bumpers are smooth, by the way.

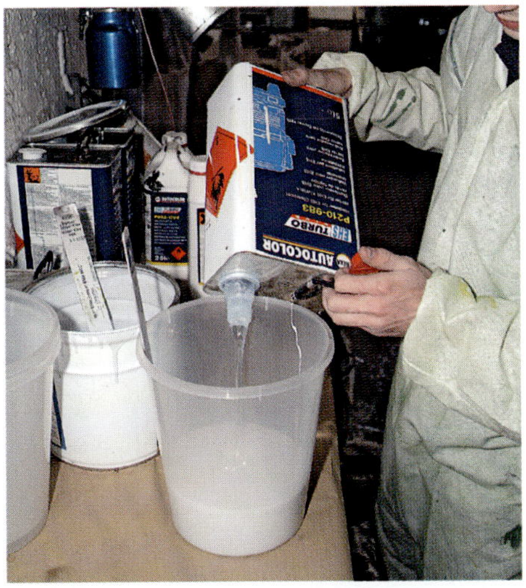

6-7-13. This primer is a 2-pack paint, and Rob mixed it with the appropriate amounts of thinner and hardener.

6-7-16. ... as well as to the grille and other individual items.

6-7-14. Dressed in full 'space walk' protective gear, Rob applied the first coat.

6-7-17. In the heat of PD Stevens' spray booth, the paint set really quickly and Rob was able to rub the surface lightly with a 'Superfine' sanding pad to remove any high spots, or 'nibs', as well as the odd small scratch in the bumper plastic that became visible. Those well-documented dimples were certainly less in evidence, too.

A COUPLE OF CAUTIONS!

SAFETY: 2-pack paint is only for use in licensed, specially equipped premises with appropriate filtration, extraction and protective gear. The spray is harmful to the environment if allowed out untamed and can be lethal if breathed in, hence Rob's safety gear. The hardened paint presents no such hazards, thank goodness!

PRIMER THICKNESS: Like a true pro, Rob spoke to ICI before carrying out this job, about the amount of primer that would be needed to make the bumpers completely smooth. He was advised against applying a sufficient depth to hide the surface dimples because there would be a possibility of cracking in future. I've learned to love the dimples, instead!

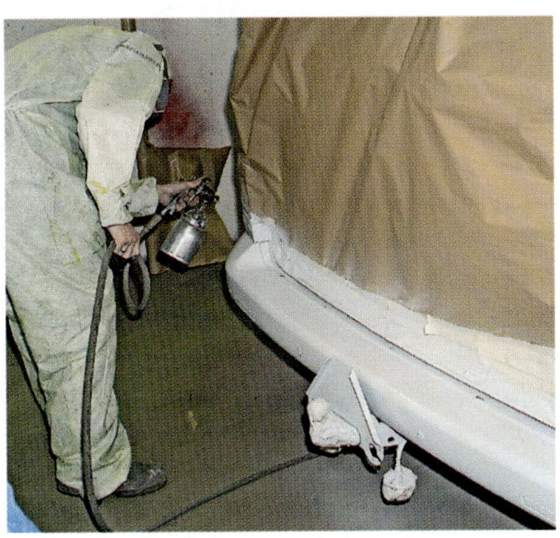

6-7-15. Rob applied three normal coats to all the bumpers ...

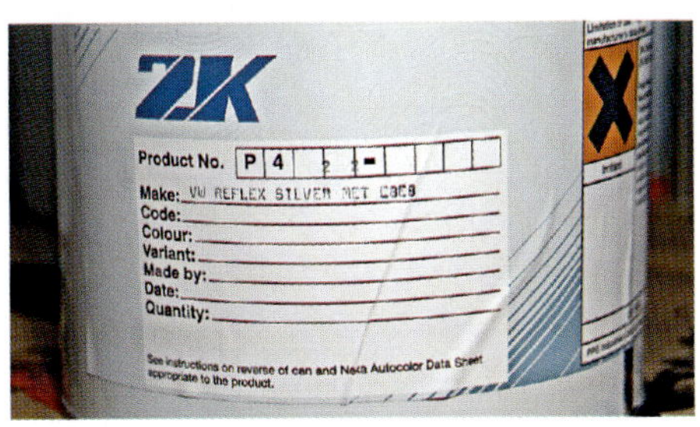

6-7-18. ICI's – or more accurately, Nexa's – famous 2K (2-pack) finish coat came next. The code, 'VW Reflex Silver E8E8' is the one that came from my vehicle details.

6-7-19. The solids in metallic paint are relatively heavy and the paint has to be well stirred. PD Stevens have mechanical stirrers to do the job but top painters always give a quick stir before mixing to ensure none of the solids have settled.

6-7-20. Rob added thinner and then hardener to the basecoat paint.

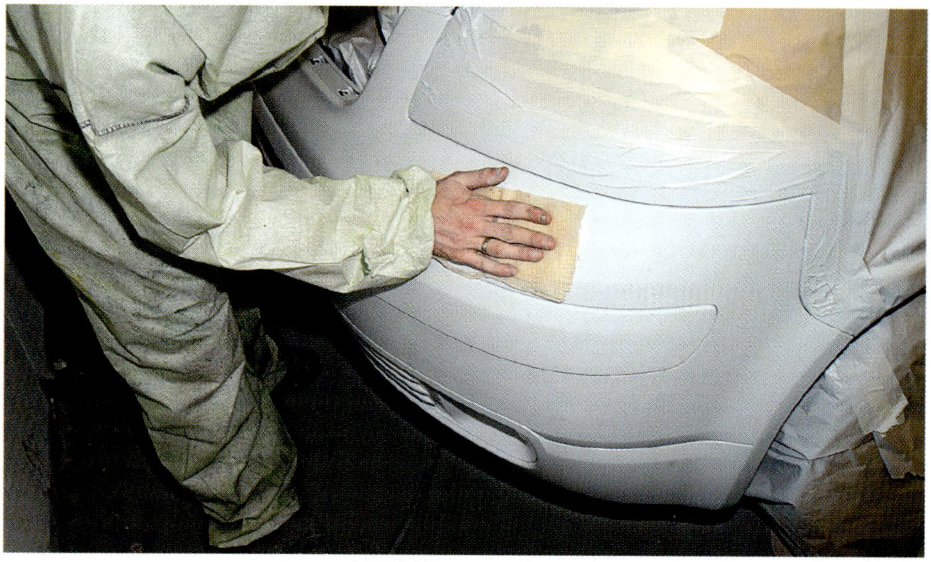

6-7-21. Immediately before applying the paint, Rob went over the surfaces to be painted with a Tak-Rag, a special sticky cloth that 'grabs' any specs of dust that might have got through the defences.

6-7-22. From outside the heated and enclosed spray booth, Rob could be seen applying basecoat paint to the smaller items on a stand.

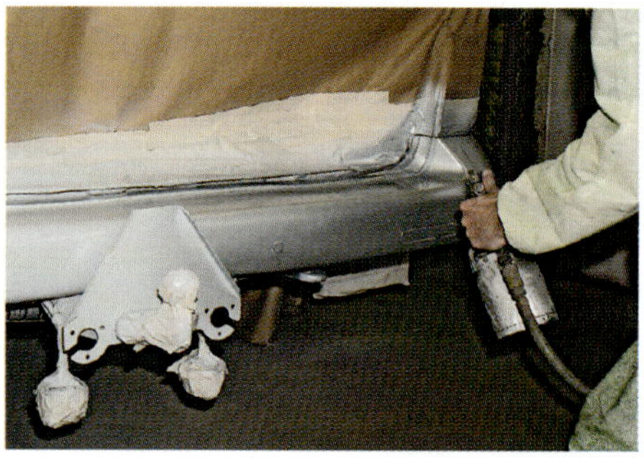

6-7-23. He worked his way around, applying the shiny-looking paint to the bumpers and other components. Note that basecoat dries matt, rather than the shiny finish that you might have expected.

6-7-24. That's because there's a coat of TurboPlus P190-155 – clear, shiny, Lacquer coat – to go on next.

Inside information

Rob told me that he applies metallic base coat with the air pressure at the gun turned up higher (so the paint comes out faster) and the paint delivery valve turned down (so it comes out finer). This allows the particles in the paint to the float to the top, enhancing the metallic appearance.

6-7-25. Once more, this is a 2K paint and Rob precisely measured the exact quantity required into the new container used for each paint mix.

6-7-26. He added the thinners and hardener as before and again in precisely measured quantities.

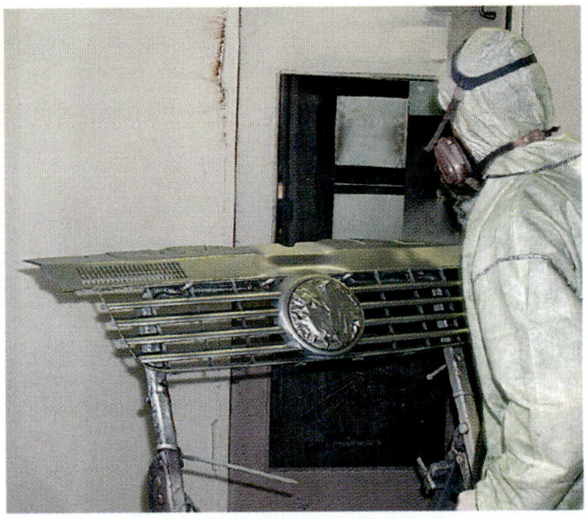

6-7-27. The lacquer coat is first applied to the removed panels ...

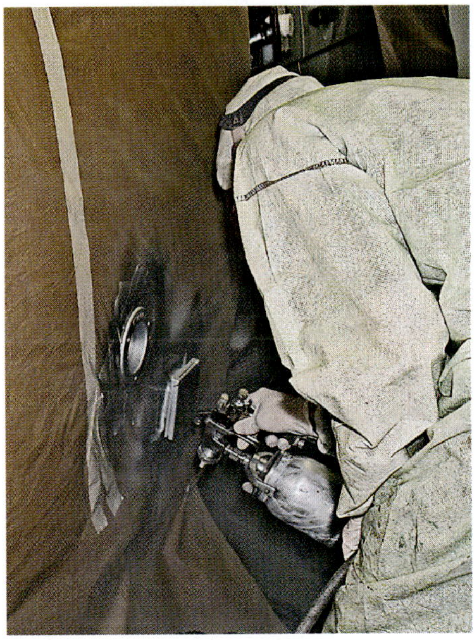

6-7-28. ... and then to the small parts still on the vehicle ...

6-7-29. ... before the main bumper sections are painted. The hot 'wind' in the booth pulls overspray into the filtration system before it can land on other sections of the vehicle.

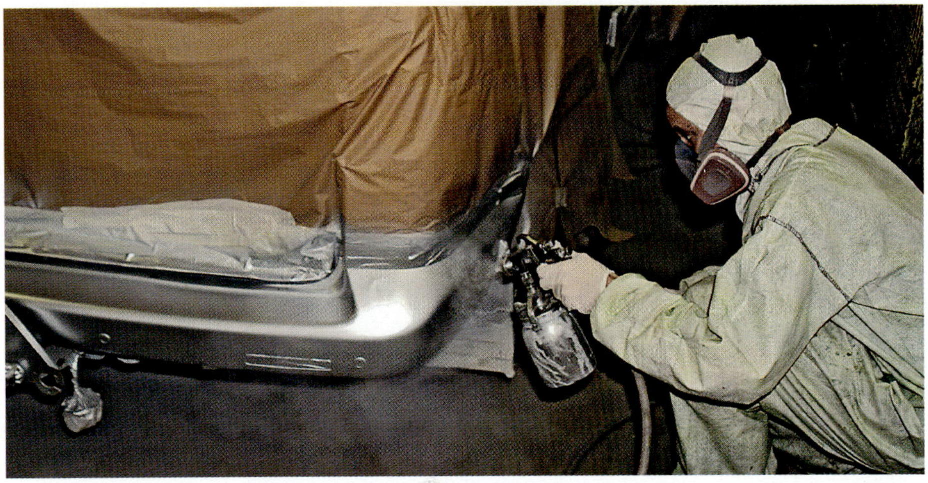

6-7-30. The lacquer coat brings up an amazing depth of shine onto the surface of the paint. It also darkens the appearance. Base coat by itself tends to look as if the paint being used is too light!

6-7-31. After five minutes in the booth, the first coat of lacquer has gone off sufficiently for the next one to be applied.

6-7-32. Rob next turned up the temperature inside the roaring spray booth, so that the paint was 'baked' as if in an oven. After an amazingly brief 30 minutes of this, the paint was hard and Rob removed the masking tape. He told me that the vehicle could immediately have been taken out into the rain, once it had cooled down, without adverse effect!

6-7-33. Because it isn't possible to mask off beneath the wheel arches, Rob used a can of black aerosol to disguise any overspray.

6-7-34. After refitting the body panels, our VW Caravelle – sorry, I mean Camper – was ready to take to the roads looking more swish than ever!

6-7-35. Colour-coding the bumpers on a motor caravan is a sure-fire way to stop your vehicle looking as if it belongs in the 'deliveries' area of the supermarket car park.

SECTION 8. SWIVELLING PASSENGER AND DRIVER SEATS

Here is what's involved in fitting swivelling front seats. Marcle Leisure carried out the fitting.

Our dear old 1985 Leisuredrive VW Transporter had a swivelling passenger seat and we used it very frequently. But when our new Volkswagen Transporter came along, we wondered if we could manage without. Only two of us; plenty of room in the back on the bench seat; what's the problem? Well, we rapidly remembered why it was that we'd used a swivelling seat when we'd got one, during every break and picnic stop. With one person sitting in the passenger seat and facing backwards, you gain lots of extra room without losing access to the living area or, even more important, the sociability that comes from facing each other.

6-8-1 An alternative to modifying the seat bases, as shown below, is to start with a swivel base that already includes access for wiring. This is the swivel available from CAK of Kenilworth. The fitting procedure is exactly the same as for the Wyvern seat shown below.

6-8-2. Jonathan Frost, the man behind CAK demonstrates the way in which the bases he supplies also include a central hole large enough for cables to pass through. The locking knob is, irritatingly, on the side of the seat where you might knock your legs against it, but the large green disk, you can just see in the swivel area, reduces rattling and free seat movement noticeably.

We decided to fit seat swivels from Wyvern Accessories, the people who made the ones fitted to our older VW. They arrived and looked pretty well identical to the ones we had before. But there was a problem. Our new-fangled Volkswagen has side airbags built into the seat backrests, seat heaters and electric lumbar supports. All these fanglements mean wires; wires that have to pass from beneath the seats and into their bases, making them veritable 12v electric chairs! And how do you get wires through solidly built seat swivels? Well, here's how I did it and it's a similar system that Wyvern Accessories is soon to adopt, I'm told. Here also, is how to fit seat swivels to your T5.

Important notes:

a) Start by disconnecting the battery.
b) In the case of some vehicles, you may need to reset the alarm after disconnecting the battery, and in almost all cases nowadays, you will need the radio code so that, when the battery is reconnected, you won't be locked out of your own radio.
c) If airbags are involved, find out the correct procedure from your main dealer. In the case of our Transporter T5, it was enough to simply disconnect the battery but it is possible that other models may require something different, such as leaving the battery disconnected for a certain period of time before disconnecting the airbag. It is essential that you check with your main dealer before carrying out the work.

6-8-3. Steve Monkley of Marcle Leisure has slid the seat back as far as it will go, revealing the nut at the front end of each runner holding it down to the seat frame. Some T5 Transporters have bolts instead of studs and nuts in this location.

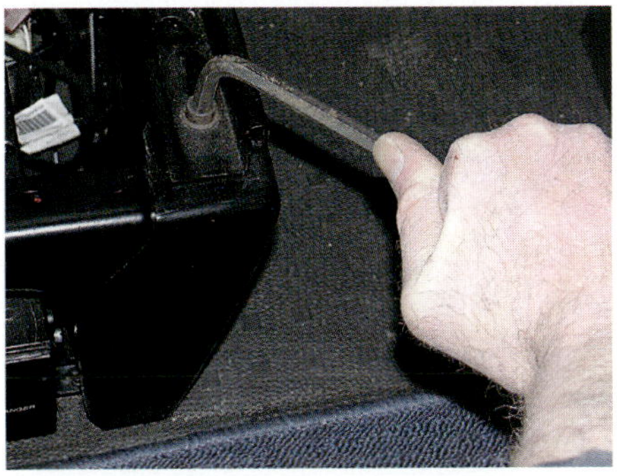

6-8-4. By sliding the seat all the way forward, Steve was able to slacken the two bolts holding the seat runners down. The correct tool to use is a Torx bit with a ratchet spanner. Steve didn't have the correct size to hand but we discovered that an Allen key was sufficient for loosening the bolts. You need the correct Torx bit for tightening, however, because otherwise there is a strong risk of damaging the bolt head.

6-8-5. With the bolts undone and the seat tipped back, Steve turned his attention to disconnecting all of the cables found under the seat. For some of them, you need to be a bit of a Chinese puzzle addict, though Steve's experience as a maintenance engineer stood him in good stead.

6-8-6. With all of the plugs and sockets disconnected, nothing was holding the seat in place. Note that, in this case, the airbag connector is the large yellow block on the right of the picture and that there were two separate clips holding the two halves of the connector in place, in typical Volkswagen belt-and-braces style.

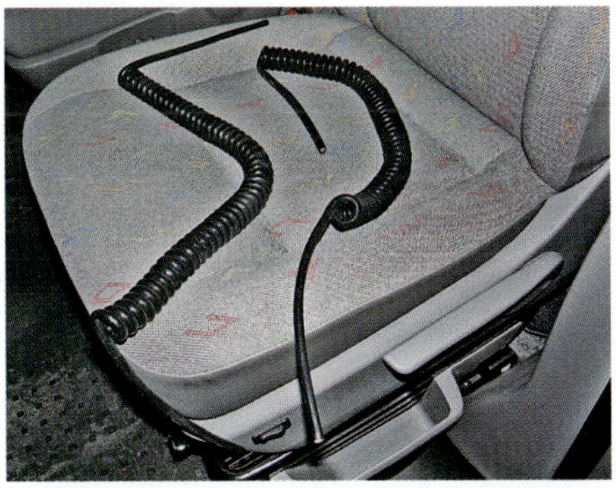

6-8-7. One solution to transferring all those wires from the seat innards to the seat base would have been to use some of these curly cables from Maypole Ltd, who have an extraordinary range of electrical fittings and components for caravanners and motor caravanners. I actively considered running a couple of these curly cables around the outside of the seat, the spiral part allowing for the seat movement without having loose cables flopping around on the floor.

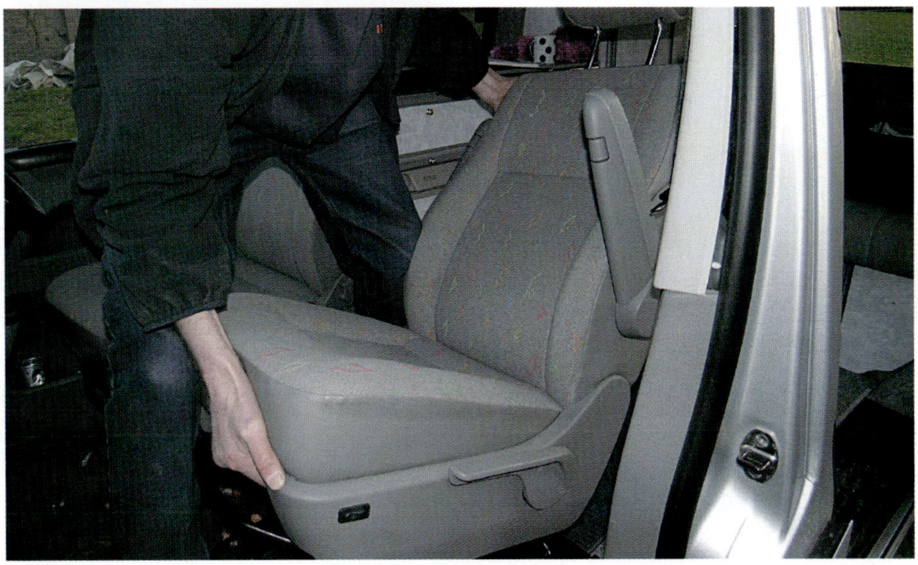

6-8-8. Steve now lifted out the passenger seat from the vehicle. Beware! They are rather heavy and you may need some assistance.

6-8-9. This is a FASP T5 left-hand swivel seat swivel base as sold by Marcle Leisure. Note that there is a small hole through the centre tubing on which the base swivels but it might not have been enough for the extra number of wires we have fitted to our seats. Other FASP swivels have a commendably large hole in the middle of the swivel.

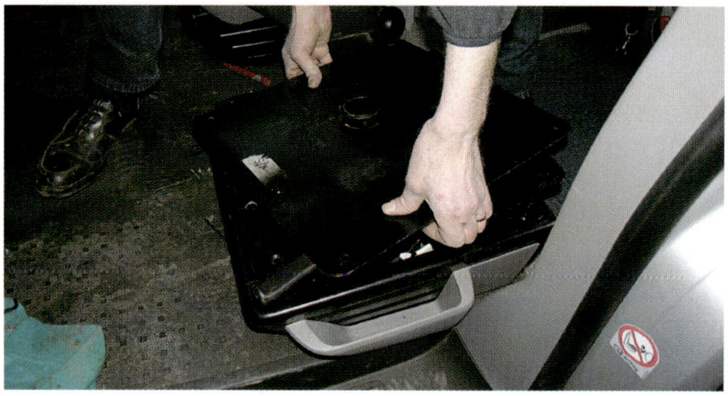

6-8-10. Steve holds my Wyvern Accessories seat in place on the seat base. You can see that, in essence, there are four holes for bolting the swivel down to the seat base and a corresponding number of holes for bolting the seat runners to the top of the swivel.

PORTER'S MODS

SAFETY FIRST!

Have an engineer carry out this part of the work for you and have him ensure that the materials used are sufficient for the loads being placed upon the seat.

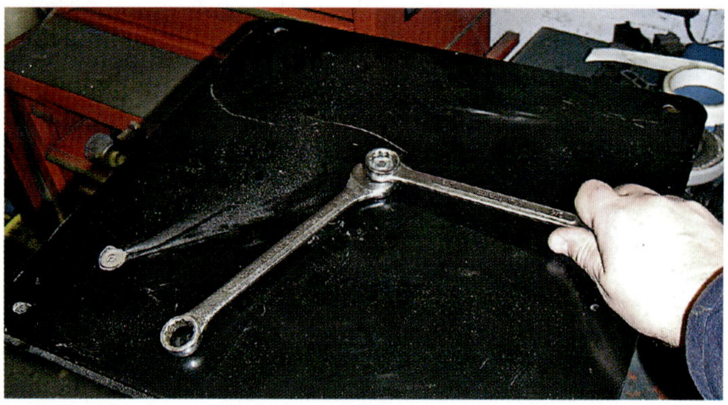

6-8-11. This was the Wyvern Accessories T5 seat swivel when it arrived with me. It swivelled on a centre bolt and there was no means of passing a cable through the middle of the swivel. My first job was to use a pair of spanners to release the locknut and remove the bolt.

6-8-12. Lifting the top part of the swivel away revealed an interesting construction. This circle of MDF carries none of the weight of the swivel. Instead, it carries the six ball bearings (arrowed) which in turn, carries the weight of the seat. The bar you can see is the arm which is used to lock the swivel in its straight-ahead position when you are driving along.

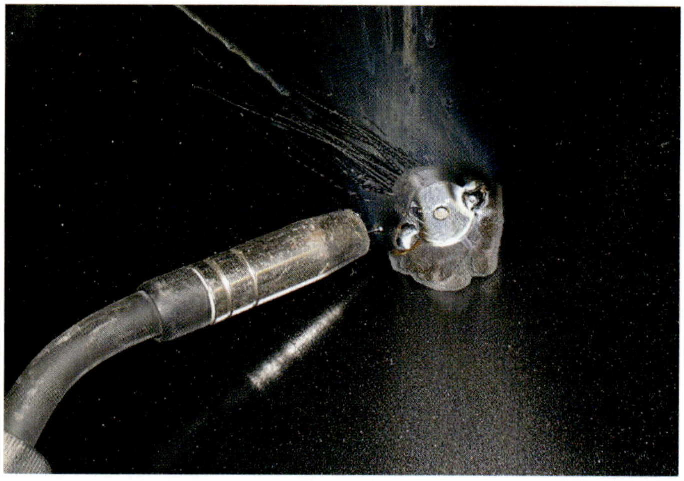

6-8-13. After taking the components apart, I needed to drill two large holes, one in the centre of each half of the seat swivel. A hole-cutter has a centre-mounted drill which acts as a pilot. The holes already drilled in the seat swivels were too large to enable me to use a hole-cutter without it wandering all over the place. I welded a washer over the hole in the seat swivel.

6-8-14. This enabled me to use the hole cutter to cut a larger hole, the washer guiding the hole-cutter and keeping it in position until it started to do its work. I've got a Clarke pillar drill and you really need such a drill for cutting holes of this type. Most hand electric drills are not sufficiently powerful and there is a risk of the drill spinning round and causing injury.

6-8-15. The hole size of 60mm had been selected to match a 60mm outside diameter threaded tube that I'd bought earlier from my local agricultural engineers.

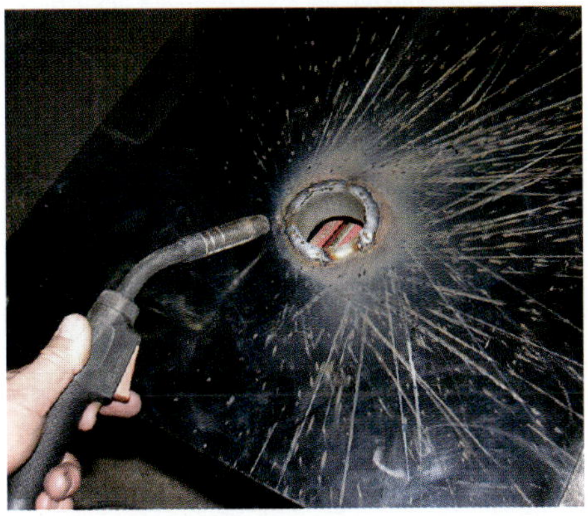

6-8-16. With the tube positioned squarely in the hole, I used the Clarke MIG welder to weld it securely in place.

6-8-17. I had to cut a larger hole in the centre of the MDF in the same way, before replacing the MDF in position, and adding a spot of Würth copper grease where each ball bearing would be fitted. You can see a clever modification that turned out to be too clever by half. I glued a strip of foam around the outside of the MDF to prevent any grease from showing up on the outsides of the swivel. Unfortunately, the grease melted the glue, the foam came off and I had to pull it out again. Ah well, not everything works!

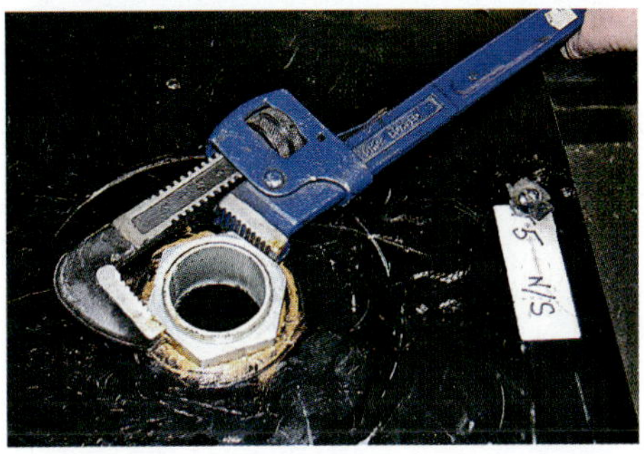

6-8-18. It took an enormous amount of effort to tighten the large nut on the threaded tube. This is because the amount of torque required on a nut of that size is huge, otherwise it doesn't bear down sufficiently tight on the swivel.

6-8-19. It goes without saying that you really don't want your seat swivel to fall apart as you're driving along! I drilled a small hole through the large nut and the tube and passed through a thin bolt, attaching a nut to it (arrowed) with threadlock.

Back to the Marcle leisure ranch ...

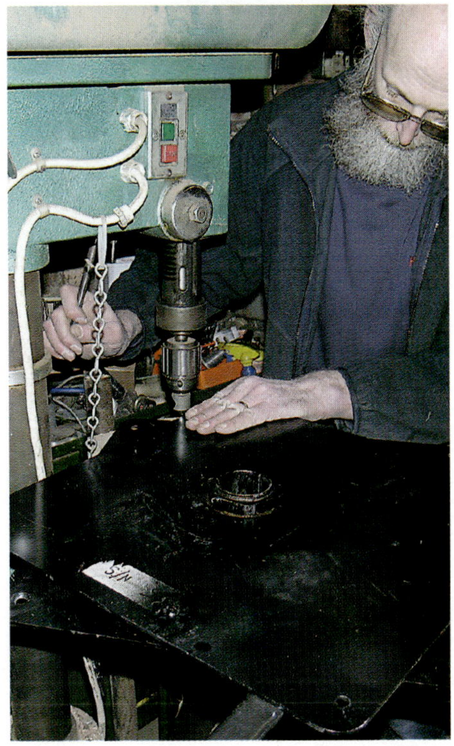

6-8-20. Having been presented with my modified seat swivel base, Steve Monkley turned to his huge selection of workshop machinery to countersink the holes in the seat swivel assembly. There was a reason for doing this which we'll come to in a moment.

6-8-21. First time around, Steve used the existing studs at the front of the seat bases to fix the fronts of the swivels in place.

6-8-22. Unfortunately, the nuts and studs sticking up fouled on the fixings for the tops of the swivels once they were in place. Steve had to drill out the studs and replace them with high tensile steel countersunk head screws with nuts offered up from beneath. Believe me, there isn't much room! Wyvern Accessories tell me that it has now modified these fixings to make them easier to fit.

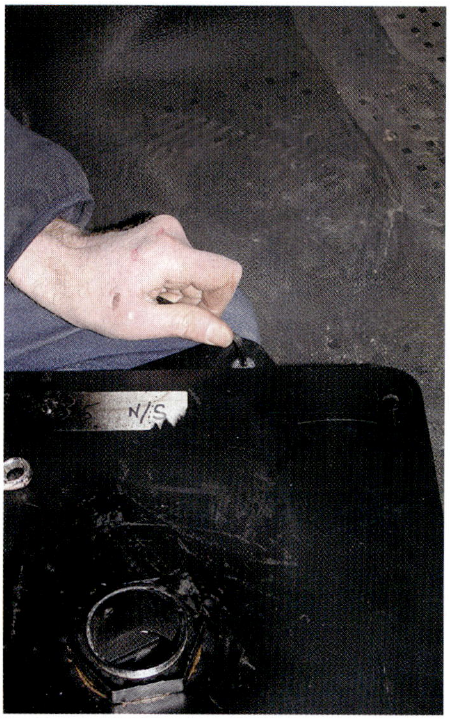

6-8-23. At the backs of the seats, there were no such problems because there are captive nuts into which the countersunk head screws are fitted.

6-8-24. Pay off time for all this effort came when Steve passed all the cables through the hole in the centre of the tube.

6-8-25. His next job was to connect everything back up again and this was greatly assisted by the fact that every plug and socket was unique and couldn't be confused with any of the others.

Important note:
If you replace any of the fixings supplied by the seat swivel manufacturers, you must only use high tensile bolts with a rating of 12.9. This figure is invariably stamped on the bolt head and on the nut used on the bolt. It's no good using a high tensile bolt with an ordinary mild steel nut because it could shear at its weakest point.

6-8-26. Steve bolted the seats themselves down to the tops of the swivels and it was at this stage that he discovered that ordinary bolts couldn't be used and all had to be replaced with countersunk screws to avoid any clashing as the swivel rotates.

6-8-27. The plastic trims on the seats had to be cut down so that the swivelling seat didn't rub on them. Steve used his circular saw to make a clean, accurate cut.

6-8-28. This enabled the trims to be refitted but it did mean that they didn't stay in place very well. Later, I drilled two holes and held everything in place with a couple of self-tapping screws.

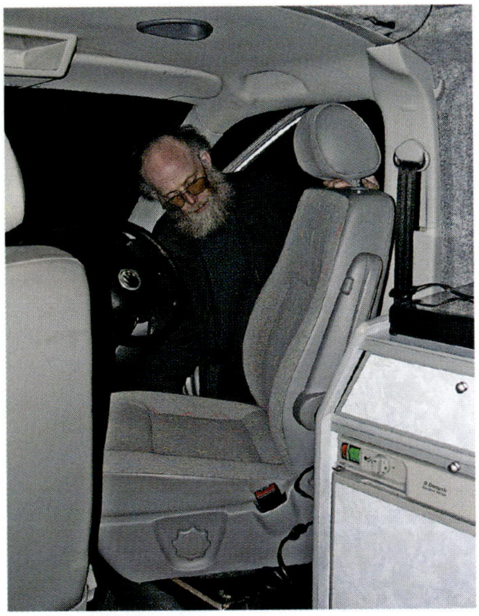

6-8-29. Steve got as far as installing the swivel seat on the driver's side but later on, I took it out again. This was because, in order to clear the handbrake, Steve had to raise the seat about 25mm using box section steel and this made the seat too high for me. I also found that the seat would only turn by 90° and this made it of limited use because there isn't much legroom in the space between the two front seats.

6-8-30. Steve Monkley seen demonstrating our new swivel passenger seat.

SECTION 9. SEAT LUMBAR SUPPORT AND SEAT HEATER

Personal question time. When on a journey in your camper:

1. Has your bum ever been numb?
2. Does your back sometimes ache like the furies?

If you answered "yes" to either of these questions, you might want to try 'Dr' Lindsay Porter's prescription, as dispensed by the motor caravan 'pharmacy' at Vehvac in Kent.

Oh, what bliss! what joy! is a warm bott on a cold winter's morn. And I've always enjoyed the luxury of that bit of extra support which you often feel the need of when you're tired or at the end of a long journey: It's then that the old back muscles become stiff and achy and can even be prone to spasms. And when the latter happens, the combination of extra lumbar support and a dab of heat where it does most good has to be experienced to be believed. I swear that my wife, Shan, who has had severe back problems in her time, would go and spend an evening in the passenger seat of our VW T5 camper now it's got Rostra lumbar supports and seat heaters, if only there was a telly in there ...

Rostra seat heaters and lumbar supports are from the country where luxury add-ons are the norm rather than the exception; the good ol' US of A. Rostra is part of the Dayna group, a massive corporation that makes Original Equipment for vehicle manufacturers, so you know that Rostra stuff will be good. And it is. I've been fitting it for over 15 years.

6-9-1. Vehvac's Keith Clark had to remove a number of dash panels in order to connect the seat heater switches where I wanted them. It seems that the more modern the vehicle, the greater the likelihood that dashboard stripping will be involved.

Now, when reading the following, bear in mind that different manufacturers' seats – and often, different models from the same manufacturer – have different constructions, but the principles shown here apply to all and, once you've thought out the way in which your seats have been put together, the work will be fairly straightforward. Vehvac had never stripped Volkswagen T5 seats before it carried out this work but Paul Thornton, one of the partners, applied his general knowledge of seats and some basic common sense to show how these seats are stripped and rebuilt.

It's worth pointing out that the tops of vehicle seats backs – the areas where headrests and, in some cases, side airbags are mounted – don't have to be fully stripped to fit these components. Bit like going to the (real) doctors to have a stethoscope pressed against your chest. You just pull up your shirt, leaving your arms in place. But don't worry; your Camper isn't fitted with lady-seats, so there are no unmentionable undies up there ...

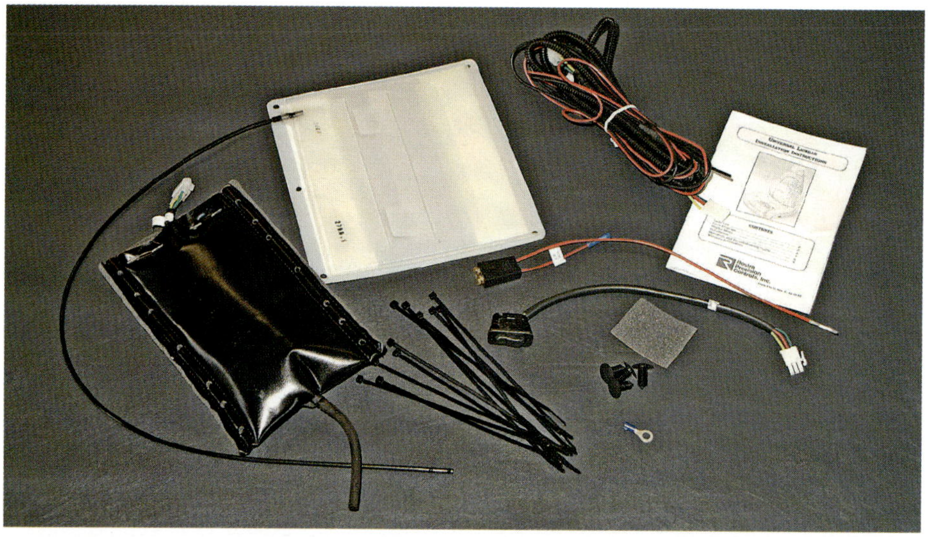

6-9-2. These are the components of the Rostra Universal Lumbar Support Kit. Reading from left to right, the major items shown here are the pump, the expandable bag, the wiring loom and beneath it the fuse and rocker switch. On the right, is the comprehensive instructions which include advice on how to strip a number of different types of seat.

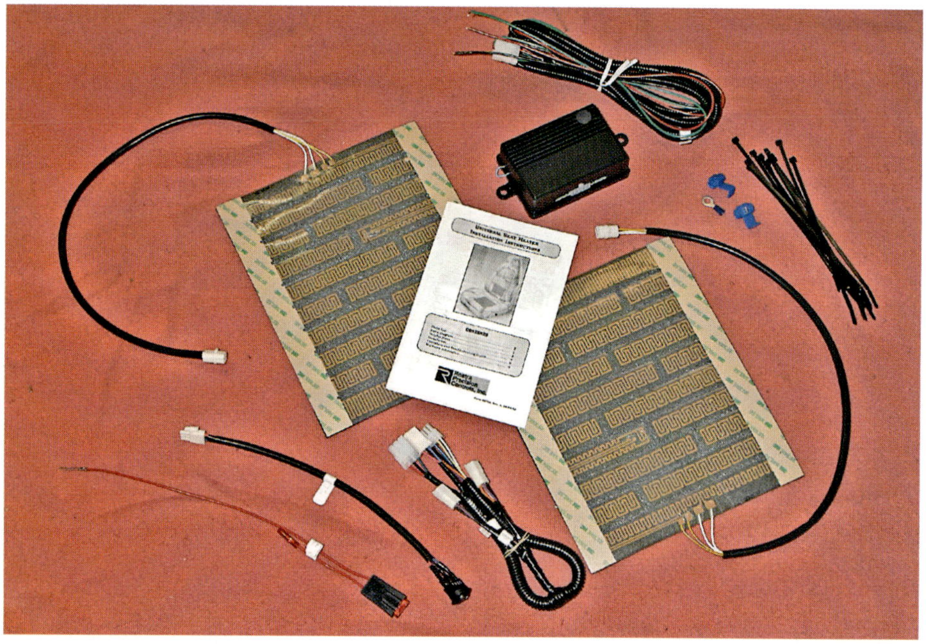

6-9-3. Similar advice on seat stripping is included in the seat heater kit where, from top-to-bottom, you can see the wiring loom and control box, the two heater pads, one for the seat base and one for the back with the instructions on top, the plug-in wiring loom with connectors already fitted, and the two-way switch and fuse unit.

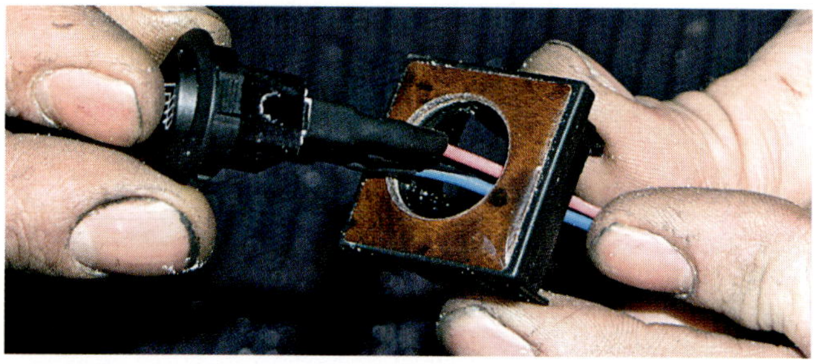

6-9-4. Keith took one of the switch blanking plates from the dashboard and drilled the size of hole recommended in the instructions so that the rocker switch clipped into place. He ran the wiring through the dash as required and in accordance with the fitting instructions.

6-9-5. The seat heater switch has two settings. You can choose during installation whether to have the whole seat heated on a higher or a lower setting; or you can choose just to have the back heated as an option to having the seat and back heated, both at the same time.

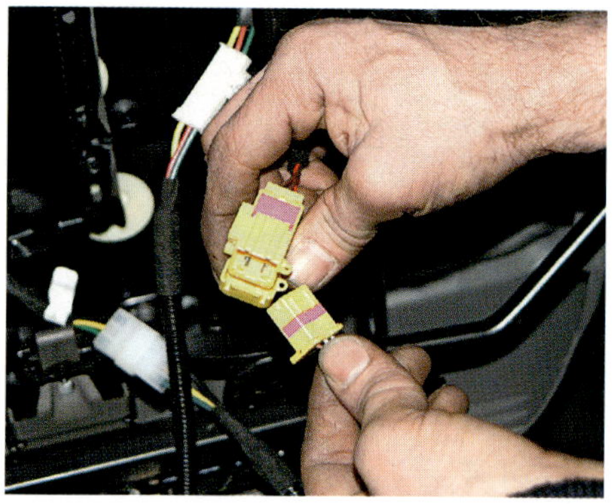

6-9-6. Vehvac decided to remove the seat from the vehicle, although in some cases, it is perfectly possible to install seat heaters and/or lumbar supports with the seats still in place. These seats are fitted with side airbags and so it was necessary to follow the manufacturer's instructions carefully, disconnecting the power at the battery before disconnecting the airbags. As long as the power is not reconnected at the battery, the airbags can stay disconnected. However, if power is reconnected with the airbags disconnected, the vehicle's ECU would probably need to be reset by a VW main dealer. Note that every manufacturer has its own procedures for airbag disconnection and these must be followed to the letter.

6-9-7. Keith next turned his attention to connecting the wiring to the components beneath the seat. The Rostra wiring diagram in the instructions is refreshingly clear and easy to follow.

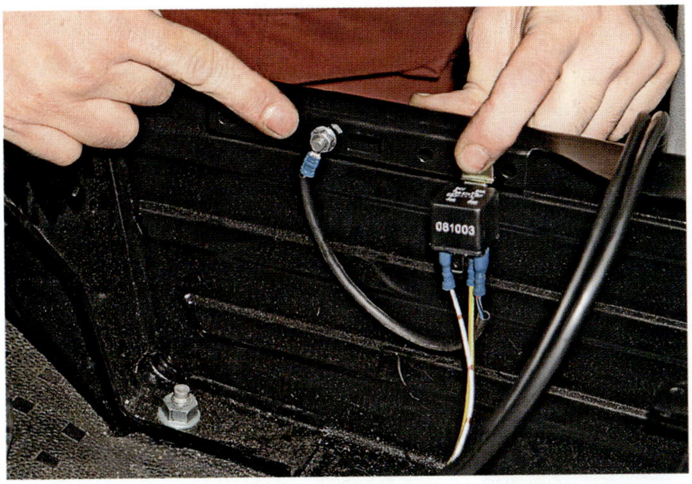

6-9-8. Keith wanted to spare the switch for the seat heater from having to carry the full current and so, in typically thorough Vehvac fashion, he fitted a relay. This is a heavy-duty switch which is operated by the user-switch. It is capable of carrying a higher current and Keith used it to pass the current from the battery to the heater. He also used the metal frame of the seat base for bolting a sound earth connection in place.

6-9-9. We both hate Scotchlok connectors because they are more prone to breaking down so Keith soldered the end of each bare cable …

6-9-10. … before crimping connectors onto their ends. Most of the connectors are already fitted to the Rostra kit but obviously, those supplying the current, the earth connections and those to the relay all had to be made up.

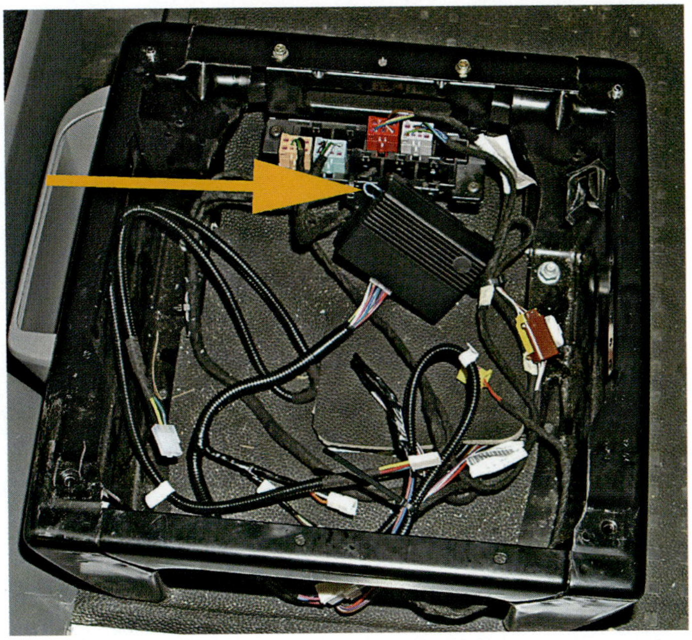

6-9-11. Finally, all of the connections were in place. This is the underside of the passenger seat and you can see the terminal ends waiting to be connected up to the seat itself when it's refitted. The wire loop (arrowed) on the control box is left intact if you want to be able to separate heat from the seat base and backrest. It is cut through if you want high- and low-level heating to both parts of the seat at once. We prefer the latter.

6-9-12. The location of the lumbar support pump will vary according to the construction of the seat but, in most cases, there is enough room on the seat frame to fix the pump (contained in its own protective bag) using the cable ties provided. Keith decided not to fit the pump at this stage because he needed access to the underside of the seat base.

6-9-13. On our Volkswagen, the seat bases are held down with screws which pass through the base of the seat frame.

6-9-14. With these screws removed, the seat base is simply lifted away.

6-9-15. At this point, Vehvac's Paul took over and started bending back the metal tabs found around the perimeter of the seat base and holding the seat trim in place. These are commonly found on many types of seat but there are other systems often involving screws. If you look carefully you can always see how the seat trim is held in place from beneath.

6-9-16. With all the tabs removed, Paul folded the plastic seam around the edge of the trim away from the seat base ...

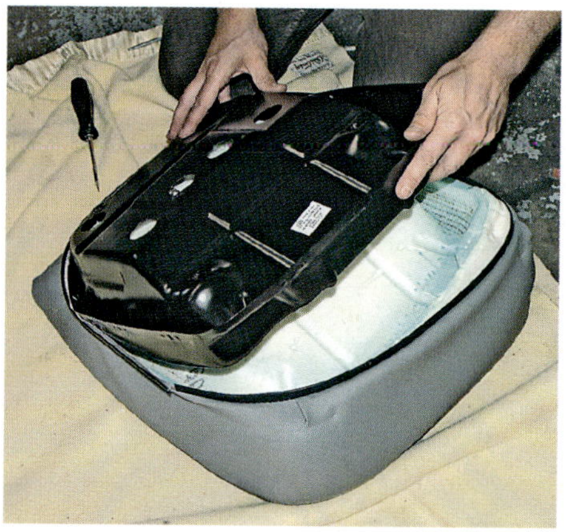

6-9-17. ... and lifted out the metal tray.

6-9-18. The seat heaters are held against the foam with 3M double-sided tape. It's very strong **so** you don't want to remove the backing paper until you are sure that you are ready to fit the seat heater in place.

6-9-19. It is common for the centre panel in the seat base to be held down by some means. Volkswagens frequently use hooks which pass over wires in the base and are simply sprung off. Many other vehicles use plastic clips which pass straight through the base and are removed from the other side. Once again, careful examination will reveal which fiendish method has been used.

6-9-20. Paul needed to establish which was the best side for the wiring to pass through the seat and having done that, he inserted the heater pad with the sticky tape backing still in place.

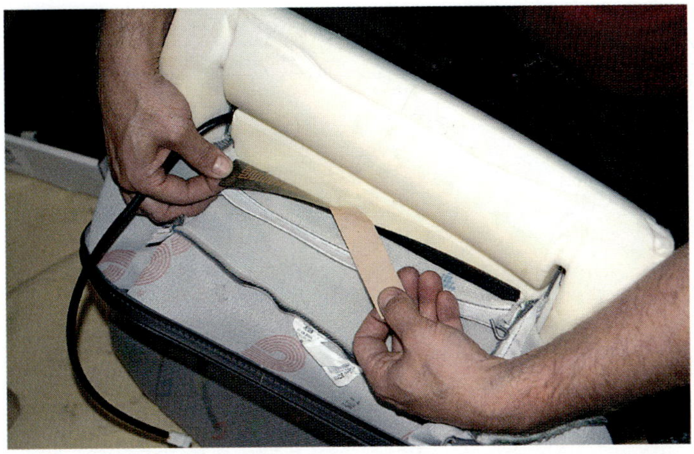

6-9-21. The tape was removed from the heater panel once it was in place. Note that the heater panel needs to go between the trim and the foam on the seat for it to work most efficiently. If placed beneath the foam, it could take ages for the heat to travel through the seat and might never be felt at all.

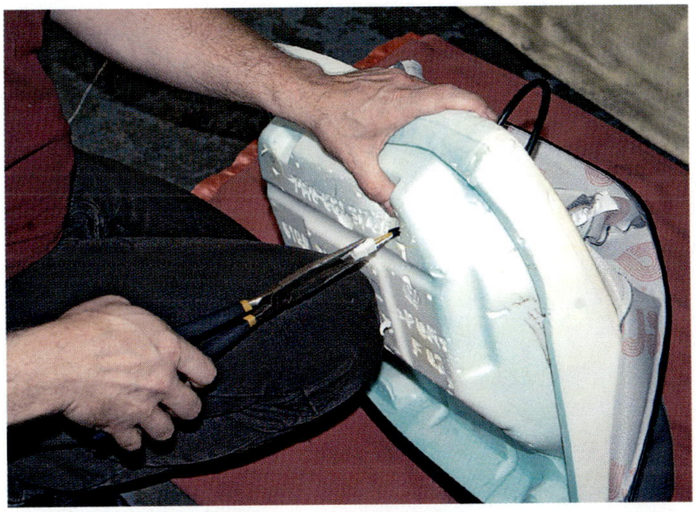

6-9-22. He made a hole through the foam in the seat base in line with a hole in the steel seat pan and passed the cable through.

6-9-23. After reassembling the seat, he used these seat trimmer's pliers to fix the tabs back into place again.

6-9-24. Here's an instance of how it may be possible to carry out this work without removing the seats from the vehicle, depending on your particular installation. The seat back trim is joined at the bottom with a plastic clip. When you tip the seat all the way back or examine it from beneath, you can always see how the seat back trim has been fitted.

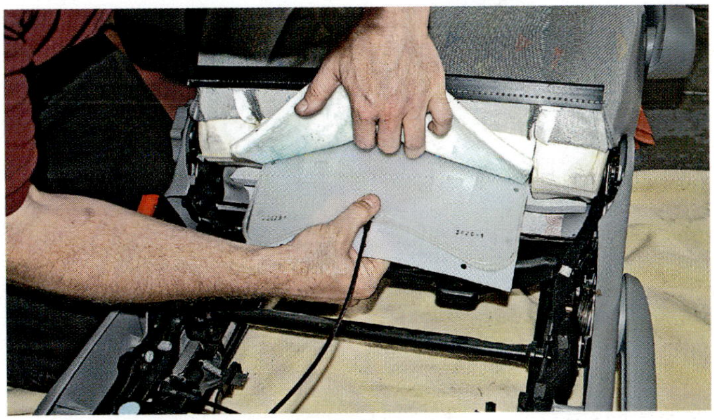

6-9-25. This is the bladder for the lumbar support and this is inserted behind the foam of the seat backrest.

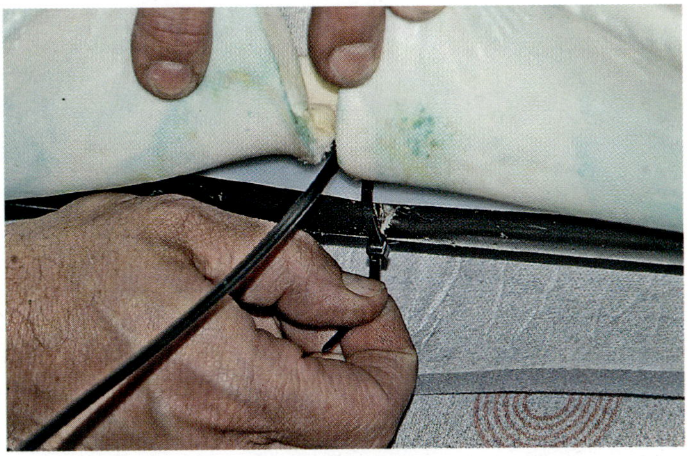

6-9-26. It consists of a flexible plastic bag on a stiffer plastic backing. The backing has holes in it and cable ties are again provided so that the backing can be clipped to the seat frame, preventing it from moving.

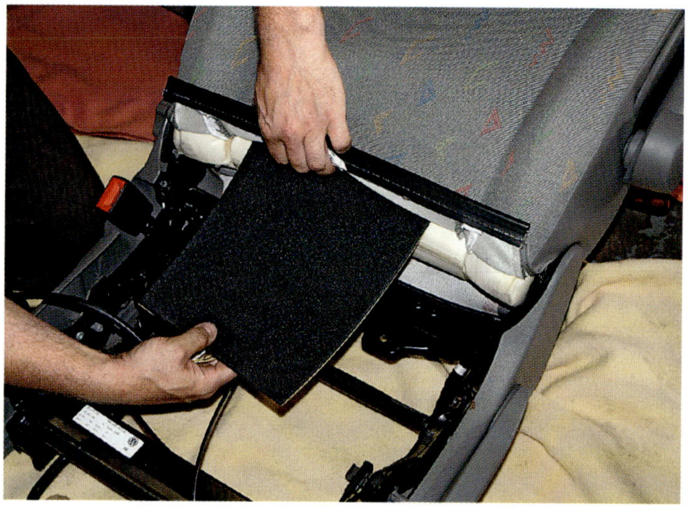

6-9-27. Once again, the heater element is fitted between the trim and the front of the foam.

6-9-28. Paul routed the air tube for the lumbar support and the electrical cable along the base of the seat foam …

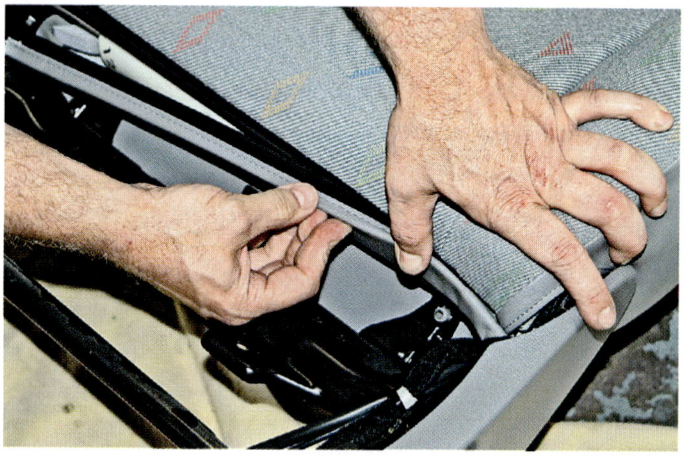

6-9-29. … before clipping the bottom of the cover back into position again.

6-9-30. The seat base was screwed back down to the seat frame. You can see the seat cable and tube connections protruding through the seat base.

6-9-31. This wonderful tool, also available from Rostra, cuts a perfectly shaped slot for taking the rocker switch for the lumbar support.

6-9-32. Paul passed the switch cable through the hole in the seat base trim …

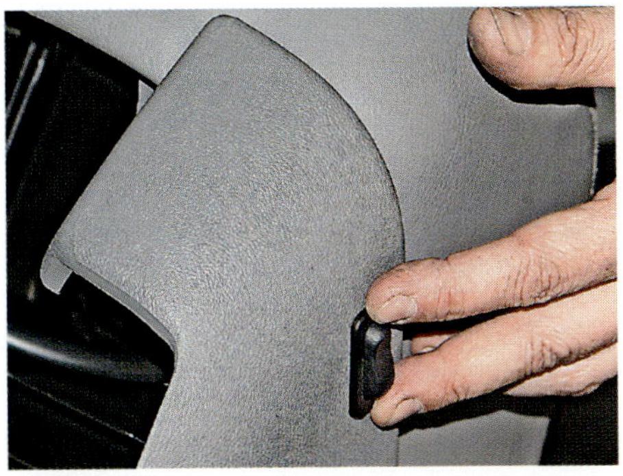

6-9-33. … before clipping the switch into position.

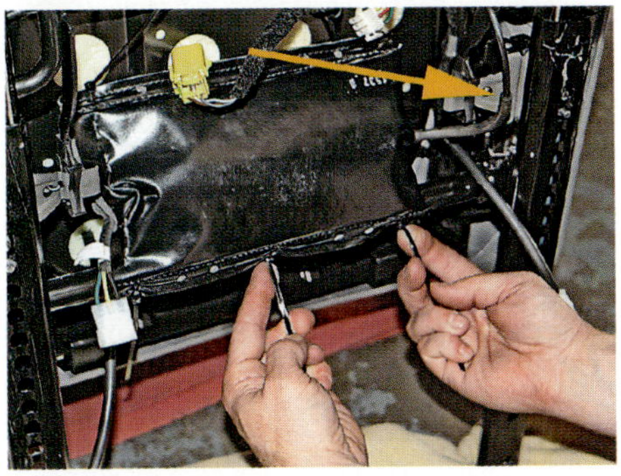

6-9-34. Paul fully fitted the pump bag to the seat base pretty much as he had established previously, having already connected the tube from the pump to the tube passing up to the inflatable bag in the seat (arrowed).

6-9-35. It then remained to refit the seats, plugging in all the Rostra connections – every plug and socket is a matching pair and different to all the others, so you can't go wrong …

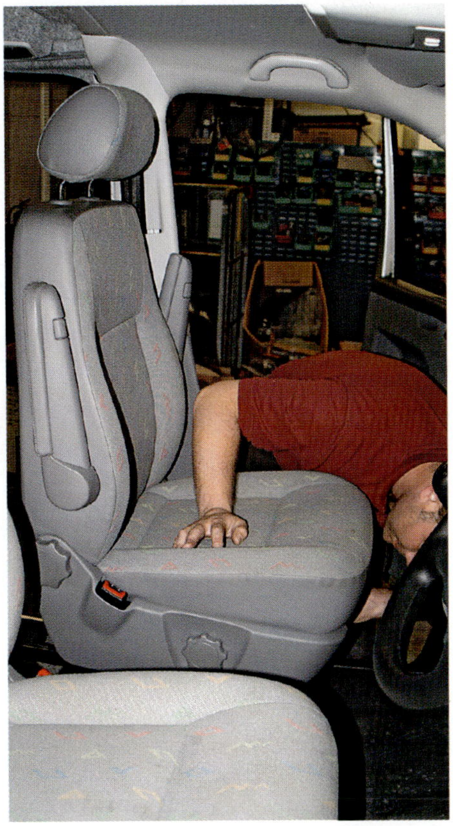

6-9-36. … and then refitting the seat frames to their bases.

SECTION 10. WOOD-STYLE DASH

Here's how to enhance the appearance of the Volkswagen T5's dash with a faux-wood-grain dash trim kit – without being stuck up about it …

There are still elements of any van conversion that give away the primary role of the base vehicle. For one thing, the van's interior will have been made with longevity in mind rather than aesthetic appeal, although the T5's is one of the best in the business. You can quite easily put carpets down on top of those hard-wearing rubber mats but the other main area of the van's appearance, the bit of the vehicle that the poor, long-suffering driver has to spend most time looking at – the dashboard – is almost invariably a featureless expanse of grey plastic, and because a van is that much wider than a car, there's so much more of it!

I decided that our Leisuredrive VW T5 needed a little attention in the dashboard department so decided to fit a 'wooden' dashboard trim from Parma Industries.

It's worth noting that it takes a while to fit the Parma kit and you really do have to take care when doing so. It's made from top-quality materials and it would be a shame to spoil it for the sake of rushing. The point is, although the job might not take you longer than a couple of hours, you really need to set aside a full day to allow yourself time to prepare properly and to spend as long as necessary to fit the trim so that it looks right and is properly aligned.

Incidentally, this is the colour known as 'Warm Brown Walnut' but there are several other colours available to special order. There are several wood-effect colours (no, it's not real tree!) plus Aluminium or Carbon Fibre for those who want something a bit trendier.

6-10-1. The new Volkswagen T5 oozes quality, although I'm told that the German-built ones are better than those built in Poland. Ours is German-built, thank goodness! The dash, though rather Passat-like around the driver's 'work station', is still a bit featureless and slab-like. Better than you've any right to expect in a mere panel van but certainly functional rather than fashionable.

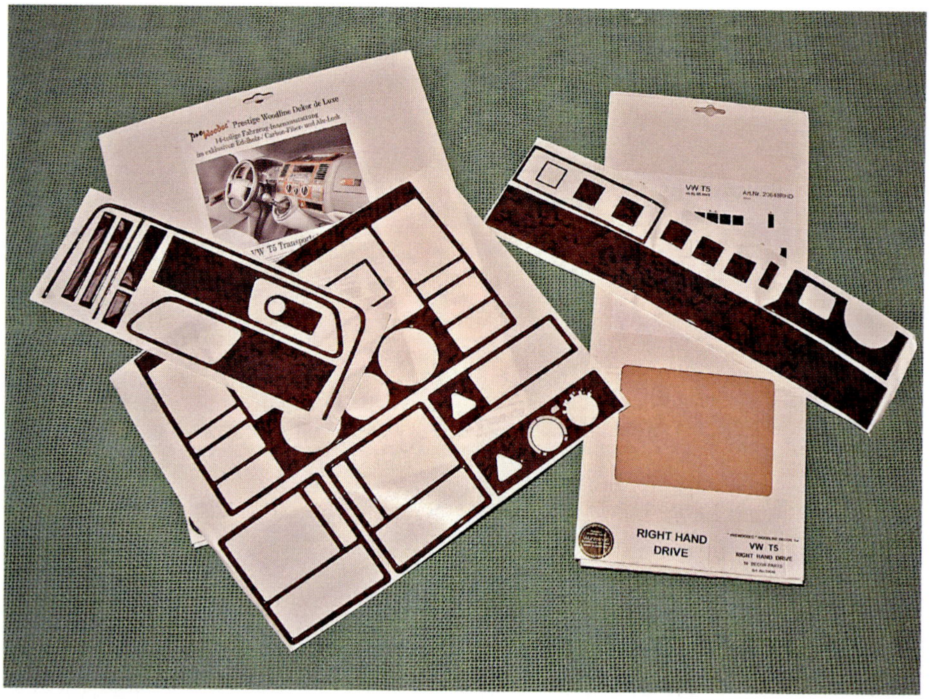

6-10-2. The Parma kit – or 'Dashboard Decor' as they call it – comes as two parts. The main part (PPW-250) is for the bulk of the dash panel while the 'Additional Kit' provides extra trim parts, including switch blank and airbag cover trim. Your first job is to get out all the parts and work out what will go where.

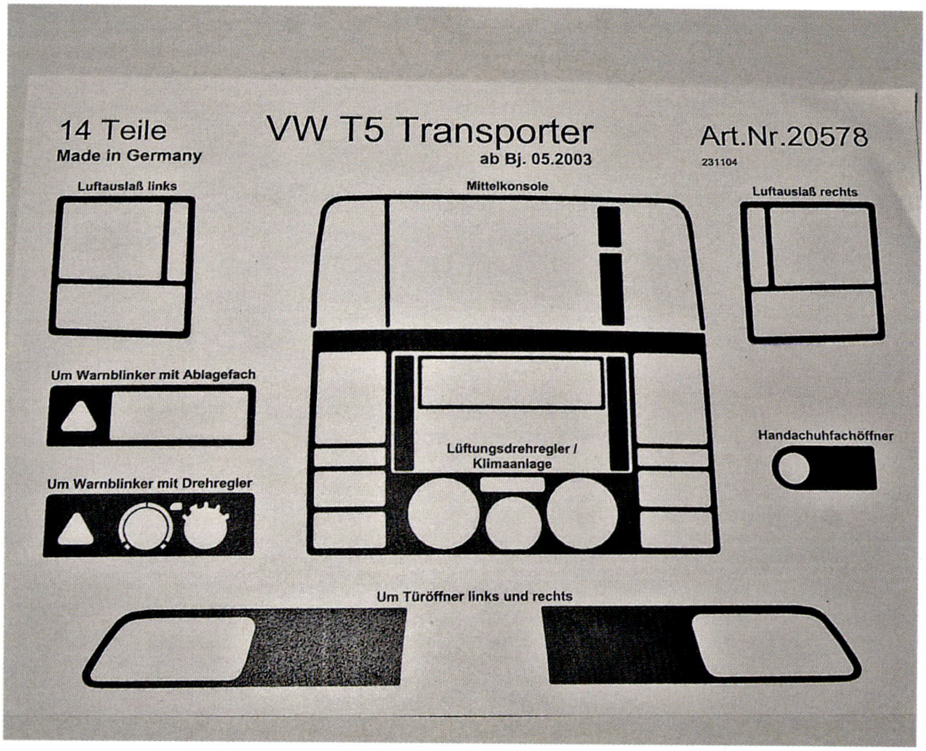

6-10-3. Included in each kit is a plan of the trim parts included in the box. It's a helpful cross-reference to the components on the sheet of trim sections but there is one serious disadvantage. Unless you know what a 'Handachunfachöfner' and a 'Um Warnblinker mit Ablagefach' is, you're a bit stuck to be honest! Even worse, German dictionaries tend to be useless with these technical, compound German words unless you know enough German to work out what the component parts of the words are so you can look them up separately. At least, that's my excuse for not being able to find them in the dictionary ...

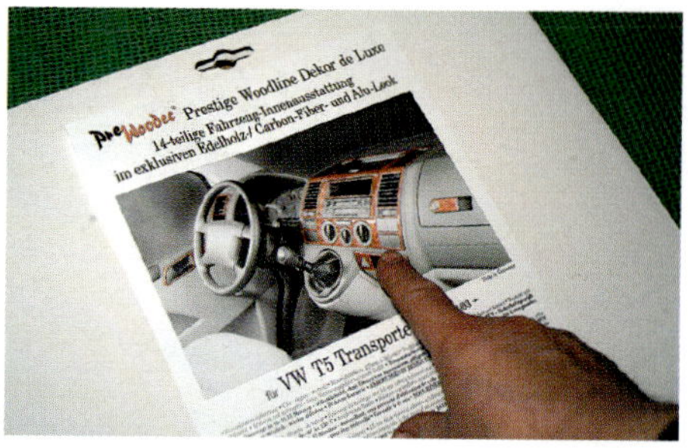

6-10-4. I found it useful to compare the picture on the front of each box with the parts list. Even though it depicts a left-hand drive vehicle, it helped to work out which parts on the list went where. If I'd had time, I could even have worked out what some of those long German words mean but I'd never have been able to pronounce them anyway!

6-10-5. If you are working in the winter months, you will need to put some extra heat into the interior of your van. If you've got a space heater, put that on. I placed the oil-filled radiator from out of our house between the front seats so that it was heating the dashboard area almost directly.

SAFETY FIRST!

- If you have a mains lead trailing into your motor caravan, be sure not to close the door on the cable.
- Modern vans have tight door shuts and there is every chance of cutting right into the cable with risk of shorting mains electricity to the body of your vehicle. Risk of electrocution!
- Much safer to use the mains connection that you would use on-site and connect to a 13amp socket inside the motor caravan.

The extra heat you will be putting into the vehicle's interior has two important benefits. One is that the adhesive on the backs of the trim sections will adhere much better when warm and the other is that the thick plastic sections will bend to shape – and stay in shape – much better than when they are cold. Each section is no less than 2.5mm thick and will be surprisingly stiff when cold. In fact, if your van has any sharper corners around which the trim needs to be folded, you will need to use the technique described right at the end of this article. New

6-10-6. Now then, this is most important! You MUST use grease and silicone remover on the dashboard before starting to adhere the trim panels. If you don't, the trim sections won't stick and there is a real risk that the adhesive on them may be made useless. They're too expensive to waste!

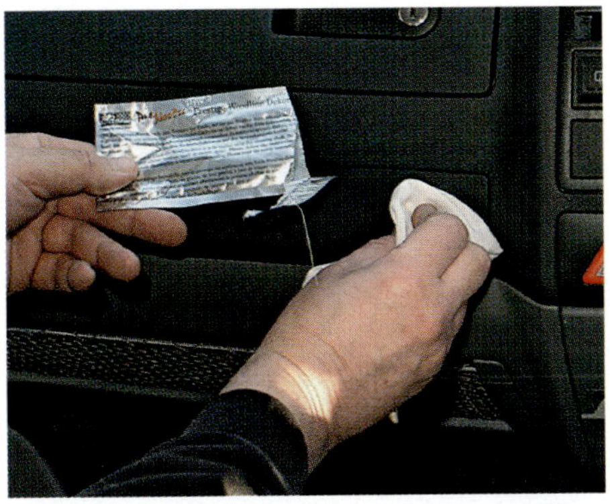

6-10-7. A small cloth impregnated with degreaser is supplied with each kit but there's not enough to do the job properly. I wiped each section of dashboard three times, using a clean rag each time, turning it frequently between wipes so that I didn't just spread silicones around between panels. You can't see those slippery silicones but believe me, they're there and they will prevent adhesive from adhering unless you eradicate them thoroughly.

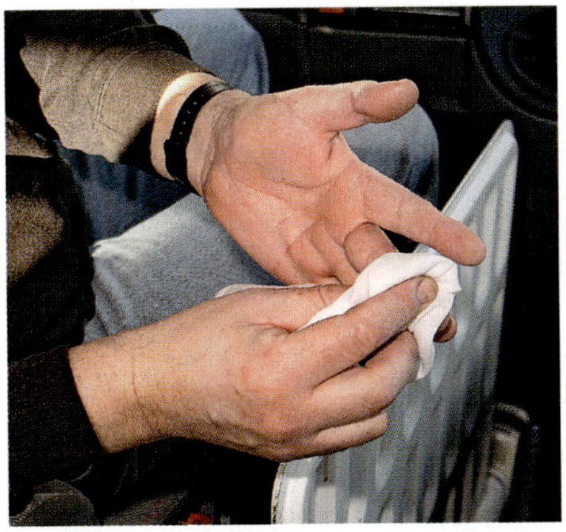

6-10-8. Grease is another enemy of adhesive and even the small amount of grease naturally created by your skin will reduce the adhesive's stickiness. I wiped my fingers before starting and a couple of times more while carrying out the work.

dashboards may have a coating of silicone on them, both from the release agent used when the plastic parts were moulded and from the heavy hands of the sales staff who sometimes seem to think that they are selling to jackdaws: Make it shiny and you make it attractive. (Or not, in my opinion.)

Older vehicle's dashes will probably have an accumulation of grease, dirt and yet more silicone. I have quite a lot to do with car bodywork and I've always got a can of Autopaint's 'Panel Wipe' handy. It's designed to remove all the contaminants described above before applying filler or paint, while not damaging vehicle paintwork or trim and it's also superb for this job. I would strongly recommend having a look in Yellow Pages for a car paint factory selling Autopaint products (it does sell to the public, unlike some manufacturers) and make sure this part of the job is done properly. You can always use the rest of the can to remove tar splashes and kamikaze fly remains from the front of your motor caravan.

SAFETY FIRST!

- All types of panel wipe are very volatile and create a strong fire risk before evaporating away. Keep away from all sources of combustion.
- Work only in a well ventilated area. The vehicle must be outside with all the doors open. Leave time between applications for fumes to clear before adding more.
- **Don't** use anything other than proprietary panel wipe. For instance, detergent won't necessarily remove silicones; cellulose thinners will melt the plastic on your dash!

6-10-9. I decide to start with the 'Um Warnblinker mit Ablagefach'. (Well you would, wouldn't you!) It was easy to see that it was the section that goes around the hazard warning light switch and it looked like a good one to learn with as it didn't seem too large.

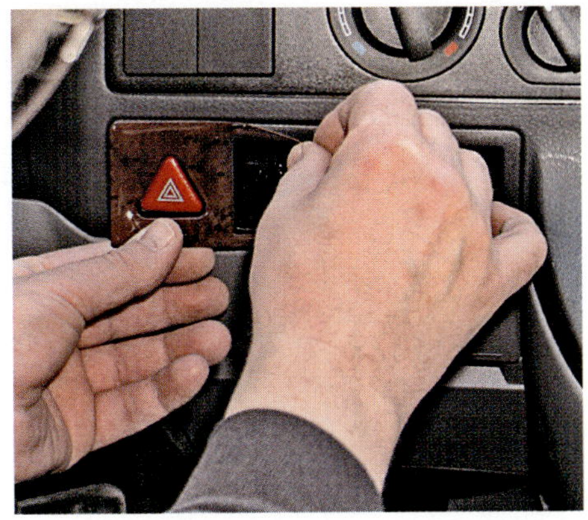

6-10-10. I started by aligning the hole in the trim with the hazard switch button – and got it wrong! So, before pressing the rest of the section down, I carefully peeled it back and lined it up more accurately.

6-10-11. The thin strips that go around the oddments tray were very flexible and it was important to make sure that the top strip was absolutely parallel to the grey plastic behind it. I reasoned that the bottom strip would be less obvious to the eye but, in the event, with the top strip in place, the bottom one 'landed' in just the right position.

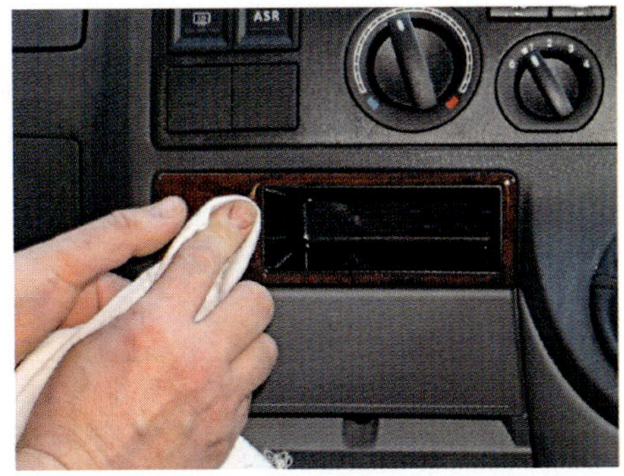

6-10-12. Finally, I used a clean, dry cloth to wipe the trim down, working from the inside-out on the larger section to remove any air bubbles that might have been trapped. Take great care not to press down too hard if the plastic is very warm because you could leave the imprint of the cloth in the plastic finish.

6-10-13. The vent surround was moderately tricky to fit because there was no larger, rigid section to fit first. I concentrated on making sure that each part of the trim was sited exactly central to the edges of the grey surround panel. I then found that the two lower strips were slightly too long. This proved not to be a problem. Provided that there isn't too much material to lose, you can stick down the outer edges, then concentrate on working the over-long strip back, towards the outer sides while smoothing it down. The plasticity of the warm plastic allows it to shrink back into itself, but don't press down too hard, too fast or you'll end up with a kink that will be difficult to get rid of.

6-10-14. This proved to be the hardest part of all to fit and it took two pairs of hands. Shan and I decided that we would start at the bottom-centre, aligning the trim with the switch gear and, after a couple of false starts and some careful pulling off of the trim, it went on really well. The very high quality of the kit really showed up here, as the complex shapes and cutouts fitted perfectly to the dash panel.

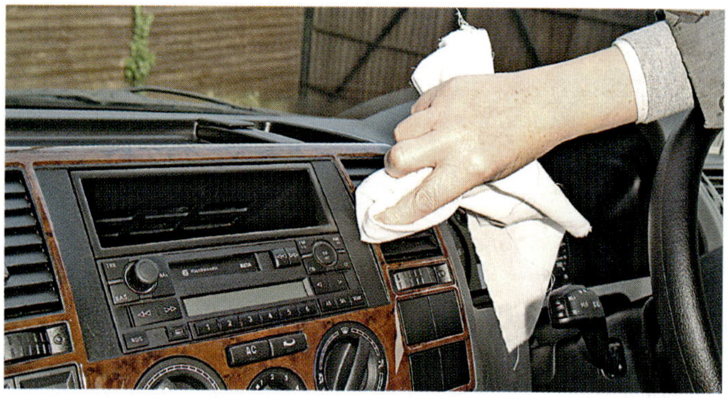

6-10-15. Once again, all the surfaces were smoothed down and all the edges pressed to make sure there were no gaps between trim and dash panel.

6-10-16. I wasn't too sure about these small sections stuck on the dash top but in fact, once fitted, they added to the effect of a complete set rather than a few random, stuck-on bits.

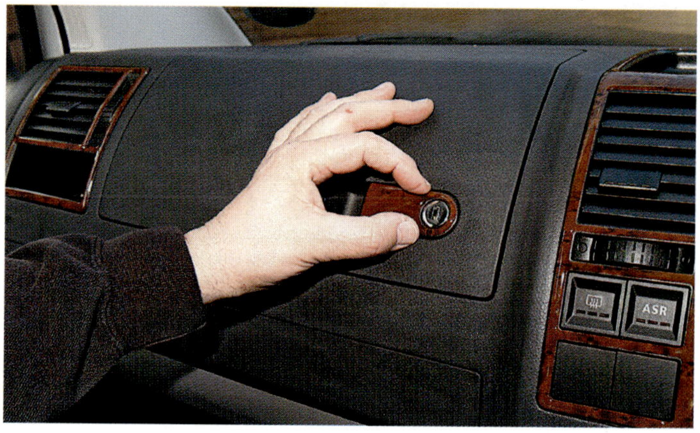

6-10-17. This small section that fits around the glove compartment door handle is even more effective because it breaks up what is otherwise one of the largest expanses of blank grey. In retrospect, this is also just about the easiest part to fit so would be a good one to start off with while you get used to the extreme stickiness of the adhesive on the back of each piece of trim. This was fitted by making sure that the hole was completely concentric to the lock on the door while also ensuring that the long, horizontal part was aligned with its background.

6-10-18. The door handle surrounds were again lined up first with the holes which they surround – the same principle as with the glove compartment door trim.

6-10-19. With the thinner sections aligned and held down, the flatter piece was smoothed down with that clean, dry cloth to squeeze out any air bubbles as it was lowered onto the door trim.

6-10-20. It took us a while to figure out where this little lad went but, once that was established, it was another of the easiest parts to fit.

6-10-21. We worked out that this long strip could only be fitted to the dash panel beneath the glove compartment door. The trouble is, this part of the dash panel is in two sections. The shorter (outer) length is fixed to the dash while the longer one is part of the airbag. You could tell by pressing carefully that they are not joined. It therefore seemed to me that there should be a break in the wood-finish trim so as not to inhibit the operation of the airbag. I trimmed the paper off one edge of the strip before removing it from the backing paper.

6-10-22. I then held it up against the dash and carefully marked the position of the gap between the airbag section and the fixed section (see inset).

6-10-23. My try square was then used to draw a line across the trim strip at precisely 90°.

6-10-24. Sharp scissors are easier to use than a knife in my view, though you do have to take care to cut exactly on the line and it's important not to leave marks between the separate cuts.

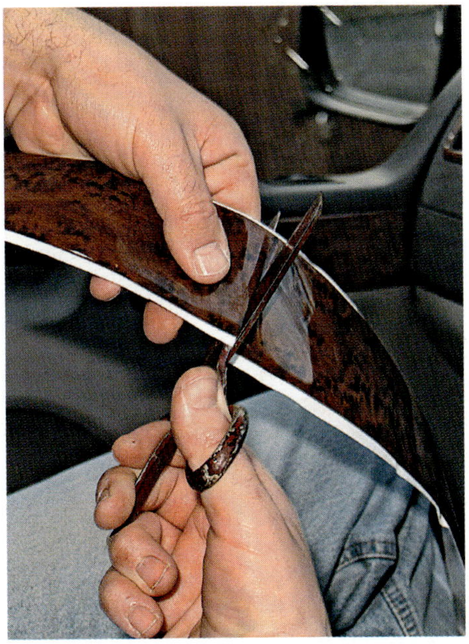

6-10-25. The smaller section was stuck down first, making sure that it left clear the joint between the two dash panels.

6-10-26. Again starting at the joint-end but taking care to leave a gap at that point, the longer section went on to the airbag trim next.

6-10-27. The length of trim had to be aligned carefully with the top edge of the trim. It had 'banana' shaped a little when in the box and I had to make sure it was pulled level as it was stuck down.

6-10-28. Perhaps the joint wasn't quite as professional as the bevelled edges seen on the rest of the trim – but I'd rather have my airbag working properly, thanks very much!

6-10-29. After concentrating so hard on the safety aspect of making the trim 'work' properly, I was taken by surprise to find that there was a fold around which the trim didn't want to adhere. Then I remembered some advice given to me by Parma Industries. He said that, if trim was reluctant to bend, you could use a heat gun – but only on a very low setting – or, better still, a hairdryer to heat and soften the material so that it will take on its new shape. I didn't want to risk wrinkling the plastic with a heat gun so out came the domestic hair dryer and that worked fine.

Inside information: The instructions supplied with the kit make it clear that the dash must be warm and that each piece of 'wood-grain' trim must be warmed before and after being fitted.

6-10-30. This thinnest piece was also one of the hardest to fit. After a couple of false starts which involved pulling the piece off and starting again, I decided to run the strip around the centres of the edges to which they were fixed and stretch or shrink the lengths as necessary.

Talking of stretching, you need to be aware that the adhesive used is very powerful and, when you remove a section of strip to reposition it, there will be a real risk of stretching it unless you take extreme care. Pull off slowly, letting the adhesive come free as you go, rather than trying to tear the whole thing off too quickly.

6-10-31. Don't do any of the pressing down and smoothing out until you really are sure that each trim section is positioned precisely. I didn't try removing any of the trim after it had been stuck well down but I should imagine that there would be a very great danger of ruining it if you tried.

Incidentally, on the subject of stickiness, you may be surprised by the extent to which the trim sections stick to your fingers. You should try to hold the edges as far as possible, though that isn't always possible. Don't press down hard on the adhesive surface with your fingers, make sure you don't contaminate it with dirt or cloth lint and, whatever you do, don't let it fold around and stick to itself. We managed to avoid this but I really don't know if you get the joint apart again without ruining the trim.

6-10-32. The Parma dash enhancement kit is not cheap but then, top quality rarely is. It's superbly well made and I think it improves the appearance of the dash beyond measure.

SECTION 11. UPGRADE ICE & SAT. NAV.

Here's how to fit speakers and make one or two other improvements to your T5 motor caravan.

6-11-1. This is the set of Blaupunkt speakers I chose to fit to our vehicle. They're called Ultraflat High Power Speaker with 120 watts capacity. The power is good for their location in the back of the vehicle and their low profile is even better because you don't want to be causing damage to your speakers if you have to load anything into the back of your vehicle.

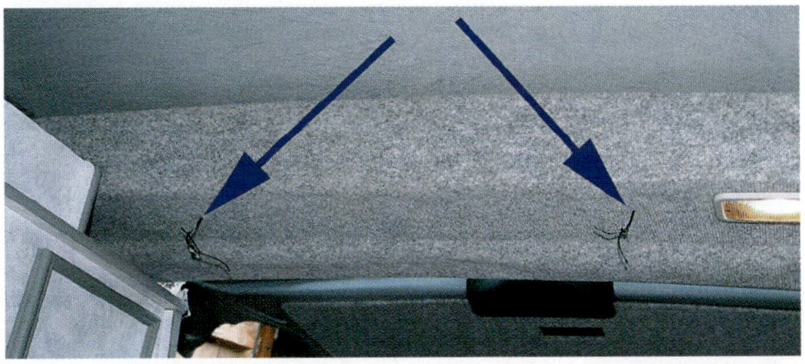

6-11-2. In the relevant sections of this manual you will see that the wires were run into place for lights and also for the rear speakers. Here, the tags of cable can be seen protruding through the hollow section at the rear of the roof.

6-11-3. Taking care not to cut through the wires, I used a jigsaw to cut out the holes to the sizes recommended by Blaupunkt.

6-11-4. First, I held the speaker cover in place and used a felt pen to mark where each screw would be going. Then, spire nuts were pushed over the edge of the plywood and carpet.

6-11-5. Each speaker and cover was fitted together as a unit using the four screws supplied in the kit.

6-11-6. I find the Blaupunkt speakers attractive and unobtrusive – and they certainly belt out the sound!

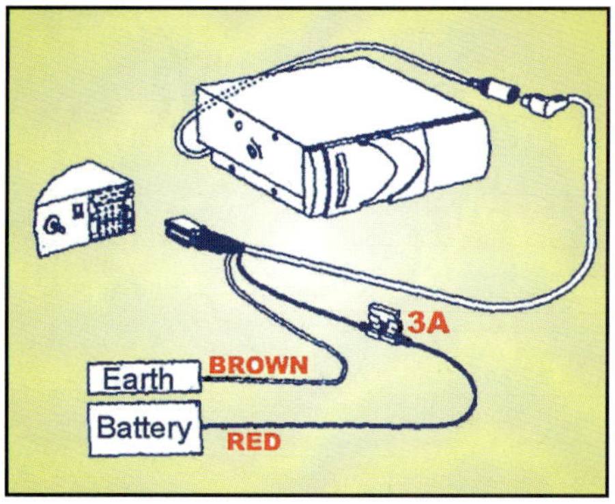

6-11-7. I also wanted to fit a Blaupunkt CD autochanger but before you do so, you need to make sure that you have the correct cables to connect your autochanger to whatever head unit you may be using, and you also need to be certain that your head unit will be capable of controlling the autochanger.

6-11-8. I used some old seat belt mountings to adapt the brackets that came with the autochanger so that they fitted existing mounting points on the vehicle.

6-11-9. Here, the mounting point extension is seen being bolted down to the floor.

6-11-10. The rear mountings were simple screwed down to the floor.

6-11-11. The hardest part of the job was in making the cutout in the plastic trim cover that goes on the back of the seat frame. As you can see, the recess in the trim is an almost perfect shape for accepting the autochanger.

6-11-12. Some versions of the Volkswagen Transporter T5 can have the VW (actually a Blaupunkt-built unit) MFD (sometimes known as 'Navi') satellite navigation systems fitted as standard. Some versions of the Transporter T5 were not specified as being fitted with this unit and, in such cases, you would need to buy your own. Purchased new from a VW dealership they are horrendously expensive but it may be possible to buy one on Ebay. There may be some risk involved in buying such a unit, especially if it is being shipped from abroad. I purchased mine through Ebay and was very pleased with it but you must look carefully at feedback reports. You may prefer to go to a specialist, one of which you might well still find on Ebay. I like this unit because the 'sat nav' facility is superb and the sound quality of the radio is also of a very high quality. However, beware that the radio does not offer long-wave (a bit of a downer for those who like BBC's cricket reports!) and, although there is a slot for a CD in the top of it, this is for the satellite navigation information and cannot be used for playing music CDs. This is why I fitted a separate CD changer to the vehicle.

6-11-13. I had the unit fitted for me by Snowden Auto Electrics in Hereford. The person supplying the unit also supplied the correct wiring harness at extra cost and you will need this if your vehicle was not specified to be fitted with the unit originally. Snowden also had to cut out the plastic housing which, on our vehicle, was two single-DIN slots and not a single double-DIN slot which is what you need.

6-11-14. The cables have to be carefully manoeuvred out of the way as the unit is slid into position.

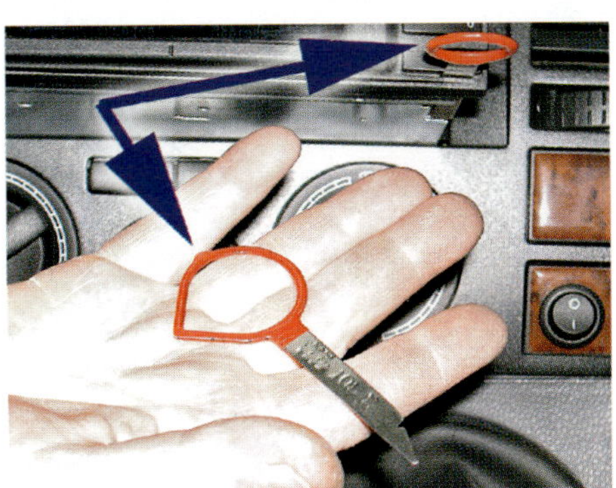

6-11-15. To remove this unit from the vehicle, you will need a removal tool of this specific shape. It can be purchased from any specialist automotive tool supplier although, once again, I bought mine on Ebay. The tool pushes into the slot which is also arrowed.

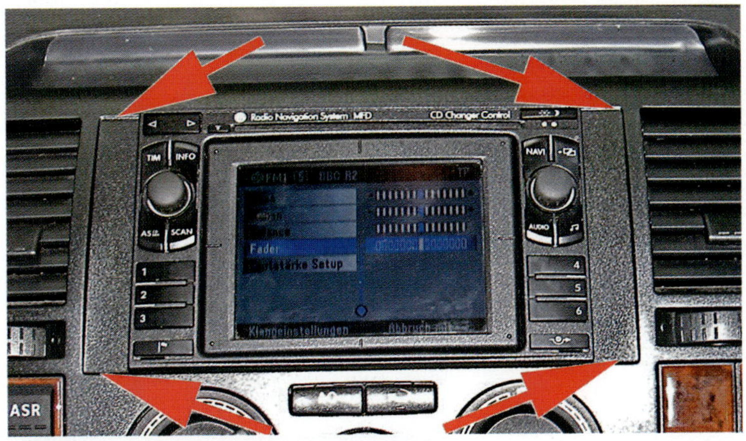

6-11-16. As this picture shows, there are four slots and it is best if you have a full set of four tools, although it is just possible to get away with two, manoeuvring one side of the unit free before inserting the other two tools into the other side and freeing it.

6-11-17. You'll need the correct mapping information to feed into whatever satellite navigation system you choose. Part of the well-known Michelin maps organisation, ViaMichelin has a wide range of up-to-date CD-ROMs, suitable for most in-car navigation systems including the one shown here. ViaMichelin works alongside the major in-car equipment manufacturers in the European market (Bosch, Blaupunkt, Becker and Siemens VDO) and major mapping content suppliers.

There are five CD titles available covering, says ViaMichelin, the whole of Europe. Unlike the VW disk which I had previously tried, the ViaMichelin disks can guide you straight to your destination, even to a specific street number, in many cities. They also combine fully updated maps and a wide selection of hotels and restaurants from the famous Michelin Guide, as well as tourist and practical information taken from The Michelin Green Guide.

SECTION 12. PROTECT UPHOLSTERY

This all started when UltraShield sent me some of its upholstery protector to try, but before I got around to using it, I managed to get an oily stain on the driver's seat of our Volkswagen tow-vehicle. "Oh deary me, what a silly chap I've been!" I said (or words to that effect) before setting out to remedy the situation.

So, if you or the kids drop curry, coffee or Coca-Cola on the upholstery, here's how you can remove some upholstery stains and block others before they happen.

SAFETY FIRST!

- The liquid and vapour are flammable and must only be used away from all sources of ignition.
- Keep out the eyes but, if necessary, wash eyes with plenty of clean water.
- Wear a breathing mask suitable for organic vapours when spraying.

6-12-1. It was after sitting on something oily and then getting into the vehicle that I managed to stain the new upholstery. A wash-off with soap and water only managed to leave a bad tide mark.

I sprayed each cushion top in overlapping patterns, horizontally then vertically. Then I turned my attention to the edges and sprayed those as well. The manufacturers say that the finer the mist, the more effective the application so set your sprayer accordingly.

If you work methodically, you won't forget which cushions you have or haven't sprayed! The UltraShield pongs slightly until it has dried and then has no odour at all, thank goodness. The application took about 40 minutes but would have taken much longer with a hand-pumped applicator. The upholstery was left overnight to dry and lose its odour, before being replaced in the caravan.

UltraShield says that its Fabric Protection is backed by a seven-year warranty from the date of application so I think it's well worth using. Just remember not to sit on the upholstery with an oily bottom before you've used it, like some people we know ...

One container of UltraShield Fabric Protection provided two coats on all the upholstery shown in this article, though this will obviously be determined by the amount you put on.

6-12-2. The first step in removing an oily stain is to dissolve it as much as you can. Autopaint's Panel Wipe, used in car bodywork repairs, did the job well without risk of damaging fabric.

6-12-3. This was followed up with Würth upholstery cleaner, applied in a thick layer of foam from the can before being rubbed vigorously with a clean cloth.

6-12-4. Another clean cloth was used to dry the fabric as much as possible and then the seat was left to dry thoroughly. In winter, you may need to leave the door open in a heated garage.

6-12-5. Once the upholstery was dry, I applied UltraShield fabric protector. It's expensive but goes a really long way. Here, I'm using the pump-up spray you can buy from UltraShield and it's fine for smaller areas such as the seats of your tow-vehicle. The manufacturers say, "UltraShield Fabric Protection penetrates deep into the fabric, forming an invisible shield around each and every fibre. This protective coating inhibits the penetration of frustrating spills such as coffee, tea, milk and fizzy drinks – without affecting the fabric's natural texture."

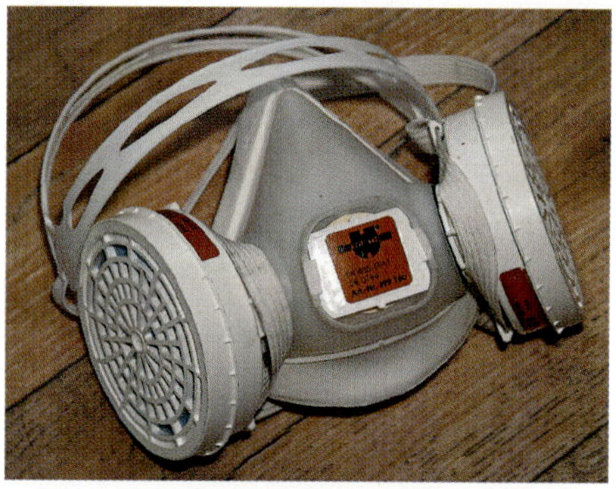

6-12-6. It's highly recommended that you apply the material only in a well-ventilated area and you should wear an adequate air-fed breathing mask such as this Würth disposable mask rather than the simpler type of mask which won't protect against vapours. The producers say, "UltraShield Fabric Protection is non-toxic and is CFC-free." but it is not sensible, in my view, to breathe in the vapourised liquid.

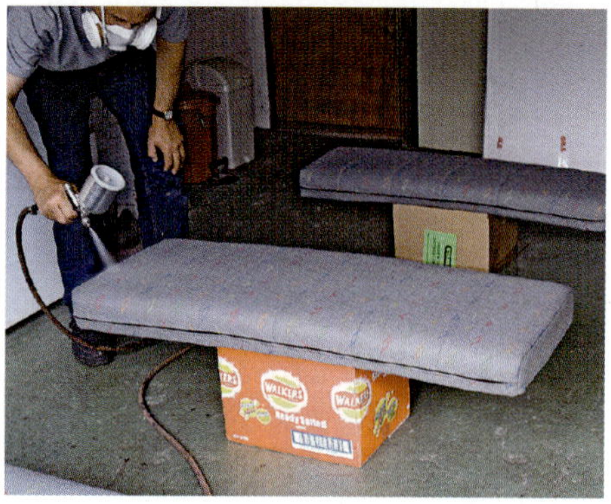

6-12-7. I also applied UltraShield to all of our caravan's upholstery. It was removed from the caravan and spread about in our garage on an assortment of boxes to keep it off the ground.

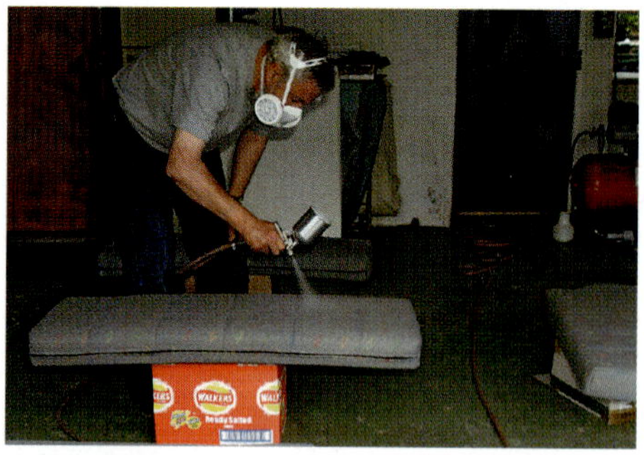

6-12-8. I used a spray gun with a compressor because the pump-up applicator would have taken ages and required a huge number of breaks for pumping up the container. The cheapest spray gun from Machine Mart would do the job. I'm lucky enough to have a Clarke workshop compressor but you could hire one or buy a small, cheap one. They're also handy for inflating a caravan's tyres without the hassle of manoeuvring in a garage forecourt.

SECTION 13. WINDOW INSULATION (CAK)

If you sleep in your motor caravan without insulating the screens, you'll find 'rivers' of condensed water running down the inside of the screens next morning. In cool weather, you'll probably be darned cold, too! Glass offers very little in the way of thermal insulation and your Camper's got lots of it!

Some owners prefer external screens; others prefer internal ones. External screens are more efficient both at keeping cold out and at reflecting the heat from the sun's rays but, when it rains and when dew falls, they unavoidably get wet. However, the choice is entirely down to personal preference.

PART A. SILVER SCREENS

This is one of motor caravanning's legendary names; so much so that all screen insulators are sometimes called 'Silver Screens', like non-Hoovers are called 'hoover'.

It's interesting to note that Silver Screens can be fitted to the inside of the vehicle, simply by starting off with fitting them to the inside of one of the doors before draping them across the windscreen and then fitting them to the other door.

The Silver Screens come with a generously sized carrying bag so you don't find yourself trying to squeeze a quart into a pint pot!

There's also an optional gauze screen which restricts vision from the outside into the motor caravan when the front screen is down.

6-13-A1. The first job is to open the door on one side of the vehicle and slide the flap on one end of the silver screen, precisely over the top corner of the door so that the seams are level with the door's edge.

> **Top tip!**
> • *If the whole thing seems too tight, remove and refit the main panel of the screen (see picture 6-13-8) moving the Velcro over to provide a little more slack in the material.*

6-13-A2. Now, close the door and make sure that the windscreen wipers are folded open and that the Velcro flaps for fitting around the rear view mirrors on the screen are undone. Drape the screen across the front of the vehicle, ensuring that it is tightly in position.

6-13-A3. Open the other door by no more than 3in and you will be able to slide the flap, on the opposite top corner of the screen, over the top of the door frame.

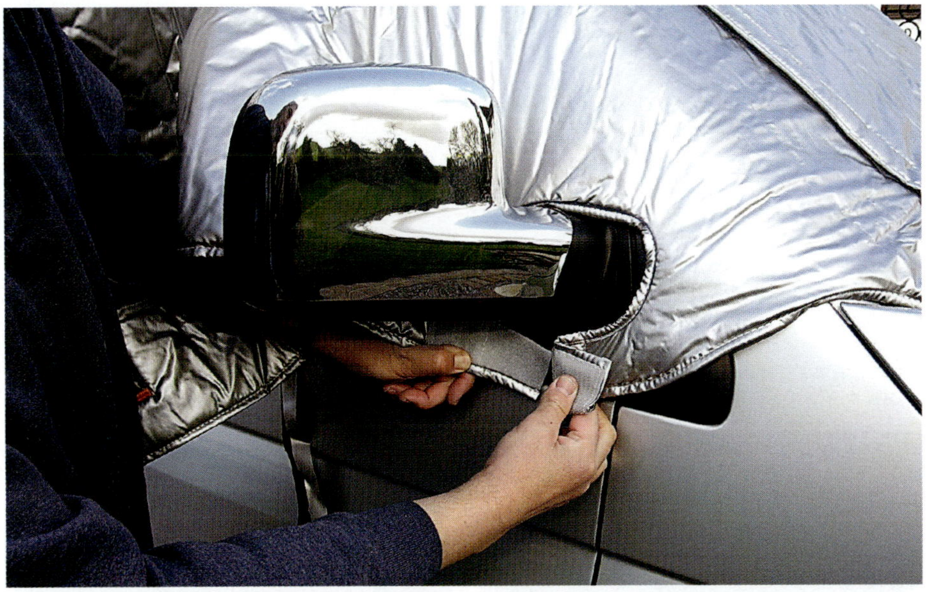

6-13-A4. You can now close the Velcro tabs underneath the rear view mirrors.

6-13-A5. To stop the bottoms of the screen from flapping, use the ties provided and attach them to the door handles.

6-13-A6. The fitted screen with the windscreen wipers, used to hold the base of the screen in place, provides a superb standard of insulation and/or reflection of sun's hot rays.

6-13-A7. If you want to stay inside the motor caravan while letting some extra light in through the windscreen, you pull on one of the tabs at the top corner which reveals the folded-over end of the Velcro tape. You can now peel this back.

6-13-A8. The front part of the screen can now be folded down to whatever height you prefer, using the Velcro tabs again to retains its position.

PART B. INTERNAL AND REAR WINDOW SCREENS

CAK sells internal screens for the T5's cab glass only – the front screen and door windows – and these are attached to the glass with rubber suckers

At the time of writing, it wasn't possible to purchase screens for any of the T5's windows other than for the cab glass but CAK sells all the parts required so that you can make your own. You'll need CAK's special quilted material with metallic, reflective surface on the outside and nylon facing on the inside, bias binding for edging the material, eyelets and eyelet tools, special fixing suckers and retaining rings. You'll also need a sewing machine and some basic tools.

6-13-B1. The first job before making your own screens is to make a paper pattern. Stick pellets of Blu Tack onto the glass ...

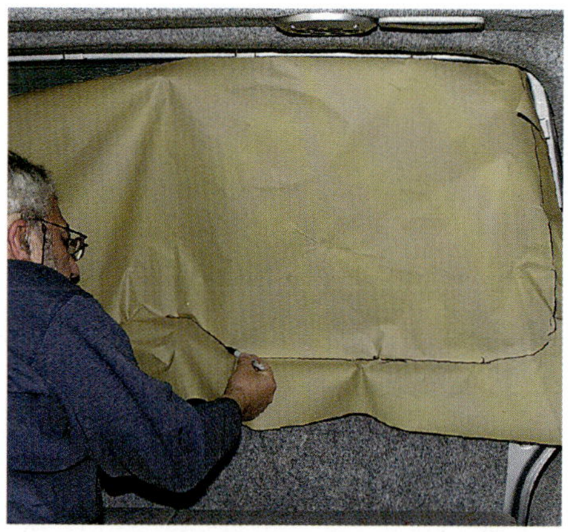

6-13-B2. ... then push an oversized piece of paper onto the glass and the window surround so that the Blu Tack holds it in place. Note that the screen really needs to be slightly larger than the glass, both for reasons of privacy and successful insulation, but make sure that it isn't too big at the same time.

6-13-B3. Having marked out the paper, this can now be trimmed. It is important that, after trimming the paper, you offer it up to the glass once more to make sure that it's right. It won't always be and it's far more economical to make changes now than it will be later!

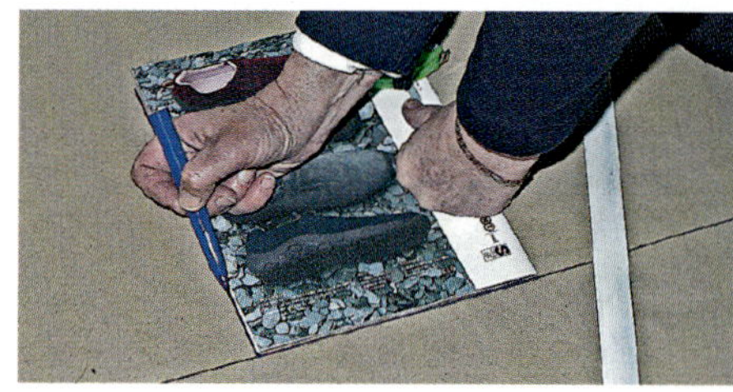

6-13-B4. In some cases, you will need to establish right angles. Where you are working with paper with a cut edge, you can create a line that's parallel to the edge through measuring but then the use of a rectangular box or magazine will allow you to draw an accurate right angle ...

6-13-B5. ... which can then be extended using your straight edge.

6-13-B6. Once the paper has been cut out and double-checked for fit ...

6-13-B7. … it can be placed on the fabric. Make sure that it's the right way up otherwise you will make a mirror image of what you need.

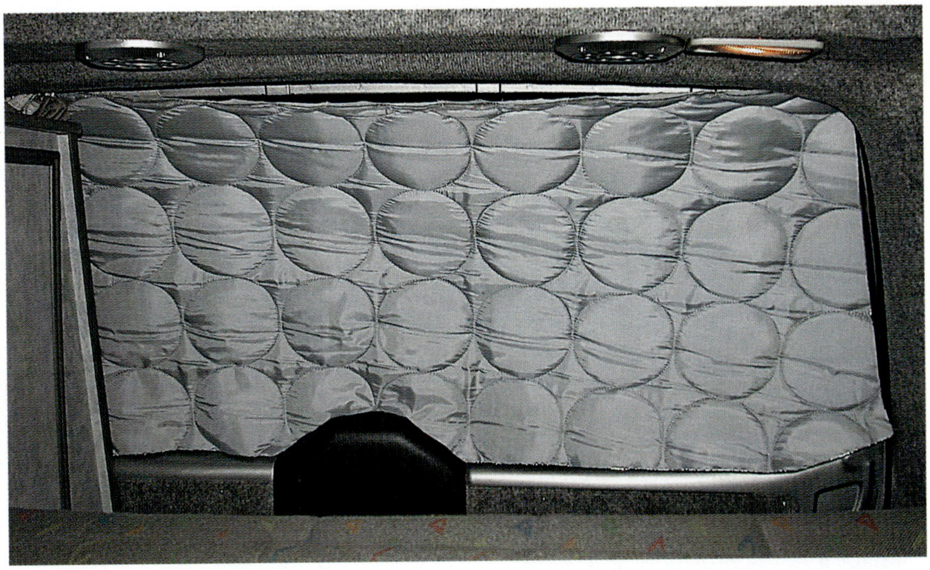

6-13-B10. Having cut out the fabric, go back to the motor caravan once more and check it for fit in the window aperture. Note the cutout that has been made here to fit around the windscreen wiper motor cover.

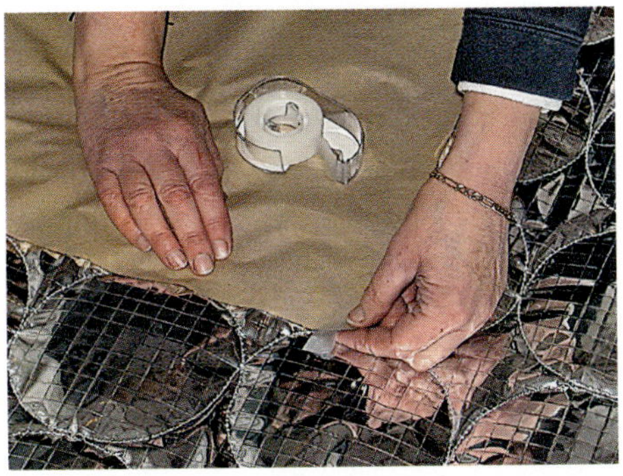

6-13-B8. Use tape to stick the paper down to the metallic surface of the fabric …

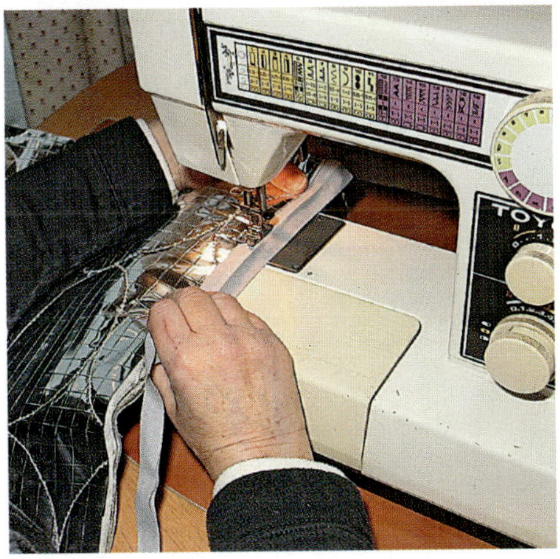

6-13-B11. Bias binding is slightly tricky to sew onto this insulating material with a domestic machine. You may find it easiest to sew the binding on once, with it held open …

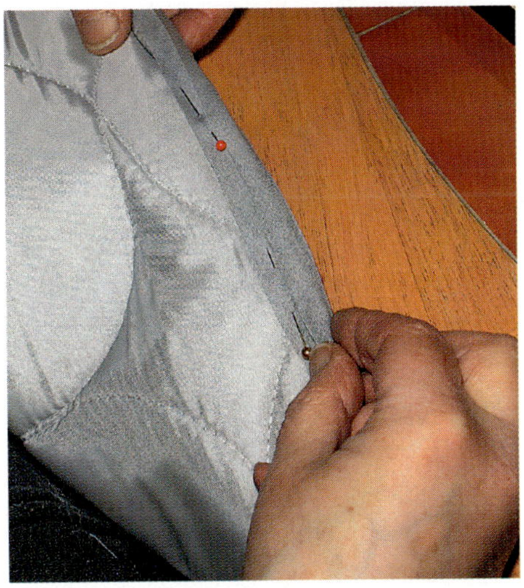

6-13-B12. … then to fold the binding over the edge and pin it down before sewing it down once more.

6-13-B9. … and cut out the fabric to match the pattern.

6-13-B13. These are the tools you may need in order to put eyelets in the screen. In addition to a hammer and a large block of wood you will need:
a: eyelet die
b: eyelet cutter and spreader
c: alternatively, you may have a hollow punch which has the correct diameter for the eyelets you will be using, which may be easier to use than the die and punch.
d: eyelet washer
e: eyelet barrel

Top tip!

- Sewing the binding down around curved corners is tricky and time consuming. You may feel, as we did, that there was little point in it and in that case, you could leave all the corners 'square' and save yourself a load of time.

6-13-14. You'll need to create a hole in the fabric through which the eyelet barrel can be pushed. Before doing so, mark the fabric with a pencil so that you know where the hole needs to be cut. It might be a good idea to do this while the material is held up to the glass inside the vehicle, so that you can be sure that the sucker will have a flat area of glass to push against. You will need to locate the die beneath the fabric, placing it on the block of wood that you will be using as an anvil and then the rounded end of the punch (not the pointed end) needs to be pushed over the die so that it aligns with it. You then hammer the pointed end of the punch and this leaves a neat hole in the fabric.

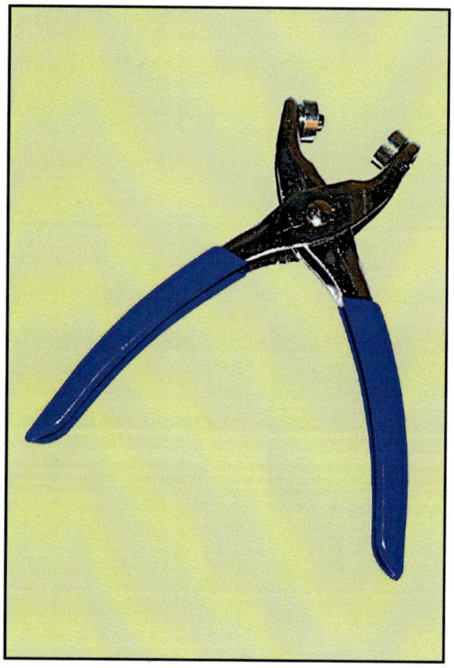

6-13-15. An alternative is to use these eyelet pliers, provided that you don't want to be making holes too far from the edge of the fabric. The advantage of eyelet pliers is that they automatically align the 'die' and 'punch' without your having to figure it out.

6-13-16. You now use the die again. Place the barrel of an eyelet onto the die, then insert the barrel through the hole you've made in the fabric from underneath.

6-13-17. With the die supported on the wooden anvil once again, the washer is used to hold down the material while you place the pointed end of the punch into the barrel of the eyelet.

6-13-18. In an ideal world, you'd have three hands for this job as you need to hold the washer down tightly over the fabric while also holding the punch but you can just do it with thumb and forefinger. Hammer the punch down into the eyelet, just enough to grip the fabric on both sides but not so much that you cause unwanted distortion of the eyelet. You have to be sure that the punch is held perfectly upright, otherwise the eyelet will look particularly squished to one side.

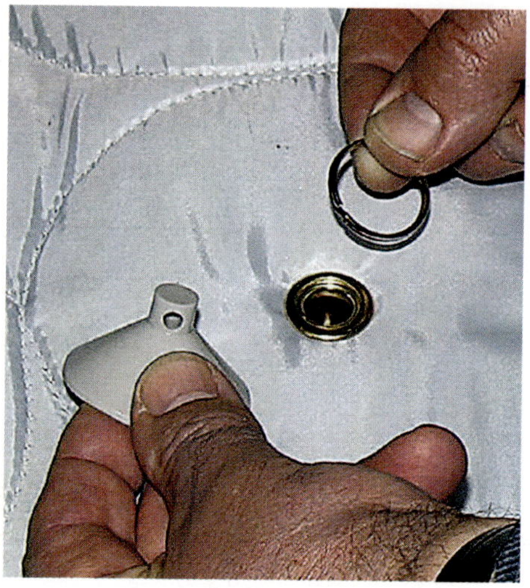

6-13-B19. The suckers provided by CAK have a hole through their stem. You place the stem of the sucker through the eyelet ...

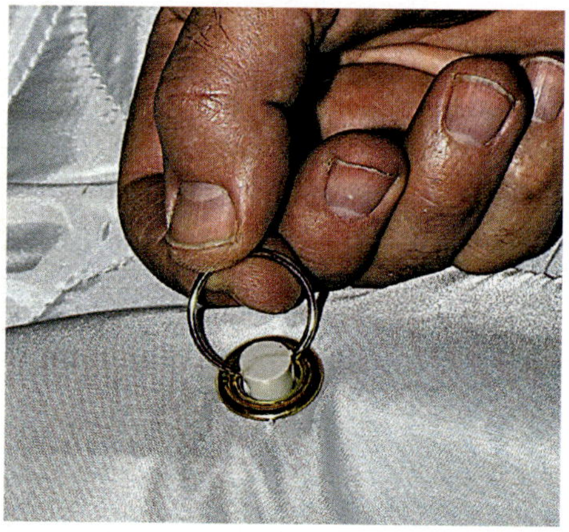

6-13-B20. ... then wind the spring clip through the holes in the stem. This retains the sucker and also gives you something to pull on when you want to remove the sucker from the glass when taking the insulating screens down.

6-13-B21. Here you can see the cab screens as bought ready-made from CAK and one of the rear screens, the one fitted to the door, that Shan and I made ourselves.

SECTION 14. SETTING UP AND USING SATELLITE TV ON-SITE

There are several ways of picking up TV on site. If TV reception is poor, you can usually rely on satellite TV. Maxview and Conrad Anderson give its advice.

6-14-1. Don't forget that you'll need a satellite receiver; you can't plug the antenna straight into the telly, like you can with ground-level transmissions. The Maxview DVB is a Freesat box (NOT Freeview – that's the aerial-based one) and it picks up over 100 TV and radio channels (including all the mainstream ones) but not the paid-for ones. For that, you'll need a box with a card slot and you'll have to pay for the extra channels. There are usually other complications too Byzantine to go into here. It's connected via Scart connections.

6-14-2. The 12v or 230v Maxview MXL014 is compact and light enough to mount on its side. The MXL014 is a Freesat box without a card slot (see above for restrictions). Its price is typically around a quarter of the price of the Kathrein UFD 540 satellite 12V receiver, which has a card slot and can be used with subscription channels at extra cost.

The case for satellite TV

- You can pick up a perfect picture almost anywhere in Europe as long as there are no immediate obstructions, such as tall buildings or trees.
- Picture quality is superb. Satellite TV tends to either work or not work with little in-between.
- As well as all the main UK channels and radio besides, there a loads of other free channels, far more than on non-satellite Freeview. Though whether any of them are worth watching is another matter ...
- A full list of channels can be obtained from the Astra website: www.ses-astra.com.

6-14-3. Before tuning a satellite dish, its base needs to be perfectly level. If it isn't, your angle of elevation will be 'out'. The Omnisat Digital Satellite Compass has an integral spirit level.

6-14-4. The Omnisat Camping Kit comes in its own box as Conrad Anderson's Steve Anderson demonstrates.

6-14-5. You'll need to carry out some assembly first.

6-14-6. Included in the box is a sucker set which you can attach to the vehicle ...

6-14-7. ... before fixing the dish and attaching the cable.

6-14-8. As an alternative, the dish can be connected to a separate structure using one of the other clamps provided.

6-14-9. Don't forget that you'll have to work out roughly where the satellite is first, so that you know where to attach the dish.

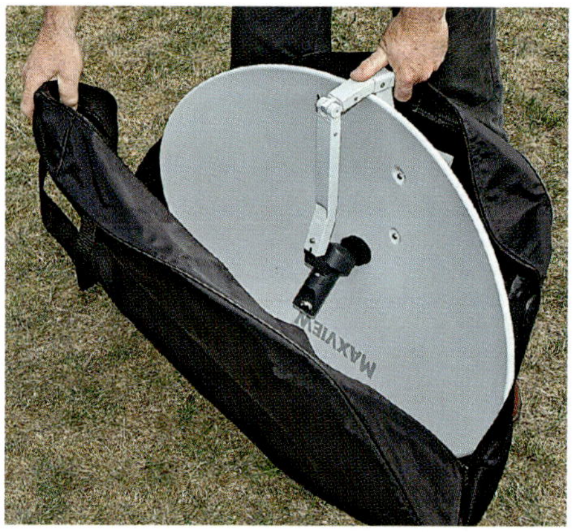

6-14-10. The larger, tougher Maxview Portable is taken out of its optional carrying case.

6-14-11. It will be fitted to a tripod which MUST be levelled precisely using the built-in spirit level, before being secured with the tent pegs provided.

6-14-12. The dish, complete with LNB on its folding arm, is then fitted to the tripod.

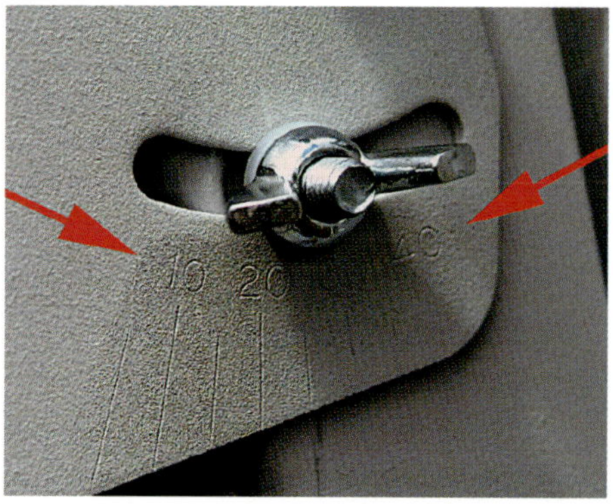

6-14-13. The first job after levelling up is to set the angle of elevation.

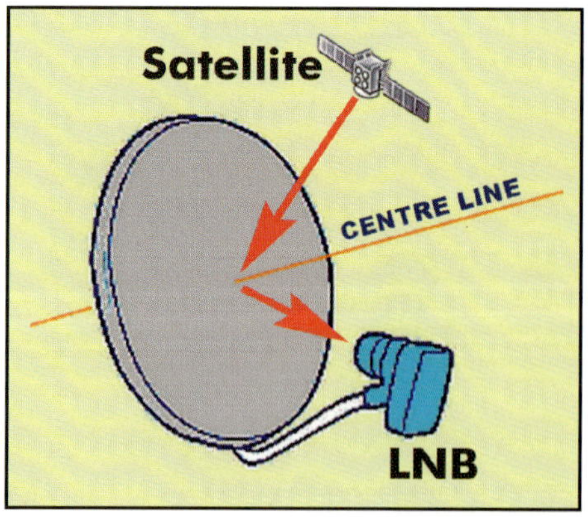

6-14-14. You don't point the dish at the satellite; you aim the satellite's beam into the centre of the dish so it is focused onto the LNB, which gathers in the signal. But don't worry; the manufacturer's markings on the antenna will have taken this into account. It's just that the dish will seem to be lower than it needs to be and could seem to point downwards in northern Europe.

Where's the satellite?

There are lots of them, but we need to look for a cluster of satellites commonly known as Astra 2, which carries our UK channels. Astra 2 satellites are in a geostationary orbit, once a sci-fi idea but now everyday reality. The satellite whizzes along, maintaining its exact position above one spot of the earth at a height of almost 22,500 miles. This means, barring catastophy, it's always where you expect to find it, but (and isn't there always a but?) while the satellite in effect stays put, we caravanners move around. So, to 'find' the satellite, you'll need a chart to tell you the the direction of the satellite from where you are, and a compass.

Here's an example of part of the lengthy chart to be found on the superb, non-commercial web site www.SatelliteForCaravans.co.uk and used with kind permission here:

6-14-15. Get the elevation right by tilting the dish to the precisely correct angle and you're more than half-way there. Don't guess; don't skimp; take your time. Set the elevation to the figure shown on the chart using the scale on the dish support.

6-14-16. This Omnisat 'Camping Kit' can even be used in its case, by adjusting the angle of the supports on the lid.

United Kingdom	Dish elevation (in degrees)	Compass bearing (in degrees)
Aberdeen	20	145
Belfast	20	141
Birmingham	26	145
Bristol	25	142
Cardiff	25	142
Edinburgh	20	144
Inverness	19	143
King's Lynn	24	146
London	26	146
Manchester	23	144
Newcastle -upon-Tyne	22	145
Penzance	24	139
Plymouth	25	141

Note: There's also an LNB 'skew' setting to compensate for the effects of the curvature of the Earth. For the UK and most of Central Europe, this can be ignored. When needed, more details are found on David Sullivan's site.

There are lots more locations all over Europe on David Sullivan's excellent site. If these figures make no sense right now, hang in there; they soon will!

6-14-17. An alternative approach, especially suitable for a coachbuilt motor caravan, is to have an adjustable dish fitted to the roof. Here, Conrad Anderson's Graham drills the roof, ready to take the mast of a Maxview Omnisat dish that can be adjusted from inside the motor caravan.

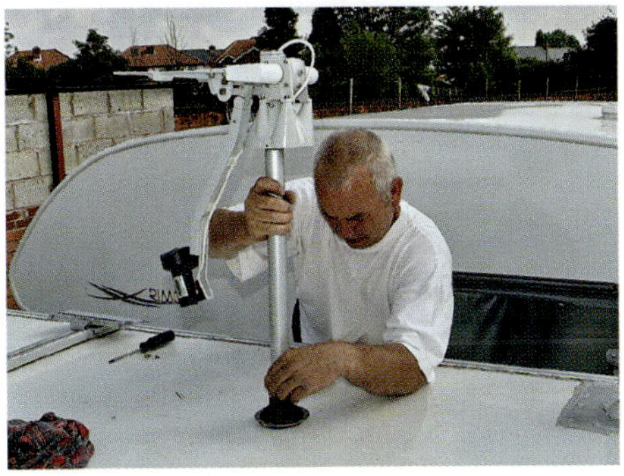

6-14-18. This is the manually adjustable MXL001 unit being inserted through the top of the roof, the sealed pivot assembly already having been fitted.

6-14-19. The dish is then bolted in place.

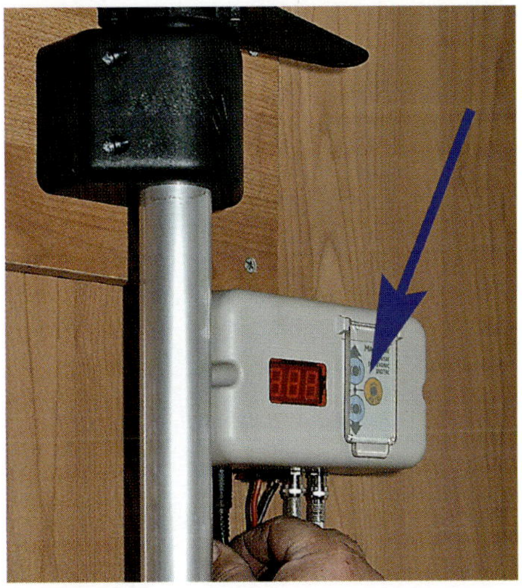

6-14-20. While the MXL001 has to be elevated manually, the Maxview Semitronic is elevated electronically, simply by pushing the button (arrowed) until the desired angle of elevation is reached. The direction of the dish is then established as for a free-standing dish (see later), except that it's also done from inside by turning the mast.

6-14-21. Next, you'll need to turn on both the TV and the receiver box. Here, the MXL014 receiver has been set to show signal strength on the TV screen and there's an audible 'beeper' option so you can see and hear when you're tuned-in.

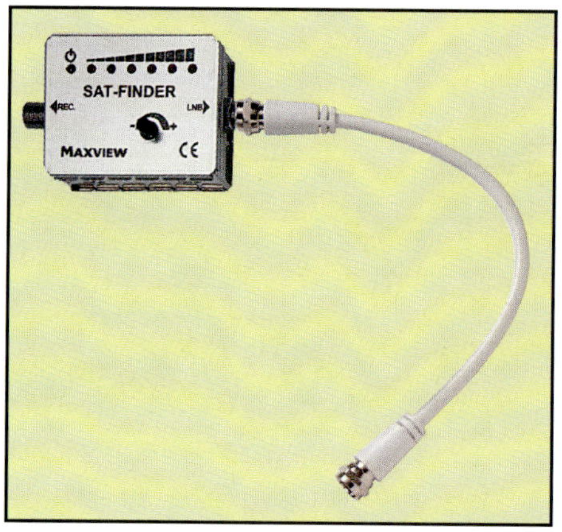

6-14-22. Another guide to signal strength is a signal strength meter. Many experienced 'sat-fans' claim that watching the TV screen is easier but if you can't see the screen from where the satellite is situated, you'll need the help of a TV watcher, or one of these.

6-14-23. Now refer to the chart once more to find out in what direction the antenna needs to be pointed. There are several different types of compass and this one clips on to the back of the Camping Kit's dish when used in free-standing mode.

6-14-24. The instructions with the compass explain how to establish approximately where the satellite is.

6-14-25. Now, here's what to do to produce a picture:
From the UK, Astra 2 is just to the East of South. Point the antenna due South initially, just 'past' the satellite.
Move the dish in small – really small – increments, towards the East, pausing briefly at each stage. This could take a full five minutes to complete.
If your compass tells you you've gone too far, you've probably moved too far, too fast. The angle is quite critical so be very patient at this stage. If you've got the previous steps right, you can't fail to 'find' the satellite because it's there all right!
If your signal strength shows you have a signal but there's no picture, you've located another satellite. There won't be a picture, though, so just keep slowly searching until you find good ol' Astra 2. When you've found it, lock the dish into position.

6-14-26. A satellite TV picture is potentially so good, you'll benefit from a quality TV to watch it on. The Avtex W151D 6-in-1 has a top quality 15in LCD screen, DVD/CD player, card reader for digital photos, RDS Radio and PC monitor option. Cheaper LCD TVs have poor pixel quality and don't show satellite pictures to their best advantage.

6-14-27. This 7-inch widescreen TFT portable TV is available from high street retailers, Maplin and might be a more useful size in a small camper. Picture quality is good and it runs from batteries, mains power supply or car cigarette lighter socket and comes with a remote.

6-14-28. Perfect for confined spaces, the Maplin SCART Freeview receiver allows you to access Freeview digital signals on a non-digital TV. It is distinguished by the small amount of space it takes up, hidden behind the set.

SatelliteForCaravans.co.uk's David Sullivan claims that it now only takes him a couple of minutes to tune-in. However, the first time you try it, you might have to spend half an hour working out just how small each movement of the dish needs to be, how many seconds you have to pause at each stage to allow the picture to fire up and just how narrow the beam is you're looking for. But once you've got the hang of it, there will be no terrors involved. Then again, it's another of those jobs that you can easily practice at home before you set out. Anyone for strawberries, cream and Wimbledon on the back lawn – on TV, of course!

SECTION 15. TINTED WINDOWS AND SUPAGLASS

My wife Shan and I have wanted to have tinted, strengthened windows fitted to our VW T5 Camper for some time, and for a variety of reasons. The first reason was to make the vehicle more secure. Imagine that you're parked on a side-street in Bruges, for example. You go to take a look around the square, the canals, the fine old buildings and you have a lovely day. However, when you come back, the day is ruined because someone has smashed the front side window and snatched your valuables, such as handbag or 'sat nav' unit from inside the cab, or passport from inside the glove box. Imagine, then, the hassle of working out what has been stolen, arranging window replacement, to say nothing of the emotional impact of the violation of your property. There have even been documented instances of a passenger side window being smashed while the vehicle is stopped at traffic lights and valuables snatched and grabbed before the driver could react – it can happen as quickly as that! It's said that smash-and-grabs – and even car-jackings – are on the increase as vehicle locks become more secure and vehicles become more difficult to steal when unattended. Approximately half-a-million UK vehicles are broken into through a smashed window every year, according to Pentagon's Craig Seckerson.

You may have heard of a Q-car; an automotive wolf in sheep's clothing. Well the second reason was to make our Camper into something of a Q-Camper – a motor caravan that doesn't look like one at first sight. Here's why:

I drive quite a lot of wildly different vehicles at different times and one thing I've noticed is the way other drivers react towards you, depending on what you're driving. Here, for what it's worth, is my personal, slightly tongue-in-cheek list of what I suddenly appear to become, according to what I'm driving:

6-15-1. A side window can be smashed and the contents extracted in a couple of seconds. It's perhaps the most vulnerable part of a modern vehicle.

Vehicle	What am I?	Other drivers' reactions
Large Jaguar	Stuck-up	"I'm not letting you into the traffic"
'Classic' Range Rover	Formidable	"OK, after you."
2CV	Laughable	"Move over – or else!"
Metro	Slow	"Get thee behind me!"
VW Motor Caravan	Boring old far... far... fella	"**Must** overtake, **must** overtake ..."

6-15-2. This dodgy-looking character is Craig Seckerson, Pentagon's Marketing Manager, smashing the glass on "the car which suffers from smashed glass more often than any other car in the country", according to Craig. It's Pentagon's demonstrator! The glass crazed (though it took two goes!) ...

6-15-4. Pentagon's new receptionist, Camille, was reluctant at first to touch the inner surface of the glass – but soon discovered it remained smooth and harmless.

Now, if I'm dawdling along, I have no objection to being overtaken and will usually pull over to make it possible. However, if I'm using the 174bhp of our VW T5 to good effect, I object to someone else driving aggressively just because they think a motor caravan stands for old, slow and overtakeable – and believe me, it used to happen! But now we're driving our VW T5 'Q-Camper', journeys are a lot more peaceful.

6-15-3. ... but, even by punching with all his might, Craig couldn't break in. As a matter of fact, he bruised his hand in trying! A large brick would have proved no more successful.

6-15-5. The glass can be forced clear from the inside, though – vital in an emergency.

6-15-6. Unprotected glass that's damaged in a collision shoots dangerous shards of broken glass around. Left is shattered toughened-glass from a Land Rover; right is a box of shards thrown from a Mercedes' laminated-glass.

6-15-7. Some motor caravans tow small cars behind so it was interesting to see this Smart car receiving the treatment among the Lambourghinis. Highly unusually, windows are removed after taking off the outer door panel, not the inner one!

6-15-8. This was our Camper parked up in the workshop before work commenced. Note how you can see right in to the rear, even through two layers of side-window glass.

6-15-9. Steve prepares to fit the tinting to the rear screen by dusting the surface with talcum powder. Note the wardrobe units in the back – now you see them!

6-15-10. After wiping a small area clean on the centre of the screen, Steve drapes the tinting film over the window.

6-15-11. After temporarily 'sticking' the film in place, Steve uses a heat gun to soften the film so that it matches the curvature of the glass.

6-15-12. The inside of the glass is now thoroughly cleaned and every trace of dirt washed out from the edges.

6-15-13. The film is now offered up to the inside of the glass and pressed into position.

6-15-14. Steve uses a knife to trim the edges so that the film fits perfectly.

6-15-15. Working from the inside-out, he fits the film onto the glass so that there are no air bubbles.

6-15-16. A little more heating and shaping is required so that the film lies flat in the curved corner of the screen.

6-15-17. There are four grades of window tint and I chose 'Smoke', the second-lightest. However, over the rear wardrobe area, Chris prepared to fit an extra layer of the darkest tint called 'Limousine'.

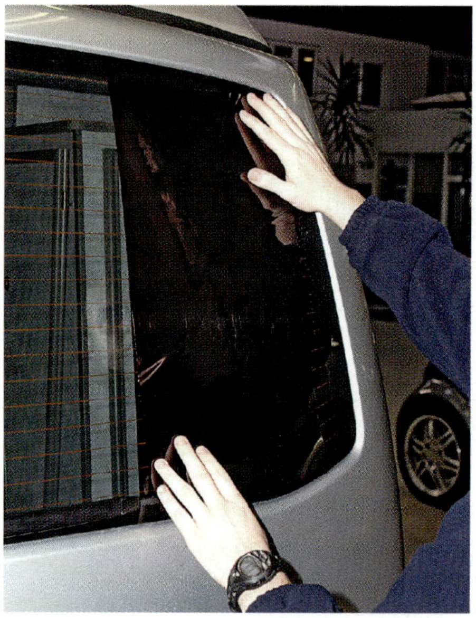

6-15-18. Chris prepared the tint material just as Steve had done and then squeegeed it into place on the glass after very carefully measuring its position.

6-15-19. Fitting SupaGlass and Window Tint to the sliding side windows meant having to remove the catches first.

6-15-20. Again, the glass was cleaned thoroughly …

6-15-21. … and every trace of dirt washed out of the edges.

6-15-22. Chris removed the protective film from the adhesive surface of the Smoke SupaGlass.

6-15-23. A special lubricant was sprayed onto the surface of the adhesive …

6-15-24. … before placing it on the glass. SupaGlass has an immense tensile strength of 29,000psi and is officially classified by British Standards as being 'Anti-Bandit'.

6-15-25. Chris squeegees every drop of the lubricating fluid from behind the sheet of SupaGlass leaving it fixed to the window.

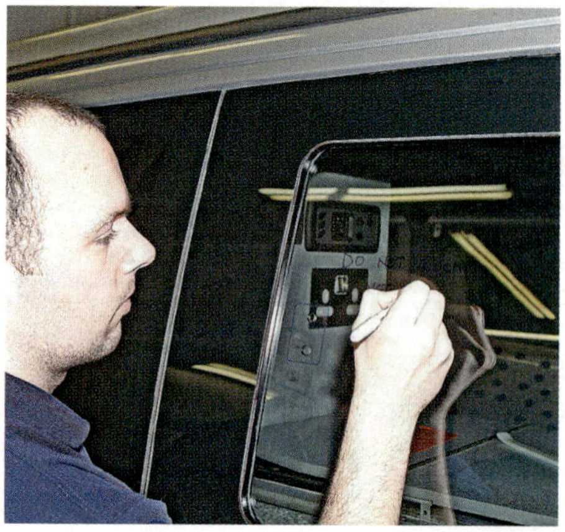

6-15-26. It was to be left to go off over night, so Chris wrote a note on the glass so that no one thinks, "Oh, I'll just finish this off!" This was all part of Pentagon's thoroughness that I found very impressive.

6-15-27. The area of the cooker that protrudes above the lower level of the window is shown being concealed with more 'Limousine' Window Tint.

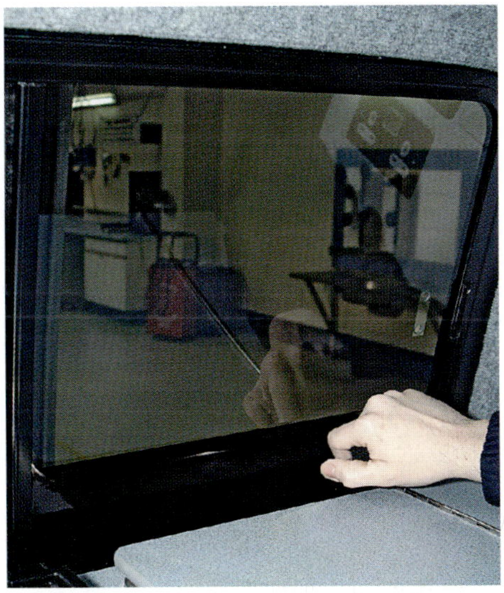

6-15-28. When in the correct position, Chris fits it to the inside of the glass.

6-15-29. Rahul lent a hand by trimming the SupaGlass from the holes to which the catches are fitted.

6-15-30. Door windows are treated differently and David, Pentagon's trimmer, carefully removed the trim and disconnected the window winder gear.

6-15-31. It's a moderately involved process but David lifted out the window glass ready for treatment.

6-15-32. Chris' brother, Dan, prepared the window for the fitting of the clear SupaGlass. I can't show you what comes next because the process is top-secret but take it from me that a purpose-made machine bonds the SupaGlass to the inside of the door window glass.

6-15-33. Dan trimmed the edges of the SupaGlass and then filed them so that they were radiused perfectly into the curvature of the glass. You really can't tell it's there.

6-15-34. David got his glass back and reassembled both doors.

6-15-35. Pentagon's last job was to clean the vehicle, making it ready to leave.

6-15-36. Pentagon kindly removed the swirly side-stripes that I was ambivalent about but which my wife, Shan, really disliked. So, what does this now look like to you? Is it a Camper? Is it a Caravelle? No, it's not Superman but it's exactly what we wanted from the visual point of view and there's the added reassurance that our Camper is a lot safer and a darned sight more secure than it was previously.

Window tinting limits

There's more to it than we've got room for but here's a taster:
You're not allowed to heavily tint the front screen or the side windows of a vehicle ahead of the B-post – the part of the bodywork that the front door shuts against. Pentagon can advise on the maximum allowed.

From there, backwards, the choice is yours but do remember that heavily tinted glass will be more difficult to see out of at night.

SupaGlass can be fitted untinted if required.

Footnotes

Pentagon claim that its SupaGlass film is specially produced and has a unique, specially developed high-tech adhesive to make it superior to any other product.

There are two drivers on hand at Pentagon, just to ferry the rich and famous around while its millionaires' machinery is receiving the treatment.

Pentagon supply the police and armed forces and are now officially approved by Aston Martin, Audi, Bentley, Mercedes, Rolls-Royce and VW Commercial Vehicles.

SupaGlass rejects between 23 per cent and 64 per cent of solar energy, depending on tint. Keeps you cool in summer!

Sobering thought

In a crash, at about 12mph, the average person loses limb control – arms flail uncontrollably. If an arm or head should flail out of a smashed window not fitted with SupaGlass as a vehicle rolls over – well, the result doesn't take much imagination, does it ...

SECTION 16. WEBASTO DIESEL SPACE HEATER

The Webasto Air Top 2000S diesel-powered space heater that Vehvac fitted to our motor caravan slots beautifully beneath the driver's seat – though it is often fitted in the rear of larger vehicles – and provides ample heat for a small motor caravan. It's also widely used in larger motorhomes as a supplement to the wall-mounted gas/electric heater and it has one enormous advantage. Unlike an LPG heater, it can be used perfectly safely and legally while you're driving along, drawing the fuel it needs from the main vehicle fuel tank.

Inside information

Some owners fit an on-board LPG tank to provide more economical fuel for heating and cooking. Unfortunately, vehicles with fitted LPG tanks are not supposed to be taken through the Channel Tunnel.

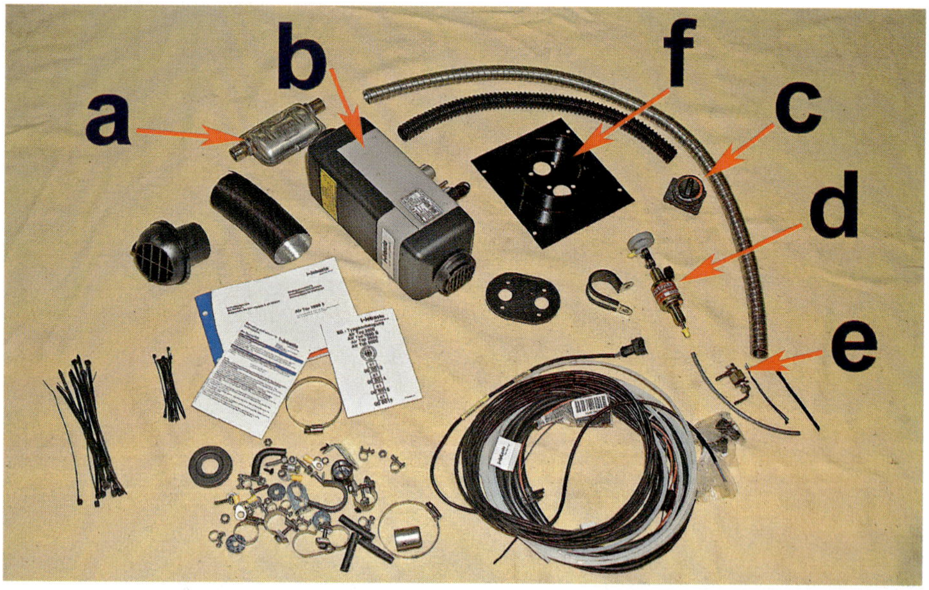

6-16-1. These are the components that comprise the Webasto AirTop 2000S kit for fitting to the Volkswagen T5. Each kit is made to fit a different vehicle and there will be detail differences such as mountings and fuel tank fittings that are model-specific. The main elements in the kit are:

a. exhaust silencer
b. burner unit
c. control knob
d. fuel pump and filter
e. fuel pick-up fitting
f. mounting plate

6-16-2. When removing the seat on a fully-equipped modern vehicle such as the T5, you have to take into account that side airbags might be fitted. In the case of our Volkswagen, the procedure is to disconnect the battery, unbolt the seat and then disconnect the airbag plug and socket from beneath the seat. On some other vehicles, the procedure for disarming the airbag may be different and it is always necessary to consult the manufacturer's manual. VW recommend plugging in a 'dummy' airbag connector while the seat is removed but as long as you are careful not to reconnect the battery and turn the key in the ignition, there won't be any problems. Otherwise, you may have to have a reset carried out by your Volkswagen dealer.

6-16-3. Keith carefully lifts out the driver's seat, giving full access to the space beneath.

Now, when Leisuredrive converted our new Volkswagen to a motor caravan, we had the option of fitting a Propex LPG-powered heater, as in our old camper. But, even though the Propex heater had always given sterling service, I had other ideas. I fancied having a diesel-powered heater and, after speaking to the installation specialists, Vehvac, I was really warming to the idea, as you might say (but only if you enjoy truly dreadful puns). The advantages of a diesel heater over an LPG unit are several:

- When you're out for a day-trip in winter, you don't need to worry about having gas cylinders on-board.
- If you travel abroad with UK specification cylinders, you'll be much less likely to use all your gas up if you're heating the living space with diesel.
- You can use the heater while you're driving along and this is wonderful for two reasons. One is that the latest high-efficiency diesel engines can be slow to warm up – ours takes five or six miles – and some modern diesel engines won't warm up at all if you're sitting in traffic, for instance. The Webasto heater comes on almost instantly.
- The second advantage is that the great big empty space behind the driver and passenger stays awfully cold when you're driving in winter – and the larger the camper, the worse it is, of course – leaving you with roasted toes and cold draughts down the back of the neck, but not if you've got a Webasto diesel space heater fitted ...

Here's what happened when Vehvac got its highly accomplished mitts on our lovely T5. The engineer for this trip is Keith and we hope you have an enjoyable journey.

6-16-4. He carefully moved the under-seat wiring out of the way and cut away the sound deadening and floor covering where necessary. This enabled him to drill a 125mm (5in) hole in the floor in the exact location. Of course, he had already checked beneath the vehicle to make sure that this point was clear although the exact location was correctly marked in the installation manual.

6-16-5. Before fitting the heater and blower motor to the floor, Keith fitted the plate shown in picture 6-16-1, item 'F', bolting it down to the floor and then fitted this rubber sealing gasket to the base of the heater unit before fitting that in turn to the mounting plate.

6-16-6. This is the heater/blower unit in place just before Keith finally connected the wiring. Before he got to that stage, he had another and slightly trickier job to carry out.

6-16-7. Vehvac insist that customers make sure their fuel tanks are as near to empty as possible before carrying out this work because the tank has to be lowered – after removing the undertray, in the case of the VW T5. Here, Keith has already disconnected the filler neck and is removing a couple of the straps holding the tank in place before supporting it from beneath.

6-16-12. … bolting it into the cap with the union at the precise angle described in the manual.

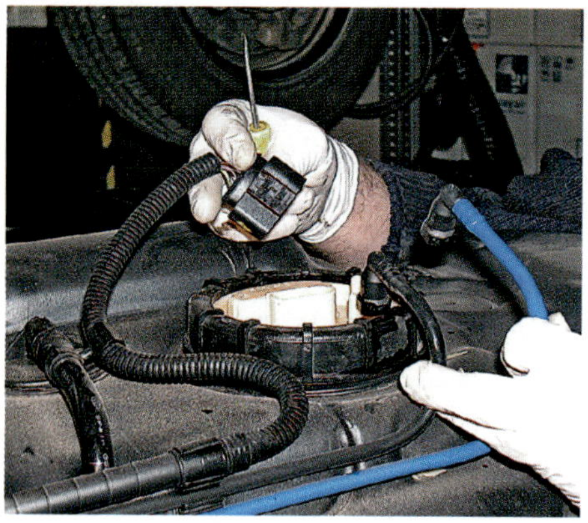

6-16-8. In this instance, Keith lifted the van upwards and off the tank, which enabled him to detach the wiring plug and diesel fuel hoses from the main tank pump and sender unit.

6-16-9. After unscrewing the knurled ring holding the unit down, he lifted it out of the tank and poured the diesel it contained back into the tank, rather than letting it spill onto the floor.

6-16-10. Following the instructions with the kit, Keith drilled an 8.5mm hole in a precise location in the cap …

6-16-11. … then fitted this specially fabricated union …

6-16-13. There are clips already fitted in the body of the pump and into these, Keith slid the pick-up pipe.

6-16-14. The upper end of it was connected to the pick-up union that he had already bolted to the cap.

6-16-15. Finally, he used the connections supplied with the kit to clamp the diesel feed pipe in place.

6-16-16. Back at the tank, the pump and sender unit was refitted, the electrical and fuel hoses reconnected and the supply pipe for the Webasto heater clipped to existing fittings on the tank top.

6-16-17. The fuel pump and filter unit were fitted together once again off the vehicle for ease of fitting and then bolted into place at a suitable location beneath the vehicle.

6-16-18. With all the scrabbling around beneath the vehicle out of the way, Keith turned his attention to the wiring. I spotted this location on the dashboard which I think is just right for the control knob. Some owners may wish to place the control knob in the rear of the motor caravan but since it is a simple matter to reach over from the rear to the front when stationary, I felt that putting the control here gave the best of both worlds.

6-16-19. After fitting the wiring to the back of the switch, Keith screwed it to the fascia.

6-16-20. There was a little dismantling and a little more detective work before Keith could run the wiring through the bulkhead, using an existing grommet, and then across the engine bay to the battery where he connected it up with its own fuse.

6-16-21. The only remaining pipework connections he had to make were the exhaust system from the base of the heater unit, beneath the cover panels and out of the side …

6-16-22. … and the heater outlet pipe which exits through the rear of the seat trim. It's important to note that the amount of heat given out at the pipe-end can be quite high and so Keith re-routed the pipe so that it was away from the kitchen unit. Otherwise it could have operated like a heat gun and damaged the surface of the laminate.

6-16-23. The outlet pipe was finally trimmed to length with a sharp craft knife and clipped securely using a jubilee clip screwed to the seat frame. The outlet nozzle can be turned to direct the flow of warm air.

6-16-24. Now, whether or not the engine is running and whether or not we are driving along, the Webasto heater that Vehvac have fitted for us provides heat in variable amounts within a few seconds of being turned on and, as an extra bonus that I wasn't expecting, runs far more quietly than any space heater I have encountered before.

SECTION 17. PROPEX LPG SPACE HEATER

The Propex blown air heater is a gas-operated heater with a 12v fan. This enables you to heat the interior of the motor caravan even when on a site without mains electricity. It's efficient and it's thermostatically controlled and although the blower is a touch noisy, it's a lot better than being cold. We have used one on winter picnic trips as well as on cool evenings when camping.

When siting the heater underneath the seat box, you have to bear in mind that there has to be an unrestricted air inlet to the heater casing. Soft items placed inside the seat box can easily block the inlets on the heater casing. I constructed a steel case to go around the heater casing, open at both ends and with an air gap of about 25mm all around the heater so that the ingress of air is far more difficult to block off.

SAFETY FIRST!

There are both LPG (gas) and electrical connections on the Propex Heat Source 1600 and these will need to be fitted by qualified personnel in the usual way.

The Propex heater also has safety requirements with regard to the exhaust of the burned gases from the combustion process. The exhaust must be suitably located away from fuel lines, electrical cables or anything flammable, either inside or beneath the vehicle. It must also be away

6-17-1. The outlet vent or vents for the Propex heater should be fitted near to the floor, and preferably near the door so that it is heating cooled air and keeping the interior of the motor caravan as warm as possible. As with so many other small fitments, it was easier to cut the hole for this vent and to fit the vent cap before the bed box was fitted to the vehicle.

from the entry door and away from any position where combustion products may enter the interior of the vehicle.

If you intend installing the Propex heater yourself (prior to having qualified personnel connect it up), consult a qualified gas engineer with regard to the siting of the heater unit and location of the hole to be drilled in the floor for positioning the exhaust. Propex strongly recommends that the exhaust pipe outlet vents beyond the outer edge of the vehicle floor, not beneath it.

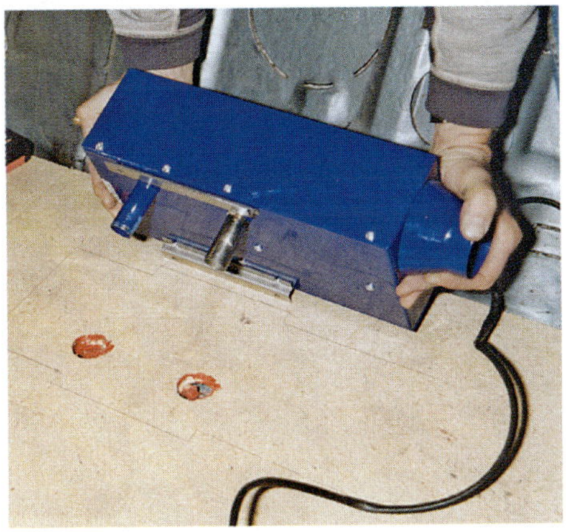

6-17-2. Here you can see the exhaust and combustion air holes, plus the larger air vent hole to the left of them, drilled in the floor of the vehicle. It's obviously important that you check the underside of the vehicle with very great care to ensure that you're not going to be drilling through chassis members, electrical, brake, fuel or any other components when drilling these essential holes in the floor.

6-17-3. The combustion air pipe and the longer exhaust pipe are both pushed onto the spigots.

SAFETY FIRST!

- Route the exhaust so that it discharges beyond the side of the vehicle.
- There must be no possibility of lethal exhaust gases seeping upwards into the vehicle.

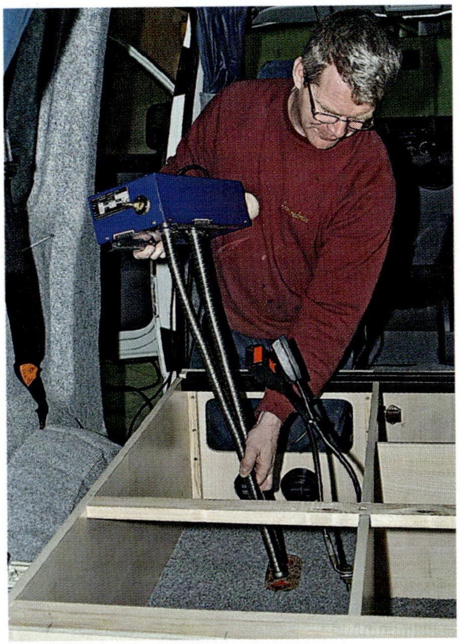

6-17-4. They are then fixed in place with jubilee clips. The bracket on the bottom of the Propex heater raises it sufficiently off the floor to enable these jubilee clips to be fitted.

6-17-5. The exhaust pipe needs to be routed well away from the hole in the floor through which it came, and well away from any other vent holes in the floor. It should also face the rear of the vehicle so that no water or debris is forced into the pipe as the vehicle is driven.

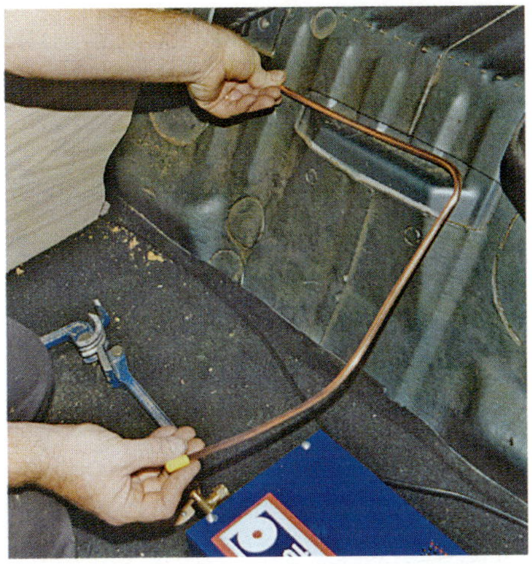

6-17-6. Bending and shaping the gas pipes before clipping them to the vehicle's bodywork is something that you can do yourself.

6-17-7. Making the gas connections to the heat source must only be carried out by a qualified gas fitter. You can now see the 'drop' vent to the left of the heat source which is a necessary requirement for any gas-operated equipment housed in the vehicle.

6-17-8. Once the bed box has been fitted to the vehicle, it's possible to connect the blower pipe to the vent on the bed box and to the heat source itself.

6-17-9. The thermostat is best located in an open space at about half-way up the height of the interior of the vehicle. In our case, the best space available was on the side of the wardrobe, as shown here. Make sure that the thermostat is not mounted in direct sunlight or above a cooker or fridge.

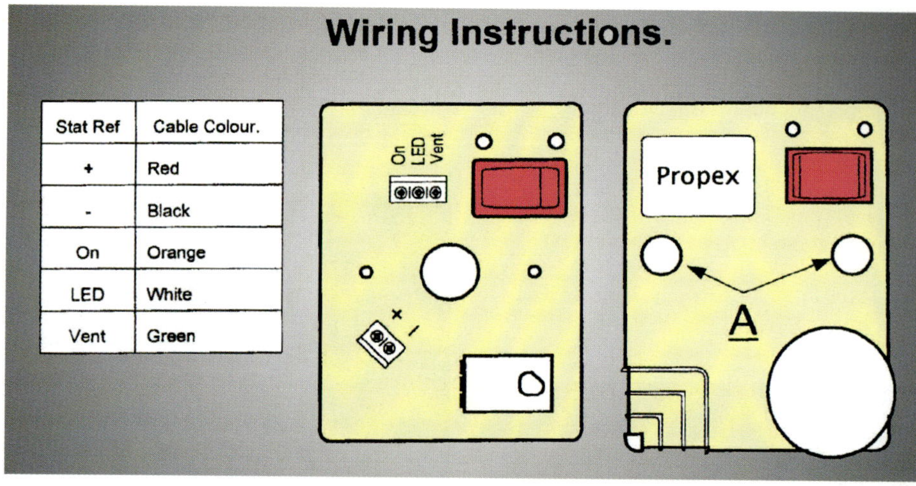

Stat Ref	Cable Colour.
+	Red
-	Black
On	Orange
LED	White
Vent	Green

6-17-10. Your electrician will need to connect up the thermostat, as well as the wiring to the heat source itself, using the colour scheme shown here.

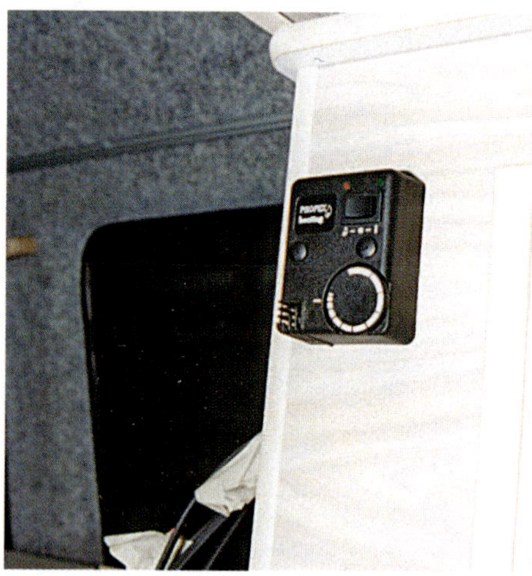

6-17-11. The thermostat, with cover in place, fitted to the wardrobe side.

FACT FILE: FITTING NOTES

1. The size of the holes for the exhaust spigots are 30mm and need to be cut with a tank cutter.
2. The hole size for the hot air outlet and recirculation air inlet vent need to be cut to a diameter of 95mm.
3. Propex recommends that the exhaust outlet should protrude a short way beyond the edge of the vehicle.
4. The combustion air pipe should terminate at least 0.5 metres away from the end of the exhaust.
5. Both pipes should have a slight downward slope to prevent any possibility of water traps.
6. The wiring to the thermostat and Heat Source 1600 is supplied with the kit and consists of two wiring looms with terminals and housings to plug into the main printed circuit board inside the heater.

SECTION 18. PORTA POTTI FROM CAK TANKS

6-18-1. In its elevating-roof models, Leisuredrive construct a compartment suitable for taking a Thetford Porta Potti 145. This is the version with wooden seat/bed base.

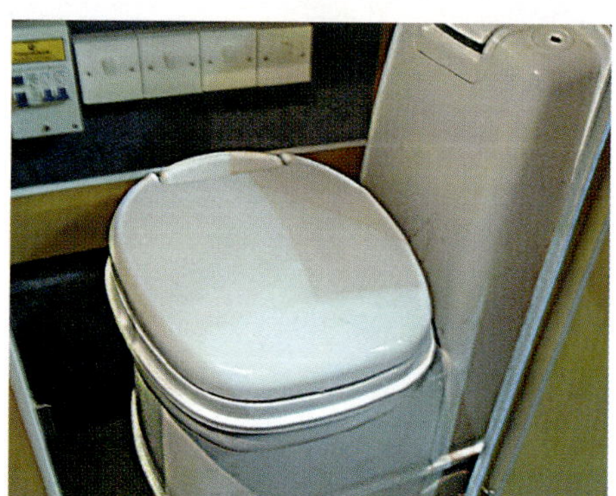

6-18-2. On fixed-roof models, a fitted unit can be installed with separate holding tank, though some owners still prefer the removable model.

6-18-3. There's no room beneath the front of the bed when a steel-framed bed base is fitted, so Leisuredrive utilize space next to the fridge and beneath the oven, when fitted. It is essential that pipes, wires and holes in the floor are kept well to one side because the WC unit can be a tight fit.

6-18-4. The alternative, on steel-framed bed versions, is to use space accessed through the tailgate door though this makes the convenience a little less convenient ...

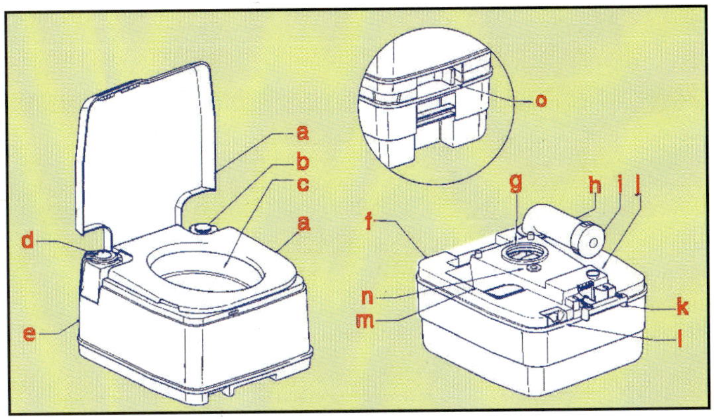

6-18-5. Our Thetford Porta Potti 145 was obtained from CAK of Kenilworth (jokes on a postcard please – or perhaps not ...) and these are the instructions on how to use the unit

PARTS

a. Removable seat cover. b. Cap, Flush water tank. c. Toilet bowl. d. Pump (differs by model). e. Flush water tank. f. Waste holding tank. g. Valve blade. h. Rotating emptying spout. i. Cap, Emptying spout. j. Vent button. k. Valve handle. l. Waste level indicator (when applicable). m. Storage for toilet fluids. n. Pressure release vent. o. Lock handle

Preparing for use

1. Slide the latch to the right to remove flush water tank from the waste holding tank.
2. Turn the emptying spout upwards and add toilet fluid for the waste holding tank. Add 2 litres of water.
3. Turn the emptying spout back into position, put cap back on and put the two toilet parts together by pressing the flush water tank down on the waste holding tank.
4. Fill flush water tank with clean water and rinsing agent.

Use

5. Open and close the valve blade once with seat and cover closed. This releases excess pressure.
6. Flush toilet by using the pump. Open valve blade to release waste into the waste tank. Close valve blade after use.
7. Disconnect toilet and take waste holding tank to an authorised waste disposal area (or normal toilet) to empty.
8. Empty waste holding tank through emptying spout. Keep vent button pressed while emptying to avoid splashing (only press it when emptying spout is pointing downwards).
9. Do not use regular toilet paper, as this may cause clogging. Use rapidly dissolving toilet paper, such as Thetford Aqua Soft toilet paper instead.

Storage and cleaning

10. Store the toilet clean and dry.
11. Remove batteries if present.
12. Lubricate seals with silicone lubricant. (Never clean with household cleaners, they may cause leakage!)

More information

For more information on your toilet or other Thetford products and services, visit www.thetford-europe.com. There you will find comprehensive sets of instructions on how to service and repair your Thetford toilet.

SECTION 19. MALAGA WATER HEATER

The Maxol Malaga E water heater is pretty well a standard fitting in good quality caravans and motor homes, although it's not often fitted to smaller motor caravans. The identical looking Malaga heats and stores hot water using gas only, whereas the Malaga E can be used from mains electricity, gas or a combination of both for very rapid water heating.

6-19-1. The Malaga and Malaga E come as complete kits of parts ready to be fitted to the vehicle. The inlet and exhaust pipes are built into the unit and are covered by the external vent plate shown here.

SAFETY FIRST!

As with so many other of the appliances shown here, installation of the gas and electrical systems are jobs for qualified personnel only.

See manufacturer's data for installation requirements.

6-19-2. You have a chicken-and-egg situation when it comes to working out the correct location of the heater. You'll need the cupboard to be in place to see where the heater will fit properly, but you'll need the cupboard out again in order to be able to fit the heater.

6-19-3. If the interior wall coverings have all been fitted before the heater is installed, you have to cut them away before deciding on the final location of the heater. Bearing in mind that the exhaust and inlet pipes are fixed, you will need to get the position of the heater right first time in relation to the outside wall of the vehicle.

6-19-4. Just to one side of the Malaga E, fit a low level vent to enable heavier-than-air gases to drop out of the enclosed space in which the heater will be situated.

6-19-5. Once the holes are drilled they should be painted to protect both the bare steel, through which you will have drilled, and the edges of the floorboard.

6-19-6. The drop vents consist of plates which are screwed to the floor ...

Important note: Before drilling any holes do make sure that there are no chassis rails beneath that part of the floor and – even more importantly – that there are no fuel, brake, electrical or other components beneath the area through which you will drill.

6-19-7. ... followed by plastic grilles which prevent the entry of uninvited furry visitors.

6-19-8. In this location, Steve works out the position of the Malaga heater, bearing in mind how far the exhaust will protrude through the sidewall. If there is any floor covering in the area where the water heater will stand, you must remove it to a width of 320mm, 450mm-inward from the motor caravan wall.

6-19-9. The curvature at the bottom of the van side might mean that you will need to make a box to raise the heater towards the more horizontal part of the van sidewall, though probably not as high as the one shown here on an earlier model of Transporter. The height of the box will also depend on the amount of headroom you have in the cupboard. Note the way in which the vent fits to one side of the box; it must not be obscured by it.

6-19-10. Ensure, by measuring and checking, that the position of the heater won't clash with anything fitted to the outside of the van. When you are certain of this, you can mark the position of the heater on the sidewall.

6-19-11. Using a small bit, drill through the top corner of each mark – the two holes corresponding with the two top corners of the Malaga heater.

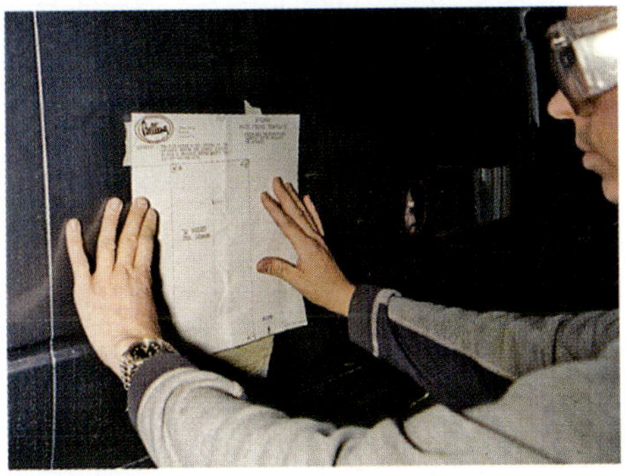

6-19-12. On the outside of the van, Steve uses the template provided with the kit and lines it up with the two holes he has drilled in the bodywork. The template is held onto the body with small pieces of masking tape, and a further two holes are drilled to mark the bottom two corner positions.

6-19-13. Several layers of masking tape are used to fulfil two purposes at once. One purpose is to mark the exact position of the cutting lines when cutting out for the Malaga heater. Having placed several layers of broad masking tape in position, each of the four holes is enlarged so that each hole is big enough to take a jigsaw blade.

6-19-14. The jigsaw is then used to cut out the exact shape required. Now you can see the second of the two uses of the strips of masking tape. The shoe of the jigsaw would normally mark paint quite badly, usually necessitating a respray. By placing several layers of masking tape over the bodywork and another couple of layers of masking tape on the bottom of the jigsaw shoe, you won't mark the paint and will save yourself a lot of extra work and expense putting right paint faults.

6-19-15. It always makes sense to cut a little way inboard of the shape that you finally want. At this stage you can trial fit the heater, making sure that it aligns correctly with the hole and, when you're satisfied that it does, use the file to remove any burrs and paint the edge of the hole to prevent any corrosion.

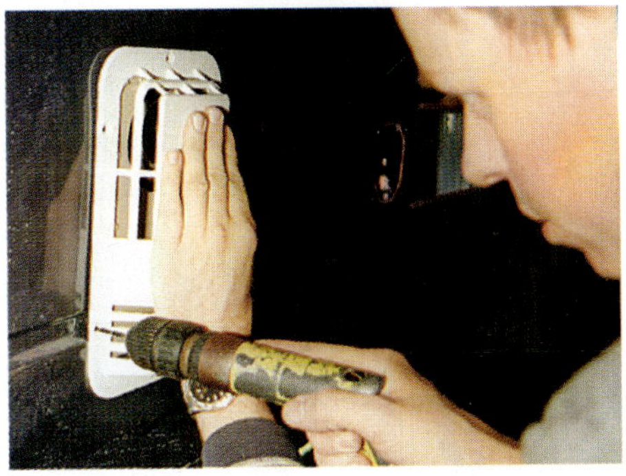

6-19-16. The next step is to screw the flue cover to the outside of the motor caravan wall. It must be centred precisely over the hole you have cut.

6-19-17. To make sure that the heater is perfectly located, draw a centre line on the floor and another one vertically up the back of the heater casing. Slide the exhaust on the heater through the flue seals on the plate that has just been fitted to the outer wall, until it reaches the stop position. Check that both the flue and the air intake pipes pass through the lip seals on the outer vent cover. Line up the vertical mark on the rear of the heater with the centre line on the floor and screw the heater to the floor.

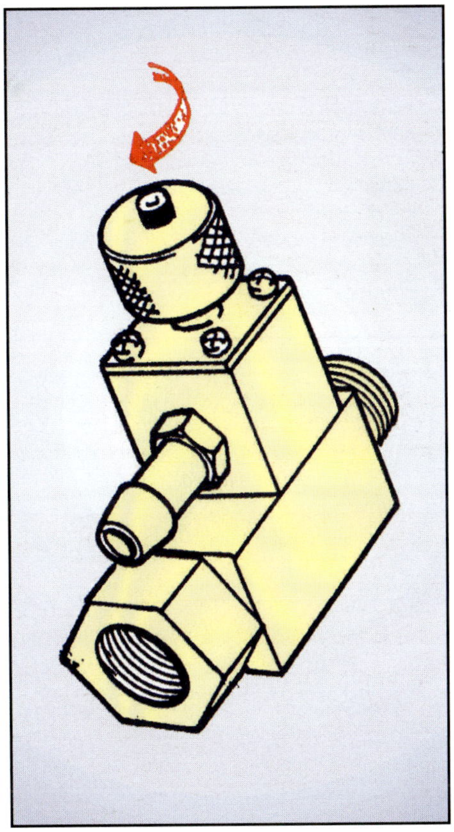

6-19-18. The drain tap will already be fitted to the heater unit – seen with the casing removed – and note that the tap is closed when the knob is turned anti-clockwise, not clockwise as would be the case with most taps.

6-19-19. In the case of a Leisuredrive conversion, there isn't enough depth for the standard water outlet (held in left hand) to be used so an elbow has to be fitted in its place.

Top tips!

- If the pipe needs to be straightened and rebent, it will work harden. In this case, scrap the pipe and use new.
- You may be able to use an automotive brake or fuel pipe bender if you don't have access to the correct plumber's tool.

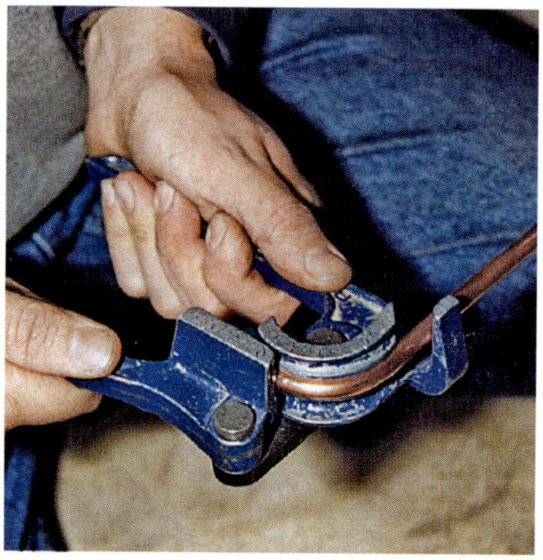

6-19-20. You can carry out this part of the work yourself but you should not make the final gas fittings. The gas pipe will have to make some tight bends in order to fit neatly within the cupboard space.

6-19-21. If you do fit the pipe temporarily in place to check its position, don't tighten the union or the olive will be squashed onto the pipe. Leave that to the professional fitter.

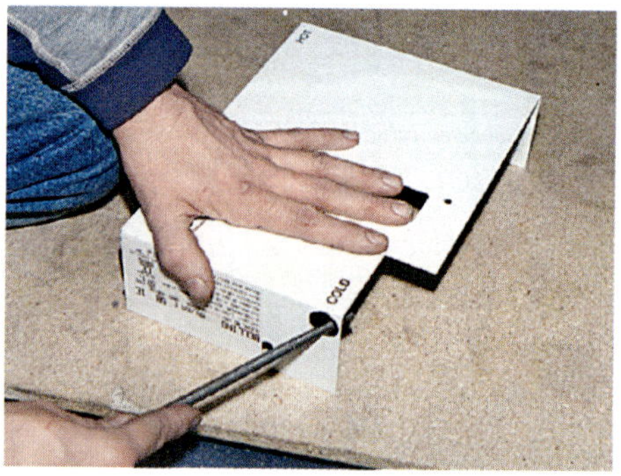

6-19-22. With the pipe in place and taken in this particular direction, it was necessary to open out and, in one place, to cut away part of the casing.

6-19-23. The casing is simply screwed onto the back of the unit.

6-19-24. You should use reinforced good quality hose. Note that the HOT and COLD connections are clearly marked and it's essential that they are connected correctly.

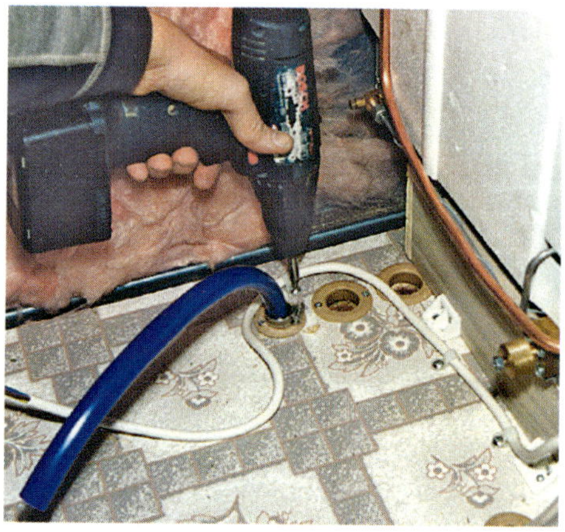

6-19-25. The electrical cable, not to be fully connected unless you are a qualified electrician, can be held in place with cable clips.

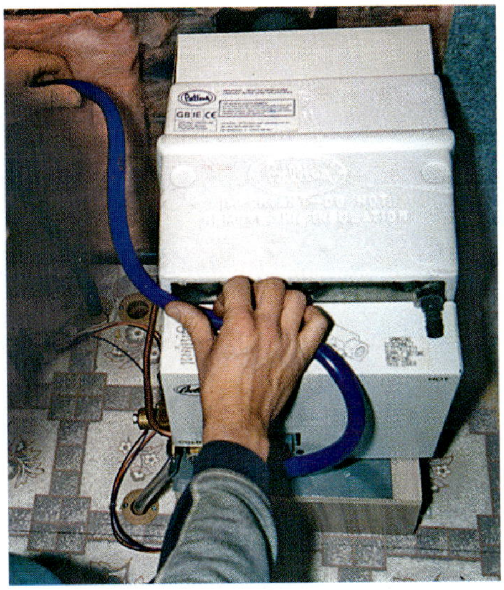

6-19-26. The water pipe should also be clipped neatly in place.

6-19-27. In the case of a T3 Transporter, the wooden box on which the heater is sited will need to be screwed to the floor.

6-19-28. The operating switch panel can be fitted to a convenient part of the kitchen unit.

6-19-29. The wiring comes with its own looms ready to be plugged in.

6-19-30. The final step for a qualified electrician, such as Leisuredrive's Steve, seen here, is to connect up the mains and 12 volt wiring feeds.

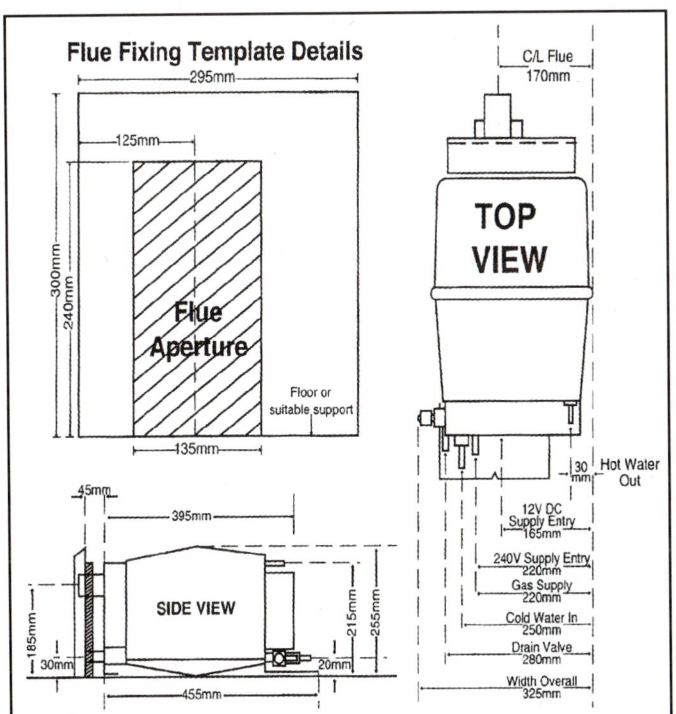

6-19-31. Installation requirements for the Malaga GE 13.5 litre model: The flue terminal position should not be closer than 300mm below an opening window or 600mm from a vertical corner.
Clearances required for installation and servicing, as seen from inside the installation:
LHS = 240mm
RHS = 5mm
Rear = 100mm
Top = 5mm

SECTION 20. ELECTRIC WATER HEATER

6-20-1. CAK's Mini 8 Storage Water Heater has been developed to provide an electric water heater of high quality construction with a stainless steel water tank. The Mini 8 comes with a tough outer protection casing, which is insulated for efficiency. Powered by a 230v mains electric element of 500w power, the Mini 8 will provide 8 litres of hot water. The compact size of 430mm (17in) long (plus electric & water connections), 230mm (9in) wide, and 230mm (9in) high, allows it to be fitted beneath the rear of the rear seat/bed base.
Further specs: Water tank capacity 8 litre. Operating pressure 16psi (1 bar). Built in pressure relief safety valve. 70°C max. thermostat. Dry weight 3kg. Filled weight 11kg.

6-20-2. CAK's proprietor, Jonathan Frost, explains that water connections for ½in PVC hose are supplied but for the push-fit plumbing we were to use, you need a 10-12mm straight reducing connector, also available from CAK. You can see that Jonathan has also supplied a drain-down valve with a stub for taking a length of plastic hose.

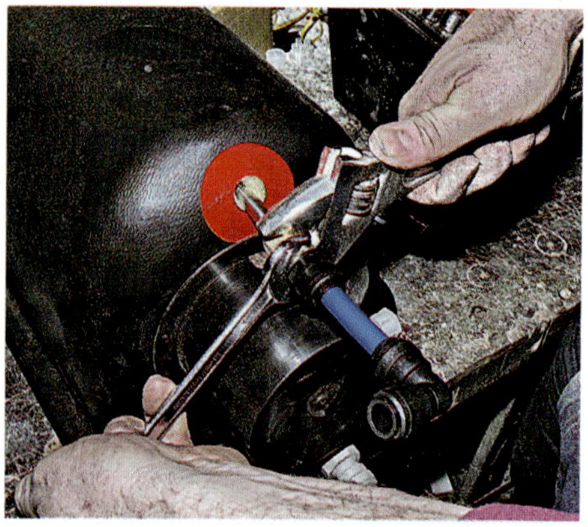

6-20-3. Before fitting the Mini 8, the reducer and a short length of push-fit pipe were connected to the outlet side.

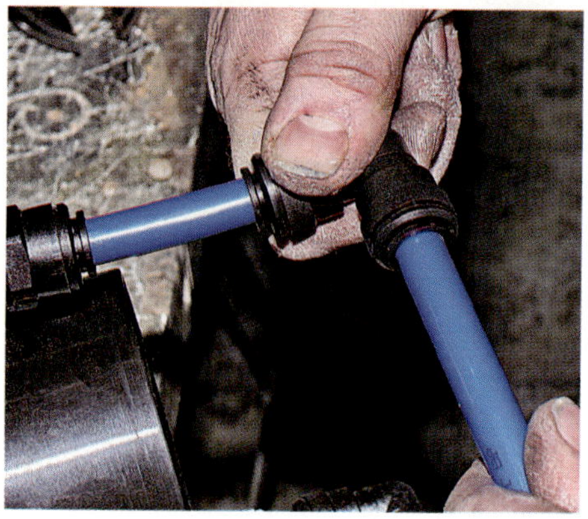

6-20-4. Roy, who was doing the Leisuredrive installation, also decided to check-fit the pipe where it continued from the elbow.

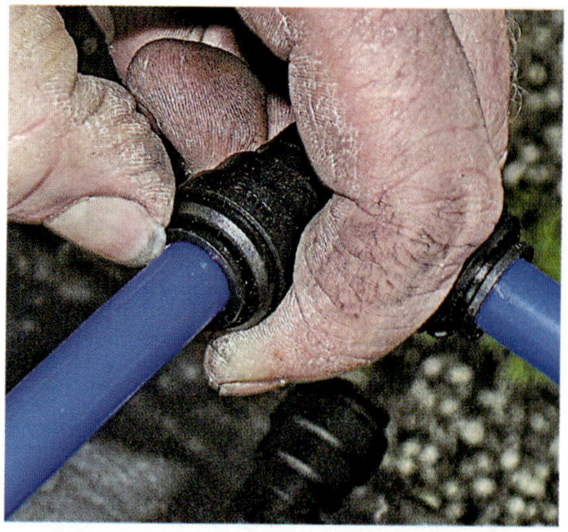

6-20-5. To remove it again, it was a simple matter to squeeze down the collar with the thumb nail and free the pipe.

6-20-6. The electrical connections need to be made by someone qualified and can be found under the protective cap on the end of the boiler.

6-20-7. Roy connected one end of his cable to the boiler before fitting it to the vehicle.

6-20-8. It was now time for Roy to offer the boiler up to its final resting place in the vehicle, although at this stage, it was not to be screwed down.

6-20-11. The switch for operating the boiler is part of the modular set of electrical components available from CAK. Here, it is being offered up to the housing which fits on the wardrobe.

6-20-12. Roy has now fed the cable through the vehicle, clipping it neatly out of the way, and the correct length of cable has been allowed for fixing to the back of the switch.

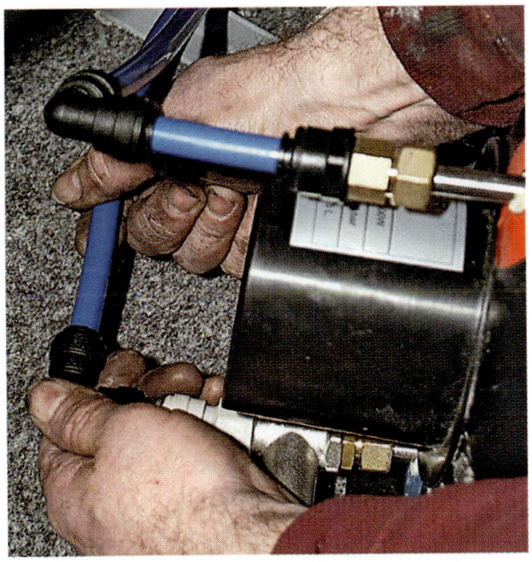

6-20-9. This was because the pipes could most easily be fitted into position now ...

6-20-13. Roy crimps spade terminals on to the cable ends before making the connections.

6-20-10. ... and the boiler finally screwed down through the flange all the way round the outside. Do bear in mind, that when fully loaded, the boiler will weigh 11kgs – be sure to make your fixings suitably strong.

6-20-14. Here you can see how the drain valve works. If the boiler is situated near a door, you can simply push on a piece of plastic hose when required and open the tap. If it is located well away from a door, you may want to permanently fit a piece of hose and to run it through a suitable drain hole in the floor of the vehicle.

6-20-15. With the wiring in place and the mains electricity connected, the boiler can simply be switched on when required.

SECTION 21. CRUISE CONTROL

Driving a Camper with cruise control makes the whole experience more restful and enjoyable, as well as the prospect of saving your license if you accidentally find yourself exceeding the speed limit. The Rostra cruise control is an aftermarket system made to OE manufacturer's standards and there are several versions available.

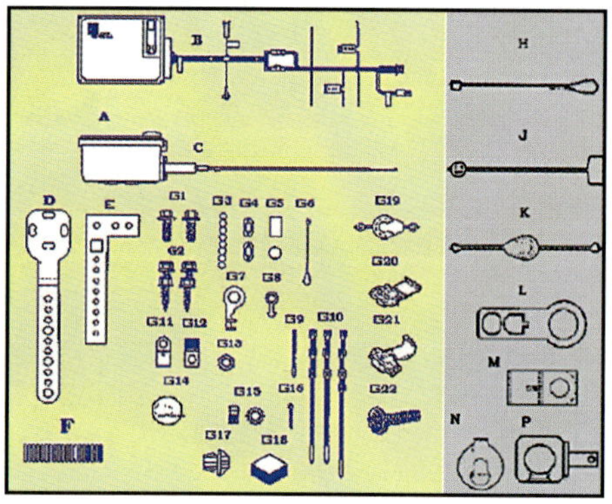

6-21-1. *Whichever kit is required, it will include all the parts needed to link up to your T5's engine. The parts in the grey box on the right are the optional accessories held by Rostra stockists, and are sometimes required, depending on the particular installation.*

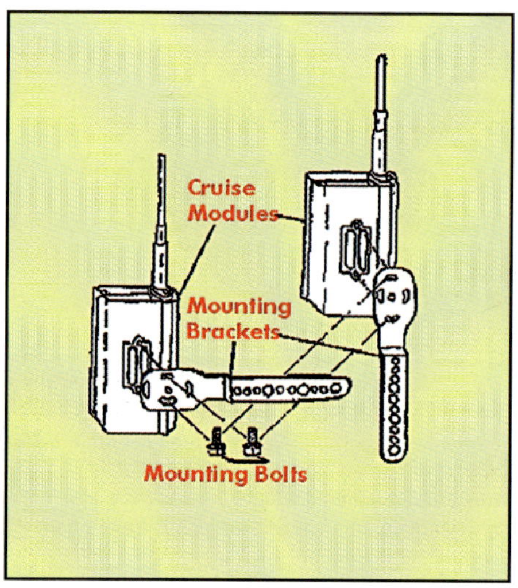

6-21-2. *The actuator motor or 'Cruise Module' can be mounted in any one of a number of locations, using the universal brackets supplied.*

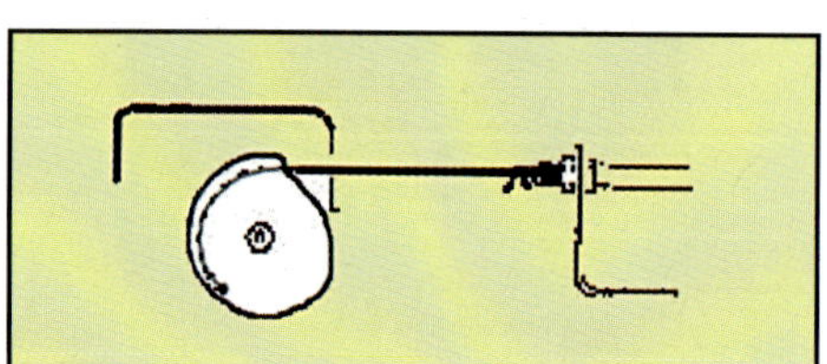

6-21-3. *The principle is that the motor pulls on a quadrant or lever operating the engine speed.*

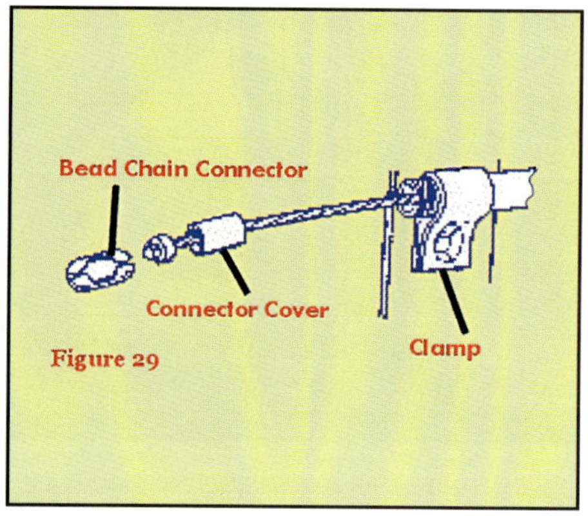

6-21-4. *The cable leading from the cruise module has to be clamped, allowing the inner to slide as required.*

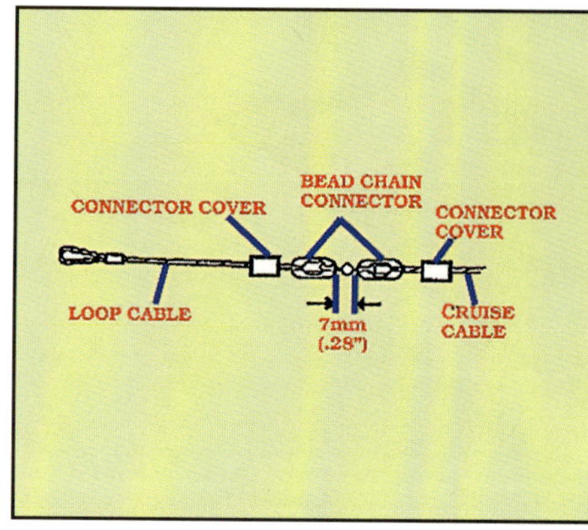

6-21-5. *There are various options available for linking the inner to the accelerator mechanism, again depending on model.*

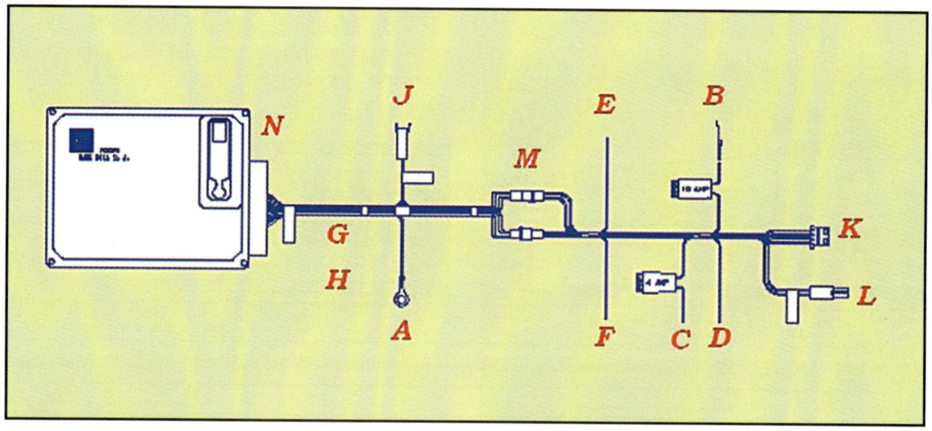

6-21-6. *The wiring instructions provided with the kit are comprehensive and simple to follow once you or your auto electrician have identified the appropriate feed and supply cables.*

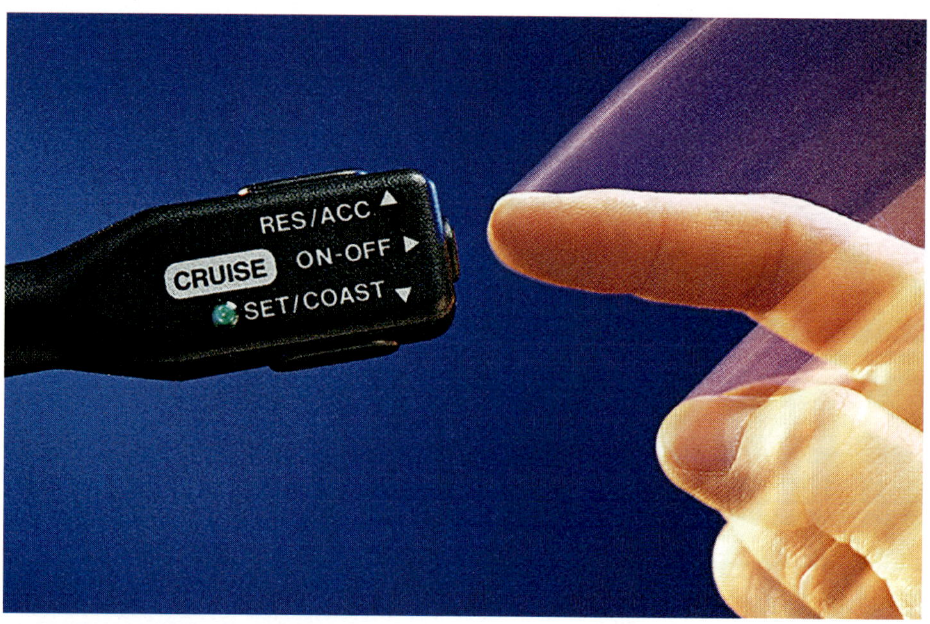

6-21-7. *The cruise control is turned on or off, reset or its speed changed using one of the several types of control knob available from Rostra. The system is also set up so that the cruise control is automatically cut if the clutch is depressed, an automatic transmission is put into neutral or if the brake pedal is touched.*

SECTION 22. XENON DRIVING LIGHTS, MAP LIGHT, FAN

The Volkswagen Transporter is a particularly well-made vehicle and, when adding accessories, it makes sense to use those of an equally high quality. Hella is one of the companies that produce 'Original Equipment' (OE) standard accessories – in fact it supplies some manufacturers – and that's why its three items are shown together, in one section; that and the fact that all three have to be connected into the wiring system. If you are not competent in carrying out electrical connections, leave it to the experts such as Conrad Anderson, specialists in motor caravan electrics and electronics, who carried out the work I photographed for this section.

Before working on the vehicle electrics note the following:

- Work must only be carried out be a competent auto electrician.
- Disconnect the battery before starting work, making sure that you have the radio code and that no other items, such as an aftermarket alarm, will be affected.

PART A. FITTING HELLA XENON DRIVING LIGHTS

Hella's smallest Xenon auxiliary lamp, the Micro DE Xenon, is ideal for low-down fitting. Its 'DE light technology' includes an elliptical reflector that directs the light to a focusing lens, which in turn projects it onto the road. A shield positioned between the reflector and the lens provides precise cut-off, making these lights ideal for low-beam and fog lamp use. I took our T5 to motor caravan electronics experts Conrad Anderson to have these Xenon driving lights fitted.

6-22-A1. The Hella DE Xenon is small enough to fit in the Transporter T5's apron and gives about twice the light output of ordinary parabolic headlamps.

6-22-A2. Xenon lights have far greater light output than halogen units but, amazingly, consume far less power. They require connecting via a ballast relay (right) in order that the lights operate 'on demand' to overcome the natural tendency of Xenon lights to otherwise come on rather slowly.

6-22-A3. The grille panels into which the lights are fitted are held in place with the two visible clips, seen here (arrowed). Here you can see the Conrad Anderson engineer levering the panel out of its recess using a non-scratching plastic tool.

6-22-A4. The brackets supplied with the lights are ideal for fitting in the space inside the housing. Conrad Anderson had to be careful on the left side of the vehicle that the light was mounted far enough forward so that it wouldn't foul on the washer bottle, found to the rear of its mounting.

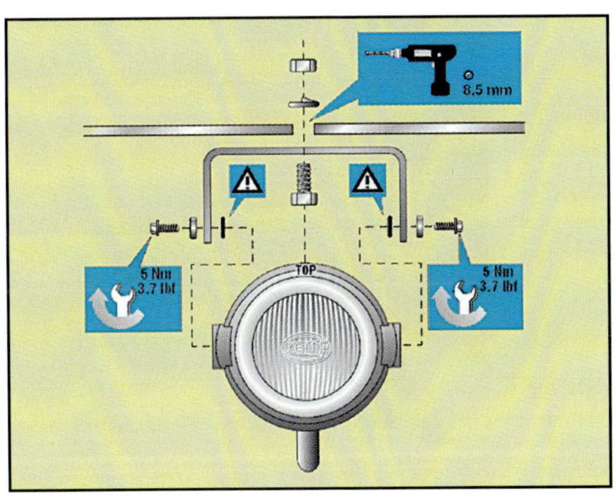

6-22-A5 These are the tightening torques and drilling sizes required when fitting the bracket and lamp into position. The central bolt holding the light unit in place is to allow for side-to-side adjustment. In our case, the two outer holes were slotted, so Conrad Anderson decided to use a pair of vertical mounting bolts after aiming the lights and brackets as accurately as possible before drilling. You have to be confident you're going to get it right – and Graham and Andy at Conrad Anderson did, first time!

6-22-A6. It was found that, when the trim panel was replaced, it fouled on part of the bracket but this was simply remedied by cutting a small part of it away and then painting it to protect it against corrosion.

6-22-A9. The light unit itself has two threaded holes allowing the light to be mounted either further forward or back according to requirements.

6-22-A10. In our case, the rear-most hole had to be used because of the proximity of the washer bottle.

6-22-A7. Having been trimmed and painted, the bracket was fitted to the inside of the recess using two bolts, rather than the one suggested in the drawing. This meant that the angle had to be just about right first time, although the holes in the bracket are slotted which allows for some adjustment.

6-22-A8. Before fitting the lamp unit into place, the ballast connector, complete with its sealing ring, was pushed through the back of the apron and securely plugged in place on the back of the lamp.

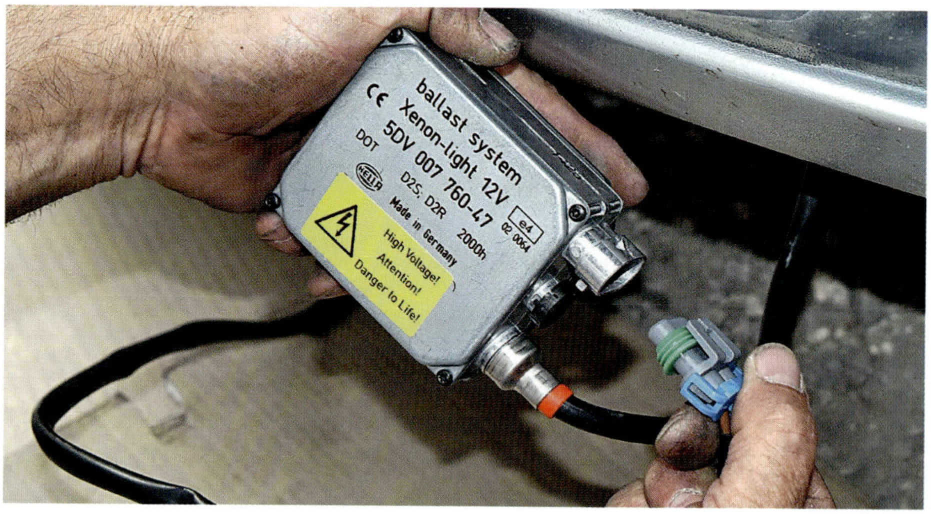

6-22-A11. The connector to the light unit is already fitted to the ballast and the power supply plug, also with its effective sealing ring, has to be clipped onto the ballast unit.

6-22-A12. The ballast unit was fitted securely beneath the vehicle with the connectors facing downwards.

6-22-A13. When both of the lights were fitted, the wiring was brought together on one side of the vehicle and the relay connected.

6-22-A15. Inside the vehicle, a certain amount of stripping down of the dashboard had to take place and cables were fed behind the dashboard and up to the switch position just above the gear stick.

6-22-A14. It was a two-man job to feed the wiring through the engine bay.

Important note: These lights were connected so that they could be turned on and off independently of the headlights. You may wish to ensure that they come on only with the headlight main beam. Alternatively, they could be wired to come on only with the headlight low beam but check with the legal requirements in the area which you live before the connections are made.

6-22-A16. There is no switch supplied with the kit so Conrad Anderson fitted an illuminated switch to match those already on the dash.

6-22-A17. A tank cutter was used to drill holes in the two panels.

6-22-A18. Firstly, one bolt holding the light in place was fitted but not fully tightened ...

6-22-A19. ... and then the other bolt was fitted. The bolt nearest to the inside of the vehicle is the most difficult to fit so it makes sense to start that one first.

6-22-A20. The final job for the Conrad Anderson technicians was to make fused connections to the battery.

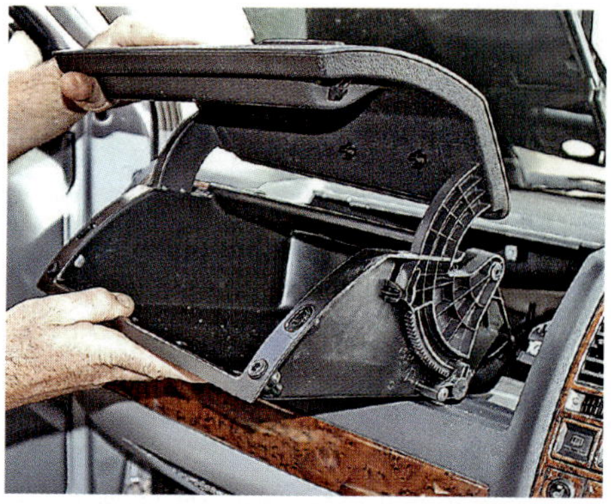

6-22-B2. ... and removing it from the dash.

6-22-B3. After careful measuring, he drilled a cable access hole ...

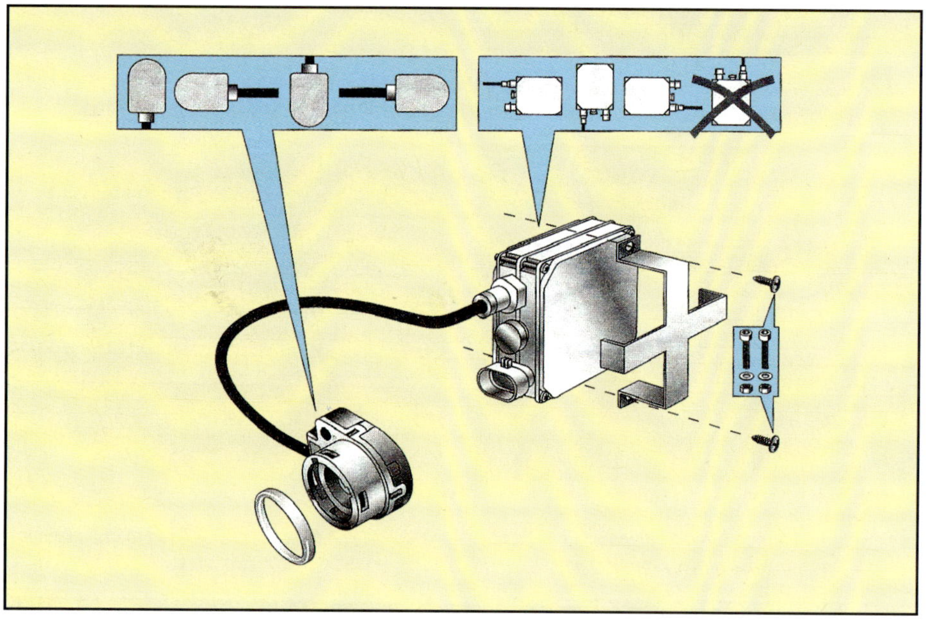

6-22-A21. DON'T FORGET! The sealing ring must be in place before the plug is fitted to the rear of the light body. The ballast device must not be fitted with the connections at the top, as shown. It must also be fitted away from driven water and road spray when the vehicle is on the road.

6-22-B4. ... screw holes for the mounting plate ...

PART B: HELLA MAP READING LIGHT

A map reading light is essential if you're navigating at night. Even when you have satellite navigation, you need to be ready for the machine's little 'errors and omissions' – and if the navigator drops a packet of mints on the floor while you're driving at night, 'sat nav' won't be any use whatsoever...

6-22-B1. I decided I wanted the Hella halogen map light fitted inside the glove compartment. It provides a light in there – there's a separate switch on the head of the light – and isn't in the way of the airbag or an accident risk in the event of a crash. Conrad Anderson's proprietor, Steve, started by unscrewing the glove box ...

6-22-B5. ... then used self-tapping screws into spire nuts on the back of the box. We decided that the plastic wouldn't be sufficiently strong to screw into direct.

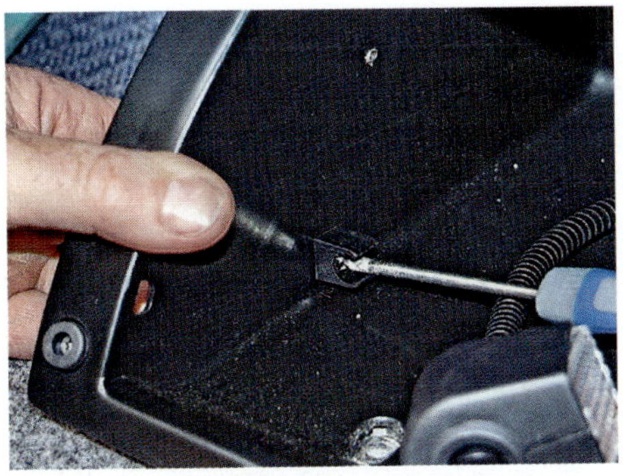

6-22-B6. This is the clip used for supporting the far end of the flexible neck.

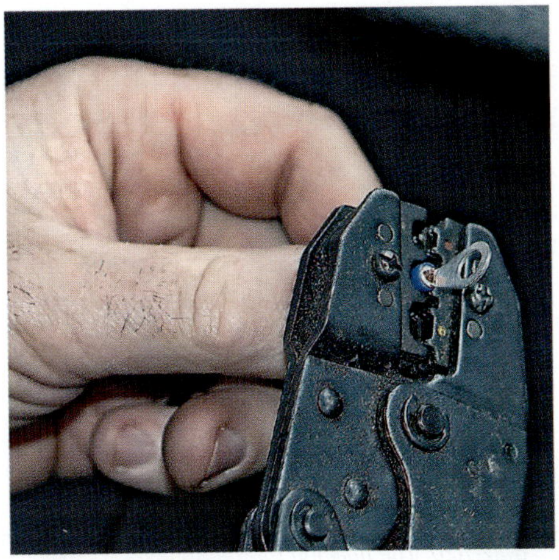

6-22-B9. The earth/ground connector from the Hella light had a connector crimped on the end of it ...

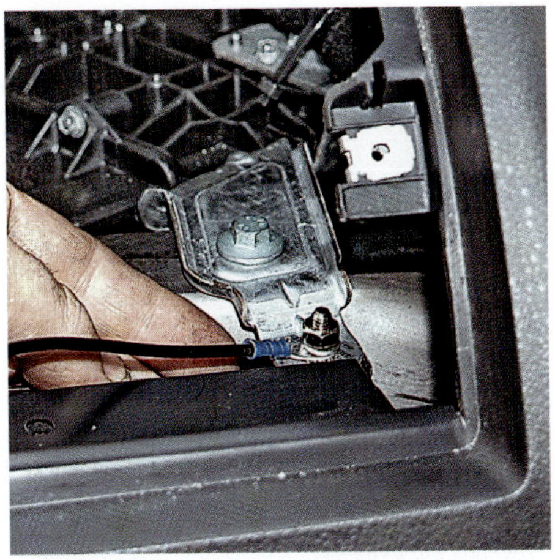

6-22-B10. ... and this was bolted to a suitable earthing point inside the dash.

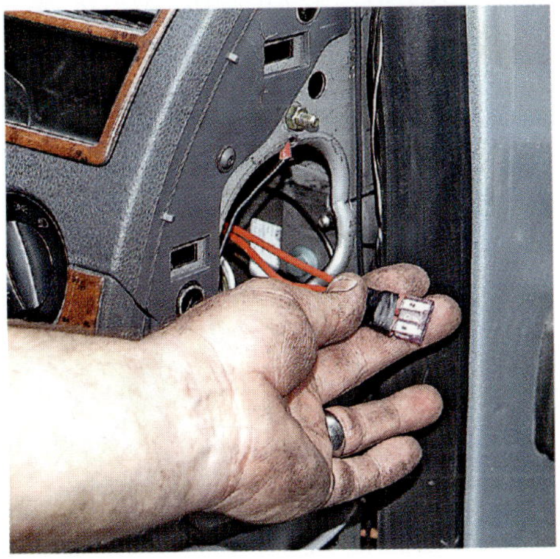

6-22-B7. The feed for the positive cable was located inside the right-hand side of the dash and was protected with a fuse. Both cable and fuse size were chosen to allow both the light and the Hella fan – see next section – to use the same feed wire.

6-22-B11. The feed cable was tapped into for the feed wire to the light, noting that colour codes vary greatly between counties and across the years. Refer to the Hella and Volkswagen manuals if you need to identify correct cable colours. The wire used by Conrad Anderson to supply power is the traditional British red.

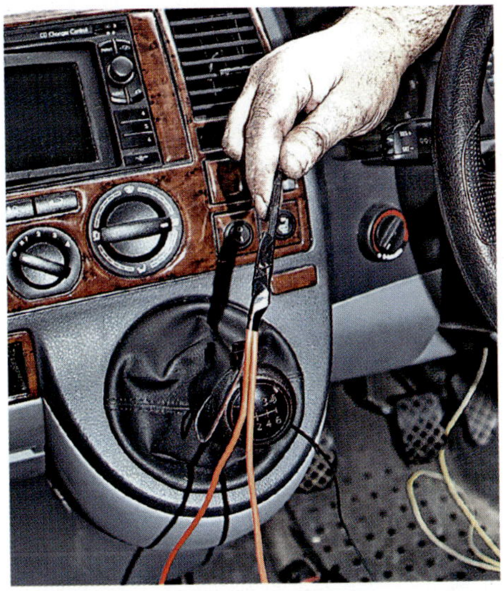

6-22-B8. Andy, who was working on that side of the dash, fed a strong but flexible, insulated fish wire through the dash, taped to it the wires he heeded to pass through, then pulled out the fish wire, leaving the electrical cables in its place.

Note: I hate Scotchloks; Conrad Anderson hate them. We recommend using only crimped or soldered connections for best quality connections.

6-22-B12. Crimped connections have been used here to add spade terminal connections at the back of the glove compartment so that the components can be disconnected if necessary in future.

6-22-B13. Steve refitted the glove compartment ...

6-22-B14. ... and when the battery was reconnected, we had a top-quality, dual-purpose Hella map and glove compartment light in place.

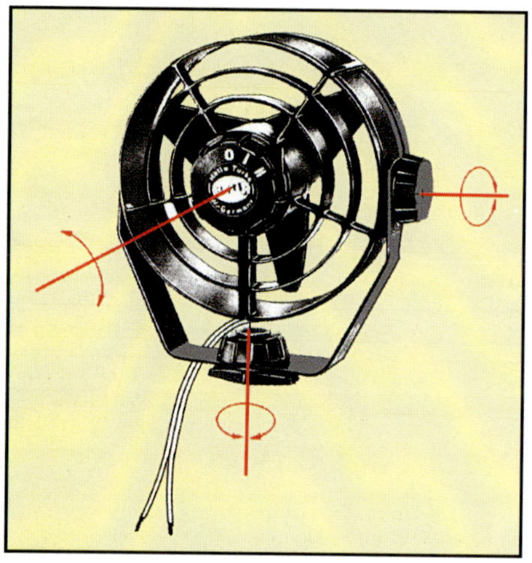

6-22-C1. The Hella Fan is quiet (when compared with cheaper fans), light in weight but relatively powerful. There are two knobs for adjusting the angle and the three-position knob on the front is an ON-OFF and speed control.

6-22-C2. As described in the previous section, a positive feed cable was located beneath the right-hand side of the dash. A new cable was temporarily strapped to an insulated 'fish' wire before being passed through the back of the dash.

PART C. HELLA COCKPIT FAN

This should be read in conjunction with Part B, above, because some of the wiring connections are shared.

6-22-C3. It is essential that the wire is fused for protection.

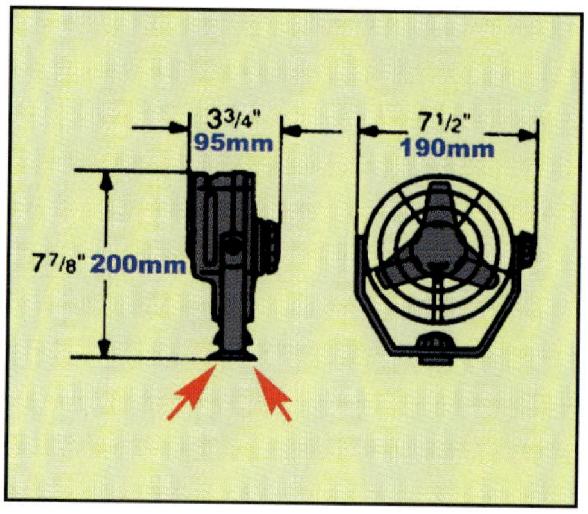

6-22-C4. The base plate of the fan is detachable and was screwed to the oddments tray on the dash using the two screw positions (arrowed), after first removing the tray by levering it up at the back.

6-22-C5. After refitting, the fan can be used to provide cool air on the face, something that the T5 lacks when the heater is on anything but the lowest settings.

SECTION 23. FITTING XENON XID HEADLIGHTS

Caution! Adapting halogen headlights to accept HID bulbs is illegal in some countries. Check with your local regulatory authority before continuing.

Xenon headlights might sound like something out of the early days of *Star Trek*, but you don't need rocket science to be able to hugely increase the power of your vehicle's headlights

Headlight bulbs, manufactured with the rare gas xenon inside a quartz envelope, are capable of producing far brighter, whiter light than traditional tungsten bulbs and are at least 250 per cent brighter than halogen bulbs. They're darned expensive, though! In addition to the cost of the rare gas, the technology required for the xenon bulbs' internal components and the need for ballast devices to provide the power required are the main reasons.

Xenon headlight systems are usually known as HID or High Intensity Discharge units. While HID Xenon headlights are several times brighter and last 10 times longer than halogen lights, the amazing thing is that they also consume 35 per cent less power and generate less heat when in use.

Here are some typical statistics:

Bulb type	Power consumption	Candela	Lumen	Hours life
Halogen	55W	67,500	1500	400
Xenon HID	35W	200,000	3200	2000

Kelvin ratings

Specifications for HID Xenon bulbs invariably seem to offer different 'colour temperature' ratings, expressed in degrees Kelvin. Don't think that this is a measure of the bulb's light output; it's not! Colour temperature is a measurement that indicates the hue of a specific type of light source, not its intensity. It is generally accepted that the best Kelvin rating for optimal human night vision is between 3800 and 6000 degrees K – the higher figure tending towards a whiter, bluer light but, above this figure, depth perception is significantly reduced and as the figure rises, the actual lighting output falls off dramatically.

Some companies have been known to claim to offer bulbs in the 8000 to 12,000 degrees K range but if this were correct, the light output would appear between dark blue and deep purple. However, moderately higher figures provide a blue-white light that some people prefer. Having said all that, it must be remembered that not all retro-fit manufacturers colour ratings are the same, so you can't compare one with the other.

It's worth pointing out, not least because it greatly affects the purchase cost, that many conversion kits do not provide Xenon HID lighting for both high and low beams. Indeed, most only offer single (low) beam. The Xenon HID kit shown here is dual-beam (I can't see the point otherwise) and the headlights work as normal on both beams. Full lighting intensity is not realised for two or three seconds, but it is said to be at least the equal of halogen bulbs when the Xenon lights are first turned on, so it's hardly a problem.

When buying a Xenon HID conversion kit, you must make sure of several key points. The kit must be:

- Fully electro-magnetically compliant to prevent interference with on-board electronics. Some cheaper systems have been said to affect ECUs, anti lock brakes, airbag systems and other vehicle electronics.
- Made specifically to fit the industry standard specs for Halogen lighting systems. Cheapskate kits that adapt the standard bulbs designed only for factory-fitted Xenon systems would require headlight housing modification and/or adaptor rings, neither of which will provide a legally acceptable beam pattern. Look for E11 (UK), A4 (German) markings as a measure of quality standard.
- Run through a relay and compatible with any bulb failure alarms which are triggered by these kits on some vehicles. Check with your supplier: If your vehicle's bulb failure alarm is triggered by the kit, there should be a 'work-round' available, requiring additional filters or load resistors.
- Legal for your vehicle. My understanding of an unclear situation is that vehicles manufactured after 1st January 2007 must only be fitted with Xenon HID bulbs if also fitted with headlight washing and automatic headlight levelling equipment. Again, check first with your supplier that this does not also apply to your vehicle even if manufactured before that date.

How easy to DIY?

If you can change an original halogen bulb, you should be able to fit a Xenon HID kit. However, on some vehicles, bulbs are particularly difficult to access, in which case you may need to have a mechanic fit them for you.

Xenon HID kits don't require the replacement of the headlight units themselves, comprising glass and reflector bodies. Unless yours are broken or rusty, there will be no need to.

It's worth remembering that, quite apart from any difficulty you may have in fitting regular bulbs, it is trickier to fit these kits into certain vehicles. A lot depends on how much room there is behind each headlight unit.

Legalities

Hella claim that retrofitted Xenon HID bulbs are illegal on any vehicle unless also fitted with automatic headlight levelling devices and headlight washers. Automatic headlight levelling devices were developed by Hella and automatically adjust the angle of tilt on the headlights without intervention by the driver, thus compensating for vehicle tilt caused by load changes.

However, though I would never say for a moment that Hella are wrong, the information I received only appears to apply to German TV regulations. Anyway, as it happens, our Transporter already has headlight levelling and will very soon be fitted with headlight washers, both of which are available through Conrad Anderson. But, legalities aside, I would suggest:

- Strongly consider fitting headlight washers to your vehicle to prevent refraction of the much brighter light produced by Xenon HID and, at the very least, keep your headlight glasses clean at all times.
- Don't fit them to a vehicle which has a propensity to rear-end sagging when loaded or when carrying passengers unless headlight levelling is fitted. Incidentally, headlight levelling devices – not necessarily automatic – have been mandatory for all vehicles in the EU since the beginning of the 1990s.
- Satisfy yourself, by contacting your supplier, that the kit being applied and/or

6-23-1. This is the Conrad Anderson 'Wide-View' Xenon HID kit. The components include a relay which, though not always essential, is best in my opinion (depending on the wiring on the vehicle) because it separates the switching on the vehicle from that on the HID kit.

fitted enables your vehicle to comply with legal requirements in all respects.

The following picture sequence was taken at Conrad Anderson - leading suppliers and fitters of electrical and electronic components to motor caravans.

Fitting instructions

6-23-2. On many vehicles, and this includes our Volkswagen Transporter T5, there is a waterproof cover on the back of the headlight unit and this must first be removed.

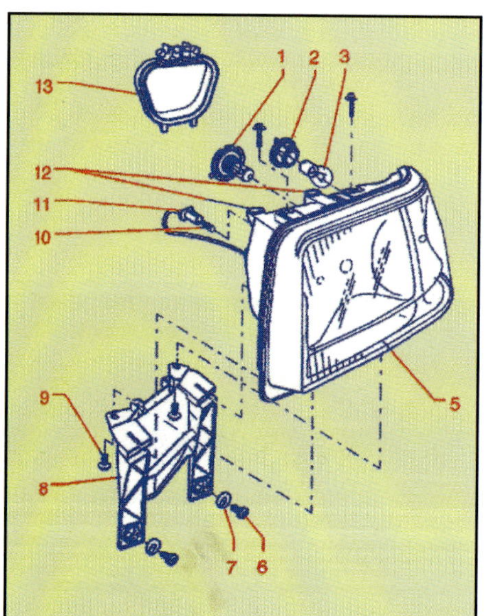

6-23-3. In this drawing, the components 6, 7, 8 and 9 are support components and are not relevant. Parts 10 and 11 are sidelight components and do not have to be touched. Parts 2 and 3 are for non-halogen bulbs and do not relate to this article. These are the components referred to in this article:
1 – halogen bulb
5 – headlight body
13 – waterproof cover

Important note: Do not, under any circumstances, touch the glass or quartz envelope on the bulb. If you do, grease from your fingers can cause the bulb to burn out prematurely.

6-23-4. Andy at Conrad Anderson unclipped the halogen bulb from the back of the headlight unit.

6-23-5. It is very helpful if you note which way up the original halogen bulb came out so that the replacement Xenon bulb (left) can be fitted in exactly the same orientation.

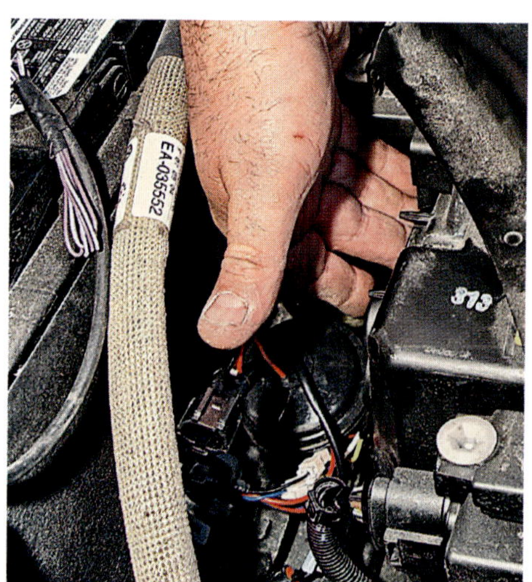

6-23-6. This is the bulb and cable connection assembly ready to be fitted to the vehicle.

Method 1

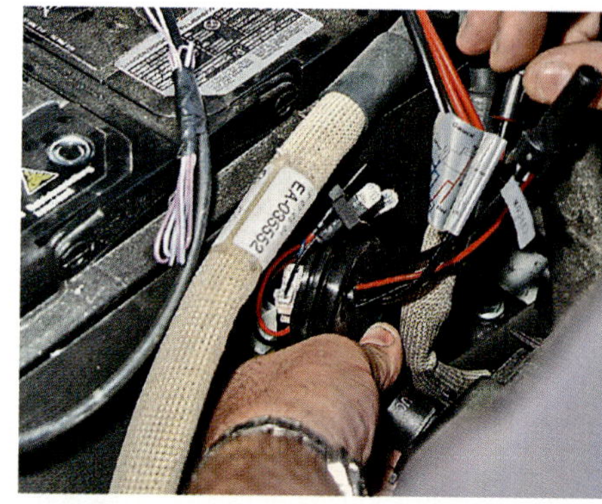

6-23-7. Depending on the room you have on the vehicle you are working on, you could now fit the Xenon bulb into the headlight unit ...

6-23-8. ... making absolutely certain that it is the right way up and firmly located. The spring clips on the back of the headlight unit must bear evenly on the bulb, which must sit flat and true in its recess. It is worth spending a lot of time making absolutely certain that the bulb mounting is correct.

6-23-9. Where waterproof covers are fitted, it is necessary to drill a 25mm hole in the plastic cover. Try to drill this hole in as flat an area of the cover as possible.

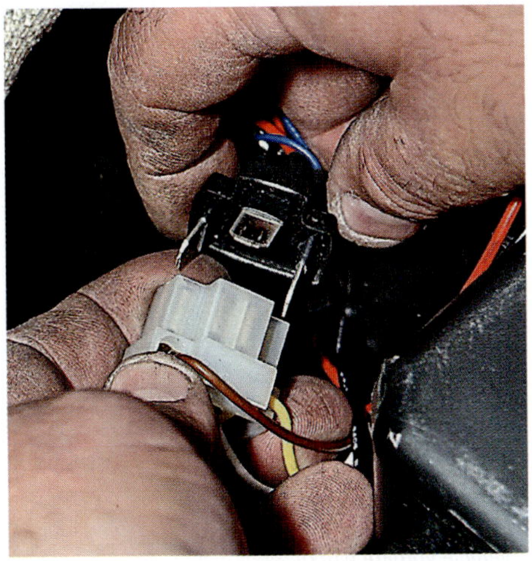

6-23-10. The three pin plug on the vehicle's wiring that previously pushed onto the halogen bulb is now connected to the three separate pins on the wiring on the Xenon kit. Interestingly, these three pins are not in a fixed block and each pin has to be pushed independently fully home. If your vehicle does not have these connections, the kit should include an adaptor connection.

If there is room to continue with the bulb already in place, follow the instructions over the next few steps. If there is not, and the bulb has to be fitted along with the cover, use the following order of work.

Method 2

6-23-11. On the battery side of the Transporter, there isn't room to follow the procedure described above, so Andy removed the bulb again and inserted the wiring, complete with the seal, into the body of the headlight cover. Note that the bulb has now been protected with the plastic shield supplied with the kit so that it doesn't get touched or knocked.

6-23-12. The rubber seal now has to be fitted into the 25mm hole in such a way that it too will be waterproof.

6-23-13. Andy removed the bulb cover and offered up the assembly to the back of the headlight ...

6-23-14. ... before clipping the bulb in place, checking it for correct fit as before ...

6-23-15. ... then pushing the waterproof cover into position onto the back of the headlamp unit.

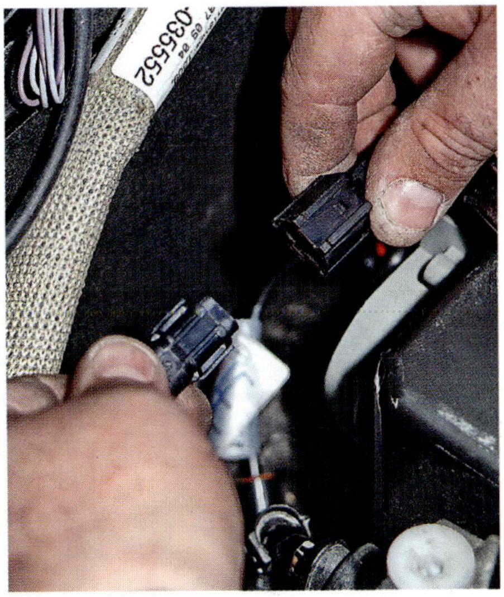

6-23-16. These are the connections from the ballast unit (of which we will see more later) and the headlight bulbs. They are handed so that you cannot confuse them.

6-23-17. The ballast unit provides the very high voltage required but only consumes 35w.

6-23-18. It should always be mounted on this plastic backing plate. The double-sided tape has already been fitted to the mounting box and is being screwed into place ...

6-23-19. ... prior to offering up and fitting the ballast unit. The backing plate provides insulation where the unit is being mounted onto metal parts.

6-23-22. On the other side of the vehicle there is more room to work, but even so, the unit has been fitted to the backing plate first.

6-23-20. These are the two plugs and sockets from the ballast to the headlight referred to earlier. They go large-to-small and small-to-large, the smaller plug fitting inside the larger socket.

6-23-23. Here, the ballast is going to be fitted to the side panel inside the engine bay and Conrad Anderson's Graham, who is working on that side of the vehicle, can be seen here wiping the panel with spirit wipe to remove any traces of grease or dirt – this is most essential if you want double-sided tape to stick. You should also do the same to the plastic backing plate, by the way.

6-23-21. Each headlight is fitted with its own relay. A hole has been carefully drilled in the front panel and a nut, bolt and spring washer are used to fix the relay in place. Before fitting the relays, make sure that they won't foul the bonnet or the bonnet stay when it is closed.

6-23-24. Graham uses the double-sided tape supplied with the kit (having wiped off the back of the ballast unit first) and fixes it to the backing plate.

6-23-25. The backing plate is also fitted with double-sided tape but, because of the shape of the panel, it also has to be screwed to the steel behind it.

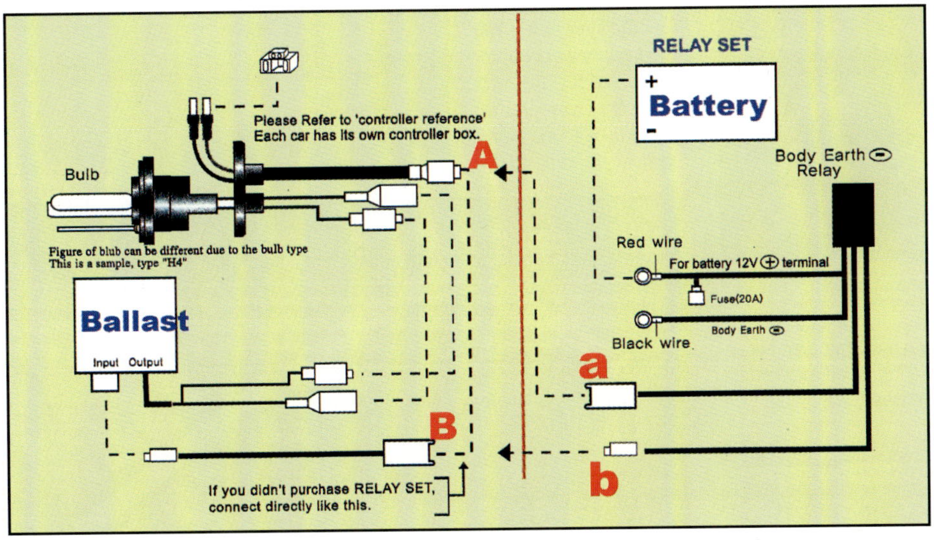

6-23-26. For reference, this is the diagram describing how the electrical connections are made. The left-hand side of the drawing shows connections without a relay (which I don't recommend) while the right-hand side shows how the relay connections are to be made. Instead of connection A being made to B, the relay is connected by connecting A to a and B to b.

6-23-27. Meanwhile, back on the battery side of the engine bay, Andy made up the terminals on the ends of the cables to fit to the battery.

6-23-28. Note that the positive cable has a fuse in it.

6-23-29. The final result is headlights that match those on the most expensive of upmarket vehicles with a clear, crisp white light, quite unlike the original halogen lights. When you first sit behind the wheel, you may be surprised at the difference. Illumination is certainly better but it's also, well, different, so you have to get used to it at first.

Important note: It is essential that you take the vehicle to have the headlight beams adjusted at an MoT testing station before using the vehicle on the road at night. It is possible that the trajectory of the beams has been changed and this will also ensure that you haven't fitted the bulbs incorrectly. These bulbs are so bright that, if used thoughtlessly or incorrectly they could be very dangerous to other road users.

SECTION 24. DRIVE-AWAY AWNING

Shan and I already owned a very lightweight, 'instant-erect' type of awning for our Leisuredrive VW T5. It's the sort with fibreglass poles and flimsy fabric. I bought it on the spur of the moment at a show and, while it's ideal for an overnighter, you wouldn't want to depend on it for any length of time or out of high season.

We were looking for a top quality drive away awning for camper vans and I found one that is designed and manufactured in Germany – which tends to be a Good Thing – called the Bregenz II and imported into the UK by Nova Leisure. It seemed to be quite adaptable and, most important of all, of excellent quality. The use of steel with passivated coating means that the weight is relatively high but, on the plus side, the Bregenz II has both strength and durability.

Panels can be rolled up or lifted for versatility, while accessory bars hold up the end panel as an extra area of shade to extend your living area still further in good weather. Pleasingly, there's also a built-in high-level vent and rainwater gutter. The Bregenz II also comes complete with vehicle anti-draught skirt, curtains, anchors and a couple of packsacks; one for the fabric and one for the poles.

6-24-1. The Bregenz II, as fitted to the left-hand drive motor caravan it was designed for, has a slight offset. This means the whole awning will be partly offset towards the front on a British van with the door on the other side but I can't see that this is a problem. The passenger door won't open on 'our' side; the driver's door stays shut on 'theirs'. So what!

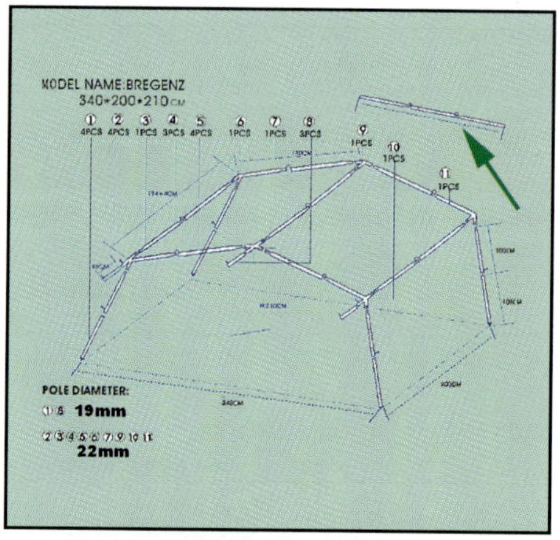

6-24-3. There's not much in the way of instructions with the Bregenz II but they include this invaluable parts list showing the correct locations of the steel poles. You have to work out for yourself that the extra pole (arrowed) is for linking up with the motor caravan, as shown later.

6-24-4. As you can see, each pole and linking section is numbered (arrowed) and the sections are clipped together using the outermost hole, making all the poles as short as possible for now. They can be expanded outward later, after the fabric cover has been added.

6-24-2. This is the comprehensive kit of parts supplied with the awning, plus the optional supports (arrowed) for the end panel to be raised as an area of shade.

6-24-5. It's always slightly tricky to push the spring-loaded button down far enough while sliding it into the edge of the female to which it is being added. You also need strong nails when separating the sections again!

6-24-6. The longer poles are linked together with internal springs.

6-24-7. You simply straighten them ...

6-24-8. ... and slot the poles together, the springs holding them close. When it's time to take the awning down, you simply pull the two halves apart and fold against each other as they were before.

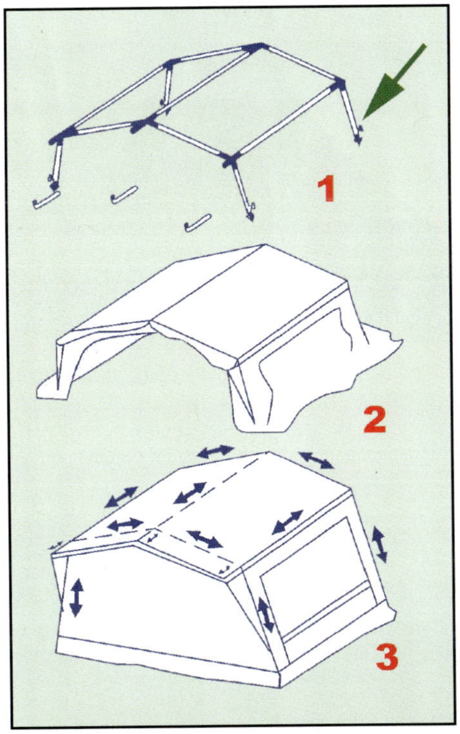

Top tip!

- Awning poles tend to flail about a little unpredictably as you are raising and lowering the legs, particularly when the heavy canvas is taken off the frame when dismantling it. It's best to assemble the awning with the motor caravan parked well out of the way and then to drive it into position later Similarly, remove the motor caravan from the danger area before taking the awning down again.

6-24-9. As always, when erecting a frame-type awning, you put the roof together first followed by the upper parts of the legs (1). On the Bregenz II, the lower parts of the legs are inserted into the uppers and clamps (arrowed) hold them in the lowered position for now. Note the extension poles which are left lying around, just where you can trip over them (no not really!), ready to be fitted after the fabric has been draped over the frame (2). The final stage involves slackening the clamps and raising the legs (3) before adjusting the lengths of the poles by moving the positions of the plungers in the holes as shown in pictures 6-24-4 and 6-24-5.

6-24-10. In the real world, it proved easy to locate the roof poles and here, Shan starts to assemble them.

6-24-11. Shan completed the roof structure ...

6-24-12. ... then fitted both corner poles on one side of the frame.

6-24-13. You can see here how the frame can twist about as Shan adds the corner poles to the other side.

6-24-14. You next need to lay out the canvas in front of the awning frame, facing it the right way and not (as we managed it the first time!) inside out. If you have the tunnel facing the side where the motor caravan will be and the roof the right way up, you can't go wrong.

6-24-15. It actually took both of us to lift the heavy canvas onto the frame but, with all the zips done up, it was very easy to push and pull into place. I don't know whether it was because of the quality or the weight but it seemed to both of us that it went together more easily than any other awnings we've put together in the past.

6-24-16. You have to make sure that the cutaway in each corner and at the top of the apex, on the side facing away from the motor caravan, goes over the extensions in the frame.

6-24-17. Further extension poles are then slipped into the frame and spikes on their upper ends are pushed through holes in the awning roof extension. There are good quality clamps holding them in place.

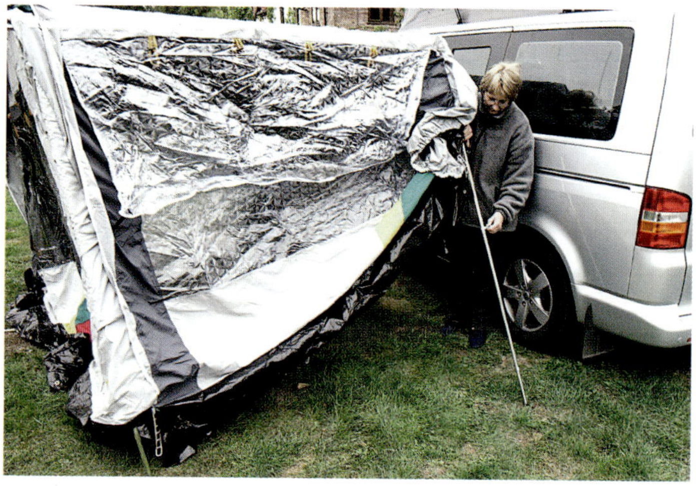

6-24-18. Either working from the outside with each corner of the canvas lifted in turn or from the inside, you have to slacken the clamp on each corner post and raise the corner posts one by one to the height you want the awning to be. The clamps should then be turned inboard so that they are not rubbing on the canvas.

6-24-19. Next, you need to get the awning and motor caravan close to each other. You can see that the access door in the awning needs to line up approximately with the side door on the motor caravan.

6-24-20. Because the awning goes further forward than on left-hand drive models, I found it necessary to fold the mirror forward, which it is designed to do (lower arrow). You can also see the clamp (upper arrow) fitted to the roof and referred to later.

6-24-21. There is a seam at the top of the tunnel where it fits against the motor caravan and into this the long pole shown in picture 6-24-3 (arrowed) is easily slid from one end.

Top tip!

- However, in the words of James Cox at Nova Leisure, "In our experience, most people do not connect the awning to the vehicle at all." It certainly seems to 'sit' nicely against the side of the T5 without requiring lashings of fixings.

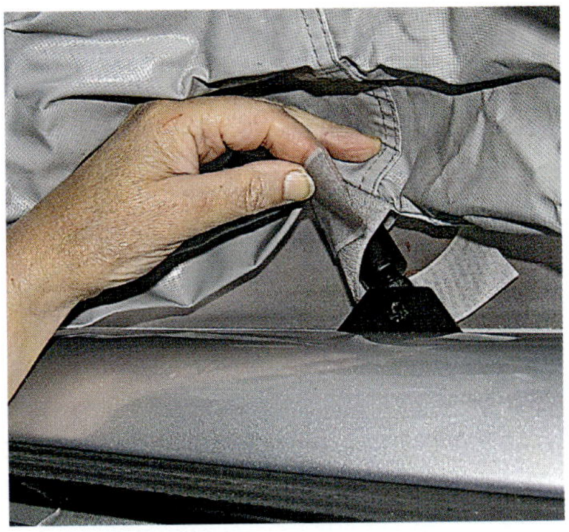

6-24-22. The clamps referred to earlier are designed to hold this pole at each end. We found that the centre of the tunnel could be fixed to the vehicle using the base of the elevating roof strut and the Velcro strips sewn into the centre of the tunnel.

6-24-23. You might be able to get the rear-most Velcro strips onto the rear of the elevating frame, but I think I'm going to have to make up a small bracket to fit to the base of the frame.

6-24-24. This is the suction clamp we saw earlier. It's superbly well made from brass and holds powerfully to a clean surface when the lever at the top is folded over, creating suction on the rubber pad.

6-24-25. We fitted the suction clamp to the front of the roof – the only place it will go on the T5 fitted with the Reimo elevating roof – you can use the Velcro strips or you can clamp the pole against the roof.

6-24-26. Even the curtain runners are very high quality on this awning. Each clip is split so that there is a small gap (arrowed) between the rollers and this allows you to push the clip onto the tape sewn into the top of the curtains.

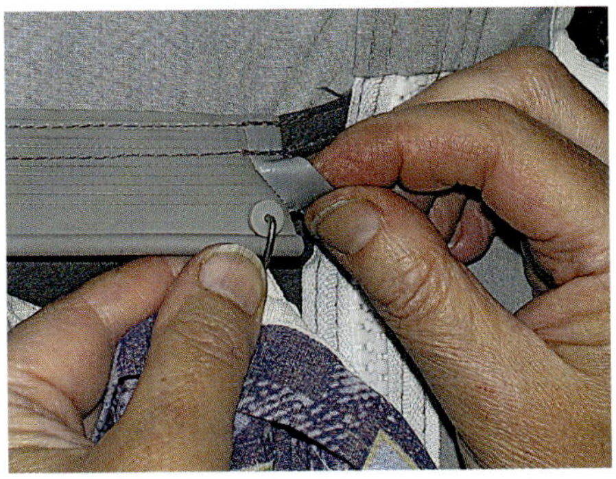

6-24-27. You then lift off the small loop of plastic from the end of the curtain runner inside the awning and slide the runners onto their rail, before replacing the loop of plastic which acts as an end-stop.

6-24-28. The final job is to peg the ladder-straps sewn into the lower edge of the awning all the way around using the standard tent pegs provided. You can then carry out the tensioning referred to earlier.

Specifications

Roof: PVC coated polyester fabric.
Sides/front/rear: Polyester/cotton with PVC film for windows.
Dimensions: Approx. 3400mm x 2000mm x 1750mm to 2100mm high. Roof extension: approx. 200mm. Weight, approx. 20kg.
Front: Zipped doorway, opening roll-up front with curtains.
Left: Roll-up side can be used as a canopy.
Right: Ventilated window and roll down 'obscured' cover.
Rear: Tunnel for joining to motor caravan. Height from 1.7m to 2.1m
Packed away: Approx. 1150mm x 350mm x 230mm (though the width does tend to 'grow' with repacking!)

SECTION 25: EXTRA LOAD SPACE – THÜLE BOX

It can be frustrating not to be able to use a top box on your camper. For obvious reasons, you can't add one to the top of an elevating roof model and going mountaineering onto the roof of a hi-top while burdened with the weight of, say, an awning might be a good way of getting the adrenalin flowing but it's not necessarily the sort of thing you want to do while packing up for a holiday. The Thüle EasyBase system is designed to place your extra carrying capacity at the rear of the vehicle, provided that you have a tow bracket fitted.

An extra bonus of the Thüle EasyBase system is that, unlike when you're towing a camping trailer, it may be possible to use a ferry or the Channel Tunnel without having to pay extra. All you would do is lift off the Thüle EasyBase system from the rear of the vehicle and put it in through the sliding door for the duration of the trip - provided that you haven't loaded that up too, of course!

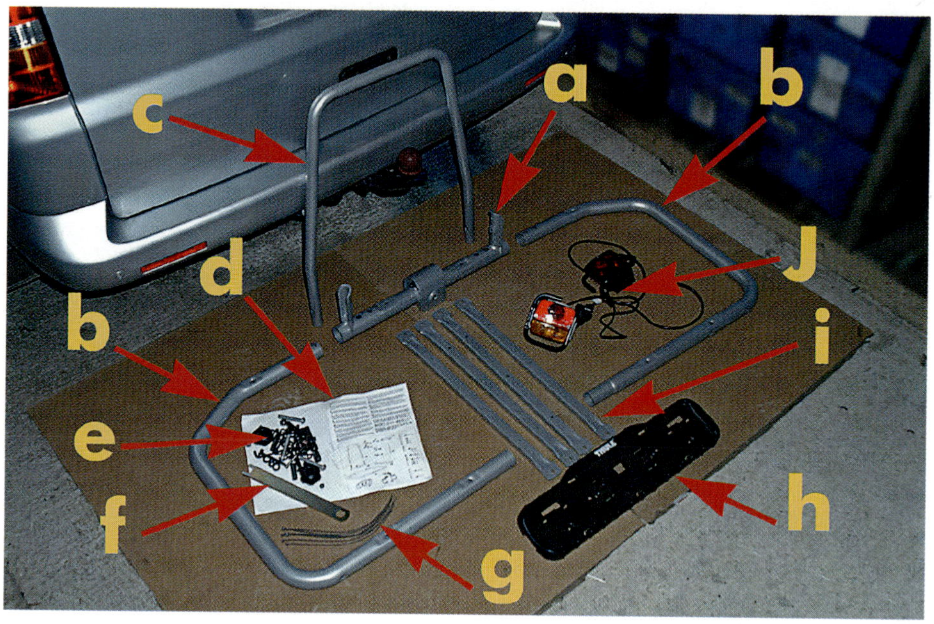

6-25-2. The basis of the system is the EasyBase which comes as a set of components for self-assembly. a. Main fixing unit. b. Sides of main frame. c. Foldable support frame. d. Instructions. e. Pack of fixings. f. Special fixing and. g. Cable ties. h. Number plate support. i. Struts. j. Supplementary lights.

6-25-1. The main attraction of the Thüle system for Volkswagen Camper owners is the 'back box' which takes the place of the roof box on smaller vehicles. This, the '900' unit, is made to the usual Thüle high standards of construction and provides a protective and waterproof method of carrying extra loads.

6-25-3. After wiping off the tow ball to make sure that it is free from grease, the central part of the frame is placed over the tow ball, the tightening screw tightened by hand as far as possible and then fully tightened with a special spanner provided.

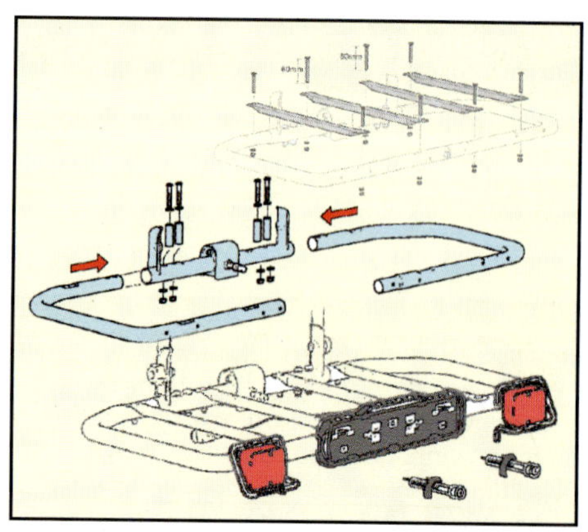

6-25-4. This exploded diagram shows how the various components are fitted together.

6-25-5. After sliding on the left-hand section of tubing, the two vertical spacer tubes shown in picture 6-25-4 are pushed into the fixing holes and the nuts and bolts fitted but not fully tightened at this stage.

6-25-6. The same is done with the right-hand section which is also simultaneously pushed onto the tubing already fitted.

6-25-7. Where the two tubular sections are fitted together, a single bolt and nut of the correct (shorter) length is used. Note that only the central hole is used at this stage and not the other hole (arrowed) where I had already fitted a nut and bolt in error.

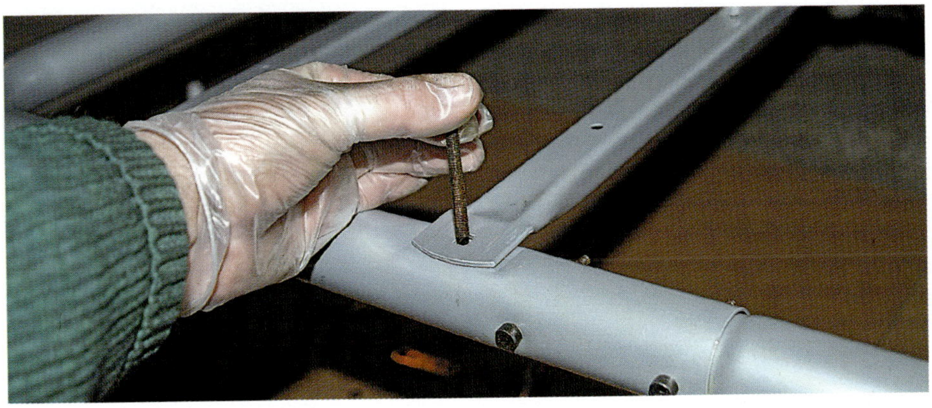

6-25-8. The support struts can now be bolted down.

6-25-9. The foldable support frame is fitted at one side using the relevant bolt and plastic knob.

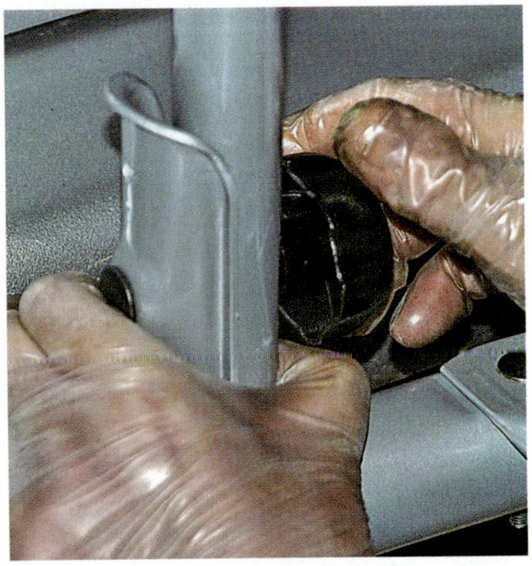

6-25-10. When fitting the other side, the tube has to be sprung into place. This is because when both knobs are sufficiently loosened, the support frame can be folded down past the fixing lugs.

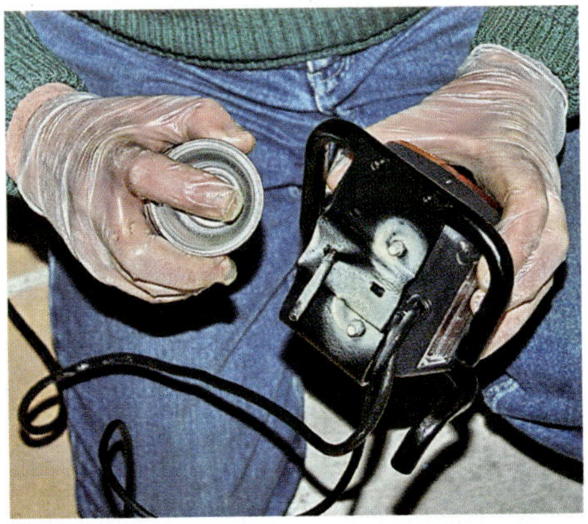

6-25-11. As with many of the 'touching' components in this assembly, I used Würth aerosol protective wax to prevent any risk of corrosion in the future. As anyone who has used a trailer board will know, the backs of light units are particularly vulnerable to corrosion and that can be a pain when, as inevitably happens, light lenses need to be replaced.

6-25-12. The bolts pre-fitted to the backs of the light units need most of their full-length to pass through the tubing to which they are attached. You have to hold the bolt head tightly in place ...

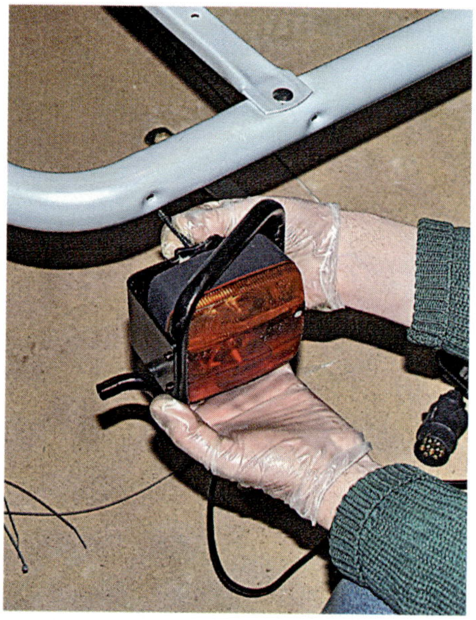

6-25-13. ... before pushing the bolt through the tube and fitting the nut on the other side.

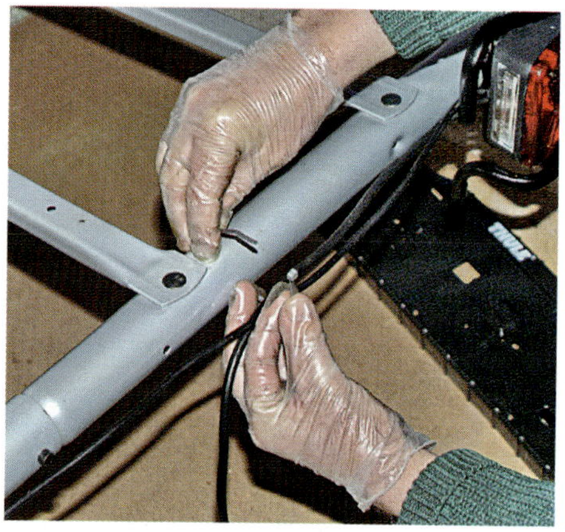

6-25-14 I used the cable ties supplied to tidily attach the electrical wiring to the frame, carrying it forward to the front of the unit using the strut nearest to the trailer socket on the vehicle. Take care not to run the cable down the underside of any of the struts because the holes in the struts are used for attaching various accessories later. Run the cable down one side of a strut.

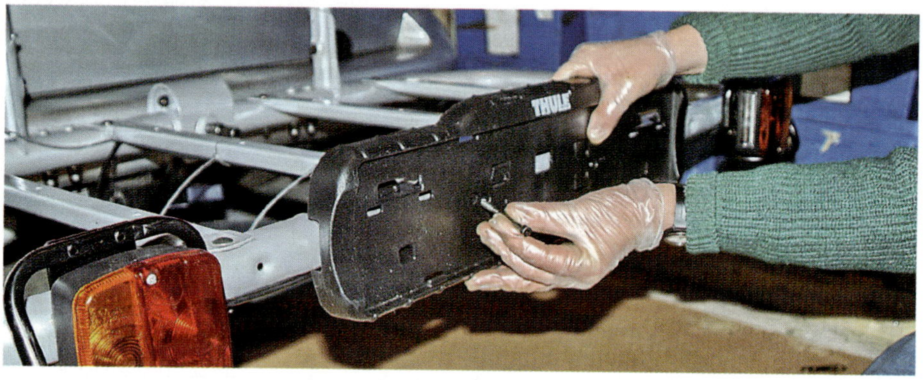

6-25-15. The two spare horizontal holes on the back of the frame are used for bolting the number plate carrier into position.

6-25-16. The number plate fixing system used is excellent. You slot the bottom of the number plate into the two brackets built into the carrier and then push out two of the four retaining pegs (which are built in to the number plate retainer), depending on the thickness of the number plate you will be using.

6-25-17. These pegs are then clipped into slots in the number plate retainer, holding the number plate securely in position. It's a simple matter to unclip the pegs and removed the number plate if you want to use the EasyBase on a different vehicle.

6-25-18. The EasyBase unit is now ready for use and can be used for attaching a wide variety of loads, up to an extremely useful limit of 60kg. However, the unit's true versatility can really be seen once you start adding some of the accessories shown here.

Accessories

6-25-19. This lightweight lock fits over the bolt holding the EasyBase to the tow ball and prevents it from being easily unscrewed.

6-25-20. The EasyBag is a strongly constructed but foldable carrier, which is also waterproof. There's a zipped opening around the top with a wide flat to protect the zip from the weather.

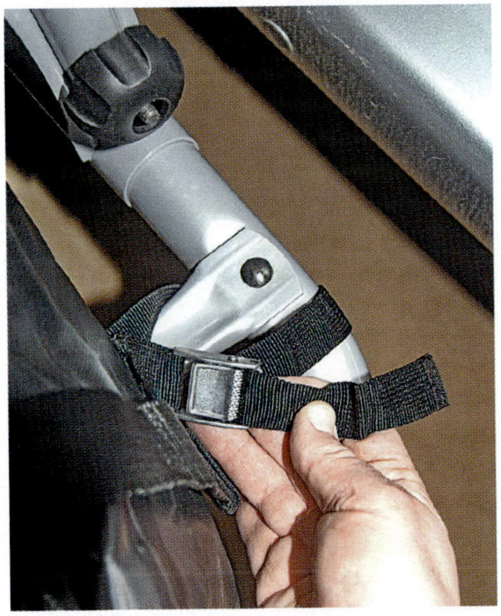

6-25-21. Nylon straps around the base are used to fix the unit to the EasyBase. There are more strong straps built into the corners of the bag, which are designed to be fixed to the outer corners of the EasyBase.

6-25-22. The greatest asset of the EasyBag is the small amount of space that it can be packed into. The rigid base collapses and the whole lot packs neatly away into the carrying case provided.

6-25-23. Another alternative is the EasyBasket which can be used to carry a wide range of bulky items.

6-25-24. The EasyBasket is quick and simple to attach and remove. Four bolts pass through holes in the EasyBasket and the struts of the base unit. The plastic washer shown here is inserted between the two, and the threaded knob is screwed on underneath.

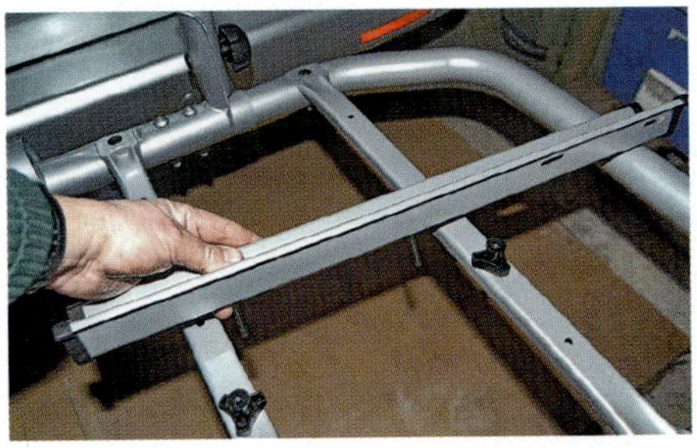

6-25-25. The accessory bike carrier, known unsurprisingly as EasyBike, consists of two steel channels which are bolting down to the relevant holes in the struts of the base unit. An instance of how well made these parts are lies in the rubber cappings which you push onto the end of each channel. They are well made, effective and look as if they will last for a long time; perhaps minor in itself but indicative of the generally high standards of construction.

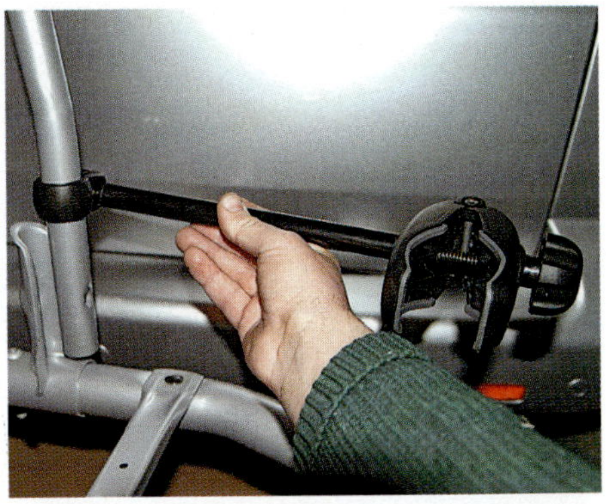

6-25-26. The top of the bike is supported by a clamp which is fed onto the foldable support frame after removing the retaining bolt from one side of it.

6-25-27 The bike is placed so that its wheels are on the channels and the clamp is tightened on the top of the frame, preventing back-and-forward movement. Note that a locking version of the clamp wheel is also available as an accessory.

6-25-28. Straps are provided for securing each wheel down to its supporting channel.

6-25-29. The EasyBike is capable of a wide range of adjustments to cater for bikes of all sizes, and I was very impressed by the solidity with which the bike is held on the rack.

6-25-30. An alternative, which will appeal to many motor caravanning couples, is the bike rack capable of supporting two bikes.

6-25-31. Exactly the same principle is used except there are clamps of differing lengths to hold the bike frames in place. By combining both kits, three bikes can be securely carried on the same rack!

6-25-32. I deliberately left what most of us will find to be the most useful of the accessories until last. The EasyBox has all the attributes of a top-box and then some. Because it's at a lower level, it is far easier and less demanding to load and unload than a box fitted to the roof. In addition, either the box, or alternatively the whole of the EasyBase assembly, could be removed from the vehicle and kept in the awning as enclosed storage when you are on site. Its capacity is nothing short of greedy!

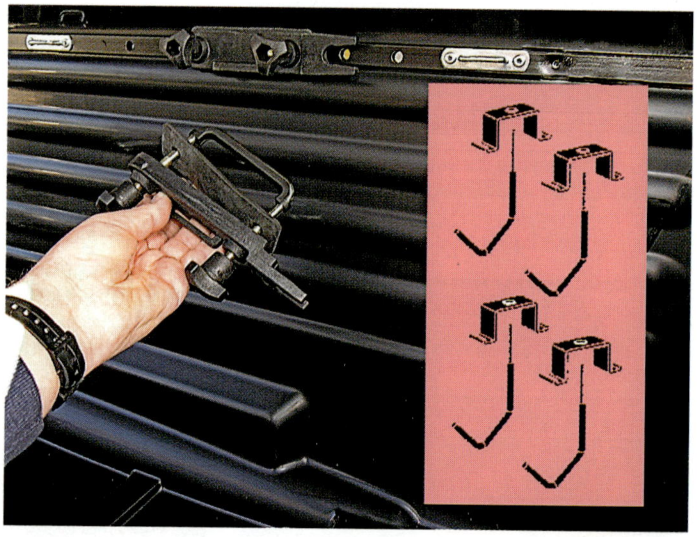

6-25-33. The EasyBox is held to the base unit using the two U-bolts at the rear and the four J-clips supplied. I really like the rubber seals and protectors supplied.

6-25-34. With an EasyBase assembly fitted to the rear of your Camper before setting out, you will greatly increase the volume of luggage that you will easily be able to take with you, releasing the inside of the vehicle for the purpose intended.

SECTION 26. PAINT SEALING

There's a lot of surface area to keep clean on your VW Camper. A paint sealant with PTFE (Teflon) lasts far longer than wax-based products and means that dirt just rinses off – brilliant! Only Paintseal Direct are licences to use DuPont Teflon in their paint protection product.

Old grime on paint can be removed with an abrasive polish which cuts away the microscopic peaks from the paint's surface then removes the grime from the troughs. Trouble is, it leaves the paint thinner each time it's used. PaintSeal fills those troughs.

6-26-1. Wax-based treatments don't compare with this stuff and you can feel the slippery difference as your bare hand glides over the surface.

6-26-2. This is the PaintSeal product - a mix containing DuPont Teflon – aka PTFE. It's so good that the product is guaranteed for five years for vehicles under six months old.

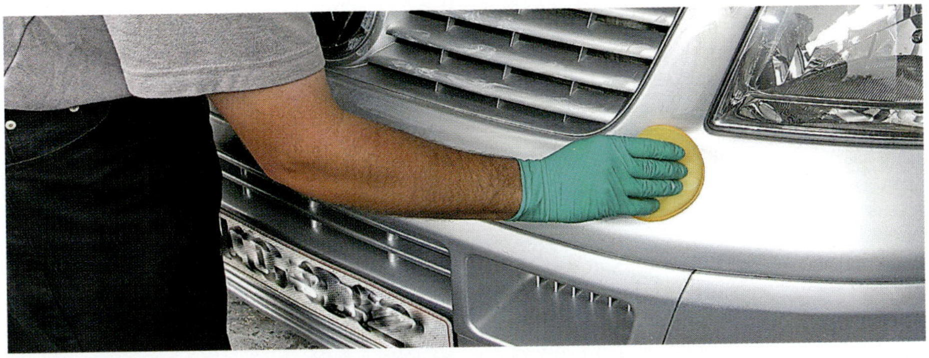

6-26-3. Mark applies a coating of PaintSeal over all the vehicle's surfaces: paintwork, ABS, fibreglass roof and all. When dry, he polishes off.

6-26-4. The treatment also works well on alloy wheels, making it much easier to remove the unavoidable layer of slightly sticky brake dust that attaches to the surfaces of braked wheels.

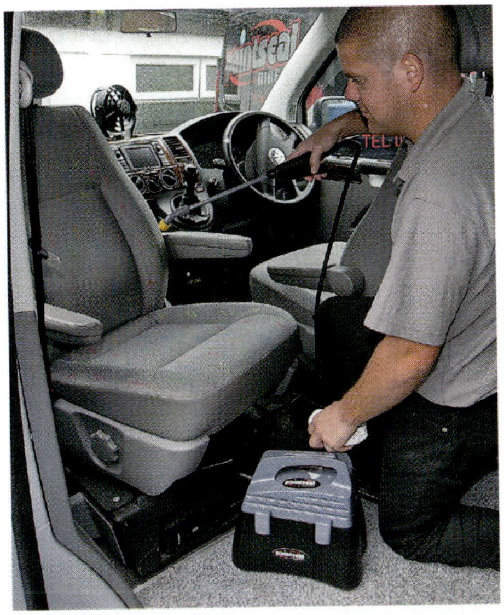

6-26-5. PaintSeal can also treat the upholstery using a similar process. Mark uses a battery powered sprayer to treat the upholstery. With open-weave cloth, spilled liquid may not 'perch' on the surface as it will with finer fabrics but it won't soak into the fibres, either.

6-26-6. PaintSeal's MD, Andy Bradbury displays the range of after-care products available by phone and online, including cleaners for several special purposes. A starter pack is supplied by PaintSeal when the vehicle is treated.

SECTION 27. SECURITY: COBRA ALARM

Here's an alarming fact! Did you know that your T5 doesn't come with an alarm as standard? No? Well nor do most owners! Because it has central locking and an immobiliser, we tend to assume that there's an alarm in there too but, unless you have one added, there isn't! I went for the biggest name of all, Cobra, once I realised that my T5 didn't have an alarm. And who better to fit it than Julian Willis, the man behind Auto Tec, and himself something of a T5 'nut'.

Fortunately, Cobra, the world's largest producer of car security systems, has developed an alarm system that is specifically for the Volkswagen and links in with the T5's integrated vehicle electronics.

Control Area Network Bus (CANBUS) wiring system means that electrical components are linked into the vehicles ECU. An untrained or amateur fitter will almost certainly cause the CANBUS system to malfunction. Ditto an alarm that has not been specifically built for the vehicle range.

Auto Tec, a Vehicle Security Installations Board accredited company, fits and recommends Cobra systems and is Cobra-approved. I was delighted with the high standards of its work with no corners cut, fully soldered joints and neatly wrapped and hidden wiring.

Ace fitter Jason told me that the Cobra system shown being fitted here – the model 4908 – upgrades the system to a Category 1 alarm from the Category 2 immobiliser already fitted to the vehicle. Other, less expensive Cobra options can provide the reassurance of an alarm siren but without the added security benefits of a full Category 1 system.

Auto Tec's owner, Julian, explained that an additional benefit of having a Cobra Category 1 system installed is that most insurance companies will provide an extra discount on premiums, emphasising the extra layer of security provided.

6-27-1. This is the Cobra system shown being fitted here. It must be emphasised that there is no way that a system such as this can be DIY-fitted. Not only are the wiring and location of the alarm components both complex and critically important, there is also the need to link in to the T5's wiring system without harming the integrated electrical and electronic circuitry.

6-27-2. The control box is fitted in a secure location 'somewhere in the vehicle', behind several panels and is thus difficult for a potential thief to locate and remove.

6-27-3. Similarly, the siren – battery backed-up on this Category 1 version – is hidden away but in a location where the sound can clearly be heard outside the vehicle.

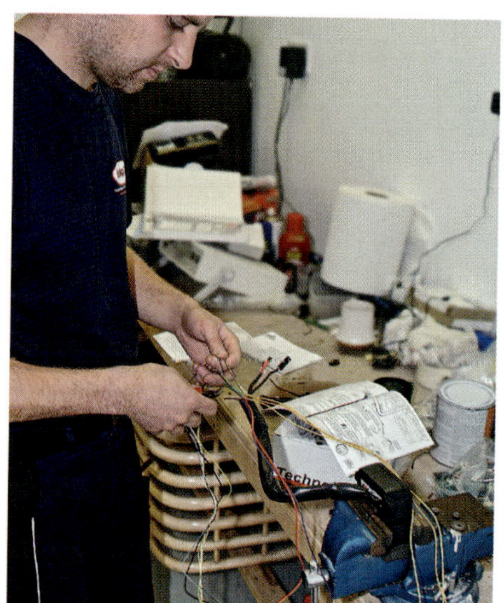

6-27-4. Jason is now seen 'looming up' the control box. He's removing wires not required for this installation and lashing together the wires required into a neat loom.

6-27-5. The new loom has to be passed carefully though the inside of the dashboard and, where necessary, inside the engine bay.

6-27-6. A pair of ultra-sonic sensors mounted (usually) on the tops of the door pillars will detect any sudden movement inside the car, including the movement created by someone breaking a side-window.

6-27-7. The T5's standard locking key fob now sets the Cobra alarm when the doors are locked. In addition to the usual flash of the lights, there's now a subtle 'beep' to tell you that the vehicle's not just locked. It's alarmed!

6-27-8. This flashing light on the dash, indicating again the neatness of Auto Tec's work – tells anyone who cares to look that the vehicle is alarmed – and warns off the ungodly! It also contains a switch that allows you to turn off the interior sensors while leaving the rest of the alarm set. This is perfect for a Camper or when leaving a dog in the vehicle.

SECTION 28. SECURITY: COBRA TRACKING DEVICE

Cobra, established in 1973, describes itself as "the world leader in vehicle security" and it is certainly one of the best known.

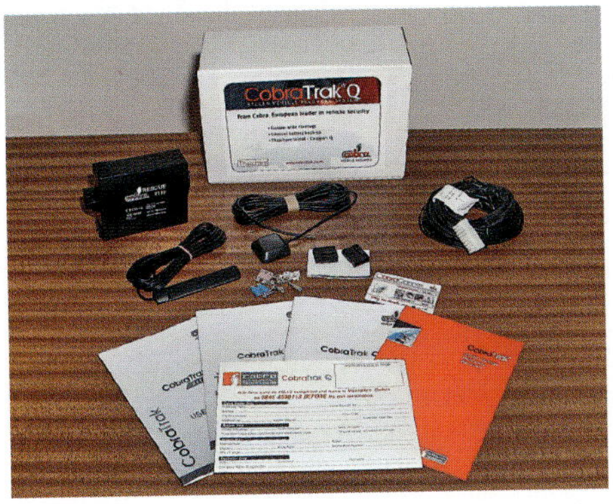

6-28-1. This is the CobraTrak kit of parts. Julian fits other makes of vehicle tracker but recommends the Cobra unit because it has several great advantages:

- *There's a satellite tracker PLUS a mobile phone tracker built in.*
- *Coverage is for all of Europe, not just those countries whose police cars have a Tracker sensor built in.*
- *If the vehicle is stolen and shipped to Europe, a guard is placed on the vehicle until it's shipped back home, all paid for by Cobra as part of the package.*
- *You can check the position of your vehicle yourself, any time you like and anywhere you've got internet access.*

6-28-2. There's a certain amount of dismantling required in order to locate and hide the control unit.

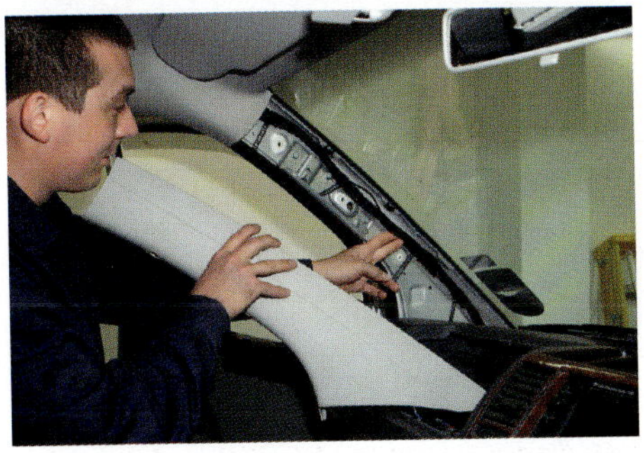

6-28-3. In addition, wires need to be run for the satellite and mobile phone sensors.

6-28-4. Even before carrying out the installation, details of the vehicle's VIN and the unit being installed have to sent to Cobra. High security!

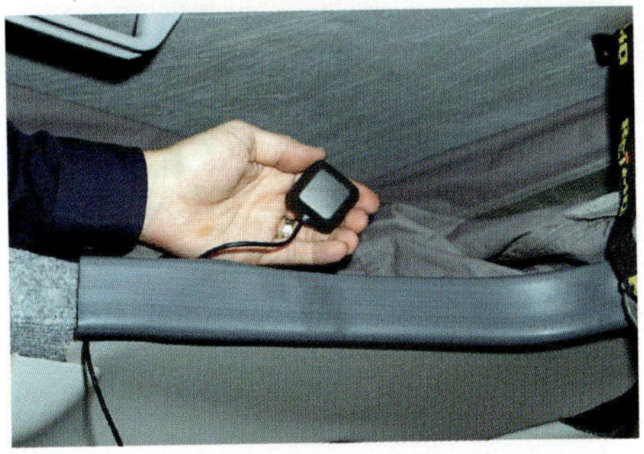

6-28-5. The satellite sensor can be placed on the cab roof where a high-top or elevating roof is fitted.

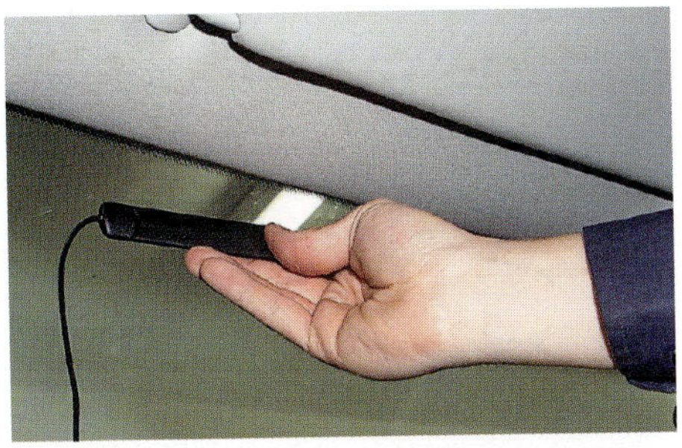

6-28-6. Likewise, the mobile phone GPRS unit is installed above the windscreen area.

6-28-7. This is the heart of the unit, the CobraTrak 'black box' unit. Of course, the potential thief doesn't know the CobraTrak is installed so it will be working away without their knowing it.

6-28-8. In the main control unit is the sim card which communicates the vehicle's whereabouts via mobile phone.

6-28-9. When ready, the control unit is plugged into the wiring harness then concealed and fixed in position.

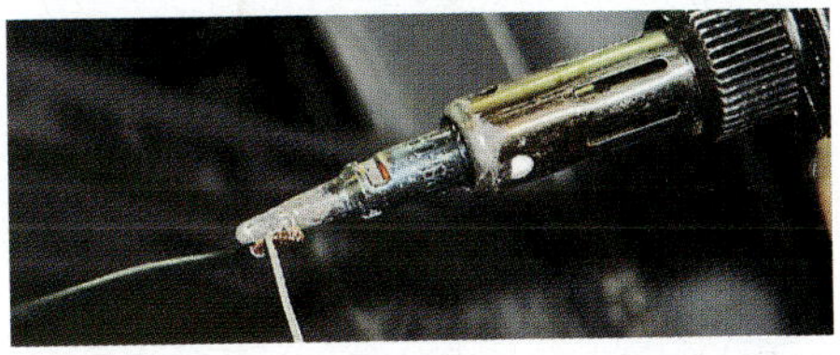

6-28-10. It's worth noting that Julian only makes soldered electrical connections. It takes a little longer but any others are prone to breaking down over time. He even uses the correct, expensive, VW-pattern insulation tape. Great attention to detail!

6-28-11. If you subscribe to the top-line 'Attivo' service, you can track the position of your vehicle online, as shown here.

The CobraTrak is a highly efficient system and arguably the best kind of security with which your vehicle can be fitted. Julian uses it on his own VW T5s. There's an annual subscription and I've opted for the 'lifetime' one since we intend keeping our Camper. However, unlike other makes, the Cobra tracker can be transferred to another vehicle if you change it.

SECTION 29. STAINLESS STEEL EXHAUST

Volkswagen T5 Campers are not like other vehicles. they're treasured, valued and capable of lasting not just years but decades in the true VW tradition. That's why a stainless steel exhaust makes more sense to a T5 Camper owner than it would to most. It's stainless so you can almost fit it and forget it! For years now I've had my SS exhausts from JP Exhausts and that's because its are the best quality exhausts I've ever come across. Here's how we fitted mine.

6-29-1. This is part of one of JP Exhausts' VW Transporter systems. As my wife said, it looks so good, it's a shame to hide it beneath the vehicle!

6-29-6. This is the full 'old' system after removal from the vehicle. You'll need the front downpipe and catalytic converter to attach to the new stainless system from JP Exhausts.

6-29-2. Inside the engine bay, the top of the downpipe is disconnected from the manifold by slackening the clamp. This is the copper gasket that must be renewed.

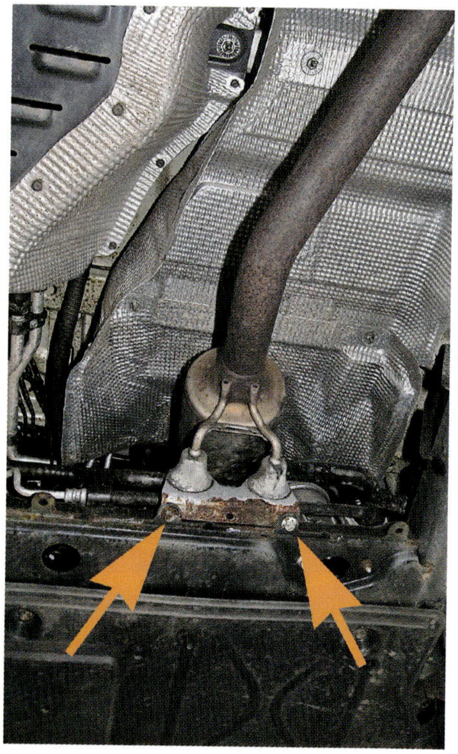

6-29-3. Viewed from beneath, looking up behind the engine, the frontpipe and catalytic converter are detached by removing these bolts (arrowed).

6-29-4. Spray releasing fluid on the exhaust hanger rubbers to allow them to be levered off – it's hard going! To the right is the VW clamp holding front section to rear.

6-29-5. Our version of the T5 had a factory-fitted one-piece exhaust. To get it out, cut it just behind the axle-line. We used a Clarke air saw to speed things up!

6-29-7. We used Würth exhaust paste on the joints of the new system. Spread it on the 'male' section then, after pushed together, push a little more into the slot then fit a new clamp. Stainless steel actually causes mild steel to corrode quickly so we used new stainless steel clamps called Mikalor clamps.

6-29-8. This shows the original VW clamp. On the VW exhaust, there is a peg on the pipe to ensure that the clamp fits correctly. If you use a VW clamp with a JP Exhausts system, mark the pipe with a felt pen to ensure the clamp sits evenly over the joint.

Appendix

Specialists, tools & equipment

ABAC, 11, Granville Way, Chaucer Business Park, Bicester, Oxfordshire OX26 4JT
Telephone: 01869 326 226
www.abacaircompressors.com

Al-Ko Kober Ltd, South Warwickshire Business Park, Kineton Road, Southam, Warks, CV47 0AL
Tel: 01926 818 500
www.al-ko.co.uk

ATS Euromaster Ltd, 1 Hagley Road, Metropolitan House, Five Ways, Birmingham B16 8AA
Tel: 0121 325 7325 for branch information.
www.atseuromaster.co.uk

Autoglass Ltd, Autoglass operate the well-known, nation-wide call-out service for emergency glass replacement.
Ring Freephone 0800 36 36 36 for details of your local branch.
www.autoglass.co.uk

Auto Tec, Supply and fit vehicle security, LED lights and electronic devices.
Walkwood Farm, Morton Lane, Redditch Worcestershire B97 5QA
Tel: 01527 541850
Email: info@myvehicle.co.uk

Avtex, 22 Merthyr Road, Whitchurch, Cardiff, CF14 1DH
Tel: 02920 610109
www.avtex.uk.com

Bernzomatic,
bernzomatic@worthingtonindustries.com
www.bernzomatic.com

Robert Bosch Ltd, PO Box 98, Uxbridge, Middlesex, UB9 5HJ
Tel: 0344 736 0109
www.boschpowertools.co.uk

Britool, Churchbridge Works, Walsall Rd., Cannock, WS11 8JR
Tel: 01902 702000

C.A.K, Aqua House, Princes Drive Industrial Estate, Kenilworth, Warwickshire, CV8 2FD
Tel: 0844 414 2324 for a catalogue or visit website:
www.caktanks.co.uk

Clarke International Ltd, Hemnall Street, Epping, Essex, CM16 4LG.
Tel: 01992 565 300
www.clarkeinternational.com

Cobra, Alarms and vehicle tracking.
Can be contacted at:
www.cobravehiclesecurity.co.uk

Conrad Anderson,
Tel: 0121 247 0619
www.conrad-anderson.co.uk

Dometic Ltd, All Dometic products should be available either from stock or to order from your local caravan dealership.
In case of difficulty, call Dometic's Call Centre on 01582 494 111 or contact them at info@dometic.co.uk

Durafix, for information on where to purchase Durafix:
www.durafix.com

Gaslow International Ltd, Manor House Stables, Normanton-on-Soar, Leicestershire, LE12 5HB
Tel: 01509 239 877 or 0845 4000 600
Email: sales@gaslowdirect.com
Download brochures: www.gaslowdirect.com

HobbyWeld, Westfield, Newbiggin Lane, Westerhope, Newcastle upon Tyne, NE5 1LX
Telephone: 0800 443 4331
www.hobbyweld.co.uk

Hodgson & Hodgson Group, (FiberForm Insulation) Crown Business Park, Old Dalby, Melton Mowbray, Leicestershire LE14 3NQ
Tel: 01664 821810
www.acoustic.co.uk

Inverter Fusion, Heath park Way, Heathpark Trading Estate, Honiton, Devon, EX14 1BB

Telephone: 01404 549791
www.inverterfusion.co.uk

JP Exhausts, Stainless steel exhausts.
Goodall Street, Macclesfield, SK11 7BD
Tel: 01625 619916
sales@jpexhausts.co.uk

Leisuredrive (FG) Ltd, Unit 4, Fishbrook Industrial Estate, Stoneclough Road, Kearsley, Bolton, Lancs, BL4 8EL
Tel: 01204 574 498
www.uk-motorcaravans.co.uk

Makita UK Ltd, Michigan Drive, Tongwell, Milton Keynes, Bucks, MK15 8JD
Tel: 01908 211678
www.makitauk.com

Maplin Electronics Ltd
All Maplin products should be available from local suppliers. In case of difficulty contact them at www.maplin.co.uk
Tel: 0870 4296000

Marcle Leisure, Much Marcle, Herefordshire, HR8 2NB
Tel: 01531 660 797
www.marcleleisure.co.uk

Maxview, Common Lane, Setchey, King's Lynn, Norfolk, PE33 0AT
Tel: 01553 813300
www.omnisat.co.uk or www.maxview.ltd.uk

Maypole Ltd, 54 Kettleswood Drive, Woodgate Business Park, Birmingham, B32 3DB
Tel: 0121 423 3011
www.maypole.ltd.uk

Michelin Tyres, Customer Service Centre, Campbell Road, Stoke-on-Trent, ST4 4EY
Tel: 0800 591 859
www.michelin.co.uk

Mobile Centre Limited, LED lighting, PO Box 222, Evesham, WR11 4WT
Tel: 01386 834851 & 0870 80 10 500
www.mobilecentre.co.uk

Morris Lubricants, Castle Foregate, Shrewsbury, Shropshire, SY1 2EL
Tel: 01743 232 200
www.morrislubricants.co.uk

NC Interiors, Nigel Cunningham.
VW Camper trim
Tel: 01204 793335

PaintSeal Direct, Paint protection.
38-40 Monson Lane, Repton, Derbyshire, DE65 6FX
Tel: 0871 200 70 70
Email: info@paintsealdirect.com

Parma Industries, 34-36 Carlton Park Industrial Estate, Carlton, Saxmundham, Suffolk, IP17 2NL
Tel: 01728 745700
www.parmagroup.co.uk

PD Stevens and Sons Ltd, Tower House, Maer lane, Market Drayton, Shropshire, TF9 3SH
Tel: 01630 6959

Pentagon Glasstech,
Tel: 0800 107 5518
www.pentagonglasstech.com

Ring Automotive, Volvox House, Gelderd Road, Leeds, LS12 6NA
Tel: 0113 213 2000
www.ringautomotive.co.uk

Rostra Precision Controls Inc,
2519 Dana Drive, Laurinburg, NC 28352 USA
Tel: 001 910-276-4853
www.rostra.com

Securon (Amersham) Ltd, Winchmore Hill, Amersham, Bucks, HP7 0NZ
Tel: 01494 434 455
www.securon.co.uk

Silverscreens, P.O Box 9, Cleckheaton, West Yorkshire, BD19 5YR
Tel: 01274 872151

Thetford Ltd, Unit 6, Centovell Estate, Caldwell Rd, Nuneaton, Warwickshire, CV11 4UD
Tel: 02476 341941

Towcraft Ltd, 20-22 Birmingham Road, Rowley Regis, Blackheath, West Midlands, B65 9BL
Tel: 0121 559 0116
www.towcraft.co.uk

Truma UK Ltd, Park Lane, Dove Valley Park, DE65 5BG
Sales: 01283 586050
Service: 01283 586020

Tyresave, 4 Dock Road, Connah's Quay, Deeside, Flints, CH5 4DW
Tel: 01244 813030
You can email Duncan Clubbe on duncan@tyresave.co.uk
www.tyresave.co.uk

Tyron Runflat Ltd,
Castle Business Park, Pavilion Way, Loughborough, LE11 5GW
Tel: 0845 4000 600
www.tyron.com

Ultraseal UK, Northgate House, St. Mary's Place, Newcastle- upon-Tyne, NE1 7PN
Tel: 0870 240 1280
www.ultrasealgb.co.uk

UltraShield Ltd, 11, Lime Hill Road, Tunbridge Wells, Kent, TN1 1LJ
Tel: 0845 6014936 (Calling an 0845 number generally charges the phone you are using with the rate of a standard local call.)

Vehvac Ltd, The Wiles Centre, Commerce Way, Edenbridge, Kent, TN8 6EJ Tel: 01732 868080
www.vehvac.co.uk

ViaMichelin UK Limited
www.viamichelin.co.uk

Witter Towbars, Drome Road, Deeside Industrial Park, Deeside, Flintshire, CH5 2NY
Tel: 01244 284 500
www.witter-towbars.co.uk

Würth UK Ltd, 1 Centurion Way, Erith, Kent, DA18 4AF
Tel: 03300 555 444
www.wurth.co.uk

Wyvern Accessories, Chelynch Road, Doulting, Shepton Mallet, Somerset, BA4 4PZ
Tel: 01749 881 122
www.wyvernaccessories.co.uk

ZIG Electronics Ltd, Units 4, 5 & 10, Phoenix Works, Thrupp, Stroud, Glos, GL5 2BU
Tel: 01453 731 700

Zygology Ltd, Over-centre catches.
2 Barnes Wallis Court, Wellington Road, High Wycombe, Bucks, HP12 3PS
Tel: 01494 437437
E-Mail: sales@zygology.com

Also from Veloce Publishing *by Lindsay Porter*

How to Convert VW Bus or Van to Camper

- Convert YOUR standard Volkswagen T3/T25 or T4 Van or Bus into a practical and stylish Camper!
- Step-by-step instructions
- Over 820 colour illustrations
- How to choose the best project vehicle for your needs
- How to plan the layout and choose fittings
- How to fit a high-top
- How to fit side windows
- Building and installing interior furniture
- Installing gas and water systems
- Fitting electrical equipment

ISBN: 978-1-903706-45-9
Paperback
224 pages

£60.00* UK $99.95* US $109.95* CAN

*All prices subject to change • p&p extra • for more info visit us on the web at www.veloce.co.uk, email us at info@veloce.co.uk, or telephone on +44 (0) 1305 260068

Also from Veloce Publishing

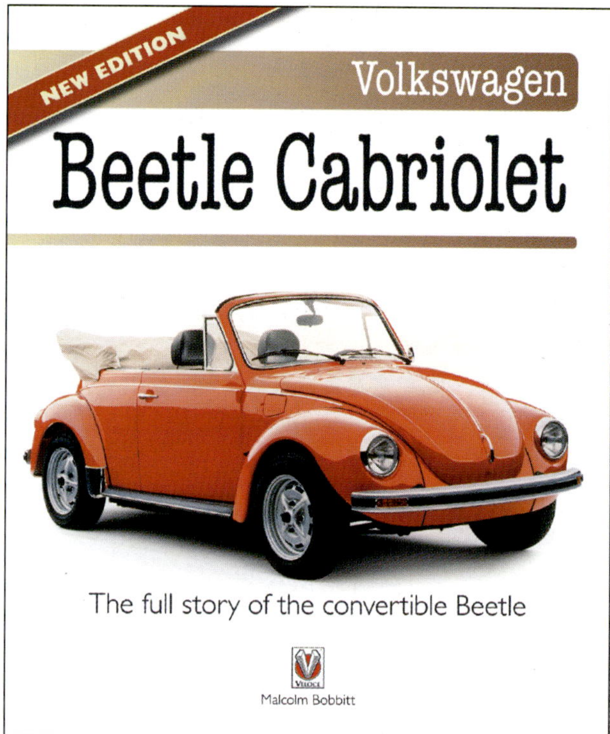

ISBN: 978-1-845840-74-7
128 pages
Paperback

£19.99* UK $29.95* US $32.95* CAN

ISBN: 978-1-845840-22-8
64 pages
Paperback

£12.99* UK $25* US $27.95* CAN

ISBN: 978-1-903706-90-9
224 pages
Paperback

£35* UK $65* US $72* CAN

Visit us on the web – www.velocebooks.com
New book news • Gift vouchers • Details all books in print • Special offers

SpeedPro Series
HOW TO MODIFY VOLKSWAGEN
BEETLE
SUSPENSION, BRAKES & CHASSIS
FOR HIGH PERFORMANCE
James Hale
Applies to all Volkswagen Beetles (does not cover front suspension of 1302 or 1303 models)

The Essential Buyer's Guide
VOLKSWAGEN
BEETLE
Your marque experts: Ken Cservenka & Richard Copping

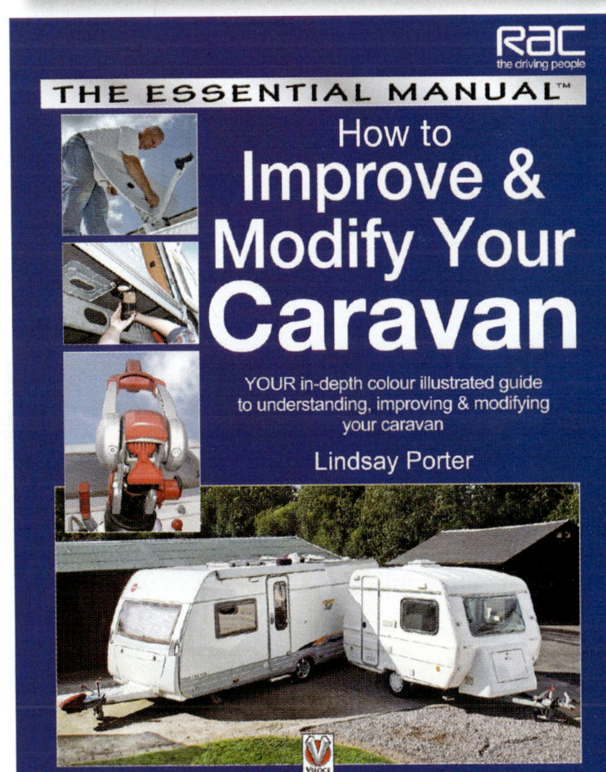
RAC
the driving people
THE ESSENTIAL MANUAL™
How to
Improve &
Modify Your
Caravan
YOUR in-depth colour illustrated guide to understanding, improving & modifying your caravan
Lindsay Porter

Index